THE CHURCH WITHOUT THE CHURCH

MERCER
UNIVERSITY PRESS

Endowed by
Tom Watson Brown
and
The Watson-Brown Foundation, Inc.

The Church Without the Church

Desert Orthodoxy in Flannery O'Connor's "Dear Old Dirty Southland"

M. K. Shaddix

MERCER UNIVERSITY PRESS | *Macon, Georgia*

MUP/ H903

Published by Mercer University Press
1400 Coleman Avenue
Macon, Georgia 31207

9 8 7 6 5 4 3 2 1

Books published by Mercer University Press are printed on acid-free paper that meets the requirements of the American National Standard for Information Sciences—Permanence of Paper for Printed Library Materials.

ISBN 978-0-88146-528-0
Cataloging-in-Publication Data is available from the Library of Congress

CONTENTS

ACKNOWLEDGMENTS

I would like to extend my sincerest thanks to Professor Stephen Matterson of Trinity College, Dublin, for allowing me such freedom in exploring my subject and for supporting my work with three years of inspired guidance. Many thanks also to Dr. Philip Coleman, Dr. Sam Slote, and Professor Gerald Dawe for their continuing support and insight.

I am indebted to the staff of the Manuscripts, Archives, and Rare Books Library at Emory University in Atlanta as well as the archivists at the *Flannery O'Connor Collection* at Georgia College and State University in Milledgeville. Special thanks to Kathy Shoemaker, Katherine Pope, and Joshua Kitchens for making my time in the archives an absolute joy.

For their generosity in allowing me to reproduce unpublished manuscript materials, my special thanks to Louise Florencourt and the *Mary Flannery O'Connor Charitable Trust*.

To my parents, Stanley and Margie Shaddix, my sister Mandy Shaddix, my niece Caroline, and my husband Dr. Shawn Doerrfeld, thank you for believing in me and for teaching me perseverance in love. Without you, there are no words.

PREFACE

In 1962, Flannery O'Connor advised her friend and fellow writer Cecil Dawkins to stay on in a township of five thousand souls in her native Alabama, not light out, as so many young authors of their generation had, for New York City. O'Connor had given in to the impulse herself and could report first hand, "That's where reality goes out the window. That is," she said, "when it ain't your reality."[1] This is good advice I would not have taken had I come across it, like Hazel Motes, say, on a stony roadside marker, somewhere between my birthplace in rural Florida and the university in western Canada where I wrote my M.F.A. After no more than a week in Vancouver, I became aware of an almost tangible disconnect between my (call it Southern) notion of the real and the global-village savvy of my mostly Canadian workshop-mates. My initial reaction was subtlety; g's were accentuated and suspicious twangs flattened. Within a month I had achieved a sound which was reasonably generic—North American, not American, and certainly not Southern.

My determination not to be mistaken, as O'Connor had been in Iowa City, for "a retarded young girl" in flight from the Southern backwater, was more or less successful; nonetheless I began to sense, in my denial of Southernness, a betrayal.[2] I was, after all, Quentin playing at Shreve; like Faulkner's suicide, I could not save tell about the place I'd come from. When I wrote, I wrote about the South, and when I tried not to write about the South, I wrote about the South and called it something else. My characters insisted upon speaking Southern and thinking Southern—a distinction I'd thought somewhat irrelevant until their language and rationale became a talking point across the workshop. At once, the self-evidence of the South and Southernness were up for debate. What did it mean to be a white woman of Southern extraction? Was my identity a construct of social and political discourse or an organic outgrowth of a very specific place in the Southern United States?

---

[1] Flannery O'Connor, *The Habit of Being*, Ed. Sally Fitzgerald (New York: Farrar, Straus & Giroux, 1979) 493.

[2] Paul Engel qtd. in Melissa Simpson, *Flannery O'Connor: A Biography* (Westport, Greenwood Press, 2005) 10.

Could I write a South able to withstand the gravity of The South? Could my point of view of Southernness, within and without fictive Souths, achieve a kind of universality?

I was not alone in my regional existentialism; since Twain, "professional" Southernness has been a viable track for artists and critics alike. Nevertheless, I developed a strange sort of homesickness, not only for the transparency of a *terra firma* South and Southern talk but for myself—The Southerner—before I'd become conscious of either geography or dialect as definitive of a manner of being. When I began this study, it was with the intention of describing souths within The South by way of local aesthetics that subvert, through self-parody and nuanced mechanics, the conventions of "Southern" literature. The project was to span the twentieth century and would attempt to triangulate, quite literally, a region-specific realism in terms of Flannery O'Connor's middle Georgia, Truman Capote's southern Alabama, and Mark Richard's tidewater Virginia. The study's opening chapter, "Monsters, Monoliths, and Middle Georgia: Flannery O'Connor and the 'Dear Old Dirty Southland,'" is the product of this initial objective.[3]

As the title suggests, my primary ambition of surveying the notional "Southern writer" by means of three authors each distinct in his or her mechanical tack, evolved into a single author study in which I undertook to read Flannery O'Connor's work against the "regional" norm. To that end, the chapter explores the historical lineage of the South as a space distinct in politics and culture, placing particular emphasis upon canonical Southern literature and the convention by which it has been asked to explain the so-called "mind of the South." My hypothesis of an apparently denigrated Southern realism is foregrounded by a contrasting of Northern and Southern ideologies from the colonial to the post-modern age. To illustrate the development and cultural impact of each regional trope, I highlight works of fiction, poetry, and drama indicative of critical points in Southern history, beginning with the romantic local-colorism of the antebellum years and the Lost Cause heroism of the Civil War, following through to Reconstruction-era degeneracy and the social upheavals of the Civil

---

[3] O'Connor, *Habit*, 537.

Rights movement and the world wars, and concluding with the relative cultural ambiguity of the twenty-first century post-South.

Interspersed within my survey of Southern history, I discuss the influence of some of the region's primary authors, including Augustus Baldwin Longstreet, George Washington Harris, Edgar Allen Poe, Joel Chandler Harris, and Mark Twain and discuss the ways in which their best known fictions—*Georgia Scenes* (1835), *Tales of the Grotesque and Arabesque* (1840), *Sut Lovingood: Yarns Spun By a Nat'ral Born Durn'd Fool* (1867), *Uncle Remus: His Songs and Sayings* (1880), and *The Adventures of Huckleberry Finn* (1885) respectively—have contributed to the concept of a prototypical Southern style. I trace the most fundamental of these tropes—the oral tradition of a region-based manner and cosmology—into the Southern Renaissance of the twentieth century during which such mannerisms were embellished and in some cases deliberately performed by a "reconstructed but unregenerate" South.[4] Of particular import are the works of the Fugitive Poets and Nashville Agrarians (*Fugitive* 1922-1925; *I'll Take My Stand,* 1930), Erskine Caldwell (*Tobacco Road,* 1932), William Faulkner (*Absalom, Absalom!,* 1936), Margaret Mitchell (*Gone With the Wind,* 1936), and Zora Neale Hurston (*Their Eyes Were Watching God,* 1937). The writers of the New South would in turn deconstruct the Southern performance with arch social realisms and, in the post-war years, a decidedly grotesque anti-realism. Caldwell is the natural progenitor of what has been called The School of Southern Degeneracy, and his work is followed by such subversives as Carson McCullers (*The Heart is a Lonely Hunter,* 1940), Tennessee Williams (*A Streetcar Named Desire,* 1947), and Flannery O'Connor (*A Good Man Is Hard To Find,* 1955). Walker Percy's *The Moviegoer* (1962), Truman Capote's *In Cold Blood* (1966), and Eudora Welty's *The Optimist's Daughter* (1973) dismantle the "Southern" real still further by interplaying an unreasonable (but believable action) within an otherwise transparent narrative. Contemporary Southern literature disengages itself somewhat aggressively from regional stereotyping, be it aesthetic or otherwise;

---

[4] John Crowe Ransom, "Reconstructed but Unregenerate," *I'll Take My Stand: The South and the Agrarian Tradition*, Ed. Lewis P. Simpson (Baton Rouge: Louisiana State University Press, 1930) 22.

Richard Ford and Bobby Ann Mason resist even the title "Southern writer," but there is also an equal impetus, witnessed in the work of Harry Crews, Barry Hannah, and Mark Richard, of reappropriating the Southern space by plumbing the still intensely personal depths of regional identity. The chapter concludes by contextualizing O'Connor within the Southern scene, both real and imagined, and suggesting a regional hermeneutic which prioritizes the text of the individual writer over that of his or her region.

The second chapter of the study, "'One Jesus [i]s Just as Bad as Another': Orthodoxy as Ecumenical Blasphemy in the Fiction of Flannery O'Connor," dismantles the image of O'Connor as absolute in her Roman dogmatism first by reviewing the short-comings of extant criticism and then by returning to primary source materials—namely the major works of St. Augustine and St. Thomas Aquinas, the *Baltimore Catechism,* and the proclamations of ecumenical councils—which have been relied upon to situate O'Connor's aesthetic indelibly within the realm of Roman dogma.[5] In my explication of O'Connor's debut novel, *Wise Blood,* I demonstrate the author's life-long affinity for fundamental Protestantism, a phenomenon which retains the Desert Fathers' personal God-seeking rarely seen in parochial Catholicism. Following that vein, I underscore the disjoint between an increasingly consumerist American Christianity and Christian fundamentalism. For her own part, O'Connor believed that writing catholically was not a case of "subtract[ing] one theology from another" but of realizing the "invisible Church" in the fullness of its reality.[6] Her preoccupation with Protestant and "heathen" characters illustrates her conviction that non-Catholics "make discoveries that have meaning." The chapter concludes with an in depth discussion of O'Connor's textual linkages with Orthodox sacramentalism and to certain linguistic idiosyncrasies indicative of her Irish-speaking ancestry.

---

[5] Flannery O'Connor, *Wise Blood*, 2nd ed. (New York: Farrar, Straus & Giroux, 1962) 176.

[6] Flannery O'Connor, "The Catholic Novelist in the Protestant South," *Mystery and Manners: Occasional Prose*, Eds. Sally and Robert Fitzgerald (New York: Farrar, Straus & Giroux, 1969) 207.

The second part of my study is distinguished by its practical application of the hypotheses put forward in part one, demonstrating, through close readings of O'Connor's second novel, *The Violent Bear It Away,* and fifteen of her stories, the ongoing development of her aesthetic irrespective of her continuing practice of Roman dogmas in her native deep South. Paramount to my analysis is the reconstruction of O'Connor's internal dialogue through published and unpublished correspondence and manuscripts of the novels and stories. Of pivotal importance are the recently opened Betty Hester letters which I had the pleasure of reviewing at Emory University's Manuscripts, Archives, and Rare Books Library in Atlanta and the unpublished manuscripts of *Wise Blood,* "Parker's Back," and "Why Do the Heathen Rage?" which I transcribed at Georgia College and State University's *Flannery O'Connor Collection* in Milledgeville. Using the collected texts and correspondence in conjunction with unpublished drafts and letters, I illustrate the profound interrelatedness of O'Connor's personal discourse and her artistic output. The archival materials are an invaluable reminder that the author's writing took place in the context of her intellectual and spiritual development and is not, as conventional criticism suggests, an intimation of a static and insular intelligence. As Brad Gooch puts it in his biography *Flannery,* "The separation between [O'Connor's] life and her art was porous..."[7] Her texts are not object-based but rather the instruments of O'Connor's critical thought and as such indicative of extratextual concerns. "The Geranium/Judgment Day," is a remarkable example of the author's progressing thought and the integration of the same with a work of fiction. The story is one O'Connor drafted at the Iowa Writers' Workshop and continued, until her final year, to revise in process with her changing conception of race and regional manners. That her fictions can be shown to have been a contiguous part of her living reality counters, in a provocative way, the New Critical approach (which O'Connor deferred to herself) of prioritizing the text over authorial considerations.

---

[7] Brad Gooch, *Flannery: A Life of Flannery O'Connor* (New York: Back Bay Books, 2009) 8.

The first chapter in part two, "Just as it is or Nothing": Flannery O'Connor's Ugly Jesus," revisits O'Connor's late stories "Parker's Back" and "Why Do the Heathen Rage?" in conjunction with their unpublished drafts to recast the sacramental symbology of the text in light of the traditions of early Christianity and the Eastern Orthodox Church.[8] The chapter draws upon the primary texts of church fathers, Sts. Climacus, Palamas, Cassian, John Damascene, Gregory the Great, and Jerome, church doctors, Sts. Augustine and Aquinas, eastern iconography, and western religious art to illustrate the symbolic expanse of O'Connor's handling of the sacrament of marriage and the performance of penance. St. Jerome is a crucial figure in my argument as he is the only Desert Father recalled by name in O'Connor's oeuvre; in "Why Do the Heathen Rage?" his presence gives bodily form to the protagonist's intellectualization of the Incarnation, and in "Parker's Back," the hero functions as a fictionalized Southern Jerome who must literally "put on Christ" to experience a penitential conversion.

Chapter four, "'Lest Ye Be Born Again': Heretical Baptism in 'The River' and *The Violent Bear It Away*," problematizes the standard reading of texts' adaptation of the baptismal rite in terms of Southern fundamentalism and Roman Catholicism.[9] Notorious for their portrayal of the deaths of two innocents, both narratives dramatize the symbolic death inherent to Christian baptism by literalizing its liturgical function. My reading of the texts involves a broadening of the sacramental spectrum to include the practices of the early Christian and Eastern Orthodox churches, for example the practice of triune submersion and the simultaneous conferral of Baptism, Chrismation, and Communion. I describe the self-baptism of Harry/Bevel by water and desire and of Francis Marion Tarwater by desire and by fire as subversions of liturgical dogmas necessary to the boys' final conversion. The manuscript drafts of both pieces as well as contemporaneous letters are

---

[8] Flannery O'Connor, "Parker's Back," *The Complete Stories* (Farrar, Straus & Giroux, 1979) 522.

[9] John 3:3, *The Holy Bible*, King James Version. King James Bible Online, 2011. www.kingjamesbibleonline.org. <http://www.kingjamesbibleonline.org> [accessed 17 Jan. 2011].

instrumental in underscoring the author's deliberate reworking of the baptismal rite as she experienced it in the Roman Church to encompass a more completely catholic sacramentalism.

The fifth chapter, "'Imagin[ing] a Vain Thing': The Undeniable Body in 'The Enduring Chill,' 'The Comforts of Home,' and 'Why Do the Heathen Rage?'" makes extensive use of the unpublished drafts of O'Connor's unfinished third novel and her correspondence with the playwright Maryat Lee to demonstrate the often radical extent to which the author continued to challenge her personal convictions in her attempts to fictionalize sex and blackness.[10] The chapter also addresses the interconnections between "Why Do the Heathen Rage?", "The Enduring Chill," and "The Comforts of Home" and traces the increasing strain O'Connor placed upon herself, from the outset of her drafting Thomas and Asbury Fox to her final rendering of Walter Tilman, to confront her own unease regarding sexuality and race. The chapter concludes with a reflection upon O'Connor's struggle, particularly in the last years of her life, with the practice of charity. The author's consideration of the charitable act was underscored by Lee's persistent subjection of self to a suffering with "The Poor," in inner-city Harlem and elsewhere, a compulsion which both incensed and inspired O'Connor.[11] Maryat seems to have embodied O'Connor's lifelong effort to "not be scandalized [by human nature] and to try to find explanations in charity."[12] Walter and his female toil Oona's exchanges demonstrate, in an unprecedented manner, O'Connor's insistence upon the orthodox deification of the body in love and her regard, nevertheless, for sacrifices made and endured by unbelievers such as Lee.

I conclude the study with a brief review of O'Connor's import in contemporary Southern Letters and in the greater American canon. The conclusion also discusses her substantial readership in continental Europe in her lifetime and posthumously and recounts the growing global audience for O'Connor's fiction and non-fiction in eastern Europe, Asia, Africa, and South America. In closing, I consider the impact of

---

[10] Ps. 2:1, KJV.

[11] O'Connor, *Habit*, 103.

[12] Ibid., 346.

trans-Atlantic exchange in O'Connor Studies and suggest further research with regard to the translation of the Southern author overseas by means of cooperatively mapping the emergence and sustainability of particular Southern writers across the globe.

Chapter 1

Monsters, Monoliths, and Middle Georgia

Flannery O'Connor and the "Dear Old Dirty Southland"[1]

In fall 1955, several months after the publication of her first story collection, *A Good Man Is Hard to Find,* Flannery O'Connor wrote a letter to Agrarian novelist Andrew Lytle—one of her lecturers at the Iowa Writers' Workshop—thanking him for his recommendation of her work to Harcourt Brace. "What you said…is what I see in the stories myself but what nobody who reviews them cares to see."[2] O'Connor's decisive vision as well as her self-explication were immediate functions of her being both a Southerner and a Catholic, birthrights she claimed throughout her career to be her art's greatest aesthetic asset. The "only thing that keeps me from being a regional writer," she confided to Lytle, "is being a Catholic and the only thing that keeps me from being a Catholic writer (in the narrow sense) is being a Southerner…"[3] In truth, the accidents of O'Connor's being a Catholic from the South were the first of many mixed blessings that would befall her, the advantage and detriment of which were compounded by her insistent self-criticism.

As strong as her sense of personal perspective was, the consensus perspective of O'Connor's contemporaries, which envisioned the South and the Roman Church as cultural monoliths, demanded habitual contention. Indeed, the creation of an aesthetic that could withstand the symbolic pressures of the Southern Judeo-Christian mythos as well as generate a discourse somehow beyond it was O'Connor's explicit project. Like the Louisiana writer Walker Percy, she had little faith in the Southern literary tradition, which she supposed did more to inform the work of the critic than it did the writer's. Where O'Connor underscored the virtue of the South's

---

[1] Flannery O'Connor, *The Habit of Being,* ed. Sally Fitzgerald (New York: Farrar, Straus & Giroux, 1979) 537.

[2] Ibid., 104.

[3] Ibid. See also Flannery O'Connor, "The Catholic Novelist in the Protestant South," *Mystery and Manners: Occasional Prose,* ed. Sally Fitzgerald and Robert Fitzgerald (New York: Farrar, Straus & Giroux, 1969) 196.

relative heterogeneity in such essays as "Some Aspects of the Grotesque in Southern Fiction," Percy likened the Southern author to Crusoe on his desert island, marooned and tending toward eccentricity.[4] It was "the very absence of a tradition," he remarked in a self-interview, "that makes for great originals like Faulkner and O'Connor and Poe."[5] In her own occasional prose, O'Connor railed against the critical rigidity of the so-called Southern School and was even less forgiving in her critique of the conventional Catholic novel. Her condemnations anticipate the trouble a postmodern Southern Catholic writer, like Percy, would find himself in if he were to take his "tradition" at its word, a dangerous self-prescription the Alabama-born writer spoke of himself in his 1985 essay "How to Be an American Novelist in Spite of Being Southern and Catholic."[6]

Percy's essay was as much a recommendation to the critical establishment as it was to the Southern Catholic writer. He shared O'Connor's frustration with mainstream American critics like Clifton Fadiman, who failed to recognize the "value of difference" in writers like Poe, Faulkner, and O'Connor. "If the writer," Percy noted, "is altogether different from the genus Writer, which is the only genus the reviewer knows, the reviewer is baffled."[7] What is needed is the recognition of "the possibility of an extraterrestrial point of view."[8] For Percy, the Southern writer was, "a value because he was somewhat extraterrestrial."[9] O'Connor had previously observed that the Southerner's relative displacement from the American mainstream was what gave him a voice worth listening to and also foresaw that the modern "Americanization" of the South and the post-modern "Southernization" of America would, in many ways, divest the Southerner of his informing alienation.[10] As a result of this

---

[4] Walker Percy, *Signposts in a Strange Land*, ed. Patrick Samway (London: Bellew Publishing, 1991) 402, 409.

[5] Ibid., 402.

[6] Ibid., 168.

[7] Ibid., 409.

[8] Ibid.

[9] Ibid.

[10] John Egerton, *The Americanization of Dixie: The Southernization of America* (New York: Harper's Magazine Press, 1974) xx. See also James C. Cobb, "An Epitaph for the North: Reflection on the Politics of Regional and National Identity at the Millennium," *The Journal of Southern History* 66/1 (February 2000) 3–24.

homogenization, the immediate Southern space—O'Connor's middle Georgia and Percy's Gulf Coast—has been obscured by a formulaic, regional South whose assumed traditions and cultural nuances are made to explain the individual experience of one of many Souths. The reader comes to the Southern novel with an in-built sense of how to read it, on the lookout for the exotic, the gothic and grotesque, the familial romance, racial violence, religious supernaturalism, and a darkening sense of place.

O'Connor had the advantage of being somewhat removed from her "native" tradition as a Roman Catholic, but her critical reception and the small industry that has been made of decoding her work have relied primarily upon identifying O'Connor as prototypically Southern and Catholic. Born into the Church in 1925 in Savannah, Georgia, and devoted to the Catholic community in Milledgeville where she spent most of her life, O'Connor was indeed a Southerner and a dogmatic Roman, but the sort of individual she was within those constructs is a point of contention typically eschewed for a standardized view of Southern and Catholic ideologies. To read O'Connor within her social and religious context, we might ask not how she conforms to regional and doctrinal norms but how her creative intellect remained remained remarkably individualized in spite of her devotion to region and Church. Nonethelss, critics have consistently forgone a more personal reading of the author in favor of an O'Connor who is more orthodox in her Southernness and in her Catholicism than she in fact was. It is as if the term "Southern Catholic," as effective as it is at scaring up images of a generic benighted South and an equally stereotyped Roman Church, is broad enough (or at least conspicuous enough) to stand as a sufficient abbreviation for O'Connor as individual and artist. The presumptions embedded in this Southern Catholic O'Connor—that she was predisposed to romantic vision and regional nostalgia, to the gothic and the grotesque, to local-colorism and dialectal fiction, religious fanaticism and, certainly, profound guilt—have been so persistently relied upon that the better part of O'Connor criticism stops short at Flannery's South, Flannery's Catholicism, or some "unhappy combination" of the two.[11]

[11] O'Connor, "The Fiction Writer and His Country," *Mystery*, 28.

It should be said that this characterization is one that can be attributed, at least in part, to the author herself. O'Connor maintained throughout her career that her vision of the real was indebted to her experiential knowledge of the South and the sacramental Church, a point I do not contend. But to appreciate the full symbolic range of O'Connor's art, the critic must consider the total experience of the text rather than deferring to a Southern or Catholic trope wherever there is the slightest shade of symbolic language. "[D]espite the themes and philosophy announced in behalf of an author by others," Mississippi writer Barry Hannah noted, "the actual art experience is much more whole. Flannery O'Connor can never be accounted for by her Catholicism. There is something rich and deep and strange in her that just doesn't get on a theorist's page...."[12] Indeed to interpret O'Connor in terms of those aspects of her aesthetic that might be called "Southern" and "Catholic" is to see only a narrow sense of both her personality and her art, yet prominent critics including Louis D. Rubin, Jr. and Sarah Gordon continue to situate O'Connor within this compressed landscape. The persistence of such conventions seems to suggest that a properly naive rendering of O'Connor's work, one that does not begin with the presumption that region and religion should be prioritized, is by and large a non-issue for her critics. If we are to revitalize O'Connor studies and effect a more complete understanding of the author and her fiction, it is crucial to recontextualize her by challenging the implicit authority of Mary Flannery as Southern Catholic. In the years since her death, critics have called up the term with such regularity that "Southern" and "Catholic" have ceased to function merely as illustrative modifiers. Their connotation is more literal than representational; as such, O'Connor's unique symbology is itself in peril of becoming overshadowed or displaced by the authority of these image systems. The significance of O'Connor's work, down to the literalness of certain details, is at risk of becoming predetermined by assumptions about the South and Southernness, the Catholic Church and Catholicism.

This is not to say that region and religion are not telling markers of narrative significance, and O'Connor, for her part, was

---

[12] James D. Lilley, Brian Oberkirch, and Barry Hannah, "An Interview with Barry Hannah," *Mississippi Review* 25/3 (Spring 1997) 19–43.

particularly outspoken about the impact that her home and her faith had upon her personal life and her vocation. Neverthelss, a more befitting, expansive criticism must suspend the notion of primacy—that the ultimate meaning in O'Connor is somehow located in one or both of these paradigms—in order to invite readings that are as interrogative and complex as O'Connor was herself. Certainly the fact that the author was a Catholic from the Deep South reveals something about who she was and, consequently, what might be significant in her writing, but these details are in no way exhaustively revelatory. "Fiction doesn't lie," O'Connor wrote in an early letter to her closest confidant, Betty Hester, "but it can't tell the whole truth. What would you make of me just from reading 'Good Country People'? Plenty, but not the whole story."[13]

Distinguishing O'Connor from her fictive South and from the South of collective imagination is a challenge matched and in some ways complicated by the task of interpreting her deceptively parochial faith. "I am afraid," she wrote to John Hawkes in 1961, "that one of the great disadvantages of being known as a Catholic writer is that no one thinks you can lift the pen without trying to show somebody redeemed."[14] This study is intended to discriminate between the literal *prima facie* O'Connor, the personae associated with her texts themselves, and the mythologized O'Connor, the popular persona who is interpretively conflated with extratextual "isms," including Gothicism, Regionalism, and Catholicism. The mythologized O'Connor derives in part from textual cues, but overall she is more the product of critical supposition. Too often certain textual distinctions—the predominance of violence and Christian motifs, for example—are isolated and used almost exclusively to interpret O'Connor's fiction and, in some instances, her personality. The result is an abbreviated O'Connor made romantic or grotesquely compelling by her many and often spurious associations with institutionalized Southernness and Catholicism. Recontextualizing O'Connor will mean deconstructing many long-held assumptions about the writing, worshipful South. It will mean owning up to a critical history of convenient delusions, which, to

---

[13] O'Connor, *Habit*, 158.

[14] Ibid., 434.

borrow from Mikhail Bakhtin, have done little but create a dead-ended philosophical monologue.[15]

Among these monologues is the so-called Southern Gothic, remarkable in that its designation is derived from an underlying irony: the critical discourse that creates and reinforces it is made itself a grotesque. The phenomenon is reminiscent of Sherwood Anderson's grotesque cosmology in the opening book of *Winesburg, Ohio*:

> [I]n the beginning when the world was young there were a great many thoughts but no such thing as a truth. Man made the truths himself and each truth was a composite of a great many vague thoughts....It was the truths that made the people grotesques.... [T]he moment one of the people took one of the truths to himself, called it his truth, and tried to live his life by it, he became a grotesque and the truth he embraced became a falsehood.[16]

O'Connor's South and its misfits require a critical gaze that can take in the regional landscape and the author's metaphorical rendering of it with an awareness of the in-built rhetorical grotesque of "Southern Gothic." Unlike the hyper-grotesques of Erskine Caldwell and Truman Capote, O'Connor's is representative of an archaic sort of realism. It creates the possibility for an awareness of the self as essentially deluding by underscoring the comic element of an inevitably errant human will. This "grotesque realism," as Bakhtin called it, insinuates that the reader shares a kinship with the inverted hero who, like Mr. Head on his way to Atlanta, assumes a posture of absolute knowledge in a world he comprehends only superficially.[17] Such an association encourages the reader to suspend the reflex to predetermine the significance of a scene or an object by means of an incidental marker. For instance, when Mr. Head and his nephew are reconciled before the "artificial nigger," the pair's vain conceptions of self and of blackness are mysteriously undone but also reinforced. Mr. Head and Nelson remain the product of a bigoted rural culture; they will continue to presume racial

---

[15] Mikhail Bakhtin, *Problems of Dostoevksy's Poetics*, ed. and trans. Caryl Emerson (Minneapolis: University of Minnesota Press, 1984) 9.

[16] Sherwood Anderson, *Winesburg, Ohio*, rev. ed. (New York: Penguin Books USA Inc., 1992) 23–24.

[17] Mikhail Bakhtin, *Rabelais and His World*, trans. Hélène Iswolsky (Bloomington: Indiana University Press, 1984) 24.

superiority, but the basis of that presumption has been irrevocably undermined by a contrary vision. "Mr. Head is changed by his experience," O'Connor wrote to Hester in 1958, "even though he remains Mr. Head. He is stable but not the same man at the end of the story. Stable in the sense that he bears his same physical contours and peculiarities but they are all ordered to a new vision."[18] O'Connor's art is replete with such transfiguring signs, and the critical dialogue they require is one of open dynamism, which assesses with equal priority the textual and extratextual discourse of the regional South but does not install an essentialized Southern reality as an interpretive baseline or endpoint.

Section 1: "The Woods Are Full of [Them]" O'Connor and the "Regional Writer"[19]

To address O'Connor's fictive South as a particular literary phenomenon not necessarily reflexive of its associated tradition, the reader must take account of the constructedness and intertextuality of the literary and critical South(s) and their engagement of geographical, political, and philosophical registers. The South is, first and foremost, a geographical space with certain historical contingencies and political nuances not unlike the West and North. In a nation as expansive and heteroglot as the United States, region has accrued strong associations with idiomatic traditions descriptive of character—a cultural shorthand, in other words. Thomas Jefferson contrasted the Northern and Southern sections of the Union with images of natural, climatic division—the cold, sober North and the warm, bountiful South—and denoted the social mannerisms of each region as endemic of their climates. Place, in the Colonial American mind, was thought to imbue character and impart distinct social valuations. Today the tradition of regional identification remains active despite the effects of mass cultural homogenization, most notably in white America where the region seems to endow a meaningful identity that whiteness does not.

Regional orientation creates an oversimplified picture of the national scene, to be sure, but its simplicity is one of its greatest virtues. It affords an approximate sketch of the American landscape,

---

[18] O'Connor, *Habit*, 275.

[19] O'Connor, "The Fiction Writer and His Country," *Mystery*, 29.

compact enough to transmute powerful automatic associations. Regional associations can be as frivolous as popular kitsch or as shortsighted as stereotype, but they are linked nonetheless to more profound and lasting intonations that have built up over time around particular locales.

More insistently than most national literatures, American literature is connotatively geographical, conjoined with real and imagined places that have intimate associations with the nation's stories and storytellers: Gatsby and Fitzgerald with greater New York, Joad and Steinbeck with California's middle coast, Huck and Twain with the Mississippi Valley. These fictionalized regions are cross-illuminated by greater geographical mythologies: the North as immigrant gateway, the far West as new frontier, and the Deep South as corrupt Eden. Set apart in spirit from the optimistic materialism of other sections, the "fallen" South has the notoriety of being the most studied region in the world.[20] Certainly, in the history of American storytelling there has been no other community, imagined or otherwise, that has produced as active or as disparate a body of images as the South. From the colonial period Southerners began to tell of themselves as a distinct community inscribed by a temperate climate and folk tradition. This American Other inspired a circuit of discourse both within and without its borders that told of a place at once seductive and horrifying, serene and hysterical, comic and pitiable—a place, in other words, unlike any other. The result of so many well-cherished contradictions is a discursive locale that challenges its two-dimensionality on the map and in its self-narration, a place that extends, for better or worse, beyond the imposition of hard data. But is the South, in fact, inherently different? Is it an organically originating entity with a unique character that is preserved by continuous dialogue, or are its differences incidental? Are they the result, not of a natural inclination in the climate or the population, but of the repeated suggestion—in literature, in popular culture, even in natural science—of Southern difference? Could the particular expressions of Southernness and the very extremity of the most glamorous and destructive of these be a function of design more so than nature, the garbled feedback of an

---

[20] John Shelton Reed, *The Enduring South: Subcultural Persistence in Mass Society* (Chapel Hill: University of North Carolina Press, 1972) 1.

almost constant inquisition of morbid curiosity not felt in any other section?

The answer for Scott Romine is in the very circuity of Southern discourse. "[S]uch circuity," he writes, "[is] constitutive of culture rather than a dead attempt to conjure or simulate it. In other words…the ghost dancing [of telling about the South] works (because culture is never something that one simply has) and, moreover, that the ghosts so produced tend to be, on the whole, friendlier ghosts than, say, those haunting Quentin Compson…"[21] By adopting Romine's outlook and directing their focus on cultural narration as a process rather than a collection of static markers that renews, creates, and destroys the image called "The South," critics might begin in earnest what many are calling the "New Southern Studies."[22] This new line of inquiry is distinguished from conventional Southern criticism by its primary assumptions; it does not, for example, suppose an essential South that is somehow lost and apparent, and which, in this real-life ghost state, actuates every piece of Southernalia, from Faulkner to the Dukes of Hazzard. The compulsion to isolate a real South from the constructed South(s), an impulse that has characterized so much of modern Southern criticism, is here abandoned for a methodology that works by first laying bare all of the insulating Southern stereotypes. In Michael Kreyling's words, "'New' southern studies surrenders its traditional claim to regional and historical distinctiveness, finds a common language in public debates over globalization of identities, and takes its chances in the dangerous, new, postmodern world where construction replaces essence."[23] If this New Southern critic were to return to O'Connor's South, in theory he would not be on the lookout for some definitive, character-giving place, but for the possibility of the creation, recreation, and even destruction of a

---

[21] Scott Romine, *The Real South: Southern Narrative in the Age of Cultural Reproduction* (Baton Rouge: Louisiana State University Press, 2008) 233. Romine refers here to a phrase coined by Rodger Lyle Brown, "ghost dancing on the cracker circuit," which Brown used in a book by the same name to describe Southern nostalgia for a never-extant, aggrandized South.

[22] See Michael Kreyling, "Toward a 'New Southern Studies,'" *South Central Review* 22/1 (Spring 2005): 4–18; Katherine McKee, *Global Contexts, Local Literatures: The New Southern Studies* (Durham: Duke University Press, 2006).

[23] Ibid., 16.

particular South at a particular moment in time and in the interpretation of the significance of those possibilities. "The image of the South, in all its complexity, is so strong in us," O'Connor wrote in 1963, "that it is a force that has to be encountered and engaged. The writer must wrestle with it, like Jacob with the angel, until he has extracted a blessing."[24] The New Southern Studies, like O'Connor's proverbial Southern writer, must confront, first and foremost, that same warring angel if it hopes to tell about a South in a way that is not primarily a reproduction of "The South" in miniature. This means distinguishing the tropological South from, say, Zora Neale Hurston's Florida or Harry Crews's Georgia, and rereading those localized Souths, not independently of South-specific tropes because it would be impossible and, I think, wrong-headed to simply discard them, but in tandem with the old tropes so that mythologized and localized South are both understood as constructed, not literal, impressions. From this vantage critics might ask how Southern discourse, oral and written, was impacted when the South was made the Grand Old South and later the Benighted South. How did these grand narratives effect the individual's South and the greater plurivocal South that existed alongside it? What kind of South was possible (or impossible) because of the construction and proliferation of such a narrative?

To address these and other questions, it is crucial to imagine the South, not as a rigid, contemporized space, but as a fluid conglomerate of past and present narratives, each superimposed one upon the other. Foremost is the contemporary post-South, a fragmented and multivocal place intent, at least in its literary circles, upon exploding the Southern typology and reappropriating the Southern space. The middle distance holds the bold promise of the New South in the form of industrial progress as well as the idealistic conservatism of the Agrarian South's "stand." In the dusky background remains the grandeur of the Moonlit Magnolia South and its grotesque counterpoint, the degenerate, morally bankrupt Southern backwater. Dissimilar as they seem, these constructed Souths are a part of the same discursive line, and like blood kin, each successive counter-image is bound to its predecessor. New Souths do

---

[24] O'Connor, "The Catholic Novelist in the Protestant South," *Mystery*, 198.

not mean new blood. Every revision of the Southern narrative is underwritten by the imprint of older and sometimes dead Souths, though a particular text may claim autonomy and maintain a seeming unawareness of its narrative lineage. The region's literature is, in this sense, a conglomerate of old and new memories. The postwar gothic carries with it the Old Southern romance as well as the rhetoric of the New South and the Agrarian pastoral, but of all the ways that lay readers and critics have reimagined the South—from Colonial Eden to post-modern Purgatory—the image they seem to have the least faith in is a realistic South. Vladimir Nabokov had it just right when he said that "'reality' is one of the few words that means nothing without quotes;" in the past century, "The South" has more than earned a pair of its own.[25] Critics have defined and redefined, deconstructed and remapped the region so many times that it seems incomplete or even naive without the quotes. They are not a sign of a South that is objectively apparent but of "The South" with its many and changeable qualifications. Reading the region therefore invokes an irony Faulkner would be proud of: the harder we try to see the real South, to authenticate it with theories and maps, the harder it becomes to see anything but "The South."

As a historical entity and an agent of political and cultural influence, the South is best described as a composite of ritualized spaces that correlate to a complex of interlocking ideologies: the colonial South, the Confederacy,[26] and the regional South, from the

---

[25] The 1997 film adaptation of Nabokov's infamous *Lolita* was relocated from its novelistic setting in the Midwest and New England to the Deep South. The change is one of very few director Adrian Lyne made to the primary material for his shooting script. On the whole, his version depicts a more faithful retelling of the novel than Kubrick's 1962 adaptation, but by resetting the story in the South, Lyne implies that the story might be infused with an atmosphere suggestive of more immediate possibility than might be found in the stereotypically lukewarm Midwest. Nabokov had quite a different picture of the American landscape, and I find it particularly telling that Lyne should decide, some forty years later, that the only place where *Lolita* could be effectively retold, the only place it could be made believable was "the South," a place which is, in itself, arguably as much a construction as Nabokov's heroine.

[26] The Confederacy comprised eleven states: Florida, Georgia, Alabama, Louisiana, Mississippi, Texas, Arkansas, Tennessee, North and South Carolina, Virginia, and several border states (Missouri, Kentucky, Oklahoma, and West Virginia) that contributed, at times, to the Confederate

highly politicized era of Reconstruction to the relatively apolitical Americanized South of the present. Economic and political allegiances between the Southern colonies and later the Confederate states made for relatively stable Southern borders, but the watermarks of discrete folk cultures often extended beyond these political boundaries. Although the notion of a regional South predates the Confederacy, sociologists, literary critics, and historians continue to debate where its borders lie and if these should conform to state lines or the contours of distinct geographical sub-regions and culture groups. As a result, contemporary maps tend to define the region more so by cultural continuities than by political borders. They include not only the Confederate states but several border states traditionally classed as non-Southern (Delaware, Maryland, and Oklahoma) and topographical regions that are in some way culturally distinctive (Southern Appalachia, the Ozarks, the Piedmont, and the Gulf Coast, or more generally, the Upland, Midland, and Lowland South).[27]

Implicit in regional mapping is an assumption of continuity between sub-sections; within the South this assumption is underscored by the customary association of place with culture where Southernness is thought to emanate organically from place itself.[28] What has been called the "Southern mind" has its roots in the

---

cause but never formally seceded from the Union. W. J. Cash argued that three of these border states (Missouri, Kentucky, and West Virginia) were "more than half Southern" in temperament, a remark that suggests a South that is more fluid and far-reaching than Confederate politics.

[27] Jason Bell references a startlingly divergent map of the South issued by the United States Embassy to Japan in his essay "'An Island in the South': Tampa's 19th-Century Regional Identity." The map redraws the boundaries of the region in such a way that the Appalachian sub-region, coastal Virginia and Delaware, and sizable swaths of Arkansas, Missouri, and Florida are no longer demarcated as a part of the South. Bell notes that this map could only be conceived and published for non-Americans because of its implication of disinheritance from regional identifications.

[28] Reed posits in his sociological survey *The Enduring South* that the "conceptual status of 'region' as an attribute of individuals (not 'regions' as geographical entities) remains unclear. Like race, and like religion, in it noncreedal aspects, region is a summary construct. It 'often captures (imperfectly to be sure) a set of historical experiences, socialization patterns, lifestyles, and…culture differences.' There is an intrinsic aspect of region, however, which sets it off from these other face-sheet data. As many

collective internalization of the Southern landscape.[29] Indeed the very concept of Southernness embodies a manner-endowing nativism that attaches preeminent value to social postures thought to be indigenous and continuous. But can we still argue, as Cash did, that the persistence of regional identification is attributable to a self-reflexive circuit of equating place with personality and vice versa? Cash was among the first social scientists to posit that Southerners are more attentive to and defensive of territorial boundaries because of the handing down of a politic that was a matter of life or death for their ancestors. Surely the same could be said, to a degree, of the Northerner. The Union lost nearly 700,000 men to the South's 500,000, and yet there is not a sense of collective "placeness" coalescent with the Civil War in the North. If New Yorkers or Vermonters think of themselves as Northern, it is secondarily. The immediacy of the borough, the city, or the state has always had more resonance than the more amorphous "North." Vanderbilt's Fugitive Poets interpreted the Northerner's relative disinterest in regional self-identity as a symptom of urbanization, which broke up the rural community and artificially transplanted it into ready-made, hyper-communities. Percy echoed their sentiments in the 1980s, claiming that the North was not a place at all: it is Nowhere.

Instead of radiating inward upon itself like the discourses of the South, Northern discourse radiates outward and is coincident with the phenomenon of Americanness. The North does not conceive itself as regional in the same way the South does for the fundamental reason that when it entered into the Civil War, it did so not to defend itself per se but to defend a greater Union. For the South, the war was waged over immediate and personal terms, among these the

---

'regionalist' scholars have observed, there are good reasons to suppose that the simple fact of residence in a particular area, implying exposure to a peculiar climate, soil, and terrain, will produce distinctive effects. If regional differences in culture and demography exist, residence alone will also determine exposure to these no-less-important 'climates'" (Reed, *The Enduring South* [Chapel Hill: University of North Carolina Press, 1972] 9; M. Kent Jennings and L. Harmon Zeigler qtd. in Reed "The Salience of State Politics among Attentive Publics" [Conference Proceedings, American Political Science Association Annual Meeting, 1968]).

[29] The phrase was first coined by the sociologist and historian Wilbur J. Cash in his seminal work *The Mind of the South* (New York: Vintage Books, 1941).

proliferation of states' rights, the justification of increased import levies, and the threat of a more generalized federal imposition. The North meanwhile was buffeted by the image of a patently righteous and self-evident American landscape, a landscape that was more the result of national myth-making than the experience of any particular place. The Southern mythos had only the fire-eating of its politicians and the now legendary heart of its soldiers to reassure itself, and even these were troubled by suspicions as to the worthiness of their cause. Nevertheless, the South remained an idea people were willing to die for. The region's tradition of fatal determination distinguished its tragedian renaissance from the turn-of-the-century American mainstream.

Initially, the sense of Southern placeness manifested itself in much cruder forms. At its most primitive, the Southern space evoked an exoticized, often carnally gratuitous, local-colorism. In Joel Chandler Harris's *Uncle Remus*, the South was the setting of living folklore authenticated by both Northern and European intrigue with the region's "magic and exotic ingredients."[30] Indeed, Harris's Br'er Rabbit can seem, at times, to be a more authentic Southerner than Remus, Augustus Baldwin Longstreet's Georgians or George Washington Harris's Sut Lovingood, even if he is a rabbit. "The Southern novelist, from Cable on," Percy claimed, "is tempted to exploit the Northern reader's gullibility and tell whoppers.[31] Even Faulkner...yielded sometimes to the temptation of 'writing Southern,' [living up] to a certain degree of exoticness expected of [him]."[32] As Percy asserts, the literary South is to some extent a self-fulfilling locale animated by the Southern writer's eagerness to amaze and the non-Southerner's eagerness to believe almost anything he's told occurs below the Mason-Dixon. This artificially trumped-up South has plagued the Southern writer with realist inclinations for generations. When O'Connor spoke about the so-called Southern Grotesque in her essay "The Fiction Writer and His Country," she describes the disjoint between the actual art experience and the expected grotesqueness of any piece of writing that comes out of the South. "Some may blame preoccupation with the grotesque," O'Connor remarked,

[30] Percy, *Signposts*, 480.

[31] Ibid., 176.

[32] Ibid., 170.

> on the fact that here we have a Southern writer and that this is just the type of imagination that Southern life fosters. I have written several stories which did not seem to me to have any grotesque characters in them at all, but which have immediately been labeled grotesque by non-Southern readers. I find it hard to believe that what is observable in one section can be entirely without parallel in another.[33]

O'Connor's work was to a large degree preempted by the texts that had come before it, by the way those texts were interpreted, and by the generalized tone associated with the Southern milieu. "In nineteenth-century American writing," she noted, "there was a good deal of grotesque literature which came from the frontier and was supposed to be funny; but our present grotesque characters, comic though they may be, are at least not primarily so....[T]heir fanaticism is a reproach, not merely an eccentricity."[34] O'Connor's own use of the grotesque, which sought to combine concrete and ultimate realties within a single image, was reduced to its mechanism of distortion by the critical apparatus associated with South Western humorists like Mark Twain and G. W. Harris and local-colorists like Longstreet.[35] The peculiar use of humor in the South suggests a further remove from the real in which "real scenes," as Longstreet called them, are presented as a transparent narrative to be read as a shared joke on place. A fictive South, in other words, is posited with an offstage wink as a literal South. This kind of humor involves the reader and yet allows him to remain apart from the scene, above, not implicated in the laughter though he might identify with the literal place that the writer has distorted for effect.

Twain's *Adventures of Huckleberry Finn* marks a definitive movement away from the insulating humor of early local-colorists to a more direct address of the reader and his conceptual South. With Huck, Twain was still playing "the old game of amazing Yankees" but with a very different end in mind.[36] He does not remove the authorial voice from its originating place through a downward-looking humor. Rather, he makes himself, his knowledge of self through place, the object of restitutive laughter. Huck makes the

---

[33] O'Connor, "The Fiction Writer and His Country," *Mystery*, 32.
[34] Ibid., 44.
[35] Ibid., 42.
[36] Percy, *Signposts*, 170.

unprecedented decision to "go to Hell" for the sake of Jim by helping him to freedom, but he also has a hand in subjugating Jim by participating in Tom's charade. There is no escape from context in Twain. Conversely, Longstreet situated the authorial voice above the local frame; his narrator introduces himself as a "native Georgian" but is ultimately so unlike the natives he encounters that he appears as an observer, alien enough to seem objective. Harris's authorial voice is embedded in the person of Uncle Remus, whose race and dialect set him apart from the reality of the anticipated reader. Huck's adventure, although left unfinished, is to draw the attention of the reader to the territorial boundaries between children and men, blacks and whites, the South and the non-South, and to demonstrate the literal and ritual value of crossing those boundaries. His story ends in anti-climax with the hero striking out for the quintessential nonplace, The Territory, where context is subsumed by a wide-open, uncreated space.

Mississippi writer Eudora Welty had an inverse method for confronting the tropological South: she struck in rather than out. Her novels explore the depth and significance of the gestures and mythologies operative in a very specific place. Where local-colorists such as Longstreet told the South chiefly by way of superficialities, Welty pushed beneath the surface to the hidden intricacies of life in a particular corner of the South. In *The Optimist's Daughter*, the heroine, Laurel McKelva Hand, returns home to Mount Salus, Mississippi, after her father's death. The town is a place she has actively disidentified herself with, and yet it seems the only place in which she is profoundly known. Here the South signifies in a very personal and lasting way as the place of original meaning. The Laurel McKelva who was created and remembered in Mount Salus survived her dislocation in Chicago and the destruction of that most intimate home place extant in mother and father. As she is leaving Mississippi, Laurel must confront her relative capability of knowing herself without Mount Salus, her girlhood clique, and her remaining family as markers. Her relinquishing the bread board to her father's spiteful widow, Fay, suggests that she needs no tokens of remembrance, that she will carry her South in the manifestation of self back to Chicago. The same question recurs in *Delta Wedding* but in reverse. How, the narrative asks, can Darby Fairchild, the very center of the bridal crush, know herself independently of the place she is so intensely identified with? The regional boundaries in Welty are internal ones, and whether self-knowledge is found in exile or in homecoming, it is the personal reconciliation with place that matters.

Truman Capote was himself an ex-patriot of the South, leaving Alabama for Manhattan, a place where he could give free reign to his inclination for performance and make the most of his Southern extraction. In effect, Capote's South is a formal caricature, highly stylized and pitched self-consciously at non-Southern attitudes and the wry slickness of the New York glossies. Capote's is an intellectualized exoticism, not as transparently bawdy as the work of Longstreet or G. W. Harris but as insistent in pulling the same gags. Within the first twenty pages of his early novel, *Other Voices, Other Rooms,* Capote references a "Yankee bandit," "Southern womanhood," and "Gothic splendor," but tone resonates more intensely than content in this passage and, indeed, throughout the book. [37] The narration is weighted with irony, but an irony that betrays what might have been a veiled feeling of indebtedness. With this first novel, Capote seems to be intentionally "doing Faulkner badly," and the result is parody with aspirations to the epic.[38] His later stories are less self-conscious in their uptake of Southern material, but it is only when he conceives his masterwork, the "nonfiction novel" *In Cold Blood,* and later the reportage sketches collected in *Music for Chameleons,* that he hits upon something that is definitely his own and not merely a reworking of the Moonlight and Magnolia trope. Very likely, it was to his benefit that the story of the rural Kansas murders came to him more or less intact. One can't help but think that the narrative comes off precisely because it is already appropriately horrendous, and the author was spared his ordinary compulsion to gothicize the real.

Distortion of the concrete and the use of the grotesque do not necessarily discount aesthetic worth, though the initial result is aimed decisively at the gut. The concrete is distorted to shock—O'Connor said as much herself—but distortion is only her first movement toward a greater intention, to illuminate what she

---

[37] Truman Capote, *Other Voices, Other Rooms* (New York: Vintage Books, 1994) 17–18.

[38] Walker Percy qtd. in *A Companion to the Literature and Culture of the American South,* ed. Richard Gray and Owen Robinson (Malden: Blackwell Publishing, 2004) 18.

conceived was an ultimate reality within the concrete. She blamed the modern championing of sentimental compassion for dulling the reader's sensibility to deeper kinds of realism. "[I]n this country," she noted, "the general reader has managed to connect the grotesque to the sentimental, for whenever he speaks of it favorably, he seems to associate it with the writer's compassion."[39] O'Connor asserted that compassion, as an all too market-friendly quasi-emotion, was not essential to the writer. She posited instead a gut-level, perspective-altering sensibility that might force the reader's own tongue-clicking compassion to the side so that he might encounter a realism capable of expanding his consciousness, not merely reinforcing the desire to be shocked and consoled. "Is it no accident," Percy asked in 1986, "that the century of terror is also the century of sentimentality. What the novelist notices is not how awful the happenings are but how peculiar it is that people don't seem to notice how awful the happenings are."[40]

The misreading of the grotesque aspect of alternative realist modes in Southern fiction is a phenomenon conjoined with the larger misinterpretation of the South as a place where grotesqueries are singularly at home. The inclination to link a piece of writing that is contextually southern to regional tropes—for instance, decadence, degeneration, supernaturalism—has inspired such terms as "Southern Gothic" and "Southern Grotesque," but these are underwritten by a troubling tautology. If the Southern Gothic can be equated to broke-down Cavaliers, miscegenation, poverty, and incest, then these same race-shifting, penniless, sister-loving Cavaliers are definitively Southern Gothic. Too easily this logic deteriorates into South = Gothic. The result is a conceptualized region where place configures meaning in a very specific and tenacious way. Writers including Faulkner and O'Connor have, to some extent, disarmed the regional trope by manipulating and recreating it in such a radical way that it cannot be slotted into the self-affirming South = Gothic/Gothic = South circuit. Faulkner's Quentin Compson (*The Sound and the Fury, Absalom, Absalom!*) was transported to an ice-gripped Massachusetts to tell about the South. "It is no accident," Percy wrote, "...that Quentin arrived at his final

---

[39] Ibid., 43.

[40] Percy, *Signposts*, 156.

solution, not in Yoknapatawpha County, ...in a Southern locale drenched in history and tragedy, ...but rather in a nonplace, wandering around the back streets of a bland Boston suburb... If [Faulkner] had set Quentin's suicide in the South against a backdrop of Gothic decor, ...it would have been robbed of its meaning."[41]

Place is doubly threatened in Percy's own "triumphant... Sunbelt" South, first by the old enemy of Southern exoticism and second by the onslaught of cultural homogenization.[42] His heroes seek a way out of the comfortable malaise of middle-class American non-identity by identifying with a literalness that brings placeness back to a mainstreamed South. Percy's *Moviegoer*, Binx Bolling, turns cinema into a ritual experience of verifying the reality of place. He watches the 1950s thriller *Panic in the Streets* in a theater that sits in the same New Orleans borough where it was shot in order to ground his immediate, trivialized real in a medium that transcends the particulars of time and self and isolates the detail of space within a signifying frame. The film, Percy remarked, "'certifies' the reality of the neighborhood in a peculiar sense in which direct experience of the neighborhood, living in the neighborhood, does not."[43]

But why should Percy's New Orleans need to be "certified"? Shouldn't Binx have that fateful sense of Southern placeness? Martyn Bone describes the paradox of Southern self-validation as post-southernness, the construction of a hyper-reality intended to reinforce another hyper-reality. Richard Ford's work might be called definitively post-southern in its offering an explicit counter to the "Southern sense of place." Ford seems to write from an anti-place, Anyplace not No Place, without allegiance to a particular locale as inherently meaningful or informing to him.[44] He actively negates his Southernness by denying and parodying the assumption that he should have a deep artistic connection with regional traditions. Bone suggests that Ford has "clinically dissected and disposed of the hoary shibboleths that supposedly define 'the South' as different from 'the North' ...[only to become] entangled in even more

[41] Ibid., 163.

[42] Ibid., 180.

[43] Ibid., 378.

[44] For an in-depth discussion of Ford's response to Percy's South, see Martyn Bone, *The Post-Southern Sense of Place in Contemporary Fiction* (Baton Rouge: Louisiana State University Press, 2004) 74–92.

pervasive and powerful myths of national identity."[45] Ford's impulse is more inclusive and outward reaching than the tradition of Southern writing seems to allow. What Percy called Nowhere, Ford calls Anywhere. The implication is one of limitlessness, of place as possibility and land as opportunity—familiar territory for the proverbial American.

The movement toward a post-southern landscape integrated subtly into the American mainstream is evident in the work of other contemporary writers like Bobbie Ann Mason and Jayne Anne Phillips. In their fictions, the conceptual borders between regions morph and dissolve. Such sudden and unpredictable shifts in the post-southern map suggest a critical unwillingness to construct a definitive place that correlates the physical and social climates of the region. Likewise a certain squeamishness underlies Southern studies, perhaps a fear of misspeaking yet again, which intimates a sense of something yet indefinable, something dynamic and detachable from, but also resonant in, the physical South. It is as if a sticky discursive fog hovers just above the southeastern U.S. to see the map the critic must look through a haze of interlocking discourse, through the old Moonlight and Magnolia South, the Agrarian pastoral, the New South, and the postmodern No-South.[46] He can be sure that no matter which of these he has hold of, the rest are not too far off, hunched behind so many figurative bushes like a gang of wary cousins.

Critical surveys of the South, like Howard Odum's, Louis Rubin, Jr.'s, Michael Kreyling's, and Richard Gray's, inevitably arrive at this disorienting crossroads between the literal and ideological South(s), Southern and non-Southern writers alike who presume to tell about the place has to travel that same shifting track. They share in Binx's quest for "the Real Right Thing," a verifiable South somewhere within "The South," but where is it exactly? Is it in the land, hunkered down in the heart of the Deep Southern states, or is it strung out along the border lands? Is it in the people, in the old Southern stock or the blow-ins, the folks who've dug in or struck out to New Jersey and California? Or perhaps the Real Right Thing is not a thing at all but, as Jefferson Humphries claims, an idea. Could it be

---

[45] Ibid., 249.

[46] James C. Cobb, *Away Down South: A History of Southern Identity* (Oxford: Oxford University Press, 2005) 68.

that the real South *is* the storied South, every story from the garden to the backwater and on to the sky-scrapers and theme parks? Nearly a century ago, Howard Odum wrote that, as a term, "'the South' is not accurate," and the same is true today, perhaps even more so. There are still "vast differences between [Southern] states and in many instances, these differences are growing. ...There [are] many Souths yet the South."[47] Cash echoed this sentiment in his infamous study, *The Mind of the South*: "[I]f it can be said there are many Souths, the fact remains that there is also one South" defined by a "fairly definite mental pattern associated with a fairly definite social pattern."[48]

Richard Gray, Great Britain's preeminent Southernist, has made a career of exploring the unstable territory between the ethereal Southern region and the many local Souths within it. His work, which spans thirty years of study, describes comprehensively the movement of Southern criticism from a pre-modern assumption of a solid univocal South to a contemporary dialogue of multiple and dynamic Souths. Gray's regional criticism begins with the relatively conservative *The Literature of Memory* (1977) and progresses to increasingly more skeptical and deconstructive texts like *Writing the South* (1986), *Southern Aberrations* (2000), and *A Web of Words* (2007). This is not to say that Gray's early work is patently naïve and therefore irrelevant; on the contrary, his first major inroad into the field is a crucial marker of conventional Southern criticism's progressive edge. While Gray does assume a relationship between the defining conceit of that criticism—that there is a preexisting physical space called the South, which is stable and contiguous and exhibits a more or less uniform cultural nuance—and Southern literature, he maintains that the conceptualization of a solid South is just that, a conceit. Nevertheless, the tradition of investing in the myth did (and does) exist; however disconnected it was with historical fact, the myth has had a pointed and lasting effect upon the local idiom, which has itself affected the character of the region's literature. "Southern tradition," Gray writes, "cannot be treated to definitive analysis. Its nature is too complicated, and its implications

---

[47] Howard W. Odum and Harry Estill Moore, *American Regionalism: A Cultural-Historical Approach to National Integration* (New York: H. Holt and Company, 1938) 523.

[48] Cash, *The Mind of the South,* xlviii.

too many, for that. But an understanding of the tendencies of its 'technique' is feasible, I think, and even necessary."[49] Gray proposed in his earliest work that the Southern context, both literal and metaphorical, fostered a certain technique for day to day living, and that by examining the "available source of ideas" in the modern Southern milieu and the ways they have been employed in fiction, critics might be able to "[estimate] the relationship of the individual writer to his regional tradition."[50] This sort of anthropological approach has its modern roots in Southern Agrarianism, a social movement that sought to preserve Southern folk traditions by promoting a rural or semi-rural lifestyle in which agricultural vocations were prioritized over industrial ones.[51] The Southern Agrarian credo, written by the Fugitive Poets, a collective of scholars and writers who met at Vanderbilt in the 1920s and 1930s, was a firm statement of supposed regional difference.[52] According to the Agrarian vision, the South was not a part of the "American or prevailing [industrial] way."[53] Like Allen Tate, Gray argues that the so-called Southern Renaissance was the result of the "breaking up" of a "relatively homogenous [agricultural] society."[54] The Renaissance writers:

> were all concerned with the history and the myth of the South, and the mutually effective tension between the two... Their freedom was limited and, in a sense, given meaning by the specifics of the contemporary situation and by the details of a shared history, which, although it was complex, was nevertheless susceptible to tentative and provisional definition.[55]

A truly critical literature could occur in the South only when it had sufficient perspective from the assumptions of its cultural

---

[49] Richard Gray, *The Literature of Memory: Modern Writers of the American South* (London: Edward Arnold Ltd., 1977) 10.

[50] Ibid., 10.

[51] Allen Tate, et al., "Introduction: A Statement of Principles," *I'll Take My Stand: The South and the Agrarian Tradition*, ed. Lewis P. Simpson (Baton Rouge: Louisiana State University Press, 1930) xli–xlii.

[52] The Nashville Agrarians included Allen Tate, John Crowe Ransom, Andrew Nelson Lytle, Robert Penn Warren, Donald Davidson, John Gould Fletcher, Lyle H. Lanier, Stark Young, Frank Lawrence Owsley, John Donald Wade, Henry Blue Kline, and Herman Clarence Nixon.

[53] Tate, *Stand*, xxxvii.

[54] Gray, *Memory*, 8.

[55] Ibid., 2–3.

tradition. "What happens when a community undergoes a radical transformation like the South did in [the early part of the twentieth century]," Gray notes, "is that suddenly the assumptions behind that community are brought into the open."[56] The most central of those assumptions was that the South was fundamentally different, that Southerners were different, and "please God, [they] always would be."[57] The theme of Southern otherness is one that Gray became increasingly preoccupied with; *Writing the South* and *Southern Aberrations* both attempt to explain the source and persistence of the idea in Southern culture. Gray's shift in emphasis from memory, which implies an independent, external South to be remembered, and difference, which implies constructedness and revision, indicates a vital movement toward the unconventional.

Unfortunately for Southern-born writers like O'Connor, the conventional image of the South and Southern writing has persisted despite critics like Gray. Certainly her local idiom, which she cited approvingly in her essays and correspondence, impacted the kind of writing she produced, but these particulars, no matter how they are trotted out, are not synonymous with the art experience itself and cannot be asked to stand in for a more exhaustive exegesis of her complex aesthetic. Too frequently critics rely on a prevailing set of characteristics associated with Southern literature to explain O'Connor's interpretation of the Southern scene. Ironically, her work exhibits very few of these traits. She was not, like Faulkner, Caroline Gordon, or the Agrarians, preoccupied with a tragic pastoral past and seems not to exhibit the most "Southern" of Southern traits, "a concern with history, [and] a deep sense of loss and defeat..."[58] Stories like "A Late Encounter with the Enemy" and "A Good Man Is Hard to Find" deride the pageantry of past-obsessed ex-Confederates and link the memory of a Magnolia South to certain doom. What's more, her narrative structuring did not affect the fragmented, looping timeline that Faulkner made famous. Her families were spare and isolated, cut off from the intricate matrix of legacies, marriages, and secret consummations evident in Welty, Faulkner,

---

[56] Ibid., 8.

[57] Howard W. Odum, *An American Epoch: Southern Portraiture in the National Picture* (New York: H. Holt and Company, 1930) 68.

[58] Jerry Leath Mills, "The Dead Mule Rides Again," *Southern Cultures* 6/4 (Winter 2000): 15.

and Gordon. She did not, like Capote, Erskine Caldwell, and Tennessee Williams, exaggerate local idiosyncrasies for effect, nor did she make grotesqueries of her characters as a means in itself. In kind, she had the most in common with Carson McCullers, a writer whose work O'Connor "dislike[d] intensely" and went so far as to say that her book, *Clock Without Hands*, was "the worst book [she had] ever read."[59] Flannery and Carson did, nevertheless, tend toward the same sort of "Poor" Southern folk but with a crucial difference. Where McCullers seems satisfied to leave her characters to a hellish isolation, O'Connor extends a terrible hand of mercy. Although typically removed from the narrative's closing action, O'Connor's insinuation of her characters' probable redemption set her significantly apart from "The School of Southern Degeneracy."[60]

In spite of these differences, O'Connor did share several foundational tendencies with the so-called Southern tradition, among them a "strong sense of place, an interest in religion, a propensity for 'gothic' elements of horror and the grotesque, [and] a strongly biblical narrative tradition."[61] What conventional criticism tends not to stress is the unique aspect each of these takes on in the hands of individual Southern writers. Margaret Mitchell and O'Connor both wrote about life in rural and metropolitan Georgia, but no one would argue that the strong sense of place inherent in their work is the same sense. By creating a rubric of Southernness, critics have promoted what Michael Kreyling calls a "casebook South."[62] If, as Kreyling suggests, there is to be a New Southern Studies, there must first be a departure from the false standardization of Southern literariness, however attractive its canon of traits has become.[63]

Louis D. Rubin, Jr. makes an attempt to revitalize or at the very least restore a sense of seriousness to Southern criticism in his later work by steering other professional southerners away from the will-

---

[59] O'Connor, *Habit*, 446, 550.

[60] O'Connor, "The Catholic Novelist in the Protestant South," *Mystery*, 204.

[61] Mills, "The Dead Mule Rides Again," 15.

[62] Michael Kreyling, "Towards a New Southern Studies," 7.

[63] Mills makes the point well in his essay "The Dead Mule Rides Again" when he proposes a new and equally arbitrary litmus for defining Southern literature: "The test is: Is there a dead mule in it?" (15).

o-the-wisp that is the "definitive, delimiting, final" Southern character.[64] In his essay, "From Combray to Ithaca; or, The 'Southernness' of Southern Literature," Rubin builds upon a relatively recent change in critical tack by which the "Southern" in Southern literature is considered, not as "an ingredient...[or] quantity...whose presence in a work of literature contributes a material substance to that work...[but as] a catalyst...whose presence causes a reaction, a change, in the components in the work without itself being effected."[65] Southern literature is a qualitative, not quantitative, denotation that describes the arrangement of narrative elements, the overall narrative effect of that arrangement, and the significance of the interrelationships between these elements. "What makes us recognize and identify certain works of fiction as Southern," Rubin continues:

> is the particular and special ways in which such elements are arranged, the characteristic shapes that they assume in respect to each other, the manner in which they cause people to behave and writers to choose metaphors. And these special ways, particular forms, traits of behavior, and resources of language come out of the Southern community experience, a community that, however much it may differ from place to place and individual to individual, so shapes the imaginative response of its literary people that when they write their stories and poems they do so, to a markedly recognizable degree, as Southern authors.[66]

Though she abhorred the thought of becoming a "regional writer,"[67] O'Connor was relatively comfortable identifying herself as a Southern writer in spite of the fact that she did not necessarily walk the critical party line when it came to writing Southern.[68] Her fiction was not intent upon social critique or reform in the same immediate way that the work of predecessors like Caldwell's, Thomas Wolfe's,

---

[64] Louis D. Rubin, Jr., "From Combray to Ithaca; or, The 'Southernness' of Southern Literature," *Virginia Quarterly Review* 66/1 (Winter 1990): 48.

[65] Ibid.

[66] Ibid., 62–63.

[67] O'Connor, "The Fiction Writer and His Country," *Mystery*, 29.

[68] See O'Connor's essays, "The Fiction Writer and His Country," "Some Aspects of the Grotesque in Southern Fiction," and "The Regional Writer" (Flannery O'Connor, *Mystery and Manners: Occasional Prose*, ed. Sally Fitzgerald and Robert Fitzgerald [New York: Farrar, Straus & Giroux, 1957] 25, 36, 51).

or her longtime mentor Gordon's was. As her writing life progressed, O'Connor became increasingly aware that she operated a good deal outside of the tradition she should have inherited. "In the thirties," she noted in her essay "Novelist and Believer," "we passed through a period in American letters when social criticism and social realism were considered by many to be the most important aspects of fiction. ...The sociological tendency has abated in that particular form and survived in another just as bad. This is the notion that the fiction writer is after the typical."[69] Out of a practical necessity, O'Connor's own stories were framed in a contemporary and sometimes topically engaged setting, but the import of the topical was always subjected to the more profound implication of an "ultimate reality" beyond the contemporary scene. She regularly condemned writers who did exactly the opposite by committing the majority of narrative authority to a topical issue. Even the ingenious Welty gets into trouble here. In a letter to Hester written in 1963, O'Connor concurs with her friend's opinion regarding "the Welty story ['Where Is the Voice Coming From?']":[70]

> it is the kind of story that the more you think about it the less satisfactory it gets. What I hate most is its being in the New Yorker and all those stupid Yankee liberals smacking their lips over typical life in the dear old dirty Southland. The topical is poison. I got away with it in "Everything that Rises" but only because I say a plague on everybody's house as far as the race business goes.[71]

Rather than politicizing the real by prioritizing one side of a topical debate, O'Connor underlines the universality of human suffering by revealing the mutually condemning and redeeming qualities of the warring parties. The bold sequences of narrative action O'Connor traded in were not intended merely to raise political awareness but to compel the reader to "feel the contemporary situation at the ultimate level."[72]

Compared to the work of her regional contemporaries, O'Connor's cosmological aesthetic appears even less Southern. Next to modernists like Faulkner, O'Connor's all-consuming vision, which

---

[69] O'Connor, "Novelist and Believer," *Mystery*, 164.

[70] Welty's story was inspired by the murder of Medgar Evers, the leader of the Mississippi NAACP, in her native Jackson.

[71] O'Connor, *Habit*, 537.

[72] Ibid., 90.

was anchored in a past far beyond the oft conjured April morning in 1861, carried with it a twinge of radical conservatism. Though her writing became increasingly existential, O'Connor never adopted a tone, like Capote or McCullers, that affected a fundamentally cynical or disillusioned outlook of the life of the spirit in the modern age. The social holocausts that had befallen mankind in the twentieth century were, for O'Connor, subordinate to our primeval status as God's most prized creation, mortal beings with immortal souls. None of the great scourges of the age—economic depression and dehumanizing work, race hate and genocide, the threat of nuclear apocalypse—could affect a change in man's ultimate predicament. Someday he will suffer death. Just how he does was a more or less irrelevant detail alongside O'Connor's primary concern of illuminating the possibility for eternal life through redemption and eternal damnation through self-delusion. Her late work retains an underlying attentiveness to the long-view despite the many and troubling symptoms of modern man's dislocation from himself, his community, and his religious sensibility.

O'Connor's greater fictive South dramatizes the cumulative effect of spiritual disinheritance; it is representative of modern humanity in the South in an immediate sense but is also metaphorically transcendent. Here the world does not appear moonlit beneath the magnolias but floodlit by the unflinching, total presence of a deified sun. It was this bold-faced look at the middle and lower-class white South that so impressed Alice Walker. In her essay, "Beyond the Peacock: The Reconstruction of Flannery O'Connor," she noted that unlike other Southern writers she'd been introduced to in graduate seminars, writers like Faulkner, Welty, and McCullers, O'Connor was not "obsessed with a racial past."[73] Where these three "seemed to beg the question of their characters' humanity of every page," O'Connor took her characters' "humanity, if not their sanity, ...for granted."[74] They were "miserable, ugly, narrow-minded, atheistic, and of intense racial smugness and arrogance,

[73] Alice Walker, "Beyond the Peacock: Reconstructing Flannery O'Connor," *In Search of Our Mothers' Gardens: Womanist Prose* (New York: HBJ Publishers, 1983) 51.

[74] Ibid.

with not a graceful, pretty one anywhere who is not, at the same time, a joke…"[75] She goes on to say of O'Connor that:

> It was for her description of Southern white women that I appreciated her work at first, because when she set her pen to them not a whiff of magnolia hovered in the air (and the tree itself might never have been planted), and yes, I could say, yes, these white folks without the magnolia (who are indifferent to the tree's existence), and these black folks without melons and superior racial patience, these are like Southerners that I know.[76]

These aspects of O'Connor's aesthetic are ones that, if they were not so consistently associated with the trademarks of writers who are also called Southern, might be considered individual in their movements against the regional grain. Of course, this is not a concern unique to O'Connor; every writer in the South, whether or not he consciously engages Southern literary tropes, is in danger of having his mule-cart—if I may rework one of O'Connor's metaphors—hitched to Faulkner's Dixie Limited. The problem of automatic association is particularly detrimental to O'Connor's project because it interprets a good deal of the ground available for dramatic play; her work comes to the reader somewhat predetermined and with certain allusions built in. For her part, O'Connor was profoundly aware that interpretative prejudice was an occupational risk she took as a writer in the post-Renaissance South. Intriguingly, she exhibited the most aesthetic resistance to the "most Southern" of Southern writers. She was singularly wary of Faulkner and noted, in several of her letters, that in her own writing practice, she was careful to give him a wide berth in case his style, which had by then become synonymous with Southern fiction firing on all cylinders, might so discourage her own "one-cylinder syntax" that she would feel compelled to "quit writing and raise chickens altogether."[77]

Most modern anthologies of Southern fiction, and a fair number of contemporary ones, lump O'Connor into that School of Southern Gothicists invariably headed up by Faulkner. "When I first began to write," O'Connor notes, "my own particular bête noire was that mythical entity, The School of Southern Degeneracy. Every time I

---

[75] Ibid., 52.

[76] Ibid.

[77] O'Connor, *Habit*, 292.

heard about the School of Southern Degeneracy, I felt like Br'er Rabbit stuck on the Tarbaby."[78] Marion Montgomery points out that, "It is quite common...to find Faulkner, Flannery O'Connor, Capote, Carson McCullers all yoked together as southern fiction writers of the same stamp."[79] *The Companion to Southern Literature* (2002), for one, lists Faulkner, O'Connor, Welty, McCullers, Caldwell, and Capote as Southern Gothicists. To be fair, the editors of this particular anthology do make an attempt to describe how each of these writers employs and interprets the Gothic, but the underlying suggestion of similarity implied by the texts' organization raises the question: does it further our understanding of individual authors and texts to persist in the claim that a generic likeness exists between them? When we are talking about this sort of companion-to-type anthologizing, yes, there is a degree of utility in generalization, but when the generalization is then interpreted as the rule and the anthology something more than a rough guide, critics begin to confuse Faulkner or Welty or O'Connor with any one or all of the marks of generic Southernness. Rather than define O'Connor by how well she represents the conventional Southern aesthetic, could she be better located through negative associations? How is she *not like* Faulkner, et al.? As previously mentioned, O'Connor does not exhibit a circuitous past-obsession like Faulkner or Welty, nor does she link up her grotesques with socio-historical circumstances like Caldwell, Wolfe, and Gordon. In fact, O'Connor does not seem to acknowledge the monolithic South except as a lost cause, refusing to give the same degree of narrative priority to it that her predecessors did. She did not, like Tate and the Agrarians, write the South as a rhetorical projection of the Southern body politic. For this reason the Fugitive project was, at times, guilty of what Bakhtin called "philosophical monologu[ing]," an attempt to "squeeze...the plurality of consciousness" in the South(s) "into the systematically monologic framework of a single worldview..."[80]

---

[78] O'Connor, "Some Aspects of the Grotesque in Southern Fiction," *Mystery*, 38.

[79] Marion Montgomery, "A Sense of Violation: Notes Toward a Definition of 'Southern' Fiction," *On Matters Southern: Essays About Literature and Culture, 1964–2000*, ed. Michael M. Jordan (Jefferson: McFarland, 2005) 54.

[80] Bakhtin, *Problems*, 9.

For O'Connor and her immediate contemporaries, the motivating image of place was no longer a monolithic South but a very specific local South some years after the Fall. At its worst, this was a South of dead-ended hysteria, a place made hopeless and hungry by the explosion of its common nostalgia. For Capote and Williams it was the negative impression of the Southern pastoral exaggerated to incredible shapes. Though O'Connor was herself an advocate of fictive distortion, she stipulated that the artist be granted the liberty to "make certain rearrangements to nature if these will lead to greater depths of vision."[81] Whether intentional or not, the greater depth of vision prompted by Capote's, Williams's, and at times McCullers's grotesques is one of morbid wonderment; unlike O'Connor's distortions, their characters appear irredeemable and often contorted to the point of inhumanity. McCullers's and Capote's characters, in Montgomery's words, "have a grotesqueness which defines them as separate from mankind, while Faulkner's and O'Connor's characters have their grotesqueness as a definition of their relationship."[82] Lay readers and critics alike are misled by certain superficial likenesses shared between Faulkner, O'Connor, Capote, McCullers, and Williams. O'Connor's heroes do share a tendency toward self-delusion with those of the other "Southern Gothicists," but the critical difference between them lies in their attitude toward that compulsion. There is everywhere in O'Connor's fiction the suggestion that her heroes suffer for the sake of their delusions; they are, as Montgomery has it, "self-responsible" as perpetrators and victims. The others seem to revel in their self-delusion, and if they suffer, they revel in that too.[83]

Perhaps the most pervasive of those delusions is the mythologized Southern space. Even in modern Southern fiction such as Capote's and Williams's that openly degrades the region's grand narrative, the underlying suggestion of that narrative—the image of a unifying, othered South—is still very much intact.[84] In an attempt to

---

[81] O'Connor, "Writing Short Stories," *Mystery*, 98.

[82] Montgomery, "A Sense of Violation," 55.

[83] Ibid.

[84] Montgomery suggests that Capote and Williams would be better described as "northern" writers who used "southern materials" in that they write through a "figuratively feminine" inactive "mood," which cannot create the necessary sense of self-responsibility he denotes in writers

understand how and why this particular delusion has survived in the literal South(s), Gray makes the vital distinction between "regional thinking (which implies…a continuous process…inviting conjecture…) and the regional mind (a rather grander term, suggesting some solid, autonomous object that is available for complete explanation)."[85] With this distinction as his guiding principle, Gray attempts to further undermine the conventional notion of a solid South. He suggests, and rightly so, that the region is not and never was a homogenous unit, but more accurately a family of sub-regions, each with its own cultural accent. "The South is an imagined community," Gray writes:

> made up of a multiplicity of communities, similarly imagined. Some of those communities are more imagined than others (where, say, there is little or no contact [between individuals]). Some individual Southerners, perhaps most, belong to several communities… Some are more active and aware in their imagining. Still, what all these communities have in common is the act of imagination.[86]

In *Writing the South* and *Southern Aberrations*, Gray explores the "Southern argument" almost exclusively in terms of what he calls "Southern self-fashioning," or the "construction" of the South(s) through "memory, …writing, talking, and telling about it."[87] Southern fiction is just one of "the various ways in which people from below the Mason-Dixon line have tried to forge the uncreated conscience of their region."[88] The notion of an original South gave credence to the ideal of a native literature; Southern writing was, in this sense, the organic outgrowth of the Southern mind. Critics such as Alfred Kazin and Lewis P. Simpson maintained that the region's literature was set apart from the main body of American literature by

---

including Faulkner and O'Connor (Marion Montgomery, "A Sense of Violation: Notes Toward a Definition of 'Southern' Fiction," *On Matters Southern: Essays About Literature and Culture, 1964–2000*, ed. Michael M. Jordan [Jefferson: McFarland, 2005] 51, 55).

[85] Richard Gray, *Writing the South: Ideas of an American Region* (Cambridge: Cambridge University Press, 1986) xiii.

[86] Richard Gray, *Southern Aberrations: Writers of the American South and the Problems of Regionalism* (Baton Rouge: Louisiana State University Press, 2000) 511.

[87] Ibid., xiii.

[88] Gray, *Writing*, xii.

virtue of its aesthetic tradition and its modern use of several uncommon devices: fragmented narrative structures, non-linear plot movements, and romantic flourishes that developed, at times, into a more aggressive "anti-realism" (e.g., Poe, Williams). Stephen Matterson notes, "The things we associate with Southern writing are often the same things we associate with [seminal writers like] Poe or Faulkner."[89] Our working definition of Southern literature is therefore based upon a relatively narrow ideal that prioritizes two things: the romantic/Gothic imagination and the overlapping circularity of social units, from family to township to region. "Most of us are considered," O'Connor noted herself, "...to be unhappy combinations of Poe and Erskine Caldwell."[90]

Leslie Fiedler is one of the few prominent modern critics who did not locate the grotesque exclusively in Southern writing. "[T]he American novel," he posits:

> is pre-eminently a novel of terror. ...Through these gothic images are projected certain obsessive concerns of our national life: the ambiguity of our relationship with the Indian and the Negro, the ambiguity of our encounter with nature, the guilt of the revolutionist who feels himself a parricide—and, not least of all, the uneasiness of the writer who cannot help believing that the very act of composing a book is Satanic revolt.[91]

Even W. D. Howells, the straight-faced Midwestern naturalist, considered grotesquerie a national inclination despite his having felt, firsthand, the effects of fictions that welled up from the Reconstruction South. He confided to Henry James that America itself "seem[ed] to be the most grotesquely illogical thing under the sun."[92] Illogical as it was, the American project was always sunnier in comparison to the credos of the ex-Confederacy, a contrast that helped to solidify the image of the South as a "cultural monolith, under threat and perhaps faced with imminent collapse."[93] Despite

---

[89] Stephen Matterson, personal interview, 11 February 2009.

[90] O'Connor, "The Fiction Writer and His Country," *Mystery*, 28.

[91] Leslie Fiedler, *Love and Death in the American Novel*, 3rd. ed. (Harmondsworth: Penguin Books, 1984) 26.

[92] William Dean Howells qtd. in Malcolm Bradbudy, "Naturalism and Impressionism: The 1890s," *The Modern American Novel*, rev. ed. (New York: Penguin Books, 1994) 1.

[93] Gray, ed., "Part I: Introduction," *Companion*, 15.

criticism that works against regional standardization, the idea of a plurivocal, heterogeneous South is one still complicated by the popular image of the Southern monolith that has conjoined, over time, with powerful narratives of Southern history, identity, and solidarity. This monolithic South is arguably the most persuasive idea in Southern letters regardless of how particular authors situate themselves within that tradition. Whether they write with the monolithic grain or against it, the pretextual idea of the South will act, in both instances, as an orientating principle.[94] It is this dependence on the Southern myth for form which makes a writer conventionally Southern. Gray and Owen Robinson contend that the distinguishing perception of the Southern writer is his envisaging himself as "someone writing from within that monolithic structure; if nobody exists like that, then there can be no such thing anymore as Southern writing. But the culture that, as a matter of self-identification—has defined itself as regional and Southern, has always been more mixed and fluid than this argument allows."[95] The image of the conventional Southern writer and his native aesthetic stands in contrast to the push in New Southern Studies to deconstruct the old regional tropes, but Gray and Robinson contest that the writing culture which produced iconic Southerners such as Thomas Sutpen, and self-deconstructing Southerners such as Binx Bolling, is essentially the same culture. "What we have now," they point out, "is an extension of what we have always had: different, developing social formations that those writers who are experiencing them choose to identify in regional terms—or, at least, choose to mark out using 'south' and 'region' as a part of their fictional vocabulary."[96] To interpret O'Connor in her proper context, New Southern criticism has shifted its attention from empirical data, such as illiteracy rates, political polls, and church rosters, to the fictional vocabulary associated with Southern discourse and the reciprocal impact of its relationship with Southern reality. O'Connor's proficiency as a realist was never dependent upon the placement of the South's borders or the ways in which its cultural quirks line up on a graph, but upon the continuing effectiveness of the Southern space as a persuasive idea capable of generating discourse.

---

[94] Gray, *Writing*, xii.

[95] Gray, ed., "Part I: Introduction," *Companion*, 15–16.

[96] Ibid., 16.

Section 2: Old South, New South, No-South: The History of Southern Self-Genesis

Contemporary critics, including Humphries and Jack Butler, suggest that accepting the South as part of a fictional vocabulary, while logical, is not a simple matter of reclassifying certain archetypes in the collective Southern memory as "fictional." As Gray has shown, Southern memory is embedded with regionalized fictions, and to deconstruct any one of them sets off an ever-complicating existential crisis. The hardest question Southern writers and critics have to face (if they decide that making such a designation is imperative to their work) is not where the South is or even what it is but *if* it is. Gray opens *Writing the South* with this very question and argues that Southern writing, if it is to be called "Southern," is to some degree a confrontation with regional self-consciousness. Humphries attempts to denote Southern existentialism in his article, "The Discourse of Southernness: Or How We Can Know There Will Still Be Such a Thing as the South and Southern Literary Culture in the Twenty-First Century":

> [W]hat we mean when we talk about the South...is not a geographical place and is only related to a geographical place by pure arbitrary contingency. The South is instead nothing in the world but an idea in narrative form, a discourse or rhetoric of narrative tropes, a story made out of sub-stories, a lie, a fiction to which we have lent reality by believing in it.[97]

The idea of the South has been a part of the American imagination for so long and is so conflated with "historical" narratives, folklore, and popular culture, that it is impossible to pinpoint where the actual stuff of South—the red clay and slash pines and slow-talking folk—stop being hard and fast things and become instead details in a narrative. For Cash, the point of diffusion came with the first rifle shot at Fort Sumter. "The conflict with the Yankee," he wrote, "[was what] really created the concept of the South as something more than a matter of geography, as an object of

---

[97] Jefferson Humphries, "The Discourse of Southernness: Or How We Can Know There Will Still Be Such a Thing as The South and Southern Literary Culture in the Twenty-First Century," *The Future of Southern Letters*, ed. Jefferson Humphries and John Lowe (New York: Oxford University Press, 1996) 120.

patriotism, in the minds of Southerners."[98] When the Confederacy fell, the story of the South became legend, elevated to a discursive space that superseded linear experience—a super-history with its epicenter located somewhere between Fort Sumter and Appomattox. Traditionalists argue that the Southern experience since the Confederate surrender cannot be disinherited from its Lost Cause, which, having been lost, is shot through with mythical archetypes and an unmistakably biblical diction. The "most inevitable and obvious" of all these "fictions," Cash wrote, "is...precisely the assumption that every planter was in the most rigid sense of the word a gentleman. Enabling the South to wrap itself in contemptuous superiority, to sneer down the Yankee as low-bred, crass, and money-grubbing, and even to beget in his bourgeois soul a kind of secret and envious awe, it was a nearly perfect defense-mechanism."[99]

Cash and successors like Reed and Humphries believe that the legendary Southern manner served Dixie far better than its rifles had; Cash recounts the way in which Southerners, tucked behind the rampart of their Great though fallen Civilization, reconstructed their cultural identity.[100] Reconstruction suggests an autonomous South that had a unified and sustaining cultural infrastructure prior to the war. Even though the "planters of the Old Dominion never managed, even in their own judgment, to create an indigenous aristocratic culture," the majority of Southerners accepted and even embellished the myth of antebellum splendor.[101] True, they had been bested by the industrial might of the North, but they were still gentlemen; they were still, as the story had it, heirs to a superior culture.[102] So powerful was this idea of tragic nobility that it continued to drum through Southern discourse long after Shiloh and Harpers Ferry were fitted with turnstiles and the grand old patriarchs had disappeared into the dust with the carpetbaggers and the sharecroppers. It managed to push its way into the twentieth century to be picked up by traditionalists like the Nashville Agrarians. "With us," John Peale Bishop told his friend Allen Tate,

---

[98] Cash, *The Mind of the South*, 65–66.

[99] Ibid., 61.

[100] Ibid., 124.

[101] Gray, *Writing*, 17.

[102] Gray, *Aberrations*, 500.

"Western Civilization ends."[103] The allure of belonging to an ancient agrarian lineage was not confined to the intellectual fringes. As Cash pointed out, "The nouveaux, the Virginians, all the South in fact, would join in asseverating and believing, that Southern culture outran not merely the Yankee's but even that of mankind's as a whole."[104]

How had the story of the South arrived at such a grand conceit? Several critics, including Cash, Humphries, and David Jansson, point North. They claim that the South was subjected, for generations, to external criticisms from England and later from the Northern United States. Initially these critiques were aimed at the South's dependence upon slave labor,[105] but over time they developed into more generalized moral assumptions, which together acted as a kind of "internal Orientalism,"[106] authorizing the persistent stereotyping of Southerners as a barbarous, "Christ-haunted"[107] hoard of provincials. "The collection of vices considered to be uniquely southern," Jansson tells us: "[were] spatialized in the sense that they [were] understood as inherent in the very landscape and social fabric of the place called 'the South.' They [were] seen as characteristic of the South in a way they are not in the rest of the country."[108]

Southerners in turn created a corrective self-narrative, "the garden of chattel."[109] The crux of Southern "cultural identity," Humphries argues, is therefore:

> a response to one's own compulsion to narrate, which in turn is almost always concomitant with the perception—accurate or not—of some Other's attempt to impose a (negative, condescending, or otherwise undesirable) narrative order from without, or of the possibility of such a narration from without. ...What we think are

---

[103] John Peale Bishop qtd. in Gray and Robinson, *Companion*, 18.

[104] Cash, *The Mind of the South*, 65.

[105] Humphries, "The Discourse of Southernness," 123–24.

[106] David R. Jansson, "American National Identity and the Progress of the New South in National Geographic Magazine," *Geographical Review* 93 (July 2003): 352. See also David R. Jansson, "Internal Orientalism in America: W. J. Cash's *The Mind of the South* and the Spatial Construction of American National Identity," *Political Geography* 22/3 (March 2003) 293–316.

[107] O'Connor, "Some Aspects of the Grotesque in Southern Fiction," *Mystery*, 44.

[108] Jansson, "American National Identity," 352.

[109] Humphries, "The Discourse of Southernness," 123.

> the way others think of us—narrate us—whether what we think bears any relation to the reality of what others think or not—determine a great deal of our response, our defensive or offensive self-narration. So what matters historically is not how many abolitionists there were in the North...but how many people in the South thought there were, and how this played on other factors that were involved in the nonsense which produced a narrative compulsion in the southern states, a desire to make sense which led to the invention of the Idea or Story of the South, which led in turn to the South itself.[110]

I do not take Humphries to mean that the South itself, the physical South, was literally altered by Southern self-imagining, but rather that it was overlaid by discourse that altered the perspective through which Southerners perceived and interpreted the physical South and the historical circumstances associated with it. This shift of aspect, though it could not change the hard stuff of the South, did transform the way Southerners understood and represented themselves and their region in manner and in discourse. "This Old South, in short," Cash wrote:

> was a society beset by the specters of defeat, of shame, or guilt—a society driven by the need to bolster its morale, to nerve its arm against waxing odds, to justify itself in its own eyes and in those of the world. Hence a large part—in a way, the largest part—of its history from the day that Garrison began to thunder in Boston is the history of its efforts to achieve that end, and characteristically by means of romantic fictions.[111]

Out of the romance of the Southern garden grew an entire population of idealized Southern folk: the gentleman planter epitomized by Thomas Jefferson, the "mysterious" and "effete literary Southerner" (E. A. Poe and Roderick Usher), the frontier Southerner or redneck (Sut Lovingood), the hero (Robert E. Lee), the tale-spinning Negro (Uncle Remus), the belle (Scarlett O'Hara), and, in the modern South, the middle class hero (the good-old-boy).[112] The story of the South became an actualized location in part because Southerners actively internalized one or many of these tropes and

---

[110] Ibid., 120–21. Humphries borrows from Tate's "A Southern Mode of the Imagination," *Essays of Four Decades* (London: Oxford University Press, 1970) 589.

[111] Cash, *The Mind of the South*, 61.

[112] Humphries, "The Discourse of Southernness," 124–28.

began to affect the manners of their mythologized counterparts.[113] "If we would know what the narrative of southernness is," Humphries claims:

> we must first admit that southernness itself is a narrative... That it was not born as a reflection of reality, or an attempt to describe it, but rather in dire response to it... Our cultural identity, as southerners is not then, or not only, the logical expression of certain physical and circumstantial factors, but rather a hysterical and, one might even say, superstitious refusal to accommodate those physical and circumstantial factors, a refusal either to run away to some other reality or to attempt to confront the unruliness of circumstances honestly and directly; this refusal, this denial, is expressed as a narrative. That narrative appears to reflect reality because, first, it may happen to resemble it, and second, having invented the story, men proceed to imitate it, to model their desires and opinions according to it. We are southerners because we, and our ancestors, and the rest of the nation, have felt a compelling need to make up stories about southerners and because we then chose to act as though those stories were as true or truer than fact itself—to imitate those narratives, to model our desires, our behavior, our thoughts, our lives according to them. We are then southerners by a perverse accident, which we have denied, repressed, exacerbated, and enshrined in a narrative that we are still in the process of telling.[114]

Cultural self-genesis, if it did in fact occur, would have had a profound effect upon Southern literature and especially upon realism. If the Southern writer internalized the Southern legend, believed in it and emulated it, his understanding of realism and the strategies he used to represent his storied real would be conspicuously unlike the realist models of mainstream America (the non-South) and Europe.[115] Furthermore, if Southerners do choose, as Gray and Humphries suggest, to view the world through their own particular mythology and then "act as though those stories were as true or truer than fact itself," then Southern realism would span a much broader discursive spectrum than mainstream realism. Indeed the Southern world-view, reared as it is on corrective mythologies, is inclined to a more romantic realism, which places as much

---

[113] Ibid., 124.

[114] Ibid., 130–31.

[115] Jansson, "American National Identity," 352.

confidence in what "might have happened [and what] ought to have happened," as in what did.[116]

Is this "tendency towards unreality…[and] romanticism" a natural characteristic of Southern thinking or is it another affected behavior?[117] Cash supposed that it was a native characteristic, wrought from the experience of the "simple" colonial Southerner in an "extravagant" and "proliferating" wilderness.[118] Like all men, he had been driven by an initial "biological pragmatism," and in the fruitful South, that drive was allowed to "relax a little."[119] Having beaten back the pine scrub and filled his larder, the Southern frontiersman became a refined hedonist. He developed an intense individualism that flared, in its less admirable moments, in "bald…assertions of ego" against his real and imagined foes.[120] To Cash's mind, the prototypical Southerner "lack[ed] the complexity of mind, the knowledge, and, above all, the habit of skepticism essential to any generally realistic attitude. …He will accept what pleases him and reject what does not, and…in general will prefer the extravagant…"[121] His was a mood in which "imagination holds unchecked sway, …in which nothing any more seems improbable save the puny inadequacies of fact."[122]

Has the Southern writer inherited what Cash supposed were the region's dominant traits of individualism and romanticism? Or has he, as Humphries claims, inherited a tradition of narrative exigency that prompts him to position himself within the collective Southern narrative which has imagined itself as inherently individualistic and romantic? Is his work orientated by the same principles as his philosophy? Humphries maintains that Southern writing is indeed effected by the kind of self-conscious posturing that he associates with the Southern temper. Whichever narrative strategy the writer chooses to negotiate the real and storied South(s)—be it with romance like G. W. Harris and Margaret Mitchell, romantic realism like Tate and Capote, social realism like Ellen Glasgow and Caldwell,

---

[116] Ibid., 43.
[117] Cash, *The Mind of the South*, 44.
[118] Ibid., 45.
[119] Ibid., 46.
[120] Ibid., 44.
[121] Ibid., 47.
[122] Ibid., 48.

or even a stripped-down dirty realism like Barry Hannah or Ford—his work is, at least in part, the product of a self-conscious impulse to narrate or re-narrate the Southern experience. Humphries implies that this process is so intensely personal (and generally defensive) that its baseline real is often several steps beyond what might be called objective reality. He claims that the Southern imagination has been shaped by habitual posturing, and therefore tends toward a world-view that is self-serving and sometimes self-fulfilling. "The reality [of the South]," Humphries writes, "reacts to this story of itself by rejecting or embracing, but in either case it grounds itself in the very narrative that is supposed to explain it."[123]

Humphries's is a very seductive argument, but how appropriate is it when aligned with Southern realism? Surely O'Connor's firsthand South has more immediate value than second- or third-hand chatter about "The South." The distinction to make here is one between the storied South and the author's perception of how that place effects his or her experience of a particular Southern space. To that end, the question to ask is not how the regional landscape has changed, though it certainly has, but how O'Connor's perception of that landscape and, conjointly, her aesthetic relationship to it evolved throughout her lifetime. In the 1930s, few would have thought to ask whether or not the South existed. Its being was taken for granted, and even though there wasn't much consensus as to how it came to be or why it was in the shape it was in, it was undeniably present. If nothing else, that fact was one all Americans, North or South-born, could agree upon. In the past fifteen years, the region's self-evidence has become a favorite point of contention among critics. Humphries and Butler underscore the very real possibility that Southern literature has been propagated, not by a natural impulse in the region, but by academic posturing and over-interpretation. Romine goes as far as to say that "the possibility exists that the South has become available exclusively to discourse and not to narrative."[124] Certainly being a "professional Southerner"—that is to say, claiming a cultural heritage that is uniquely Southern and, by association, the authority to confer the title to others—has become, in Butler's words,

---

[123] Humphries, "The Discourse of Southernness," 123–24.

[124] Scott Romine qtd. in John A. Staunton, "Shadowing Grace and in the Post-Southern South: 'A Roadside Resurrection' and Larry Brown's Narratives of Witness," *Religion and Literature* 33/1 (Spring 2001) 45.

"a small industry."[125] Southern critics have persisted in being Southern critics by continuing to ask the question, "Is there such a thing as Southern writing, ...and if there is, what makes it Southern?"[126] Answering that question once, Butler quips, "brings in some useful if not life-changing checks, and it doesn't hurt your reputation either. If you answer [it] two or three times, you're an expert."[127] The problem here is, again, one of circuity; as Butler points out, "answering the question is one of the things that infallibly identifies you as a southern writer," and Southern writing is, therefore, whatever the self-made Southern writer/critic decides it is.[128] It is impossible to say just how far removed this manufactured Southernness is from the beingness located in the region itself, however unstable. The critic cannot return, as Gray reminds us, to a South that is unwritten or without self-consciousness, but he can authenticate the critical South by setting aside the notion of the literary South in favor of an author by author and sometimes a text by text interpretation of the region.

There is in the impulse to create, recreate, or reclaim the South in academia, an ironical undertone, a reaction that is conventionally "Southern" even if it comes at a remove. Telling about the South has been the compulsion of Southerners as long as there has been a non-South to square itself against. "North and South," Lewis P. Simpson claims, "needed to invent each other in order to invent themselves," and indeed a steady volley of regional stereotyping is apparent between the industrial North and the agrarian South from the colonial era.[129] Nearly a century before the Civil War, Thomas Jefferson recorded the most common of these characterizations in a letter to his friend François Jean Chastellux. "In the North," he wrote, "they are cool, sober, laborious,...[and] chicaning....In the South they

---

[125] Jack Butler, "Still Southern After All These Years," *The Future of Southern Letters*, ed. Jefferson Humphries and John Lowe (New York: Oxford University Press, 1996) 33.

[126] Ibid.

[127] Ibid.

[128] Ibid.

[129] Lewis P. Simpson qtd. in Humphries, "The Discourse of Southernness," 121.

are fiery, voluptuary, indolent,...[and] candid."[130] Presumptuous and oversimplified as they were, these regional types stuck fast in America's collective imagination, shaping identities on both sides of the Potomac through the Revolution and the Civil War and on into the present.[131] The staying power of these stereotypes would suggest more than mere political rivalry. Ritchie Watson suggests that the social tensions between North and South were compiled by a "deep cultural and racial division that had originated over two hundred years ago in England," in what he describes as, "the antagonism between Puritan and Cavalier."[132]

There is much debate as to the dominant presence of Cavaliers in the Colonial South. In 1941, Cash noted the steady "heaping up" of "a mass of evidence" by modern historians "that actual Cavaliers or even near-Cavaliers were rare among Southern settlers."[133] Even traditionalists like Frank Owsley and John Gould Fletcher claimed that most of the colonists in the South were "of the yeomanry" not "the gentry," and if they were descendent of Cavalier blood, they were themselves dispossessed and poor "broken-down cavaliers."[134] The relatively small number of true gentle-folk in the Colonial South and the longevity of the Cavalier myth suggest that the desire to point to and exaggerate a supposed difference in blood was always a defining aspect of the Southern identity.

---

[130] Thomas Jefferson, "Letter to François Jean Chastellux," *A Jefferson Profile As Revealed in His Letters*, ed. Saul Kussiel Padover (New York: John Day Co., 1956) 28.

[131] Jefferson's regional types were echoed in 1855 by the "fire-breathing" South Carolina politician William Lowndes Yancey: "The climate, soil, and productions of these two grand divisions of land have made the character of their inhabitants. Those who occupy the [North] are cool, calculating, enterprising, selfish, and grasping; the inhabitants of the [South] are ardent, brave and magnanimous, more disposed to give than to accumulate, to enjoy rather than to labor" (William Lowndes Yancey qtd. in Richard Gray, *Aberrations* [Baton Rouge: Louisiana State University Press, 2000] 499).

[132] Ritchie Devon Watson, "Antebellum Race Mythology and the Development of Southern Nationalism," *The Southern Literary Journal* 35/1 (Fall 2002): 13.

[133] Cash, *The Mind of the South*, 3.

[134] Frank Lawrence Owsley, "The Irrepressible Conflict," *Stand*, 69; John Gould Fletcher, "Education, Past and Present," *Stand*, 98.

The Old Dominion "claim to gentility," according to Cash, evolved through the Civil War and Reconstruction into a general assumption of genetic difference in the common Southerner.[135] The relative isolation of communities in the rural South and the circularity of blood ties within these communities helped to propagate the idea. "If being a poor white farmer," Cash explained, "you knew that your planter neighbor was a kinsman, you were normally going to find it as difficult to hate him as to think of him as being made of fundamentally different stuff from yourself..."[136] Cash asserted that it was more intuitive for the common Southerner to underline his kinship with the local aristocracy rather than the economic status he shared with poor Northern town-folk. Despite the fact that he had more in common with the latter in the practical matters of day-to-day living, he would always assume to be philosophically aligned with the planter and would tend to define himself in terms of the values of Southern chivalry he imagined he shared with his wealthy cousins. Here, gentlemanly values were the defining measure of character and material status was merely a superficial embellishment, potentially awe-inspiring but virtually meaningless if a man were not, first and foremost, a gentleman. Southern men aspired to this persona by inheritance or affectation to such a degree that the collective South presumed it was alone predisposed to gentlemanly virtue. Regional wisdom had it that Northern men did not inherit this gene; for them, the dollar always trumped the grand gesture.

These extremes have been whittled down over time and displaced, to a certain extent, by the subsequent and all-consuming myths of national unity and progress. In an age of relative homogeneity in white America, it seems somewhat unaccountable to suggest that the historically dominant populations in the North and the South, the narrators of each region's grand narrative, are ethnically different when they share a common language and a common Western European ancestry. But consider the way Jefferson generalized each of these groups—the sober and exacting Puritanical North and the impassioned but lackadaisical Cavalier South. Aren't these "primitive portraits" of the Yankee and the Southerner still

[135] Cash, *The Mind of the South*, 35.

[136] Ibid.

resonant in the national psyche?[137] The descriptive language embedded within these two has lost its formality, but stark differences in mannerism and motivation remain. Could the prioritization of certain social rituals, commerce in the North and communion in the South, have generated two sets of contrasting manners in each region? Much has been made of this difference in manners, and for O'Connor the distinction was one upon which she based the resolving logic of her fiction. Her "artificial nigger," for instance, would not have worked the same symbolic miracle in a non-Southern milieu. The ritualized action of a region's manners are, in Lionel Trilling's words, that culture's "hum and buzz of implication."[138] They reflect "the whole evanescent context in which its explicit statements are made" and are "that part of a culture which is made up of half-uttered or unuttered or unutterable expressions of value."[139]

The tradition of enmity between North and South corresponds to a parallel tradition of implied difference in cultural valuation. Might the persistence of this concept of oppositional realities have led each group to emphasize different objects and gestures in their attempts to represent real life in fiction? Sociological surveys, like Odum's and Reed's, suggest that even though the cultural North and South could be further divided into innumerable internal splinter groups, each with its own learned airs, they shared a firm association with a generalized Northern or Southern folkway that lent a sense of familiarity and unity to an otherwise disorienting mesh of competing linguistic registers. Certain patterns of images associated with the monolithic South overlap in the fiction written within various of these splinter groups. Although these images have been manipulated in different and sometimes contrary ways by each local interpreter, there is a sense of connectivity in each individual appropriation that

---

[137] Gray, *Writing*, 27.

[138] Lionel Trilling, "Manners, Morals, and the Novel," *The Liberal Imagination: Essays on Literature and Society* (Oxford: Oxford University Press, 1981) 194. See also Tate's discussion of Southern manners in his essay, "A Southern Mode of the Imagination." He offers a Southern response to Emerson's famed adage, "Manners are the invention of a wise man to keep a fool at a distance." "[M]anners are not inventions," Tate quipped, "but conventions tacitly agreed upon to protect the fool from consciousness of his folly" (*Essays of Four Decades* [London: Oxford University Press, 1970] 585).

[139] Ibid.

each writer had linked to an image heritage that could engage a cache of phrases, scenarios, and tones capable of tripping the same internalized store of images and linkages between images in the reader. When Faulkner wrote about men who made their living by pumping air into the hides of nag mules (*The Hamlet*) or by farming mud on country roads (*The Reivers*), the reader who shared in the author's image heritage, who knew a thing or two about the motions and grand resolutions of the Southern swindle, could participate more actively with his stories because they were implicitly aware of when to laugh, when to cringe, and why. This is partly what O'Connor meant when she said that the South was a place where you could still make belief believable.[140] In the non-South, the inflated mule is a fantastic object; in Mississippi he is literal. Even if he is not actual, he is credible because of his embeddedness in the image heritage of actual Souths, places where he might exist, and if he doesn't could yet.

If the South was a place where mythologized mules could be made believable, the North was where another animal, much grander in style and dimension, was conceivable: the prospering American. At the turn of twentieth century, Northern discourse, from economics to politics and poetics, was preoccupied with the national myth. The psychological center of ascending American super-power had its roots firmly in the industrial North. Southern discourse was meanwhile caught between two opposing but equal urges: to invest in the Unionized American dream or to hold fast to the region's agricultural tradition. The majority of the population in the South (the lower and middle classes) was scandalized in the 1920s and 1930s by the supposed importation of Northern values into New Southern social praxis. "The South is at last to be physically reconstructed," John Crowe Ransom wrote in his essay, "Reconstructed but Unregenerate."[141] "...But it will be fatal if the South should conceive it as her duty to be regenerated and get her spirit reborn with a totally different orientation toward life."[142] True as that might have been, many of the South's social elite were eager to strike up business alliances with Northern industrial giants. Gray

---

[140] O'Connor, "The Catholic Novelist in the Protestant South," *Mystery*, 208.

[141] John Crowe Ransom, "Reconstructed but Unregenerate," *Stand*, 22.

[142] Ibid.

notes that after the Civil War, "control shifted from [the planters] to new forces, openly committed to industrialization, accomplished under Northern direction by Northern capital, [which reduced] the South to a colonial status and [fastened] on it a colonial psychology."[143]

The proposition of still greater change, of a New South rehabilitated in the image of the economically superior North, led to a deep internal schism between traditionalists, Yankees, and their Southern partners, the "Southern Yankees."[144] "In effect," Gray writes, "the Mason-Dixon line became a kind of moral demarcation, crossed only by the occasional contaminating influence."[145] Traditionalist social movements like the Agrarian "stand" grew out of conservative fears of fatal "contamination" from the North which would underwrite and eventually collapse the authority of "superior," "native" codes. The Agrarians, for example, clung to their generations old motto of self-sufficiency and "production for use rather than profit."[146] For staunch followers of the movement like Tate, economic infrastructure was a direct correlative of moral intent. "Economy," he once said, "is the secular image of religious conviction."[147] In the North where economy was "based upon a possession of cash" rather than "a comparative use and enjoyment of nature," religious conviction was, to Tate's mind, essentially hollow because it was divorced from mankind's true "vocation."[148] Almost certainly there were corners of the industrialized North that felt a similar pang of misgiving in the modern super-world, but the rhetorical power of the national myth was strong enough to discourage the backward-gaze associated with its Southern counterpart. "Perhaps because it had so little else to give its people," Irving Howe ventures, "the South nurtured in them a generous and often obsessive sense of the past."[149]

---

[143] Gray, *Writing*, 88.

[144] Humphries, "The Discourse of Southernness," 128.

[145] Gray, *Writing*, 41.

[146] Gray, *Memory*, 3.

[147] Allen Tate, "Remarks on the Southern Religion," *Stand*, 175.

[148] Andrew Lytle, "The Hind Tit," *Stand*, 214; Tate, et al., "Introduction," *Stand*, xlii.

[149] Irving Howe, "The Southern Myth and William Faulkner," *American Quarterly* 3/4 (Winter 1951) 357.

Whether it is considered the result of discursive tradition or genetics, the implication of the regional binary is that a fundamental difference exists between Americans on either side of the Mason-Dixon. North and South have become, at least in our minds, cultural sovereignties, and the difference between them is perceived as "quasi-ethnic."[150] O'Connor's obsessive revision of one of her earliest stories, "The Geranium," suggests that this was a difference she felt acutely. The story, which dramatizes the cultural divide in the person of an elderly Southerner who is relocated to the North, testifies to her interest in exploring the subtleties of regional attitudes. O'Connor intuited that it was here, in the interplay of two contrasting but intimately related traditions, that symbolic meaning could be made literal and resonant. She concludes her final revision of "The Geranium," which she renamed "Judgment Day," with old Tanner broken and delirious on a tenement staircase, just steps away from the mirage of home on the ground floor. The change in plot suggests that, for O'Connor, a final judgment of meaning requires a homecoming of sorts, a confrontation with the place that bestows upon us our first means of judgment.

The need to acknowledge our origins and to make some sort of judgment about that place is one of the most recognizable characteristics of our national literature, and one which functions sub-textually as a defense of American actuality. The politics of regional identification betray a further need to associate the self with something more immediately knowable. This urge to distinguish oneself from the greater American scene that is alternately unwieldy and unnaturally pat manifests itself in modern Southern literature almost entirely in negative terms. The prosody of the Fugitive poets, for example, is marked by a haunting mortality very much at odds with the brash images of consumable immortality manufactured by corporate advertising.[151] Ironically, the primary criticism against the Agrarians' political agenda was their use of a like method of romance; the lost South of their literature was at times as self-consciously mythologized as any Madison Avenue spread. Tate's

---

[150] Reed, *Enduring*, 91.

[151] See John Crowe Ransom, *Poems about God* (New York: Henry Holt and Company, 1919); John Peale Bishop and Edmund Wilson, *The Undertaker's Garland* (New York: Alfred A. Knopf, 1922); Allen Tate, *The Swimmers* (London: Oxford University Press, 1970).

"Ode to the Confederate Dead" lends a Homeric air to the lost Rebel cause. John Crowe Ransom's collection *Poems About God* harkens back to a Southland that is sound and purposeful in its god-fearing labor, and in which the folk seem a natural extension of the landscape. The metrical tightness of their work imposes a further sense of order which reiterates the dimension of New Jeffersonian regionalism in their politics.

The Fugitive resurrection of the dream of a classless South populated by a benevolent rural nobility is one radically turned on its head by Caldwell. The social politic of novels like *God's Little Acre* and *Tobacco Road* is based not on an assumed antique order but on the insane logic that follows when outmoded regional aphorisms are overlaid upon an impoverished New Southern scene. The plight of Lester Jeeter and his line is their compulsion to enact the refrain "Cotton is King" indefinitely and regardless of the results. Their action exaggerates the region-wide temptation to invest in temperamental cash crops. The almost mechanical behavior of the Jeeters sets them apart from other white-trash archetypes like Faulkner's Snopses who are horrifying because of the deliberate, exacting nature of their actions. The Jeeters horrify because of their general oblivion. Anti-heroes like Lester and his precursor Ty Ty Walden dramatize Caldwell's criticism of the New South's lust for upward mobility. The get-rich-quick scheme is the motivating priority of both of these men, and it takes precedence over their own and their family's most basic needs. The only sensible characters in the novel are the ones least associated with sense by Southern convention; Black Sam and Uncle Felix, Ty Ty's field hands, ask for food not gold.

The outright ridiculousness of Caldwell's characters is counter-balanced by their animal enthusiasm for all things taboo: incest, adultery, voyeurism, kidnapping, theft, battery, even the starvation of the family matriarch. The tone Caldwell uses to describe such evil-doing is essentially comic, but the horror evoked by these acts is not entirely disarmed by humor. Unlike Twain, Caldwell does not attempt to diffuse the reader's unease with the suggestion that his grotesques aren't meant to be taken seriously after all. Jeeter may be the engine that drives most of the gags in *Tobacco Road*, but his representation of a very real horror—that of the share-croppers' South—saves him from being merely a joke. The underlying seriousness of the Jeeters' plight left in suspension distinguishes Caldwell and other grotesque realists like O'Connor from the main body of American literature which, Leslie Fiedler reminds us, "likes to pretend...that its bugaboos are all finally jokes..."[152]

The turn in Southern fiction in the early twentieth century from local-color humor to a more devious satirical humor has had considerable consequences for the region's image. The exaggerated elements of Caldwell's parodic Georgia, for instance, were read by many as straight realism. The nagging suspicion among outsiders that Southern folk were, at the core, a species of violent sexual degenerates was rallied if not confirmed. Increasingly the South was classed by the non-South as a sort of nether-region divorced, by virtue of its strange nature, from the national mainstream. By association, Southerners were displaced from greater America whether or not they exhibited the brutish individualism or social conservatism of the regional stereotype. Popular media encouraged this image, overwhelmingly casting the Southerner in these behaviors and further encouraging the general public to assume that he was naturally predisposed to violent and backward behavior. O'Connor's grotesques, when viewed through this lens, were interpreted negatively as a reinforcing echo of an old stereotype; their redemptive qualities are overshadowed by the ready-made image of the defective Yokel. "The result of [this] spatialization of...human vices," Jansson explains, "[meant] that they [could] be projected onto and contained within the South, thus erasing them from the national identity."[153]

Not surprisingly the South did not take kindly to its being dubbed the dumping ground for America's sins. One of the most dramatic of its discursive counters came from the "post-North" era of the early twentieth century when Southern manners were once again the subject of scathing critiques.[154] Articles like H. L. Mencken's "The Sahara of the Bozart" picked up the familiar image of a destitute post-war South and attached it to the ascending image of a modern South crippled by an inborn provinciality. The Southerner was now the bearer of a morally corrupt past and a culturally inferior present. When the stereotype was working at full tilt, the

[152] Fiedler, *Love and Death in the American Novel,* 26–27.

[153] Jansson, "American National Identity," 352.

[154] Cobb, *Away*, 233.

South was the exact cultural inverse of the non-South: conservative rather than progressive, religious rather than analytical, rural rather than urban. Nowhere could you find the opera houses and galleries that Mencken claimed he came across in even "second-rate" cities in the North.[155] For him and the majority of the Northern literati, no high culture meant no culture.[156] The cultural artifacts of the South did not fit the Northern or European models Mencken prized and so were patronized or ignored completely. His criticism became a prototype of the modern Northern gaze which continues, through its disparate set of manners and aesthetic codes, to misinterpret value in the Southern idiom.[157] Mencken exaggerated the negative possibilities of the Southern context by fixing an oversimplified causality to "negative" Southern traits. His work and the work of later critics who operated under a similar reductive code tended to "[name] and [identify the South] against the historical tide."[158]

Of course, the South was not without culture at the turn of the twentieth century. As Donald Davidson points out in his essay "A Mirror for Artists," "The South has been rich in the folk-arts, and is still rich in them—in ballads, country songs and dances, in hymns and spirituals, in folk tales, in the folk crafts of weaving, quilting, [and] furniture making," but these were generally disregarded by outsiders as the stuff of a "pathetic" peasant class of "poor white trash" who had lost the best of their numbers to Northern arms and industry.[159] Cash attributed the "drainage" of "Southern strength and brains" to the "great intolerance of the savage ideal" in Southern

---

[155] H. L. Mencken, "The Sahara of the Bozart," *The American Scene: A Reader*, ed. Huntington Cairns (New York: Alfred A. Knopf, 1977) 161.

[156] Although Mencken was a native of Maryland, a border state, his sentiments were distinctly Northern.

[157] In *Writing the South*, Gray argues that the critical temptation to explain cultural artifacts, like literature, by historical or sociopolitical means is wrong-headed: "The main assumption seems to be that literature can be explained entirely in terms of historical circumstance, and its emergence or absence ascribed to laws of causality that are strict and systematically applicable. ...Historical circumstances...do not determine the state of literature, its presence, or its character when it is present; they merely provide a context, of positive and negative possibilities" (*Writing the South* [Cambridge: Cambridge University Press, 1986] 35–36).

[158] Gray, *Aberrations*, 499.

[159] Donald Davidson, "A Mirror for Artists," *Stand*, 55.

academies and colleges[160] while Mencken maintained that the region's cultural vacuity had been caused by a literal bloodletting, claiming that the region had, after the Civil War and Reconstruction, "simply been drained of all its best blood."[161] A powerful subtext underlies Mencken's claim one which has become an American truism. In the hands of the mass media,[162] ithas proved a terribly influential idea: the South, that place "down there," does not or cannot exhibit (high) culture because it is genetically morbid.[163] The soul-crushing effects of poverty and re-colonization were interpreted as expediting circumstances to the South's essential problem which was innate.[164] The place was a wasteland, not because it was economically depressed, but because its (white) people were genetically inferior.

The Southern "race" was not always addled by such images of moral and intellectual bankruptcy. Even Mencken supposed that the best of America's men had come, not from the North, but from the "Old Dominion" South.[165] His revival of the Grand Old garden is just as striking an artifact as his critique of the modern South; it underlines the breadth of influence, in time and across borders, of the old tropes. The nostalgia which infuses Mencken's use of the garden narrative indicates, in Kirby's words, "the quasi-Marxist, liberal-chic intellectualism... [that] reinforced the embarrassing New

---

[160] Cash, *The Mind of the South*, 320.

[161] Mencken, "The Sahara of the Bozart," 161.

[162] Cash noted a "curious Janus-faced attitude" in the Yankee, which led to his indulgence in "romantic Southern themes." "In Northern literature and even more in Northern theater [these themes] grew constantly in popularity, until in the 1890s they were near to dominating all other" (*The Mind of the South*, 125). For more on the media manipulation of Southern tropes, consult Jack Temple Kirby, *Media Made Dixie: The South in the American Imagination*, rev. ed. (Athens: The University of Georgia Press, 1986) and John Shelton Reed, *Southern Folk, Plain and Fancy: Native White Social Types* (Athens: The University of Georgia Press, 1986).

[163] Mencken, "The Sahara of the Bozart," 157.

[164] Cash's "savage ideal" further illustrates Mencken's point that post-war "whites were thrown backwards not only politically and economically, but culturally, too" (Kirby, *Media Made Dixie*, 82). "In the end," Cash claimed, "almost the only pleasures which might be practiced openly and without moral obloquy were those of orgiastic religion and those of violence" (*The Mind of the South*, 133).

[165] Mencken, "The Sahara of the Bozart," 160.

South-grand Old South dichotomy."[166] As powerful an image as the Southern Sahara was for Mencken, he was compelled to counter it almost immediately with the Edenic green of the "Ur-Confederate['s]" "late empire."[167] He went so far as to install a pair of gentlemen on a proverbial veranda, the "torch bearers" of what he believed was the only true civilization in Colonial America. Leisure, he asserted, was the ultimate aim of this Southern gentry. "[They] liked to toy with ideas. [They were] hospitable and tolerant."[168] They had "that vague thing we call culture."[169] The Northern elite had merely installed a government.

Mencken implies that the Northern aristocracy, for all its market savvy, lacked the easy manner and imagination of its Southern counterpart; it affected the airs of the common bourgeoisie more so than it did the hypothetical "Yankee gentleman."[170] In spite of his opera houses, Mencken's modern Yankee maintained the dry, exacting manner of his colonial ancestors. He bears a striking resemblance to Jefferson's archetype; preoccupied by his market-mind, never completely at ease, he invests what imagination he has in material enterprise. The crux of the New Southern problem, for Mencken and later for the Agrarians, was the displacement in the Southern upper classes of the gallant manners gleaned from colonial Virginians by the "worst traits of the Yankee sharper."[171] "The tone of public opinion [in the modern South]," Mencken wrote, "is set by an upstart class but lately emerged from industrial slavery into commercial enterprise—the class of 'bustling' business men, of 'live wires,' of commercial club luminaries, of 'drive' managers, of forward-lookers and right-thinkers. ...The old repose is gone. The old romanticism is gone."[172] There is a degree of truth in Mencken's sense of loss; "the Compsons and Sartorises were," as Percy put it, "not only defeated by the Snopses but were actually joining them."[173] There is another thread of feeling in modern Southern literature, a

---

[166] Kirby, *Media Made Dixie,* 67.

[167] Mencken, "The Sahara of the Bozart," 158.

[168] Ibid.

[169] Ibid.

[170] Ibid.

[171] Ibid., 168.

[172] Ibid., 167–68.

[173] Percy, *Signposts,* 4.

stronger thread that tells of a place where the much coveted repose of Southern legend is not gone. In O'Connor and Welty, Hannah and Mark Richard, the old manners are alive and well, but they have changed hands. They are fleshed out, not by gentrified landowners, but by the good-old-boy and the redneck, the lapsed Baptist and the credit card orphan, none of whom conjure the same sense of cultural aptitude as the colonial planter did. For Mencken and his followers, the modern South was without culture because it was without the positive aspects of Northern culture; today it is without gentlemen because the gentlemen are counted from the bottom up, not the top down. "The formality that is left in the South now," O'Connor wrote in 1954, "is quite dead and done for of course...," but "traditional manners, however unbalanced, are better than no manners at all."[174] "[B]ecause we [Southerners] are losing our customary manners, we are probably over conscious of them. "[T]his," she added, "seems to be a condition that produces writers."[175]

Section 3: "It's Better Than the Theatre, Isn't It?": An Argument for Southern Realism[176]

The South's emotional attachment to its social custom and the anxiety it experiences when that custom is perceived as threatened suggests that differences in regional manners illustrate not only superficial contrasts of behavior, tastes, and market trends but also more profound dissimilarities. At the turn of the twentieth century, Gray notes that, "The sense of accumulating differences went beyond the economic..."[177] The figurative cleavage between South and non-South began to signify not only political divisions but spiritual and philosophical ones as well. Gray argues that this was "largely because as the Northeast moved into the industrial age the orthodoxies of its old theocracy were...replaced by the liberalisms of

---

[174] O'Connor, *Habit*, 70; and "The Catholic Novelist in the Protestant South," *Mystery*, 200.

[175] O'Connor, "The Fiction Writer and His Country," *Mystery*, 29.

[176] The Canadian Shrevlin McCannon, also known as Shreve, makes the above remark to Quentin Compson as the latter divulges his interpretation of the Sutpen family drama (William Faulkner, *Absalom, Absalom!* [London: Vintage Random House, 2005] 217).

[177] Gray, *Memory*, 19.

the nineteenth century."[178] It was this liberalizing Northern manner that the South closed ranks against, a reaction which cannot be summarily accounted for by the abolition of slavery or any other political skirmish. If, as Trilling claims, "Our attitude toward manners is the expression of a particular conception of reality," then the Southern defensive is not merely a political move but an expression of a much deeper-reaching faith in a Southern mode of reality.[179] The heroes of Southern literature, regardless of whether they rail against or ape the Old Southern manner, portray a particular spectrum of reality in which those actions have meaning. In other words, they participate in the constructedness of their regional identities, and that very action—of owning or disowning the South—is what has lent Southern fiction its sense of relative coherence. It is no accident that the progenitor of Southern Gothicism, E. A. Poe, was himself enamored of the act of performing Southernness. While Poe's actual links to the region are famously suspect, his decision to underscore his ties with Virginia, not Massachusetts, to "become" Southern as it were, suggests that even if regionalisms are arbitrary, they affect our sense of what is actual.

When such contrasting conceptions of real value were engaged by early modern realist narratives, they tended to generate variant generic conventions which mirrored the "assumptions and rationalizations [each culture group has made] about the world."[180] In the North and South, they generated two distinct genres: a national realism traditionally aligned with the North and a "regional" realism in the South. Each genre reflects the implicit value judgments of its folk and demonstrates the divergent narrative strategies used in each region to connote those judgments. The wild look of a Southern realism like O'Connor's does not, as many have supposed, betray a penchant for unreality but for a more profound, sometimes meta-physical aspect of reality. Such deviant realism is not a South-specific phenomenon; Henry James's romantic realism, which O'Connor counted among her chief influences, was the prototype for the Northern trend. What has been called romance in the North and grotesquerie in the South is in some ways a

---

[178] Ibid.

[179] Trilling, "Manners, Morals, and the Novel," 195.

[180] Mack Smith, *Literary Realism and the Ekphrastic Tradition* (University Park: Pennsylvania State University Press, 1995) 2.

misconception of authorial attempts at a more inclusive sort of realism. The tonal qualities of James's and O'Connor's work are inescapably reflexive; both might elude to a greater meta-physical real, but the stuff of immediate social gesture is New England British and middle Georgian respectively. In this regard, as Mack Smith points out, "a realist text refers as much to its own philosophic origin and processes of validation as it does to an extratextual reality."[181]

Although manners and the discursive registers attached to them overlap in border communities and intermix with migrating populations making distinctions between these values increasingly subtle, there is still a palpable feeling in the contemporary United States that the "ethnic" differences between the North and South cannot be lost to corporate homogeneity, popular culture, or changes of address.[182] A conspicuous tension remains between the "unified" national language of the non-South and the heterogeneous language of the regional South(s). Some critics, like Ihab Hassan, credit this tension with sustaining the narrative potency of the Southern story. "Part of the vitality of Southern fiction derives its energy," Hassan claims, "from the energy of opposition, which is but another way of saying that the Southern novel, insofar as it has a regional identity, is more openly hostile to those popular assumptions the country entertains at large."[183]

"There is a familiar series of oppositions at work here:," Gray explains, "'southern' versus 'American'/'Northern,' place versus placelessness, past versus pastlessness, realism versus idealism, [and] community versus isolation."[184] The persistence of the idea of "Southernness" and "Northernness" suggests that border-blurring has in fact amplified the urge in both groups to maintain the local distinctions that they associate with a common past and a common understanding of cultural value. In the South, this collective association with the local rather than the national is, Gray writes, "a matter of language and communal ritual: the human habit of positioning the self with the help of the word and others—giving a local habitation and a name to things to secure their and our identity,

---

[181] Ibid., 3.

[182] Gray, *Aberrations*, 499, 503–504.

[183] Ihab Hassan, *Radical Innocence: Studies in the Contemporary American Novel* (Princeton: Princeton University Press, 1961) 102.

[184] Gray, *Aberrations*, 499.

and establishing a connection or kinship with other people that is also an anchorage, a validation of oneself."[185] The ritual aspect of the Southern performance manifests in the recurrence of certain "aberrations" in the region's literature, though I would be careful to attach a causal significance to any of these. The conventional canon acknowledges five predominant elements as characteristically Southern, in Butler's words, a strong sense of "place, …the darkness and splendor of families, …a way of talking, …the Bible, and…black[s] and white[s] locked into a mutual if inharmonious fate."[186] The predominance of these five elements seems to imply a very specific kind of knowledge, a way of perceiving the real world and making discursive sense of it that is peculiar to the South. Butler claims that when these elements are brought together, "a recognizable world, a single defined realm against which we [can] distinguish human motivation with remarkable clarity" is thrown into relief.[187] That recognizable South is not a literal place so much as a recitation of what makes such a place recognizable. This formula-South can predetermine the Southern story by reducing it to a combination of certain pre-named elements within a frame of black water and kudzu. The individual vitality of text and place is lost in generalization. Faulkner, O'Connor, and Hannah may have been Southern writers who wrote about Southern people, but we haven't really begun to talk about *Light in August* or *Wise Blood* or *Ray* when we say that Joe Christmas, Hazel Motes, and the Doctor are motivated by the same things, that these are Southern motivations, and that the three of them exist in the same fictional realm.

The regionalist impulse in Southern criticism is limited by the arbitrariness of the Southern proof and its tendency to interpret texts by means of a predetermined standard. What makes this mode so persuasive is the connotation of a historical South within the proof itself. It is hard to read Joe Christmas independently of the miscegenation saga or to envision Hazel Motes without conjuring the roadside preacher. At the first mention of blackness and Bibles, we know where we are. The aura of the South, that pervasive mist of literal and imagined placeness, comes at us as landscape—the black pines and the tar-paper shacks—and the bigger-than-here symbol—

---

[185] Ibid., 504.

[186] Jack Butler, "Still Southern After All These Years," 35.

[187] Ibid.

the forbidden lover and the fallen Christ. In the South, landscape and symbol have colluded to such a degree that the land itself has become symbolic and the symbol regionally inflected. At no time was the distinction between regions more apparent than in the modern age when the Southern imagination, with its basis in a storied past, was scaled against the Northern imagination with its perennial design for the future. The South was still "a place," as Hassan put it, "where the Protestant mind and the folk spirit [had] not succumbed entirely to business ethics and urban impersonality."[188] The consequence of this difference was a distinct but undervalued cultural literacy. The Southern imagination was degraded precisely because of its persistence of faith in folk reality over abstraction. From the outside looking in, it seemed the Southerner "[did] not analyze because he [would] not make the exertion…[or] that his education [had] not brought him up to the level of analysis…"[189] Richard Weaver claimed that "both of these have a degree of plausibility. Yet…both miss the true factor, which is that the Southerner rebels against the idea of analysis because his philosophy or his intellectual tradition, however transmitted down the years, tells him that this is not the way to arrive at the kind of truth he is interested in."[190] The kind of truth the Southerner is interested in has everything to do with his range of perception. "It is his habit," Weaver continues, "to see things as forms and large configurations, and he senses that the process of breaking these down (which is nearly always done for some practical purpose) somehow proves fatal to the truth of the whole."[191] "Analysis is," in other words, "destructive to the kind of reality he most wishes to preserve."[192] Weaver suggests that the Southern mind does not restrict reality to practical knowledge; it ventures beyond the hard facts of a transparent real to the indirect and mysterious elements of a transcendent real, and it does so without so much as a blink. The

---

[188] Hassan, *Radical Innocence*, 79.

[189] Richard M. Weaver, "Aspects of the Southern Philosophy," *Southern Renascence: The Literature of the Modern South*, ed. Louis D. Rubin, Jr. and Robert D. Jacobs (Baltimore: Johns Hopkins University Press, 1953) 15.

[190] Ibid.

[191] Ibid.

[192] Ibid.

personal knowledge of mystery, as subjective and incomplete as it is, is as tangible a part of the Southern real as cast iron and cornbread.

If there is anything unique about the "Southern mind" it is its seemingly automatic acceptance of mystery as a meaningful part of the real. Of the four elements which Weaver indicates as unique to the Southern tradition, "a feudal theory of society, the code of chivalry, the ancient concept of a gentleman, and a religiousness that leads to the acceptance of life as a mystery," the final element—the unconscious equation of mystery with normalcy—has had the strongest and most enduring influence upon Southern thinking and writing.[193] O'Connor's is a particularly persuasive case; even as a relative outsider in the dominant Protestant tradition, her Catholic ideology was very much at home in the South. O'Connor's religious universalism prompted her to seek a reality of extended vision which coincided with the Southern inclination toward a total real that is coincidentally knowable and unknowable, or to put it another way coincidentally doctrinal and mystical. "[Southerners] have a large enough sense of reality," Robert Heilman points out, "not to exclude all enlightenment that is not laboratory tested. For them, totality is more than the sum of the sensory and the rational."[194]

This is not to say that the Southerner experiences a fuller reality than the non-Southerner but that he has developed a unique way of perceiving and interpreting the world and of describing that phenomenon in language, a mode that is, to borrow from Tate, predominantly "realistic" because it is couched in a "religious mind...[that] calls upon the traditional experience of evil which is the common lot of the race."[195] Tate believed that the South was unique in its world-view because of its tendency to base its sense of order on the inevitability of human failures rather than an "irrational" assumption of "omnipotent human rationality."[196] Tate condemned the non-South for its "worship" of a principle of perpetual returns and for its practice of an empirical religion which he felt was only half realized and ultimately "bad" in its ability to "predict only

[193] Weaver qtd. in Gray, *Writing*, 275.

[194] Robert M. Heilman, "The Southern Temper," *Southern Renascence: The Literature of Modern South*, ed. Louis D. Rubin, Jr. and Robert D. Jacobs (Baltimore: Johns Hopkins University Press, 1953) 11.

[195] Tate, "Remarks," *Stand*, 159.

[196] Ibid., 158.

success."[197] The non-Southern mind began to disassociate itself more actively from its founding Calvinism, replacing the imaginative influence of brimstone with the consumable stuff of science turned to capital. In turn, the national spirit pitched away from a want of comfort in an afterlife to a demand for comfort in this life. A growing sense of entitlement coupled with the image of modern America as the bountiful mechanism capable of answering any demand reinforced the belief that man was master of the knowable world. "Once reason," Tate wrote:

> ceased to be the instrument through which its purely qualitative features could be contemplated and enjoyed...it began to see the natural setting as so many instances of quantity; that is nature began to see the practical possibilities of knowing herself. The symbol and the myth meant that nature was largely an inviolable whole; once the symbol and the myth were proved to be not natural facts, but unnatural fictions that fitted into no logical series tolerable to the rational mind, nature became simply a workable half. It now thinks that it is a Whole of limitless practicability.[198]

The South was not unaffected by the national shift from New Jerusalem to corporate Shangri-La. There were dramatic and lasting changes in the New Southern marketplace; Atlanta, Birmingham, and Dallas became consumer meccas in their own right. Nonetheless there remained in the rural South a dissident feeling of skepticism with regards to the Northern "cult of Progress." There was, of course, a whiff of hypocrisy in the South's conservatism; as surely as it resisted radical industrialization it filled its garages with automobiles and washing machines from Michigan. But the world itself, the mysterious beingness of animate and inanimate matter, was still viewed with "essentially naïve, direct, and personal eyes."[199] O'Connor's work is balanced between these two impulses; the struggle of her protagonists culminates in their choice between an incarnate and a discarnate vision.

Often that choice is ironically passive. Hazel Motes's story is not resolved until he stops resisting his inherited total vision by acting out a naturalistic impulse to destroy that vision through blasphemy. The virtue of O'Connor's protagonists has its basis, more often than

---

[197] Ibid.

[198] Ibid., 165–66.

[199] Cash, *The Mind of the South*, 35.

not, in what they cannot do, a mode which doubly subverts the national rhetoric of dreams made possible through action and the regional embarrassment of lasting spiritual conviction. When the novel was reissued in its second edition, O'Connor reintroduced Hazel through the lens of this central and unifying problem:

> That belief in Christ is to some a matter of life and death has been a stumbling block for readers who would prefer to think it a matter of no great consequence. For them Hazel Motes's integrity lies in his trying with such vigor to get rid of the ragged figure who moves from tree to tree in the back of his mind. For the author Hazel's integrity lies in his not being able to. Does one's integrity ever lie in what he is not able to do? I think that usually it does, for free will does not mean one will, but many wills conflicting in one man.[200]

O'Connor's initial audience, especially that part of it which was made up of reformed and born-again Southerners, suffered from an internal conflict similar to Hazel's: Did they carry on in the old way, did they import a new way, or did they make an easy compromise by accepting neither old nor new but imitating both? Many of O'Connor's characters, especially her mothers and grandmothers, choose the last of these. The old way was, for them, too precious to abandon outright; to do so would have been to disown the better part of their own personalities which had been twinned, for generations, with the traditional image of Southernness. The New South was not so new that it disallowed these aging belles their habitual flourishes. There is, in the actions of characters like Julian's mother ("Everything That Rises Must Converge") and the grandmother ("A Good Man Is Hard To Find") an almost maternal affection for the Old South which is at it boldest when that South is made to seem, by more progressive characters, outmoded. As they would for themselves, these women desire that this South be left to its eccentricities and, perhaps, even be allowed a certain degree of ridiculousness in its old age. Such was the posture that became more or less representative of the New Southern mind. As Gray notes, there was no "great revolution" in Southern thinking during the modern era.[201] "All the signs are that the non-material culture of the region, although not unaffected by changes in the material culture,

---

[200] O'Connor, *Wise Blood*, 4.

[201] Gray, *Writing*, 225.

[was] less substantially altered than one might expect."[202] Reed makes the point well in *The Enduring South*. When he asked white Southerners to describe themselves, the words they "used most frequently were conservative, tradition-loving, courteous, and loyal to family ties."[203] This same sample described Northerners as "industrious, materialistic, intelligent, progressive, and sophisticated."[204] The "American people" in general were thought to be "materialistic, industrious, and pleasure-loving."[205] "In effect," Gray writes, "the Southerners interviewed associated the national system of values with one quite alien to their own. They tended to see themselves as a distinctive minority, not nearly as 'American'—nowhere near as much a part of the cultural mainstream—as most observers of the South's material development would like to believe."[206] This evidence suggests that even though Southerners and non-Southerners shared certain kinds of non-empirical knowledge there were still dramatic differences in the ways each group managed that information. Non-Southerners tended to cordon off non-empirical knowledge with disclamatory tags that suggest a disjoint between a particular experience and the more general experience they called reality. The compartmentalization of ordinary and extraordinary experiences was, in the Agrarians' view, proof of the displacement of religious conviction by scientific idealism in the Northern mind:

> Religion is our submission to the general intention of a nature that is fairly inscrutable; it is the sense of our role as creatures within it. But nature industrialized, transformed into cities and artificial habitations, manufactured into commodities, is no longer nature but a highly simplified picture of nature. We receive the illusion of having power over nature, and lose the sense of nature as something mysterious and contingent. The God of nature under these conditions is merely an amiable expression, a superfluity, and the philosophical understanding ordinarily carried in the religious experience is not there for us to have.[207]

---

[202] Ibid.

[203] Reed, *Enduring*, 27, 29.

[204] Ibid.

[205] Ibid.

[206] Gray, *Writing*, 226.

[207] Tate, et al., "Introduction," *Stand*, xlii.

O'Connor poked fun at modern secularized logic in *Wise Blood* when Hazel's love interest, the self-proclaimed bastard Sabbath Lily Hawks, solicits the advice of a newspaper columnist:

> I says, "Dear Mary, I am a bastard and a bastard shall not enter the kingdom of heaven as we all know, but I have this personality that makes boys follow me. Do you think I should neck or not? I shall not enter the kingdom of heaven anyway so I don't see what difference it makes." ...Then she answered me in the paper. She said, "Dear Sabbath, Light necking is acceptable, but I think your real problem is one of adjustment to the modern world. Perhaps you ought to re-examine your religious values to see if they meet your needs in Life. A religious experience can be a beautiful addition to living if you put it in the proper perspective and do not let it warf [sic] you. Read some books on Ethical Culture."[208]

Mary Brittle's advice to Sabbath is to adjust herself to the modern world by interpreting religion in general and the Bible in particular figuratively rather than literally. O'Connor does not tell us where Mary Brittle is speaking from herself but she makes a point of underscoring her subtle way of pointing to the general leveling off of peculiarities in regional cultures by a national politic that promotes intellectual conformity through industry, the marketplace, education, and the popular arts.

Certainly the most striking characters in *Wise Blood* are the ones who have not adjusted to modern life in the South. Even Hazel whose aim is to debunk the Southern Jesus does not seem to have lost his inherited sense of a divinely ordered, primarily mysterious reality. He does not exhibit as active a consciousness of distinction in the way more integrated characters like George Rayber (*The Violent Bear It Away*) and Julian ("Everything That Rises Must Converge") do. The result is a conspicuous alloy of spiritual and physical knowledge. Hazel catalogues all of his experiences beneath the same heading, treating each of them, from the mundane to the fantastic, as a part of the same general experience of an ultimately mysterious existence. He does this even when he does not desire belief in that mystery. Indeed Hazel's aggressive denial of his tradition, his risk of the ultimate blasphemy, and his eventual reversion imply a radical change in the intellectual climate in the South, one that has had an effect on traditional thinking but has not, by any stretch, eradicated

---

[208] O'Connor, *Wise Blood*, 119.

the peculiarly Southern habits of being. The foremost of these remains a literalizing Christian spirituality. Davidson contended that, "This consciousness, too often misdescribed as merely romantic and gallant, really signifies a close connection with the eighteenth-century European America that is elsewhere forgotten."[209] He claims that this European "social inheritance," which flourished in the agrarian South, fostered the region's totalizing consciousness. "The manners of planters and countrymen did not require them to change their beliefs and temper in going from cornfield to drawing-room, from cotton rows to church or frolic."[210]

The Southern inclination toward cumulative consciousness is evident in the fiction of Southern writers as disparate as O'Connor and Faulkner, but it is unclear if the tenacity of such "Southern" mindedness can be equated to the "hallmarks" of the region's writing. O'Connor's case is especially ambiguous. She seems to exhibit the Southern tendency toward comprehensive vision, but she does not always conform to the conventions associated with the Southern myth such as epic diction, romance, narrative circularity, timelessness, and compulsive repetition. It might be that these image patterns are arbitrary or that critics have placed too much emphasis upon them and in so doing have created an independent, self-perpetuating South that looks suspiciously like the real South(s) but is, in fact, only superficially related to it. Gray's later work certainly supports this kind of introspective, meta-textual reading of the region, its literature, and its critical baggage, but the larger industry of Southern-ism, even when it attempts a more skeptical outlook, is generally preoccupied with the wrong question, that is which came first: the uncreated, organic entity or the critical terminology? The danger here is not in exposing the South(s) as constructions (which are, for critical argument, the only Souths that matter) but in reasserting a discursive camaraderie between post-modern criticism and the monolithic, soon-to-be-extinct South. Embedded in this gesture is the assumption of the existence of an original, unadulterated South which has been irredeemably altered by negative and corrective interpretation. Gray's early discussion of the Southern renaissance, for instance, assumes an original South by

---

[209] Davidson, "A Mirror for Artists," 53.

[210] Ibid.

implying an uninterrupted legacy of knowledge created by the imposition of history upon a virgin South. "The things [the renaissance writers] say, and the way in which they say them," he writes, "seem to have been defined with extraordinary completeness—you could even say circumscribed—by the paradoxes implicit in what their history has taught them."[211]

Late modern Southern writers participated, like Faulkner and the Fugitives had, with the assumption of a unifying historical consciousness, but their work also demonstrates a growing cynicism for the "Southern tradition." The country wisdom of O'Connor's most infamous characters can be read, on one level, as a parody of traditional Southern thinking, but O'Connor was not primarily interested in caricature. She wrote, on several occasions, regarding the value of working within a regional tradition even if that tradition had become unbalanced in places and diluted in others. She felt that her greatest debt to the Southern tradition was to the communal knowledge of "sacred history" which she believed created ties between ordinary people and the "universal and holy, which allow the meaning of their every action to be heightened and seen under the aspect of eternity."[212] The South was changing but not so fast that the Scriptures no longer functioned as the region's most powerful shared discourse. "Sam Jones's grandma read the Bible thirty-seven times on her knees," O'Connor noted in her essay, "The Catholic Novelist in the Protestant South."[213] "[T]he rural and small town South, and even a certain level of the city South, is made up of descendants of old ladies like her. You don't shake off their influence in even several generations."[214]

When a subconsciously biblical world-view is applied to narrative realism certain generic conventions have to be stretched and reconfigured to accommodate another mystery, what Welty called "the mystery…[of using] language to express human life."[215]

---

[211] Gray, *Memory*, 1.

[212] O'Connor, "The Catholic Novelist in the Protestant South," *Mystery*, 203.

[213] Ibid., 201. Samuel Porter Jones was a famed Methodist revivalist of the late nineteenth century.

[214] Ibid., 202.

[215] Eudora Welty qtd. in Gray, *Aberrations*, 504.

Like Henry James,[216] the Southern realist seems to be interested in the "real"—"the things we cannot possibly not know, sooner or later, in one way or another"—and the "romantic"—"the things that, with all the faculties in the world, all the wealth and all the courage and all the wit and all the adventure, we never can directly know."[217] He is a romancer in that he has inherited the social and spiritual myths of his region and the reflex to interpret even the most fantastic of these literally. His native idiom creates a perspective so unlike that of the non-Southern mainstream that the harder he tries to write "straight" realism the more romantic he sounds to the non-Southern ear. This is not to say that he is unable, by virtue of his cultural surroundings, to write a more naturalistic realism. It is rather an irony of terms: the more persistently the Southern realist follows a regional aesthetic, the further he gets from the standardized notion of realism. O'Connor put it much more succinctly: "The South is a story-telling section. The Southerner knows he can do more justice to reality by telling a story than he can by discussing problems or proposing abstractions. We live in a complex region and you have to tell stories if you want to be anyway truthful about it."[218] "In a work of art," she went on to say, "we can be extremely literal, without being in the least naturalistic."[219] O'Connor is unique amongst her peers because she affirms a literalizing view of the spiritual real while maintaining a straightforward narrative technique. Her stories are set in a Georgia which is recognizable enough to be convincing to the modern reader and distorted enough to jolt him back to an elemental vision of being as transcendentally grotesque. Her work is reminiscent of Byzantine triptychs in that past, present, and infinite being are folded one on top of the other. All three are coincidental and interactive, each effecting and effected by the perceived actuality

---

[216] James wrote against the predominant aesthetic of the North just as his Southern counterparts did. I include him here because of this proof of aberration within the Northern literary scene and because of his particular influence on Southern literature, including the work of O'Connor (*The Habit of Being*, ed. Sally Fitzgerald [New York: Farrar, Straus & Giroux, 1979] 99).

[217] Henry James qtd. in Richard Chase, *The American Novel and Its Tradition* (Baltimore: Johns Hopkins University Press, 1957) 27.

[218] Flannery O'Connor qtd. in *Conversations with Flannery O'Connor*, ed. Rosemary M. Magee

(Jackson: University Press of Mississippi, 1987) 103.

[219] O'Connor, "The Nature and Aim of Fiction," *Mystery*, 70.

of the others. Such a narrative encourages a gaze which can see backward beyond the boundary of Southern history, downward into the present particular, and forward into the future unknown.

Southern realism like O'Connor's has been called many things—romantic, gothic, grotesque—but it is rarely aligned with the tradition of realism which Americans gleaned from Eliot and Flaubert. When the term is used to describe Southern literature it is always accompanied by an expositive word like "social" or "dirty." These imply that realism, when it does occur in Southern writing, is not Realism proper but a subordinate regional variety that is defined by a demographic or stylistic quirk. This is a gross over-simplification to be sure. What makes realism "Southern" is not the simple addition of Southern elements but a total re-imagining of the realist genre so that the form might accommodate a persistence of belief in the South of the ineffable aspect of the real as immediate and straight-faced as the antebellum cracker's or New England Romancer's. This tendency to force the boundaries of conventional realism outward was especially true of O'Connor. In her work, the same denotative relevance is attached to the unknowns of human intimacy and the supernatural as to the hard truths of nature. Real life in the South for O'Connor was not a calculable mass of dropped g's and red clay but an intricate mesh of overlying objects and images, some earthly, some not; when they were fictionalized, they established a multi-form realist aesthetic that was necessarily more pliable than the national standard. O'Connor's frequent distortion of the literal Southern object—the pine hollow, the back water—and the fictionalized Southern trope—the country drifter, the soapbox prophet—was not anti-realist in its departure from transparent representation. It was in line, rather, with a much older tradition of folk-realism that began in earnest with Chaucer and by which reality is made palpable through fantastic, idiomatic exaggeration. O'Connor's realism singularly melds the romantic and otherworldly image systems of the South with the more literal elements of regional character and landscape, each of which was underpinned by a universalizing "sympathy between narrator…character…and reader" drawn from the regional sense of communal experience.[220] O'Connor once said, "A great deal of the Southern writer's work is

[220] Gray, *Memory*, 144.

done for him before he begins, because our history lives in our talk."[221] By engaging this active feeling of shared reality, she was able to imbue her fictional South with a more immediate drama that reminded the reader that he shares "in the experience[s the author describes] rather than merely [observing] them."[222]

The first instance of a mature Southern realism—that is a realism which worked within the local idiom without pandering to or exploiting it—is also considered by many, including Hemingway, to be the progenitor of "all modern American literature."[223] Twain's *Huckleberry Finn* adopts a way of telling about the South which, in Gray's words:

> is neither the language of the "realist" in *Life on the Mississippi* nor that of the "romantic," but another form of speech entirely which accommodates both of those languages and then raises them to a higher power. ...It reconciles the demands of the pragmatist with those of the dreamer, the progressive impulse with its nostalgic equivalent—and manages to treat the alphabet of the river as a medium of communication and as an object of its own peculiar beauty.[224]

O'Connor used the alphabet of the Southern landscape in much the same way. Her work reveals a distinct interpretation of the realist model made to integrate with the Southern context. It spans a broad technical spectrum, incorporating elements from folkloric traditions (oral story-telling, local-color realism) and the supernatural or gothic (grotesque realism) to a grimy minimalism (Kmart or dirty realism). In her deliberate combination of realist and romantic language, O'Connor shares a distinct kinship with Twain. Where early Southern fiction tended toward one extreme of picturesque local-colorism and modern mainstream realism tended toward the opposing empirical extreme, modern and contemporary Southern realism cuts out a middle way, walking the line between a "self-destroying mysticism...on the one hand and a self-destroying naturalism and practicality...on the other."[225]

---

[221] O'Connor, "Writing Short Stories," *Mystery*, 105.

[222] Gray, *Memory*, 144.

[223] Ernest Hemingway, *The Green Hills of Africa*, rpt. ed. (New York: Simon and Schuster, 1963) 22.

[224] Gray, *Memory*, 114.

[225] Tate, "Remarks," *Stand*, 163.

What was once a question of empirical reality—is the Southern experience so unlike the non-Southern that the real in the South seems fictionalized and, therefore, Southern fiction must be more romantic than it is realistic—has become a question of aesthetics. Realism in the South, though it may engage some of the conventions of traditionally non-realistic genres (romance, myth, and folk-tale) should not be classed as either Romance, Myth, or Folk-Tale or some combination of these as it so often is by critics who read the Southern mode against the conventions of mainstream realism. This method oversimplifies the particularities of the local aesthetic by isolating unreal elements which do not conform to the national standard and generalizing their effect.[226]

With this trend in mind, we should also consider that part of the Southern narrative which has been drafted by non-Southerners. For the outsider, the South was and in some ways continues to be a country apart, wondrous and terrible, almost too good (or bad) to be true. "The fact is simply," Weaver wrote in 1952:

> that for the North the South is too theatrical to be wholly real; therefore it is "history" and not "real life." The South appears to the North as a kind of tableau. It is interesting, even fascinating, to look upon with its survivals of medievalisms, its manners that recall vanished eras, its stark social cleavages, its lost cause, its ballads and sentimental songs. But the very presence of these causes the typical American to view it with the same dubious credulity that one shows toward the exhibit in the glass case at a museum. It is so strange that one cannot conquer the feeling that it must be in some degree fictionalized.[227]

Certainly part of the reason the South inspires feelings of other-worldliness or sub-reality is because some aspects of the Southern narrative have been fictionalized. But which and by who? Humphries suggests that when North and South move to represent their notion of the real in literature, objectivity will be at the mercy of their need to explain themselves in regards to a projected other:

---

[226] The general reception of Southern fiction as unrealistic has its roots in the conventional adoption of Poe and Faulkner as the progenitors of the region's best writing. This line of criticism emphasizes the "most Southern" (or un-Northern) elements in a text and assumes that all Southern fiction exhibits, to a greater or lesser extent, shades of a Southern gothic tradition identified with Poe and Faulkner.

[227] Weaver, "Aspects of the Southern Philosophy," 28.

"Both the negative and the positive [versions of the narrative South] may be, and probably are, entirely arbitrary and bear little relation to fact; when there is an attempt at moderation, if not objectivity, it usually falls on deaf ears on both sides because it appeals to neither's narrative desire..."[228] I do not mean to suggest anything so sinister as a hegemony of realism imposed upon localized Southern aesthetics by Northern critics and publishing houses. The Southern realist operates at a different register not because he is consciously subverting an oppressive non-Southern aesthetic but because he is following a very different kind of expressive impulse that grew out of an oral narrative tradition. The delivery of the tale and the unrepeatable quality of performance are of primary importance to the Southern storyteller, whereas content and resolution, which are almost always known to the listener *a priori*, are subordinate considerations. Faulkner hardly introduces Thomas Sutpen, and the Southern reader knows ruin is eminent because he recognizes in Sutpen other stories of Southern patricians and their epic desires and lost causes. He knows that Sutpen will be undone in his striving to become like these ghosts. "[L]ike the Greeks," O'Connor noted, "you should know what is going to happen in this story so that any element of suspense in it will be transferred from its surface to its interior."[229] Because the audience is aware, at the outset of the narrative, of what will become of Sutpen, Faulkner could turn his attention to the internal working of the plot in the hero and in the reader-foil, Quentin, whose purpose it is to dramatize the audience's discursive relationship with the South.

The sympathy, as Gray calls it, between teller, tale, and audience meant that the distinction between one form of telling and another could be disregarded for the sake of the performance. Faulkner, to my mind, blended fantastic and historic rhetorical elements to create a Southern diction that moved freely between generic borders and prioritized the "dramatic point of the story" above its fidelity to empirical reality.[230] The result was a relatively uniform idiomatic connotation that was available to the teller whether he was performing a tall-tale or a family legend, a sermon or a speech. "Storytelling is a ritual [in the South]," Gray writes, "that

[228] Humphries, "The Discourse of Southernness," 123–24.

[229] O'Connor, "A Reasonable Use of the Unreasonable," *Mystery*, 109.

[230] Weaver, "Aspects of the Southern Philosophy," 208.

helps authenticate the lives of those who tell and listen; it enlivens memory and familiarizes by linking the extraordinary with the ordinary, the present with the relevant past."[231] Poe, Twain, and Faulkner were all ritual storytellers who sustained a unique dramatic intensity through the synthesis of fantasy and history. Most critics would hesitate to call them realists because, as Eric J. Sundquist puts it, their "reckless, imaginary [selves] refused to yield to the literalizing demands of a strict realism."[232] Like these three O'Connor departed, perhaps necessarily, from the generic standard when she moved to compress her local reality into an empirical language. Such deviation suggests that the realist aesthetic in the South is derived from the conventions of its local idioms rather than the scientific conventions of naturalism or a more conventional Western realism. While it does not disregard empirical language, the Southern idiom seems to have more faith in the stylized conventions of myth, romance, and humor as a means of describing the Southern real. "If we admit, as we must," O'Connor wrote, "that appearance is not the same thing as reality, then we must give the artist the liberty to make certain rearrangements of nature if these will lead to greater depths of vision."[233] For many writers in the South and especially for O'Connor, realism is not meant to dispel the mystery of life by way of explication but to draw attention to and if possible to deepen that sense of mystery.

Howard Odum and John MacLachlan argued that the Southern faith in non-empirical knowledge was the by-product of the region's rural, agrarian heritage. They claim that Faulkner's definitive "Southern" aesthetic, his:

---

[231] Gray, *Aberrations*, 507. Eric Cheyfitz links this process of ritual storytelling to the reader's overall conception of the real: "[I]f reality is nothing but a process of community storytelling, then reality, conceived of as a substantial realm prior to this process, is a romance, a figure in a story, a figure believed in with such force of conviction that it seems to take on that substantial priority that can tell each member of the community who he or she is" ("A Hazard of New Fortunes: The Romance of Self-Realization," *American Realism: New Essays*, ed. Eric Sundquist [Baltimore: Johns Hopkins University Press, 1982] 44).

[232] Eric J. Sundquist, ed., *American Realism: New Essays* (Baltimore: Johns Hopkins University Press, 1982) 4.

[233] O'Connor, "Writing Short Stories," *Mystery*, 98.

> sense of the final in the immediate and the universal in the particular...has found no voice among [American city dwellers]. Such sensitivity and sensibility seem to come to metropolitan minds ex post facto: reading it they grasp it, only to forget it straightway again; the grasp is half-handed, "intellectual," unfelt, lacking that strength which goes with a sense of elemental reality.[234]

The familiar dichotomy between the rural South and the urban North is used here to illustrate a possible source of power in Southern fiction. For Odum and MacLachlan, the modern Southerner's proximity to elemental reality translated into a narrative style that could be more deeply felt because it spoke to the most basic of human desires. The city-dweller, being removed from the drama of life on the land, has become less motivated by his primitive desires—he has no need to grow his own food or build his own shelter—and is preoccupied with the more abstract desires he has developed in the city. This is, admittedly, a rather dated observation; the post-modern South is, in many ways, as ready-made a space as Odum's urban North ever was, and there are very few Southerners who could claim a truly self-sufficient, rural lifestyle that is beyond the reach of urban commerce. But Southerners have maintained, in spite of its industrial evolution, a "sense of being rooted in a dear, particular place and, with that, a feeling for the past that is part of their earth and therefore a part of them."[235]

O'Connor believed that the fiction writer should be especially wary of straying too far from his own "elemental reality." She advises her friend Cecil Dawkins that the younger writer would "be better off in any town, population under 5,000, in south Alabama than [she] would be in New York City. That's where," she continued, "reality goes out the window. That is, when it ain't your reality."[236] For O'Connor the contexts of action, in life and especially in literature, were crucial to meaning. If you were to superimpose the gestures of her characters upon a non-Southern landscape, few would translate. As Percy points out, "Even Erskine Caldwell, out to

---

[234] Howard W. Odum and John MacLachlan, "Literature in the South: An Exchange of Views," *Southern Renascence: The Literature of the Modern South*, ed. Louis D. Rubin, Jr. and Robert D. Jacobs (Baltimore: Johns Hopkins University Press, 1953) 102.

[235] Gray, *Aberrations*, 498.

[236] O'Connor, *Habit*, 493.

profane, had to have something to profane. Try to imagine...Lester Jeeter blaspheming in California. Who would care?"[237] Discursive value corresponds directly to the localized place where human drama occurs, where there is a sense of shared history or "some communicable tradition or idiom according to which a personality can be identified."[238] "The interrelationship of personal and cultural history," Frederick J. Hoffman notes, "provides for a balance in human events that enhances meaning and locates it."[239] In fiction, "the nature of objects arranged in a scene tells something about the quality of the acts; they depend indispensably upon their relation to place for any values that may exist beyond their distribution in space."[240] Hoffman implies that narrative action is inescapably idiomatic and that, when dislocated from a grounding cultural space, meaning becomes increasingly abstract. Action therefore demands a cultural context to refer back to, and if that context is based on superficial constructions or is exaggerated the actual value of the action is misconstrued or even lost. In Hoffman's words, the actions cannot engage with the "types of knowledge and kinds of emotional commitment" encoded within place.[241]

This is not to say that the people O'Connor wrote about could not exist outside of the South but rather that what they say and do means the most in the South. The imprint of a shared cultural heritage is strong in the South whether or not the particulars of that heritage are literal, exaggerated, or completely false. O'Connor used that cache of images unreservedly to her own adventure. In pairing her sacramental vision with place, she conjured a broadened and at times contradictory picture of Middle Georgia. On one hand there exists a fiercely personal South which divined its truth through an elaborate set of learned narratives, and on the other a unified, all-consuming Catholic cosmos. At the moment of dramatic climax, O'Connor's narratives achieve an equation of like value between the particular and the universal while maintaining an appearance of

---

[237] Percy, *Signposts*, 178.

[238] Frederick J. Hoffman, "The Sense of Place," *South: Modern Southern Literature and Its Cultural Setting*, ed. Louis D. Rubin, Jr. and Robert D. Jacobs (New York: Doubleday, 1961) 60.

[239] Ibid., 60–61.

[240] Ibid., 61.

[241] Ibid.

opposition. "For me," O'Connor wrote in an early letter to Hester, "the visible universe is a reflection of the invisible universe."[242] She believed, as St. Augustine did, that, "the world poured forth from God in a double way: intellectually into the minds of the angels and physically into the world of things."[243] In this total real, there are no hierarchies of being; the supernatural is not supplementary to nature nor superior to it. It is an intrinsic and visible part of the natural world. Just how visible the supernatural is and in what form it manifests depends upon where an individual is in time and space. O'Connor's South describes one such intersection.

Like the Souths of so many of her contemporaries, O'Connor's Georgia was marked by a literal interpretation of the Bible.[244] Her habitual juxtaposition of Christian imagery with visceral local details suggests that she intuited a compatibility between the mysteries of her faith and her dead-pan, South-born aesthetic. She considered her narrative voice an extension of her spiritual beliefs. "I have heard it said," she wrote in her essay, "The Fiction Writer and His Country" (1957) "that belief in Christian dogma is a hindrance to the writer, but I myself have found nothing further from the truth. Actually, it frees the story-teller to observe. It is not a set of rules which fixes what he sees in the world. It affects his writing primarily by guaranteeing his respect for mystery."[245] In a later essay, O'Connor continued this thought by saying, "We write with the whole personality, and any attempt to circumvent it whether this be an effort to rise above belief or above background, is going to result in a reduced approach to reality."[246] O'Connor's was, in a rapidly

---

[242] O'Connor, *Habit*, 128.

[243] Ibid.

[244] Frank Lawrence Owsley claims in his essay "The Irrepressible Conflict" that the South became "devoutly orthodox and literal in its theology" as a result of Northern criticism (which was considered by fundamentalists to be shamelessly liberal) against an institution which was more or less "benevolent" and certified by the scriptures (*I'll Take My Stand*, ed. Lewis P. Simpson [Baton Rouge: Louisiana State University Press, 1977] 81).

[245] O'Connor, "The Fiction Writer and His Country," *Mystery*, 31.

[246] O'Connor, "The Catholic Novelist in the Protestant South," *Mystery*, 193. Just prior to the publication of this essay, C. Ross Mullins asked O'Connor about the relationship of spiritual belief and the project of literature. She replied that, "Distinctions of belief create distinctions of habit,

modernizing American scene, a minority opinion. She spoke openly about her fear that the nation's literary sensibility, which she believed reflected a deeper spiritual deficit, was being degraded by the secular ideology of the marketplace (best-sellers) and the laboratory (positivist and naturalist aesthetics). Whatever the reason, O'Connor's own work was overwhelmingly misunderstood by her critics. She admits to Hester her frustration with reviews that confused her adherence to a regional aesthetic, that sees grace in even the most horrific of places, with a secularized aesthetic, which sees only horror. "I am mighty tired of reading reviews," O'Connor wrote:

> that call A Good Man is Hard to Find brutal and sarcastic. The stories are hard but they are hard because there is nothing harder or less sentimental than Christian realism. I believe there are many rough beasts now slouching toward Bethlehem to be born and that have reported the progress of a few of them, and when I see these stories described as horror stories I am always amused because the reviewer has hold of the wrong horror.[247]

The persistence of traditional realist models which prompted negative interpretations of her own realism would problematize O'Connor's reception throughout her career. What best captured the real to her mind read as fantastic or brutal to an audience steeped in non-Southern realist conventions.[248] The majority of O'Connor's Northern contemporaries did not share her literal sense of God's grace in the world—what she called "Christian realism"—nor did they sympathize with her equally unsentimental Georgia humor. In

---

distinctions of habit make for distinctions of feeling. You don't believe on one side of your head and feel on the other" (qtd. in Magee, ed., *Conversations*, 106).

[247] O'Connor, *Habit*, 90.

[248] O'Connor described her intentions for "A Good Man Is Hard to Find" in a letter to an anonymous English professor. He had apparently misinterpreted O'Connor's stylized realism as a "dream" fantasy. "There is a change in tension from the first part of the story to the second where the Misfit enters," O'Connor explained, "but this is no lessening of reality. This story is, of course, not meant to be realistic in the sense that it portrays the everyday doings of people in Georgia. It is stylized and its conventions are comic even though its meaning is serious" (*The Habit of Being*, ed. Sally Fitzgerald [New York: Farrar, Straus & Giroux, 1979] 437).

effect, they subjected O'Connor's "grotesque realism"[249] to their own aesthetic rubrics, perpetuating inverted descriptive terms: "[A]nything that comes out of the South," O'Connor claimed, "is going to be called grotesque by the Northern reader, unless it is grotesque, in which case it is going to be called realistic."[250]

This is not a trend specific to Southern or American literature. Bakhtin proposed that the stylistic range of generic realism was constricted comprehensively when writers broke from the medieval and Renaissance traditions of grotesque realism which he traces from Rabelais and Cervantes to Balzac and Dickens.[251] "Breaking away from this tradition diminished the scope of realism and transformed it into naturalist empiricism. ...This degeneration," he claimed, "was linked with the specific limitations of the bourgeois world outlook."[252] Contemporary realism seems to have been defined by an idiom that was locked into a limited, perhaps bourgeois world-view, and as a result Southern fiction, which adopts its realist aesthetic from the medieval and Renaissance traditions is seen, not as a revitalization of "grotesque realism," but the Grotesque. Here again, we see that "[T]he relation of individual works to a system of literature or realism is culturally determined."[253] "In this context," Smith posits, "'realism' can be described as a term that rival representational paradigms define separately and then contend with one another to culturally legitimate."[254]

In order to reappropriate the term realism so that it resonates within Southern contexts and specifically within O'Connor's fiction, criticism must reconsider the genre's aesthetic boundaries and the regional and sub-regional idioms from which those boundaries were constructed. As Davidson points out, "The...tradition in which... [Southern] writers would share has been discredited and made artistically inaccessible; and the ideas, modes, and attitudes that

---

[249] "Grotesque realism" is a term first used by Bakhtin in his study of *Rabelais* to describe a critical but often neglected element which "manifests" itself within the "entire range of realistic literature" (*Rabelais and His World*, trans. Hélène Iswolsky [Bloomington: Indiana University Press, 1984] 24).

[250] O'Connor, "Some Aspects of the Grotesque in Southern Fiction," *Mystery*, 40.

[251] Bakhtin, *Rabelais*, 52.

[252] Ibid.

[253] Smith, *Literary Realism and the Ekphrastic Tradition*, 9.

[254] Ibid.

discredited it, largely not Southern, have been current and could be used."[255] If the conventional definition of realism is largely non-Southern, if it does not take into account the variance in regional thinking and aesthetic tack, it is not a complete definition and cannot be meaningfully applied to generic aberrations in either Faulkner's Mississippi, O'Connor's Georgia, or Percy's Louisiana.

There is also a need to reevaluate what critics mean when they attach seemingly objective geographical labels like regional and Southern to literature from the South. These are terms which are misleading because they imply a relationship between particular authors and texts, their "native" region, and the popular image of that region. To prescribe to this kind of logic is to presume to know something of the essence of Welty's craft simply because you've read Faulkner or of O'Connor's because you've read McCullers. "The trouble is," Percy wrote:

> that the term "southern novelist" connotes too powerfully in the public consciousness, so powerfully that the connotation tends to close off the class so that all instances of the class tend to get assigned to the class like a Disposall. You can imagine, for example, a non-Southerner browsing in a non-Southern bookstore, picking up an interesting-looking new novel and inquiring of the non-Southern clerk, who may say something like, "she's one of the best young Southern novelists," whereupon the non-Southern customer is apt to put it back in short order, thinking he knows all he wants to know about Southern novelists, including female Southern novelists—which is one reason why Southern novelists don't sell many books.[256]

This accordion of easy associations has prompted many contemporary Southern writers, like Richard Ford, to actively disassociate themselves from the South and the interpreting terminology that comes along with it. But where did these terms come from, and how do they affect our baseline reading of Southern fiction? The notion of the American region seems to originate coincidently in both Southern and non-Southern discourse from the Colonial era with post-war and contemporary Southern criticism tending to emphasize regional difference as the function of a fortunate fall and non-Southern criticism tending, especially

---

[255] Davidson, "A Mirror for Artists," 59.

[256] Percy, *Signposts*, 154.

throughout the modern age, to emphasize a mainstream American tradition. The result is a chain of critical polarities—National and Regional, American and Southern—which identifies regional Southern literature as subordinate to a greater American literature. Deviant aesthetic traditions are thereby decentered with tags that connote some definitive sub-standard, and the mainstream gaze is prompted to default to conventional Southern stereotypes and to interpret Southern literature by attaching a non-Southern "othered" South to it.

Whether or not they are intended to indicate a negative critical difference, regional tags carry the automatic association of predominantly negative stereotypes. The Southern canon inevitably subsumed these negative associations, and the result is a critical inclination to associate Southern writing, in general, with a low-grade aesthetic, e.g. provincial writing and local-colorism. The more Southern fiction is identified as regional, the further it is pushed into the canonical margin. The Southern canon is thereby othered, existing, for the majority of critics, as an outlier to American literature proper. Exceptions were made for Faulkner's work, but because it was so lauded by mainstream critics, it was considered by many to be a remarkable fluke in an otherwise unremarkable canon.[257] Lesser known modern writers like O'Connor struggled against the regional conception of their work for the duration of their careers. In her oft-quoted essay, "Place in Fiction," Welty notes that "Regional…is a careless term as well as a condescending one because what it does is fail to differentiate between the localized raw material of life and its outcome as art. 'Regional' is an outsider's term; it has no meaning for the insider who is doing the writing because, as far as he knows, he is simply writing about life."[258]

Since the turn of the twentieth century, the need for a pluralism of terms has been increasing in time with the accelerated blending of

---

[257] Even Faulkner "did not win popular acclaim…until after he received the Nobel Prize in 1950. Despite the critical notice," Kirby notes, "it would seem, the book-reading middle class found [him] turgid, puzzling, and 'difficult'" (*Media Made Dixie*, 51).

[258] Eudora Welty, "Place in Fiction," *Welty: Stories, Essays & Memoir*, ed. Richard Ford and Michael Kreyling (New York: Literary Classics of the United States, Inc., 1998) 796.

regional communities with "the messy rest of America."[259] "What is happening everywhere, and also in the South, is a very rapid mixing," Butler writes:

> Not that detail is lost, but the level of detail shows an increasingly fine grain. One of the things this means to writers is that larger and larger amounts of energy are going to be required to establish background and character. Before you had a lot of givens in the culture. You could shorthand some of the information and still get 3-D effects. It isn't that Flannery O'Connor didn't use supremely good details. But her details had the whole culture backing them up. …If you try that now, the detail may seem antiquated or worse, clichéd.[260]

If New Southern critics are to talk in a meaningful way about the South and Southern writing, we need to develop a critical apparatus that is accessible to both insider and outsider. This double-headed reading would allow us to deconstruct the historical significance of the conjoined priorities and reciprocal influence of Southern and non-Southern aesthetics without favoring either tradition. Critical details like Southernness or gothicism pose a problem for American criticism because they have the whole culture backing them up, a culture prone to Disposall interpretation which has made "Southern" an increasingly arbitrary distinction. To institute a theory of Southern realism that is to be truly dynamic, its methodology must refer to national and local registers and interrogate them both with equal disinterest. To make sense of the Southern canon, to decode native action and its correlative forms, criticism first has to redefine the parameters of conventional realism so that its terminology resonates within its context. Southern realism must be defined on its own terms, which will require, in many cases, a re-contextualization of the Southern writer. For O'Connor, this reclaimed South must be delimited to middle Georgia and let go into the furthest reaches of transcendental realism. The author put it best herself when she declared to the Georgia Writer's Association that, "To call yourself a Georgia writer is certainly to declare a limitation, but one which, like all limitations, is a gateway to reality."[261] The

---

[259] Butler, "Still Southern After All These Years," 34.
[260] Ibid., 38.
[261] O'Connor, "The Regional Writer," *Mystery*, 54.

"realism of each novelist," in the South or anywhere, "will depend on his view of the ultimate reaches of reality."[262]

[262] Ibid., 40.

Chapter 2

"One Jesus [Is] Just as Bad as Another"

Orthodoxy as Ecumenical Blasphemy in the Fiction of Flannery O'Connor[1]

Much has been made of the ultimate reach of Flannery O'Connor's informing reality. Contrary to the interpretive through-line posited by critical orthodoxy which holds that O'Connor's fiction can be reduced essentially to a logic of absolute Roman Catholicism, the author's own scholarship describes an ongoing interrogation, in spite of sacramental ties, of her inherited church and the doctrines of a broader Christian tradition. To maintain that O'Connor's work is fundamentally reflexive of her patronage to the Church of Rome is to disengage it artificially from her persistent theological querying. Her fiction stands as an irreducible element of process in which O'Connor tested her faith in the Christian mysteries against the varying but interrelated cosmologies of the Hebrews, the early church, Eastern Orthodoxy, and Protestantism. The pat Catholic theology which critics like Joanne Halleran McMullen (in her early work), Guy Reynolds, and Patrick Samway, S. J. have attributed to O'Connor might describe her sacramental devotion, but steadfast as she was in adhering to Roman dogma, her theology extended, even in her childhood, beyond Rome. O'Connor's tendency toward orthodoxy is described by her repetition of social blasphemies motivated by the ironic disavowal of those first terms. Hazel Motes lies with the prostitute Leora Watts because he does not believe in the resurrection of his body. Ruby Turpin "occupie[s] herself... naming the classes of people" because she believes few to be better than herself. [2] Neither is stricken by an other-worldly judgment, but gradually they perceive these slights as theological betrayals. Hazel has the fateful realization that he is "not clean" while Ruby envisions herself as least in the Kingdom.[3] "The Church, as institution, doesn't

[1] O'Connor, *Wise Blood*, 176.

[2] O'Connor, "Revelation," *Complete Stories*, 491.

[3] O'Connor, *Wise Blood*, 224.

come into it one way or another."[4] By destabilizing and at times inverting the surety of civic gnosticism, evangelical Protestantism and, in stories like "A Temple of the Holy Ghost" and "The Enduring Chill," Roman Catholicism, O'Connor held forth a debate that was at once deliberately personal and inconclusive.

Recent scholarship has seen a decisive shift away from pre-emptive Roman explication in spite of the prevailing and somewhat cultish image of O'Connor as Catholic ideologue. In his review of Brad Gooch's biography, *Flannery*, Ralph C. Wood observes that, "It has become virtually standard procedure, among interpreters of Gooch's kind, to say that O'Connor's life and work must not be confined or reduced to her Catholicism, that she had not merely one but many strings on her fiddle, that we deny the variousness of her fiction by concentrating chiefly on its religious quality."[5] Wood concedes that there is a "small truth contained in this charge."[6] O'Connor did not "confine herself within a religious cocoon[7] but was keenly attuned to writers as various as T. S. Eliot…, Guy de Maupassant, Caroline Gordon…,William Faulkner, and even J. D. Salinger…and was remarkably alert to popular culture."[8] Wood correctly notes that what is overlooked in Gooch's description of O'Connor's non-Catholic pursuits is the "significance" of characters like Enoch Emery who are "cut off from religious rituals that might have given redemptive shape to [their lives]."[9] O'Connor's fictions

---

[4] O'Connor, *Habit*, 290.

[5] Ralph C. Wood, "Such a Catholic," Rev. of *Flannery: A Life of Flannery O'Connor* by Brad Gooch, *National Review* 61/4 (March 2009): 38.

[6] Ibid.

[7] Josephine Hendin was one of the earliest proponents of a non-Catholic reading of O'Connor: "Because I think O'Connor told more than religious tales, I propose to view her fiction not for the dogma it illustrates, but for the themes it suggests. To assume that her work is merely a monologue on redemption is to see it only in part, to ignore much of its meaning, and to lose sight of the believer behind the belief" (*The World of Flannery O'Connor* [Bloomington: Indiana University Press, 1970] 17). Although I disagree with Hendin's argument that a psychoanalytical approach is the more appropriate reading, I do agree that O'Connor has been made a "spokesman for the Roman Catholic Church," and while this categorization has led "to a number of insights into her work…it has also tended to distort—to reduce it to a series of illustrations of church dogma" (3).

[8] Wood, "Such a Catholic," 38–39.

[9] Ibid., 39.

suggest that the Church Christ left has been lost and that religious and irreligious alike seek a new church and a new jesus, one tangible to the modern world. In 1961, she wrote to Hester in reply to her friend's leaving the Roman Church: "The natural comes before the supernatural and that is perhaps the first step toward finding the Church again."[10] O'Connor's fictive seekers, especially her blasphemers, testify to the misplacement of the real, in Catholic and Protestant faiths alike, as the conduit of revelation. The early church envisioned an immemorial continuity between the natural and the supernatural, and Orthodox still maintain, with their Hebrew forebears, that "the invisible things of Him from the creation of the world are clearly seen, being understood by the things that are made, even his eternal power and Godhead…"[11] In scripture, the Deity speaks through the mattered world: a desert bush, a whirlwind, a man; in O'Connor, the real is likewise taken up as a tenuous but faithful revelation of an ultimate reality.[12]

Deprioritizing the Roman perspective in O'Connor opens the field of interpretation to a broader range of informing story cycles which partake of a more ancient realist aesthetic. O'Connor's private reading was, of course, framed by the traditions and parochial ideologies of the Church of Rome, but it was by no means an exclusively Catholic scholarship. Her fiction is very much indebted to literature that predates or diverges from the Roman Church, notably the books of the Old Testament, the cosmological myths of the ancient near east and Medieval Europe, the lives of early saints, and Protestant theologies. The Catholic apparatus as it has been made to explain O'Connor gives only a cursory nod to the author's intellectual ecumenism, and it would be shortsighted to insist that her doctrinal orthodoxy within the Catholic Church precludes a devotional life that extends in time and expression beyond the teachings of pre-Vatican II Catholicism. To be sure, a catholic is one who intuits himself as a vital part of the apostolic tradition, and that tradition, since the Great Schism of the 11th century, has been divided between competing but complimentary theologies in the East and West. Carter W. Martin remarks that O'Connor "accept[ed] her Christian Orthodoxy as naturally as if schisms never occurred, as

---

[10] O'Connor, *Habit*, 453.

[11] Rom. 1:20, *KJV*.

[12] Exod. 3:2; Job 38:1; Isa. 6:1–10, Jer. 1:1–19, *KJV*.

seriously and as stringently as if she were a contemporary of Geoffrey Chaucer rather than of John O'Hara..."[13] Her self-governed church was contemporary to Christ, to the Church Fathers and the Desert Copts, and to Scholastics like St. Augustine and St. Thomas Aquinas.[14] Her letters reveal a spirituality that was dynamic, habitually reevaluating faith against the strain of personal doubt and the modern culture of unbelief. She was a cradle Catholic, but her dutifulness to the Church did not come without her subjecting its rites, as Christ did of the Temple, to prayerful skepticism. Her biblical foil, therefore, is not the law-driven Pharisee but the faith-driven father who, when faced with the mystery of salvation, cries, "I believe; help my unbelief!"[15]

From childhood, O'Connor was indoctrinated toward an awareness of herself as inevitably participant[16] in what St. Thomas described as Being as "becoming," the medieval catholic sense of actuality made comprehensible by the experience of the "going-on-ness of creation" by the intellectual soul.[17] While the evolution of O'Connor's theology begins and ends in the sacraments of the

---

[13] Carter W. Martin, *The True Country: Themes in the Fiction of Flannery O'Connor* (Nashville: Vanderbilt University Press, 1969) 20. See also Carter W. Martin, "The Catholic Commitment as a Phenomenological *Vorhabe*: Flannery O'Connor," n. date, "Sally Fitzgerald Papers," MS 1101, Box 53, FF 2, *Flannery O'Connor Collection*, Manuscripts, Archives, and Rare Books Library, Emory University, Atlanta.

[14] Robert Drake describes this aspect of O'Connor's theology as "classical[ly] Christian." Drake qtd. in Steven Robert Watkins, *Flannery O'Connor and Teilhard de Chardin: A Journey Towards Hope and Understanding in Life* (New York: Peter Lang Publishing, Inc., 2009) 4.

[15] Mark 9:24, *The Holy Bible*, New Standard Revised Version, Catholic ed. (New York: Harper Collins, 1989).

[16] It should be said that O'Connor was not always a willing catechumen. She wrote to Hester in 1956 of her routine childhood brawls with her guardian angel: "I went to the Sisters to school for the first 6 years or so...at their hands I developed something the Freudians have not named—anti-angel aggression, call it. From 8 to 12 years it was my habit to seclude myself in a locked room every so often and with a fierce (and evil) face, whirl around in a circle with my fists knotted, socking the angel. This was the guardian angel which the Sisters assured us we were all equipped. He never left you. My dislike of him was poisonous" (*Habit*, 131–32).

[17] Marion Montgomery, *Hillbilly Thomist: Flannery O'Connor and the Limits of Art*, Vol. I (Jefferson: McFarland and Company, 2006) 350.

Roman Church, it is also crucially punctuated by the extra-liturgical writings of the early Church Fathers, Eastern Saints including Cyril of Jerusalem, Basil of Caesarea, and Jerome, Medieval mystics such as St. John of the Cross, and by neo-Thomists like Jacques Maritain and Christian evolutionists like Teilhard de Chardin. Though she defended the doctrines of Rome in practice, O'Connor was by no means proto-typically Catholic; on the divided doctrine of the Roman and Orthodox Churches, she sides implicitly with the latter, which is to say with pre-schism orthodoxy. She did not exhibit any particular devotion to the Bishop of Rome nor to the Virgin Mary.[18] In one of her earliest missives to Betty Hester, O'Connor wrote that she, "Of course…[did] not connect the Church exclusively with the Patriarchal Ideal. The death of such," she went on to say, "would not be the death of the Church, which is only now a seed and a Divine one."[19] O'Connor was also no great believer in the Catholic Indulgence in spite of her prayers for the intercession of saints. "Penance rightly considered," she said, "is not acts performed in order to attract God's attention or to get credit for oneself. It is something natural that follows sorrow."[20] As to the decisive issue of papal infallibility (*ex cathedra*), O'Connor maintained that the human element of the living Church would inevitably err, and one can only assume that she included the Pope within the ranks of God's people. "[T]he Church is crucified in time…by all of us…" she wrote to Dawkins in 1958:

> Christ never said that the Church would be operated in a sinless or intelligent way, but that it would not teach error. This does not mean that each and every priest won't teach error but that the whole Church speaking through the Pope will not teach error in matters of faith. The Church is founded on Peter who denied Christ three times and couldn't walk on water by himself. …To have the Church be what you want it to be would require the continuous meddling of God in human affairs, whereas it is our dignity that we are allowed more or less to get on with those graces that come

---

[18] When compelled by her mother and cousin to visit the shrine at Lourdes, O'Connor said that she guessed the "only way to stand it [would] be to indulge temporarily in Quietism, cut [her] motor off so to speak and be towed" (*Habit*, 250).

[19] O'Connor, *Habit*, 99.

[20] Ibid., 354.

through faith and the sacraments which work through our human nature.[21]

On the equally schismatic point of the *filioque,* O'Connor espoused that the Holy Spirit descended into matter in a mysterious way and was content to leave its source (Father or Son) a mystery. If pushed, she tended to emphasize the *through* Him of the Sprit's descent in Christ, anticipating the shift that would come with Vatican II. Purgatory was one of the few peculiarly Roman doctrines that O'Connor espoused, but her notion of that state, the slow purging of vice through the revelation of the self in God, was decidedly more attuned to the thirteenth than the twentieth century. It is no accident that she calls the vision of Ruby Turpin purgatorial which she holds as a counter against Protestant and (Vapid) Catholic assumptions of total conversion.[22] "I don't think," she confided to Hester, "of conversion as being once and for all and that's that." "I think once the process is begun and continues that you are continually turning inward toward God and away from your own egocentricity and that you have to see this selfish side of yourself in order to turn away from it."[23] Self-judgment, O'Connor contended, is the first step towards purgation. "Part of Purgatory," she claimed, "must be the realization of how little it would have to take to make a vice into a virtue."[24]

Critics too often apply a standardized version of the Catholic mind—the very persona O'Connor derides in her essay, "Catholic Novelists and Their Readers"—to Flannery and interpret her work as if she were writing immovably from that perspective.[25] In his study

---

[21] Ibid., 307.

[22] Ibid., 577.

[23] Ibid., 430.

[24] Ibid., 155.

[25] See Patrick Samway, S.J., "Toward Discerning How Flannery O'Connor's Fiction Can Be Considered 'Roman Catholic,'" in *Flannery O'Connor's Radical Reality*, ed. Jan Nordby Gretlund and Karl Heinz-Westarp (Columbia: University of South Carolina Press, 2006) 162; Guy Reynolds, "There are So Many Horrible Examples of Regional Writers, and the South Is Loaded: Flannery O'Connor 'Every Action is Weighted With an Eternal Consequence,'" *Twentieth Century American Women's Fiction: A Critical Introduction* (New York: St. Martin's Press, 1999) 114–45. Reynolds describes O'Connor as "categorically adherent to the Roman faith." See also Margaret Earley Whitt, *Understanding Flannery O'Connor: New Perspectives* (Columbia:

Risen Sons: Flannery O'Connor's Vision of History, John F. Desmond suggests that this sort of criticism "regard[s] [O'Connor's] religious thought as monolithic and prescriptive and assume that [her] relationship to it was an overtly static one of passive acceptance."[26] The significance of this projected Catholic O'Connor is elevated to a staggering degree by McMullen in her book *Writing Against God*, so much so, in fact, that all shades of extra-liturgical influence, including O'Connor's sustained interest in the Early Church and Medieval and Eastern Christian theologies, her interaction with modern popular culture, and her struggle with religious doubt are down-played or disregarded entirely.[27] "[W]hile…an increasing number of O'Connor's commentators have sought to newly contextualize O'Connor's religious impulses within the political and social issues of post-World War II American and Southern culture," Stuart C. Chapman writes, "a steadfast group of critics continue to advance Saint Flannery's religion as something that transcends the cultural situation in which it was produced."[28] Despite the challenge afforded by socio-political framing to long-standing assumptions regarding O'Connor's provinciality, the orientation of studies like Jon Lance Bacon's *Flannery O'Connor and Cold War Culture* is wholly

---

University of South Carolina Press, 1995); Joyce Carol Oates, "The Action of Mercy," *The Kenyon Review* 20/1 (Winter 1998): 157–60.

[26] John F. Desmond, *Risen Sons: Flannery O'Connor's View of History* (Athens: University of Georgia Press, 1987) 7.

[27] In her early work, McMullen interprets O'Connor in view of a Roman model radically influenced by modern liberalism, especially in her insistence on the gentleness of Christ in Catholic orthodoxy (*Writing Against God: Language as Message in the Literature of Flannery O'Connor* [Macon GA: Mercer University Press, 1998] 26). In a more recent essay, "Christian but Not Catholic: Baptism in Flannery O'Connor's 'The River,'" McMullen is correct in her impulse to extend her interpretation beyond the Roman tradition, but her litmus (does Harry/Bevel's baptism constitute a legitimate Catholic rite?) is somewhat beside the point as O'Connor's rendering of the sacramental event was never so arbitrarily limited to Roman doctrine. Conversely, Ted R. Spivey offers a firsthand account of O'Connor's intellectual interaction with heterodox scholars, contemporary social concerns, and biblical exegesis not necessarily included in the Roman canon in his study *Flannery O'Connor: the Woman, the Thinker, the Visionary* (Macon GA: Mercer University Press, 1995).

[28] Stuart C. Chapman, Rev. of *Flannery O'Connor and the Mystery of Love* by Richard Gianonne, *Modern Fiction Studies* 46/4 (Winter 2000): 1026.

contemporaneous, interpreting O'Connor in terms of her most immediate contexts. The troubling suggestion which follows is that O'Connor was in a meaningful way typical of the post-war South and the Irish-American Church.

O'Connor's own library, which Kathleen Feeley cites as one of the "finest theological libraries in the country," suggests that she was neither typical of her region nor her Church; it includes the writings of medieval Scholastics, saints and mystics of the early Eastern and Roman Churches, and modern theologians, both Protestant and Catholic.[29] O'Connor was also a reader of such decidedly anti-religious thinkers as Freud, Jung, and Nietzsche.[30] The breadth and variability of her reading life, notably her habitual study of primary Christian literature, implies that O'Connor's interpretations of Roman doctrine were neither naïve nor static. She was, Wood reminds us, "a self-declared advocate of thirteenth century Catholicism." [31] Her attachment to Medieval Catholic cosmology placed her nearer in sensibility to the early church in regard to Christology and the corresponding human experience of being in time. The Christ of the early church is not merely symbolic of a code of ethics; He is the actuality of man transfigured unto God, indicative of creation fulfilled and immediate in the human person. "For O'Connor," Wood writes, "a civil religion of 'Do Unto Others' will never do. It has no metaphysical foundations to undergird it [and] no sacramental or prophetic communities to sustain it."[32] Of O'Connor's medieval influences, most notable is St. Thomas Aquinas with whom she shared a belief in the essential goodness of mankind. Both held

---

[29] Kathleen Feeley, S.J., *Flannery O'Connor: The Voice of the Peacock* (Chapel Hill: Rutgers University Press, 1972) xii. In addition to the oft cited works of Augustine and Aquinas, O'Connor was influenced by Protestant scholars, including Karl Barth and Paul Tillich, by Jewish theologians, including Martin Buber and Hannah Arendt, by German "pre-Reformation Christian[s]," Baron von Hügel and Eric Voegelin, and such Roman ex-communicants as Simone Weil (O'Connor, *Habit*, 196, 294, 297, 303, 305–306, 523, 540).

[30] Although I disagree with Arthur Kinney's claim that O'Connor's personal library reflects a "staunch Catholicism," his catalogue of the same is invaluable: *Flannery O'Connor's Library: Resources of Being* (Athens: University of Georgia Press, 2007).

[31] Wood, "Such a Catholic," 38.

[32] Ibid., 41.

the human inherence of the good as displaced by the Fall but not irrevocably. Aquinas' vision of the church and the baptized (both within and without institutional Catholicism) as the earthly manifestation of the mystical and actual body of Christ, a tradition inherited from Hebrew Christians, was also a defining aspect of O'Connor's personal theology.[33] American parochial Catholicism, in her lifetime, tended to de-emphasize the people's participation in the Real Presence through their "transubstantiation into a reconciled community," in other words their role as bodily "members" of the church in which Christ is the unifying head. The congregation was imagined as simply representative of the mystical body, not as a contiguous and reciprocating part of Christ's actual self.[34]

Furthermore, O'Connor was critical of the manner in which Christianity in the post-industrial United States has been uniquely integrated into the national ethos as a function of the founding capitalist ethic. As such, the American Christian finds himself in the uneasy situation of submergence in a culture where "Catholic and Protestant alike...have made the gospel of Jesus Christ seem all too much like the gospel of the United States."[35] O'Connor's more notorious protagonists are renderings of the sort of outmoded visionary who intuits himself a part of a providential rather than a political organism. The movements of Hazel Motes and Francis Marion Tarwater toward that end are repeatedly confused and obstructed by the national claim on reality which manifests in a Christianity so insistently state-friendly and independent of catholic sacramentalism it has been subsumed by the secular politic of liberal humanism. O'Connor's modern prophets are evocative of the historical consciousness displaced by the American religion—what Desmond and Claude Tresmontant describe as the biblical view of man in history—which has its roots in the Hebrew Book of Genesis

---

[33] See Acts 9:1–5, *KJV*.

[34] Stanley Hauerwas and Ralph C. Wood, "How the Church Became Invisible: A Christian

Reading of the American Literary Tradition," *Religion and Literature* 38/1 (Spring 2006): 63.

[35] Hauerwas and Wood, "How the Church Became Invisible," 62. See also Harold Bloom, *The American Religion: The Emergence of the Post-Christian Nation*, 2nd ed. (New York: Chu Hartley Publishers, 2006); Christina Beiber Lake, *The Incarnational Art of Flannery O'Connor* (Macon GA: Mercer University Press, 2005) 32–35.

and its implied resolution in the Second Coming.[36] "I think," O'Connor wrote, "that what [God] began when Moses and the children of Israel left Egypt continues today in the Church and is meant to continue that way. And I believe all this is accomplished in the patience of Christ in history and not with select people but with very ordinary ones—as ordinary as the vacillating children of Israel and the fishermen apostles."[37]

The persistence of a hermeneutics that limits the scope of this view to any one of its informing parts—to, say, the Roman tradition, Christian humanism, the New South, the psyche—artificially installs a sense of primacy to paradigms which O'Connor interrogated with a more or less uniform skepticism.[38] Not least among these was the

---

[36] Claude Tresmontant, *A Study of Hebrew Thought*, trans. Michael Francis Gibson (New York: Desclee Co., 1960) 8–9, 11. See also Lake, *The Incarnational Art of Flannery O'Connor*, 7.

[37] O'Connor, *Habit*, 337.

[38] Sarah Gordon argues that O'Connor's fidelity to the dogmas of the Roman Church belies her choice "not…to question the authority and rigidity of the Church and its teachings" (*Flannery O'Connor: The Obedient Imagination* [Athens: University of Georgia Press, 2000] 235). Robert Brinkmeyer divides O'Connor's heteroglossia into two discrete categories, Catholic and Fundamentalist, implying first that there are no further distinctions to be made with regard to the author's extratextual influences or her voicing and, second, that there is no interaction between these two competing modes of vision (*The Art and Vision of Flannery O'Connor* [Baton Rouge: Louisiana State University Press, 1993]). Robert M. McCown and David Eggenschwiler describe O'Connor's theology as Christian Humanist (McCown, "Flannery O'Connor and the Reality of Sin," *Catholic World* 188 [January 1959]: 285–91; Eggenschwiler, *The Christian Humanism of Flannery O'Connor* [Detroit: Wayne State University Press, 1972] 17–19). Jon Lance Bacon, Patricia Yaeger, and Sarah Gordon opt for a social historicist read of O'Connor, while John Hawkes, Claire Katz, and Jeffery Gray approach her psychoanalytically (Bacon, *Flannery O'Connor and Cold War Culture* [Cambridge: Cambridge University Press, 1993]; Yaeger, *Dirt and Desire: Reconstructing Southern Women's Writing, 1930–1990* [Chicago: University of Chicago Press, 2000]; Gordon, *Flannery O'Connor: The Obedient Imagination* [Athens: University of Georgia Press, 2000]; Hawkes, "Flannery O'Connor's Devil," *Sewanee Review* 70/3 [Summer 1962] 395–407; Katz, "Flannery O'Connor's Rage of Vision," *American Literature* 46/1 [March 1974] 54–67; Gray, "'It's Not Natural': Freud's 'Uncanny' and O'Connor's *Wise Blood*," *The Southern Literary Journal* 29/1 [Fall 1996]: 56–68). See also John R. May, "The Methodological Limits of Flannery O'Connor's Critics," *Flannery O'Connor Bulletin*, Vol. XV (1986): 16–28.

Church of Rome. O'Connor poked fun at her fellow congregants by referring to them variously as "Cathlicks" and "Catlicks" and to certain of the clergy as "idiot priests," "idiot nuns," and "simmernarians."[39] Her derision of the institutional church is an oft-neglected fact of her faith, and one driven home by her admission that she, "[u]sually…[thought] that the church's motto [wa]s The Wrong Man for the Job…"[40] She believed it was her "business to change the external faults of the Church—the vulgarity, the lack of scholarship, the lack of intellectual honesty—wherever [she] found them…"[41]

No doubt it was because of her intimacy with the Church that O'Connor felt compelled and in some ways justified in her criticisms of its modern institution. "I was brought up in the novena-rosary tradition," she told John Lynch, "…but you have to save yourself from it some way or dry up."[42] She spent six and a half years in Catholic schools in Savannah but admitted that she was "always just as glad" to be without them in middle Georgia.[43] She felt herself particularly disconnected from the "nice vapid-Catholic distrust in finding God in action" characteristic of modern Catholic literature. [44] Her personal antidote was to remain faithful to dogma but skeptical of doctrine. "[D]octrine *develops*," she told Dawkins in 1959; it moves through the actual body of the church—the clergy and the congregation—and is therefore simultaneously fallible (to the degree that human nature is prone to error) and perfectible (to the degree that the observance of dogma, which O'Connor held to be the "guardian of mystery" and a primary conduit of grace, are

---

[39] O'Connor, *Habit*, 215, 274, 309, 511.

[40] O'Connor, *Habit*, 474. In this sentiment, she echoed the judgment of Dante who, in his *Inferno*, names clerics—from the most inconsequential of monks to infamous cardinals and popes—in the fourth and sixth circles of Hell where the avaricious and the heretical are made to suffer (*The Divine Comedy*, trans. C. H. Sisso [Oxford: Oxford University Press, 2008] 74, 88.). It should be noted that the skeptical humor O'Connor directed at the institutional Church was alike in kind to the criticisms she aimed at modern "interlecktchuls."

[41] O'Connor, *Habit*, 308.

[42] Ibid., 139.

[43] Ibid., 520.

[44] Ibid., 139.

efficacious).[45] Her seemingly paradoxical claim that a good Catholic should be "properly anti-clerical," "dangerous" in his creative thinking, even antagonistic, is clarified by her underlying conviction that the "Church is mighty realistic about human nature" and that "Ideal Christianity doesn't exist..."[46] "[A]nything the human being touches, even Christian truth, he deforms slightly in his own image. Even the saints," she said, "do this."[47]

When the early church instituted its various dogmas, it did so with the intention of safe-guarding a right attitude in the communicant, an openness to all reality that is "larger than human understanding."[48] O'Connor believed that Christian dogma "preserves" a depth of human vision that is only verbalized in doctrine and which has a spiritual "significan[ce]...that we cannot fathom."[49] She was aggressively critical of the habitual pieties of "unimaginative and half-dead Catholics who," she was sure, "would be startled to know the nature of what they defend by formula."[50] Her peculiarly antiquated sense of Catholic doctrine has its locus some several centuries previous to the conservative reactionism of the Council of Trent. From this vantage, she could say "the Church cannot be identified with Western culture" despite her life-long commitment to it because what it is, its mystical actuality, is most like Christ when it is least like an institution.[51] "Writers like myself," O'Connor remarked, "who don't use Catholic settings or characters, good or bad, are trying to make it plain that personal loyalty to the person of Christ is imperative, is the structure of man's nature, his necessary direction... The Church, as institution, doesn't come into it one way or another."[52]

---

[45] Ibid., 364–65. Italics in typescript.

[46] Ibid., 262, 346, 516, 571.

[47] Ibid., 516.

[48] Ibid., 365.

[49] Ibid.

[50] Ibid., 366.

[51] O'Connor, *Habit*, 299.

[52] Ibid., 290. O'Connor's orthodoxy was, not surprisingly, based in logic more so than mysticism: "It is not logical to the Catholic to believe that Christ teaches through many visible forms all teaching contrary doctrine... If Christ actually teaches through many forms than for fifteen centuries, he taught that the Eucharist was his actual body and thereafter he taught part of his people that it was only a symbol. The Catholic can't live with this kind of

O'Connor's Southern sensibility resulted in a Catholicism of a decidedly down-home cast, akin to Protestantism in its suspicion of religious hierarchy and amenable to supernatural interjections. The attendant politics of institutional religion and the ongoing doctrinal conflicts between nations, races, and sects were very much beside the point in both her theology and fiction, though she was attentive to the goings on of papal and ecumenical councils abroad and of the competing forces of liberalism and conservatism in American churches and synagogues.[53] "[F]or me," O'Connor wrote, "[the thing]...that is...of the gravest concern...is always the conflict between an attraction for the Holy and the disbelief in it that we breathe in with the air of our times."[54] Numerous distinctly American phenomena including Transcendentalism, Deism, and dozens of churches further reformed beyond Calvinism and Lutheranism grew from a like concern.[55] As rapidly as the nation displaced its need for "the poor man's insurance system" it created new and amended modes of belief to counter a growing spiritual discontent.[56]

Section 1: "A Nasty Dose of Orthodoxy": O'Connor's Catholic Vision[57]

O'Connor's preference for apparently Protestant heroes and anti-heroes follows from her sense that fundamentalism, in its return to a biblical hermeneutic that reads the gospel as inextricable from and fulfilling of the Old Testament, shares a doctrinal kinship with Catholicism. "The fact is...now," she wrote Ted R. Spivey in 1959, "that the fundamentalist Protestants, as far as doctrine goes, are closer to their traditional enemy, the Church of Rome, then they are

contradiction" (ibid., 341).

[53] O'Connor once noted, "People are always asking me if I am a Catholic writer and I am afraid that I sometimes say yes, depending on who the visitor is. Actually the question seems so remote from what I am doing when I am doing it, that it doesn't bother me at all" (ibid., 353). See also *Habit*, 551.

[54] Ibid., 349.

[55] Most conspicuous among these were Evangelical Protestants (Methodists, Baptists, Pentecostals, and Adventists), Mormons, and Quakers.

[56] O'Connor, *Habit*, 231.

[57] Ibid., 510.

to the advanced elements in Protestantism."[58] That doctrine, to borrow from O'Connor, is crypto-catholic, which is to say that all of its dogmas and practical laws can be reduced to the foundations of the Nicene Creed. "The religion of the South," O'Connor explains:

> is a do-it-yourself religion… It's full of unconscious pride that lands [its practitioners] in all sorts of ridiculous religious predicaments. They have nothing to correct their practical heresies and so they work them out dramatically. If this were merely comic to me, it would be no good, but I accept the same fundamental doctrines of sin and redemption and judgment that they do.[59]

Five years later she confessed to her friend Sr. Mariella Gable that she was "more and more impressed with the amount of Catholicism that fundamental Protestants have been able to retain. Theologically our differences with them are on the nature of the Church, not on the nature of God or our obligation to him."[60] When O'Connor called herself a Catholic writer she did not mean Roman per se but rather "catholic as opposed to parochial," "universal religion as opposed to sect."[61] As far as a man is disposed to the vision of prophesy, which is to say as far as he is able to perceive the gospel in the world, he is "a natural Catholic."[62] "The true prophet," O'Connor said, "is inspired by the Holy Ghost, not necessarily by the dominant religion of his region."[63] She is perhaps most conspicuously a Thomist in her view of the prophet, affirming, in characters like Francis Marion Tarwater, St. Thomas's conviction that "prophetic vision is dependent on the imagination of the prophet, not his moral life…"[64] The various acts of such visionaries as Tarwater (the younger) "may not have been good," but O'Connor's subtle implication is that some "good," though very likely unknowable to us, "did come out of [it]."[65] St. Thomas writes in his *Summa Theologiae*: "As Augustine says: 'Since God is supremely good, he would not allow any evil at all in his works if he wasn't sufficiently

---

[58] Ibid., 341.
[59] Ibid., 350.
[60] Ibid., 518.
[61] Ibid., 302.
[62] Ibid., 407.
[63] Ibid.
[64] Ibid., 367.
[65] Ibid., 178.

almighty and good to bring good even from evil.' It is therefore a mark of his unbounded goodness that God allows evils to exist and draws from them good."[66]

O'Connor was set somewhat apart from the modern Roman church in her understanding of the nature of evil which she derived from Medieval Catholic and Eastern Orthodox theology. As in the Eastern liturgy, O'Connor seems to emphasize the necessity of human corruption and evil as the occasion for grace in her fiction.[67] The sense of joyful celebration in Augustine's *felix culpa* is nowhere felt in the *Baltimore Catechism*'s discussion of the Fall. Rather it attributes a vaguely sadistic intention to Providence, suggesting that God forbade Adam and Eve to eat of the Tree of Knowledge so that he might "try their obedience."[68] The Catholic Church in America was, no doubt, influenced by the predominance of Puritanical theology. Lutheranism and Calvinism both stressed the judicial function of the Incarnation as the lawful justification of the elect who, in faith and good works, merit salvation by grace. Man's nature, Calvin believed, had been "utterly corrupted" by the Fall; it is therefore bound to Providence and predestined to eternal life or eternal damnation through the irrefutable power of grace.[69] The insistence of the early reform churches on faith as a condition of grace and on good works as meritorious are oddly superfluous alongside the doctrine of predestination. The Roman Church maintained a more orthodox view, which comes to bear in the first sacrament of Baptism; by this rite, original sin is completely

---

[66] St. Thomas Aquinas, *Summa Theologiae,* 1a.2.1–3, 202.

[67] The Eastern Churches continue to celebrate the *felix culpa* as the joyous cause of the coming of Christ by insinuating the message of the Easter Vigil throughout their liturgical calendar. See Nicholas Arseniev, *Mysticism and the Eastern Church,* trans. Arthur Chambers (Oxford: A. R. Mowbry and Co. Ltd., 1979) 42, 77. The Roman Church reserves the overt praise of man's "fortunate fall" for the *Exsultet,* which is sung at the Easter Mass.

[68] Third Council of Baltimore (1891), *The Baltimore Catechism,* No. 2 (New York: Benziger Brothers, Inc.) Lesson 5th, Question 41. *www.bostoncatholicjournal.com*. 24 September 2010. http://www.pcpbooks.net/docs/baltimore_catech ism.pdf (accessed 24 September 2010).

[69] John Calvin qtd. in Wilhelm Niesel, *The Gospel and the Churches: A Comparison of Catholicism, Orthodoxy, and Protestantism,* trans. David Lewis (Philadelphia: Westminster Press, 1962) 234.

eradicated, not merely forgiven.[70] Rome reiterated a further tie with the East at the Council of Trent with its claim that man's free will and God's grace act cooperatively toward the soul's justification and that this same will can reject the gift of grace.[71] As Niesel puts it:

> Rome does not deny original sin but regards it simply as an absence of gifts man once possessed. It is *original guilt*. The life of man, fallen from communion with God, is therefore assessed in an altogether positive and tolerant way... Evangelical theology can regard man only in the light of revelation. Just because it does so it knows him to be, in and for himself, in utter darkness and utterly lost... Roman theology, on the other hand, thinks...that in his reason and freedom of will, man possesses an important "point of contact with the Sublime."[72]

To the minds of church doctors such as Augustine and Aquinas, evil is not a by-product of man's essential corruption but "the defective use of good" still inherent in his soul.[73] Evil, as such, contains not simply the possibility for reversal but a continuous probability of the same. "Hazel knows what the choice is and the Misfit knows what the choice is," O'Connor wrote to John Hawkes in 1959, "—either throw away everything and follow Him or enjoy yourself by doing some meanness to somebody..."[74] For O'Connor, even a man of murderous calculation like the Misfit is "redeemable" in that he possesses a consciousness of the probability of his using good effectively.[75] His struggle, like Hazel's, has been to actively deny the probability of the good within himself. "To see the reality of one's own will participating in creation," Marion Montgomery posits, is to see the Misfit's "dilemma."[76]

As an immigrant church in the United States, the Catholic faith lost its decisive connection with the orthodoxy of the early and Eastern Churches, namely that doctrine of "original guilt" which belies our "participation in...and co-responsibility for Adam's

---

[70] Council of Trent qtd. in Niesel, *The Gospel and the Churches,* 60–61.

[71] Ibid., 57–58.

[72] Niesel, *The Gospel and the Churches,* 55.

[73] O'Connor, *Habit,* 129.

[74] Ibid., 350.

[75] Ibid.

[76] Marion Montgomery, "Flannery O'Connor and the Jansenist Problem in Fiction," *The Southern Review* 14/3 (1978): 447.

perverse choice."[77] In the U.S., Orthodoxy's emphasis on the church as a community of faith co-operative with the triune God has been displaced radically by two hallmarks of the early reform churches: the prioritization of individual salvation and the relegation of divine actuality to the a-temporal, disincarnate realm of metaphysics. I make the distinction because critics, including Wood in his early work, have regarded O'Connor as an orthodox Roman of Augustine's type through narrowed allusions to the saint's early writings and the impact certain of these articles had on the thinking of Luther and Calvin.[78] I have in mind the oft-pared statement made by Augustine in his *Enchiridion* that, "After the fall [the human will] was able to choose only evil."[79] Calvin misappropriated the statement to arrive at his singularly bleak view of the human situation; expelled from the Garden for his sin, man persists in a state of utter corruption. But in his endearment to Augustine, Calvin overlooked the latter's account of evil. To Augustine, evil represents that aspect of imbalance within the fallen will made actual by its inclination to choose a lesser good over a greater. In his *De Natura et Gratia*, Augustine wrote expressly against the notion of humanity as irreconcilably corrupt. "Man's nature, indeed," he averred, "was created at first faultless and without any sin," and although the soul now requires a "physician" because it is no longer wholly sound, "all good qualities which…it *still* possesses in its make, life, senses, and intellect, it possesses from the most high God."[80] What critics have

[77] John Norman Davidson Kelly, *Early Christian Doctrines*, 5th ed. (London: Continuum International Publishing Group, 2000) 364.

[78] Wood argues that O'Connor is theologically closer to Augustine than to Chardin with regard to her "dark estimate of human sinfulness" (*The Comedy of Redemption: Christian Faith and Comic Vision in Four American Novelists* [Notre Dame: University of Notre Dame Press, 1988] 92). Wood has since revised his thinking in his reading of Mason Tarwater who, he writes, "is too orthodox a Christian to grant evil any sort of dualistic equality with good" (*Flannery O'Connor and the Christ-Haunted South* [Grand Rapids: William B. Eerdmans Publishing, 2005] 228).

[79] I have yet to encounter a critic who, when discussing O'Connor's Augustianism, takes into account Augustine's *Retractions* in which he clarifies his most controversial pronouncements. See *The Retractions: Fathers of the Church*, trans. Sr. Inez Mary Bogan, rep. ed., Vol. LX (Washington, D.C.: Catholic University Press, 1999).

[80] St. Augustine of Hippo, *De Natura et Gracia* qtd. in *Anti-Pelagian Writings: Nicene and Post-Nicene Fathers of the Christian Church*, ed. Philip

interpreted as "pessimism" in Augustine is in fact "eschatologically optimistic."[81] Original sin "weakens" man's natural goodness, degrading his likeness which makes the soul desirous of the good and gives cause for his redemption through an inherited concupiscence, but it does not corrupt him utterly. Concupiscence is a corruption of "measure, form, or order," not of the eternal spirit itself.[82] "[E]very nature," Augustine wrote, "which can be corrupted is also itself some good."[83]

O'Connor had an intimate knowledge of Augustine's primary works including his *Confessions* and scriptural commentaries. The details of his biography she gleaned from J. M. Flood's *The Mind and Heart of Augustine* and Romano Guardini's *The Conversion of St. Augustine*. The saint's admission to a debilitating pride became the template for such protagonists as O. E. Parker, Francis Tarwater, and Hazel Motes; in like fashion Augustine "disdained to be a little one" before the truth Christ declared discernible to children in holy scripture and "took [him]self to be a great one."[84] "It seems to me," O'Connor confided to Hester, "that all good stories are about conversion...," and conversion calls first for the annihilation of pride.[85] Her heroes' ultimate self-denials agree with Augustine's defining credo: "Always you renounce a lesser good for a greater; the opposite is what sin is."[86] O'Connor also made the point, contrary to the image of Augustinism as morbid asceticism, that she did not "assume that renunciation goes with submission, or even that

Schaff, Vol. V (Whitefish: Kessinger Publishing, 2007) 122. Italics my own.

[81] Lorine M. Getz, *Nature and Grace in Flannery O'Connor's Fiction* (Lewiston: Edwin Mellon Press, 1982) 37.

[82] St. Augustine of Hippo, *De Natura Boni Contra Manicheans* qtd. in *Writings Against the Manicheans and the Donatists: Nicene and Post-Nicene Fathers of the Christian Church*, ed. Philip Schaff, Vol. IV (Whitefish: Kessinger Publishing, 2004) 352.

[83] St. Augustine of Hippo, *De Natura et Gracia* qtd. in *Four Anti-Pelagian Writings: Fathers of the Church*, ed. William J. Collinge and John Arthur Mourant, Vol. LXXXVI (Washington, D.C.: Catholic University of America Press, 1992) 24.

[84] St. Augustine of Hippo, *The Confessions of St. Augustine*, trans. Edward B. Pusey (New York: Pocket Books, 1952) 35.

[85] O'Connor, *Habit*, 275.

[86] Ibid., 126.

renunciation is good in itself."[87] On the way "to the Father of souls," she reminded Hester, "...it is necessary to pass the dragon."[88] It is not as if, upon conversion, the conflict of wills evaporates and the soul ascends in a vacuum, secure in total submission to divine insight. The wills are all the more inflamed in the convert to strain, as Aquinas put it, "against mere nature."[89] Purity, O'Connor told Hester, "is something that comes either with experience or with Grace," and grace can be refused even by the convert.[90]

O'Connor's book reviews and correspondence reveal an unflagging dissension with the "parochial [Catholic] aesthetic" which "separat[es] nature and grace as much as possible...reduc[ing the] conception of the supernatural to pious cliché."[91] The "Catholic" aesthetic is "able to recognize nature in literature in only two forms, the sentimental and the obscene."[92] O'Connor's distrust of the Pious Style made her an unlikely proponent of the sort of intellectual individualism associated with Protestantism.[93] The parallel is perhaps not so remarkable when we consider that Luther and Calvin imagined themselves as Catholics in spite of their rejection of the hierarchies of the Church and most of the lesser rituals of the Latin Mass. Their intention was not to create many disparate reform churches but to reform *the* Church. O'Connor was particularly sympathetic to this impulse in Protestantism which she believed to be only politically disassociated from Rome. Despite the fact that she was, in her own practice, a firm believer in apostolic succession as well as the tradition of the Latin liturgy,[94] O'Connor was a constant

---

[87] Ibid.

[88] St. Cyril of Jerusalem qtd. in O'Connor, *Habit*, 126.

[89] St. Thomas Aquinas qtd. in O'Connor, *Habit*, 343.

[90] Ibid.

[91] O'Connor, "The Church and the Fiction Writer," *Mystery*, 145, 147.

[92] Ibid., 147.

[93] O'Connor complained of the offending sensibility of the "American-clerical tone." "Smugness," she wrote, "is the Great Catholic Sin" (*Habit*, 131).

[94] In 1961, she bemoaned the advent of the English missal. "The Latin," she wrote to Rosalyn Barnes, "had been translated to make it appealing to idiots, everything in baby-English... So many of these attempts to get the Mass nearer the participants are misdirected" (*Habit*, 432). In an unpublished letter to Hester she declared, "I am one of the laymen who RESIST the congregation yapping out the Mass in English & my reason besides neurotic

affirmer of the kinship between Catholics and Protestants, convinced that the truth of the gospel was visible in both faiths, albeit from different vantages.[95] Fundamentalist Protestants retained a sense of immediacy in their worship not often felt outside of Catholic orders; their expectation of God's call suggests an orthodoxy that is in line with the Old Testament prophets and the Desert Fathers.

O'Connor's attempts to write the Protestant spirit catholically were, in the main, ill-received. After the publication of her second novel, *The Violent Bear It Away*, she chided William Sessions for:

> ...judging the old man [Tarwater] as if he should act like a Catholic. The prophets were Jews and old Tarwater is a Protestant and his being Protestant allows him to follow the voice he hears which speaks a truth held by Catholics. One of the good things about Protestantism is that it always contains the seeds of its own reversal. It is open at both ends—at one end to Catholicism, at the other to unbelief.[96]

O'Connor's sense of Christendom is revealed in her certitude that the reform churches contain catholic truth and are a part of Christ's church, incarnate in the presence of the gospel. Institutional hierarchy, for the author, was secondary to the Real Presence of Christ, and that presence was not, in her estimation, exclusively won by the apostolic claim of the Roman Church. She declared the message of Christ irrelevant if some portion of mankind was cut off by virtue of institutional nuance from the revelation of man as an unending analogy of the resurrection. "We miss the point," the

---

fear of change, anxiety, early bed-wetting and laziness is that I do not like the raw sound of the human voice in unison unless it is under the discipline of music" ("Correspondence with Betty Hester," 17 October 1959, MS 1064, Box 2, FF 1, *Flannery O'Connor Collection*, Manuscripts, Archives, and Rare Books Library, Emory University, Atlanta). It is my sense that the author was mourning the loss of the modern Church's connection with its incantatory tradition which reinforces the ritual sensibility of the "unsearchableness" of the divine will.

[95] So close were Catholic and Protestant doctrine in O'Connor's thinking that she felt at ease in saying she was herself a "good Protestant" by virtue of being a good Catholic. "I am glad," she told Maryat Lee, "you find me a good Protestant. That is indeed a compliment. All good Catholics have the best Protestant qualities about them; and a good deal more besides; my good deal more besides I try to keep from view lest I offend your delicate sensibilities" (ibid., 418).

[96] Ibid., 410–11.

theologian William Lynch wrote, "if we only say that Christ is the gate and do not also add that man is the gate."[97] The Roman and Eastern catechisms hold that the Church is Christ, a point upon which O'Connor concurred so far as the Church was allowed to represent not only the communion of souls within the orthodox tradition but also that portion of the presence displaced by the Reformation.[98] The Second Vatican Council was, only after her death, reordering its priorities toward ecumenism while Protestants and Catholics in the South remained segregated, at times violently so. The Depression-era KKK's most infamous slogan was "Kill the Kikes, Koons, and Katholics."[99] Still, O'Connor persisted in the belief that opinions, even volatile ones, did not divide the church in an essential way. "When you leave a man alone with his Bible and the Holy Ghost inspires him," she told Gable in 1963, "he's going to be a Catholic one way or another, even though he knows nothing about the visible church. His kind of Christianity may not be socially desirable, but it will be real in the sight of God."[100]

O'Connor used narrative blasphemy to remark upon the many and subtle ways the American religion has contorted the universal church from a living sign of the fulfillment of creation to a

---

[97] William F. Lynch, S.J., *Christ and Apollo: The Dimensions of the Literary Imagination* (New York: Sheed and Ward, 1960) 176.

[98] In his article, "The Catholic Faith of Flannery O'Connor's Protestant Characters: A Critique and Vindication," Ralph C. Wood inverts the notion of the Reformers as displaced Catholics to illustrate his claim that "O'Connor was so committed to her own distinctly Catholic form of Christian faith that she makes even her Protestant characters its advocates" (*Flannery O'Connor Bulletin,* Vol. XIII [1984] 16). The difference Wood perceives between O'Connor's Catholicism and "radical Protestantism" cannot be reduced to the Protestant emphasis on God's "election of us" and the Catholic emphasis on "our choosing [Him]" (18). The very idea of divine election comes from St. Augustine who said that faith is not dependent upon the free choice of man's will to believe or not to believe but upon God's irresistible grace. "[I]n the elect the will is prepared by the Lord" (*De Praedestinatione Sanctorum* qtd. in *Nicene and Post-Nicene Fathers,* Vol. V, ed. Philip Schaff [New York: Cosimo, Inc., 2007] 503).

[99] KKK Parade of Forty Thousand Men, Washington D.C., 1925 qtd. in *The American Pageant: A History of the Republic,* ed. David M. Kennedy, Lizabeth Cohen, and Thomas Andrew Bailey (New York: Houghton Mifflin Co., 2001) 730.

[100] O'Connor, *Habit,* 517.

moralizing "Elks Club."[101] The "politer" Christians who populate her stories are ashamed at the sight of fanatics like Mrs. Greenleaf and Hazel Motes who insist upon dragging Jesus into the open air. Mrs. May and Ruby Turpin are content to leave Him tucked safely in their hymnals each Sunday lest He inflict Himself upon their actual affairs. With healers and heretics alike, O'Connor revealed the American gospel as it is made a function of social desirability. In her own church, she criticized the over-stress of ritualized dogmas which she believed had come to signify a social mandate more so than a biblical one. "The foundation of religious life lay not in the Church or the Sacraments," Douglas Robillard has said of O'Connor's theology, "but in the private and often terrifying experience of divine grace."[102] He describes her as a "Pentecostal Catholic," an epithet that appropriately identifies her with the prophet's desire for an unmediated "baptism" in the Holy Spirit. "[I]n affirming her link with a biblical type left undeveloped by the Church," Frederick Asals observes, "[O'Connor] seems characteristically to have been asserting both her traditionalism and her independence."[103] She repeatedly faulted the church for its liturgical emphasis on the New Testament and blamed the same for her own incomplete view of sin. Two years before her death, she remarked that, "The fact that Catholics don't see religion through the Bible is a deficiency in Catholics."[104] "[I]n the last four or five centuries," she went on to say, "we in the Church have over-emphasized the abstract and consequently impoverished our imagination and capacity for prophetic sight."[105] With the hope of recovering the prophetic voice underlying doctrine, O'Connor advocated a "biblical revival" which would proceed from the combined wisdom of now disparate traditions: the scriptural conviction of the Jews and Protestant fundamentalists, the mysticism of the early church, and the retention of sacramental literalism in

---

[101] Ibid., 337.

[102] Douglas Robillard, Jr., *The Critical Response to Flannery O'Connor* (Westport: Praeger Publishers, 2004) 169.

[103] Frederick Asals, *Flannery O'Connor: The Imagination of Extremity* (Athens: University of Georgia Press, 1982) 215.

[104] Joel Wells, "Conversation with Flannery O'Connor," *Critic* XXI (September 1962) 4.

[105] O'Connor, "The Catholic Novelist in the Protestant South," *Mystery*, 203.

Eastern and Roman Orthodoxy. O'Connor imposed her enlarged view of Christendom upon her protagonists, suspending their post-Christian aversion to religion as historically actual, contemporaneously manifest, and limiting in its archaic social provisos.

Despite the national pledge to the contrary, most Americans of O'Connor's generation viewed history in terms of "civilizational cycles" rather than, as Eric Voegelin put it, "history as existence under God" and an "exodus from civilization."[106] To make the "leap in being," as the Israelites did in their faith to Mosaic law, the self must relinquish the illusion of its discreteness in exchange for salvation. America's modern liberalisms and reactionary conservatisms have effectively deposed the ancient orthodox perception of God as "non-other," and have replaced the Deity with a prohibitive usurper and a fearsome, inescapable Other.[107] Conversely, orthodoxy proclaims that:

> The God disclosed in the hypostatic union…is not distinctive in a conventional sense, but rather non-contrastingly other. …[He] is not so much somewhere else (that would make him only a distant finite thing) but somehow else, and this particular mode of His transcendence is made plain precisely in the act by which He becomes non-interruptively close to the world.[108]

O'Connor's protagonists are therefore caught in the ironical act of protecting an autonomy which, to the orthodox mind, does not essentially exist. "Whether you are a Christian or not," O'Connor wrote to Hester, "we worship the God Who Is. St. Thomas on his death bed said of the Summa, 'It's all straw,'—this was in the vision of that God."[109]

Whether "True Believer" or "Apostate," O'Connor's critics are inevitably met with the author's insistent self-commentary and its declaration that the authoritative baseline in her fiction is Christian orthodoxy.[110] Thomas F. Haddox posits that contemporary criticism

---

[106] Ibid., 294.

[107] Nicholas of Cusa qtd. in *Blackwell Companion to Catholicism*, 269.

[108] Robert Barron, *Blackwell Companion to Catholicism*, 269.

[109] O'Connor, *Habit*, 93.

[110] Timothy P. Carron, "'The Bottom Rail Is on the Top': Race and 'Theological Whiteness' in Flannery O'Connor's Short Fiction," *Inside the Church of Flannery O'Connor: Sacrament, Sacramental, and the Sacred in Her*

centers "not on the interpretation of [O'Connor's] text[s], but on the proper context to choose for the interpretation of the text..."[111] Certain accidents of the author's social circumstance—her Southernness, her speculative maidenhood, her prolonged illness, and her (Roman) Catholicism—have been unremittingly relied upon to explain her most provocative preoccupations—the grotesque, mother-daughter relationships, death and divine judgment. None of these parameters is without critical validity, but their frame of reference is one detrimentally limited to biographic contemporality which implicitly subordinates the influence of ancient and classical philosophy and theology upon O'Connor's creative intellect.

There have been recent exceptions to this tendency, beginning with Carol Shloss's insistence, in her 1980 study *Flannery O'Connor's Dark Comedies*, that the author was "at no time simply a Catholic apologist..."[112] In 1986, Robert Brinkmeyer Jr. proposed that O'Connor's work reflects an identification with both the Roman Church and Southern Fundamentalism. "[A]t its most basic level, her closeness to the fundamentalist manifests itself in her desire to communicate, usually in violent terms, to the modern non-believer. This desire to evangelize," Brinkmeyer concludes, "was anything but a Catholic trait."[113] John F. Desmond calls attention to the breadth of O'Connor's orthodoxy in *Risen Sons...* (1987).[114] Richard Giannone aligns O'Connor's theology with the early church of the Desert Fathers, Medieval mystics, and saints in his complimentary studies *Flannery O'Connor and the Mystery of Love* (1999) and *Flannery O'Connor, Hermit Novelist* (2000). McMullen argues against the typical sacramental view of O'Connor's "Roman" Catholicism in her essay, "Christian but Not Catholic: Baptism in Flannery O'Connor's

---

Fiction, ed. Joanne H. McMullen and John Parrish Peede (Macon GA: Mercer University Press, 2008) 138.

[111] Thomas F. Haddox, "On Belief, Conflict, and Universality: Flannery O'Connor, Walter Benn Michaels, Slavoj Žižek," *Flannery O'Connor in the Age of Terrorism: Essays on Violence and Grace*, ed. Avis Hewitt and Robert Donahoo (Knoxville: University of Tennessee Press, 2010) 233.

[112] Carol Shloss, *Flannery O'Connor's Dark Comedies* (Baton Rouge: Louisiana State University Press, 1980) 28.

[113] Robert Brinkmeyer Jr., "A Closer Walk with Thee: Flannery O'Connor and Southern Fundamentalists," *The Southern Literary Journal* 18/2 (Spring 1986): 6.

[114] Desmond, *Risen Sons*, 6–31.

'The River'" (2007). "[The author's] treatment of baptism," McMullen writes, "is foreign to the *Baltimore Catechism* and the Council of Trent…yet traditional O'Connor critics repeatedly ignore the nuances in her text that assign contradictions with orthodox pre-ecumenical Catholicism."[115] Brad Gooch notes a "growing fascination" in O'Connor's later work ("The Comforts of Home," "Why Do the Heathen Rage?") with the Eastern Desert Fathers in his article "Thirteenth Century Lady" (2007).[116] W. A. Sessions links O'Connor's understanding of the Eucharist with Roman and Eastern Orthodox liturgies in his essay, "The Real Presence: Flannery O'Connor and the Saints" (2007).[117] Steven Robert Watkins responds to Ruth Johansen's comparison of O'Connor narrative strategy with the mythological Trickster (*The Narrative Secret of Flannery O'Connor: The Trickster as Interpreter*, 2009) by noting that, "There is a mysterious operative force working in O'Connor's literature, but it is not necessarily a traditionally Christian (Roman Catholic) force."[118] Anthony Di Renzo classes O'Connor as a biblical historicist, linking her theology to the early church in his article "And the Violent Bear it Away: Flannery O'Connor and the Threat of Apocalyptic Terrorism" (2010), and Jacqueline A. Zubeck applies an Orthodox theology to O'Connor in her article, "Back to Page One in 'Parker's Back': An Orthodox Examination of O'Connor's Last Story" (2010).[119]

---

[115] Joanne H. McMullen, *Inside the Church of Flannery O'Connor*, ed. Joanna Halleran McMullen and Jon Parrish Peede (Macon GA: Mercer University Press, 2007) 187.

[116] Brad Gooch, "Thirteenth-Century Lady," *Flannery O'Connor Review* 5 (2007): 31.

[117] W. A. Sessions, "The Real Presence: Flannery O'Connor and the Saints," *Inside the Church of Flannery O'Connor*, ed. Joanne H. McMullen and John Parrish Peede (Macon GA: Mercer University Press, 2007) 24.

[118] Steven Robert Watkins, *Flannery O'Connor and Teilhard de Chardin: A Journey Together Towards Hope and Understanding about Life* (New York: Peter Lang Pub., Inc., 2009) 4.

[119] Anthony Di Renzo, "And the Violent Bear It Away: Flannery O'Connor and the Threat of Apocalyptic Terrorism," *Flannery O'Connor in the Age of Terrorism*, ed. Avis Hewitt and Robert Donahoo (Knoxville: University of Tennessee Press, 2010) 3–24; Jacqueline A. Zubeck, "Back to Page One in 'Parker's Back': An Orthodox Examination of O'Connor's Last Story," *Flannery O'Connor Review* 8 (2010): 92–116.

Their consummate message seems to be that "modernism's God is not O'Connor's God."[120] "In her stories," Christina Bieber Lake contends:

> God is not a distant authoritarian figure who passes judgment on sinners, but a being whose primary aim is revelation (and not necessarily explanation). When O'Connor's God permits violence, it is always to prove to her protagonists that they are created beings who are not as independent as they would believe. ...[T]he triumphant birth of the self is replaced by a much lowlier birth at the hands of others, a birth usually triggered by a humiliating encounter with the physical world.[121]

O'Connor's incarnating orthodoxy was of a more ancient strain than was typical of parochial Catholicism in post-war U.S. "The Catholic Church in America is largely an immigrant Church," O'Connor wrote to Dawkins in 1958; as such it was preoccupied with social integration and the seemliness of impeccable morality.[122] "Culturally," the author stipulated, "it is not on its feet. But it will get there. In the meantime," she added, "the culture of the whole Church is ours and it is our business to see that it is disseminated throughout the Church in America.[123] The "whole Church" O'Connor references is not merely the Church of Rome but the "universal [catholic] church," the church that is "Christ continuing in time" and therefore inclusive of all of His followers irrespective of doctrinal or political divisions.[124] "You don't serve God by saying: the Church is ineffective, I'll have none of it," O'Connor told Dawkins. "Your pain at its lack of effectiveness," she wrote, "is a sign of your nearness to God. We help overcome this lack of effectiveness simply by suffering on account of it."[125]

O'Connor considered the divisions within Christendom unnatural and was particularly grieved by the "awful loss" of the "separated [Protestant] brethren."[126] She followed the doctrinal pronouncements of "the one visible Church" with a profound

---

[120] Lake, *The Incarnational Art of Flannery O'Connor*, 34.

[121] Ibid., 34–35.

[122] O'Connor, *Habit*, 308.

[123] Ibid.

[124] O'Connor, *Habit*, 302, 337.

[125] Ibid., 308.

[126] Ibid., 341.

awareness of persevering catholic thought in Orthodox and Protestant Churches,[127] envisaging the "faith and passion" of Southern Protestantism as an antidote for the "lazy" "satisfied" "cultural insularity" of the "parochial aesthetic."[128] Her champion was the churchless protestant, a prophet as unprotected as the Desert Fathers from the "vicissitudes of [his] own nature" and additionally ignorant of the sacraments.[129] His aspiration to a sensible theophanic "calling" might disassociate him from institutional orthodoxy, but it also allows him to make spiritual "discoveries" known to the rest of the Christian world at the considerable remove of scriptural documentation and religious orders.[130] "People make a judgment of fanaticism by what they are themselves," O'Connor wrote to Sr. Gable in 1963:

> To a lot of Protestants I know, monks and nuns are fanatics, none greater. And to a lot of the monks and nuns I know, my Protestant prophets are fanatics. For my part, I think the only difference between them is that if you are a Catholic and have this intensity of belief you join the convent and are heard from no more; whereas if you are a Protestant and have it, there is no convent for you to join and you go about in the world getting into all sorts of trouble and drawing the wrath of people who don't believe anything much at all down on your head.[131]

O'Connor's own theology was primarily incarnational, extending into "strange places…not totally congenial" to her Roman upbringing.[132] The mattered world, in her sight, was always recreating the paradox manifest in Christ of imperfect flesh become the conduit of transfiguring love. Her grotesqueries foreground the Incarnation by dramatizing the potential, in the most profane of bodies, for perfectibility. They represent "that part of reality that cannot be tidied up or explained away," a tangible fragment of

---

[127] Ibid.

[128] O'Connor, "The Catholic Novelist in the Protestant South," *Mystery*, 207; and "The Church and the Fiction Writer," *Mystery*, 145.

[129] O'Connor, "The Catholic Novelist in the Protestant South," *Mystery*, 207.

[130] Ibid., 208.

[131] O'Connor, *Habit*, 517.

[132] O'Connor, "The Catholic Novelist in the Protestant South," *Mystery*, 206.

vision into the mystery of creation.[133] In O'Connor's words, "it is the fact of the Word made flesh…[t]hat is the fulcrum that lifts my particular stories. I'm a Catholic but this is in Orthodox Protestantism also, though out of context—which makes it grow into grotesque forms."[134]

O'Connor's perception of Protestant orthodoxy as inherently "out of context" intimates a further remove in her thinking from the predominant religious ethic of the South. To the moment of crisis, protagonists like Hazel Motes and Francis Tarwater act out the extremity of the "Protestant temper," striving for an experiential knowledge of the "spiritual directly rather than through matter."[135] O'Connor was, in this manner of thinking, indebted to Jacques Maritain, a Catholic convert also profoundly sympathetic to the Protestant temper, who described the "root of Martin Luther's error [as] consist[ing] "in an inordinate desire for sensible experiences of divine grace, a perversion of [Johannes] Tauler's mysticism—leading to a despair of ever being a *friend of God*, and to search for salvation by a kind of faith—trust operating without good works and unvivified by charity."[136] American Reformation theology, influenced directly by Lutheranism and Calvinism and indirectly by Manichaeism and Jansenism, aspired to a religiosity of pure spirit. To hardline Protestants, the body was no longer the tangible point of collusion between man and his incarnational redemption through Christ but the origin of evil through his original sin. Where Eastern and Roman orthodoxy underline the New Creation born of Christ and the possibility He creates for total reconciliation with God, fundamental Protestantism stresses the depravity of the flesh despite the coming of Christ. As the Orthodox catechism puts it, "The Protestant churches accept that the nature of man…was lost wholly, and replaced with a nature wholly corrupt and ethically dead."[137]

---

[133] Lake, *The Incarnational Art of Flannery O'Connor*, 37.

[134] O'Connor, *Habit*, 226–27.

[135] Ibid., 304.

[136] Jacques Maritain, "Introduction," *St. John of the Cross*, ed. Fr. Benedict Zimmerman, O.D.C. (New York: Sheed and Ward, 1932) 91.

[137] Rev. Constas H. Demetry, D. D., *Catechism of the Eastern Orthodox Church* (Fort Lauderdale: The Saint Demetrios Greek Orthodox Church, 31 January 2001) 19. *www.christusrex.org*. http://www.christus rex.org/www1/CDHN/catechis.html (accessed 28 August 2010).

Numerous critics, including Joyce Carol Oates, have implied that Roman orthodoxy, as represented by Augustine and Aquinas, shares with fundamental Protestantism a foundational vision of human depravity. On the basis that O'Connor participated in the dogmas of the Roman Church and had an interest in the works of Augustine and Aquinas, they ascribe to her a vision of man unsympathetic to the point of misanthropy, a sense of nature as essentially menacing, and of God as attainable only through the transcendence of matter. Oates claims that, "O'Connor's writing is so stark…and so difficult to absorb into a recognizable world because it insists upon a brutal distinction between what Augustine called the City of Man and the City of God."[138] The fault of Oates's interpretation is her reading Augustine, Aquinas, and O'Connor out of the context of their developing thought. The definitive clause of *De Civitate Dei*—that "two cities have been formed from two loves: the earthly by the love of self, even to the contempt of God; the heavenly by the love of God, even to the contempt of self"—seems to imply a Manichean disconnect between the realms, one that contradicts orthodox Christology.[139] Oates glosses over Augustine's (and O'Connor's) conviction that part of the heavenly city "sojourns on earth and lives by faith [in the resurrection]," and that man, "the son of the resurrection, lives in hope…"[140]

Conversely, O'Connor's Augustinianism, which sustains the vital interconnectivity between heaven and earth, is far more sympathetic of man and his inclination to glory in himself than most critics allow. Her emphasis, like Augustine's, is directed at God's faithfulness to man's free will, not, as Oates suggests, to the faithlessness of man: "God judged it better," Augustine wrote, "to bring good out of evil than to wipe out evil and his flawed creation with it. …This saving work extends to the bringing back of the human will to its original balance, able freely to choose between good and evil."[141] Augustine approached evil-doing as a condition

---

[138] Joyce Carol Oates, "The Visionary Art of Flannery O'Connor," in *Flannery O'Connor*, ed. Harold Bloom (Philadelphia: Chelsea House Publishing, 1986) 43–53.

[139] St. Augustine of Hippo, *The City of God*, Book XIV, ch. XXVIII, trans. Marcus Dod (Lawrence: Neeland Media, 2009) 359.

[140] Ibid., Book XIX, ch. XVII, 519; Book XV, ch. XVIII, 378.

[141] Ibid.

that creates the circumstance for a more complete communion with ultimate being through the efficacy of grace.[142] His most infamous proclamation, that fallen man "was able to choose only evil," takes on a softer cast when read within its framing conviction of a more glorious potential for man risen by way of the New Covenant of Christ, the second Adam.[143] The Augustinian view of the Fall as *felix culpa* survives in Eastern Orthodoxy and, less emphatically, in the Church of Rome. O'Connor dramatizes this aspect of pre-schism Catholicism more explicitly than any other, contemporizing the ancient promise of a reciprocating union between humanity and the sublime will, more intimate than what Adam possessed in the Garden in that it seeks man in every possibility of his nature. Her telling of man's encounter with God has been interpreted against the Western letter and, therefore, has been read in terms of the Church in the West whose American translation O'Connor resisted as philosopher and aesthete, if not as a dogmatist. "[T]he dominant theological motifs (and in Roman Catholicism and Protestant Scholasticism almost the only motifs)," Donald Fairbairn argues, "are legal in character. Salvation is the state in which one possesses the righteousness of Christ. While certainly part of the biblical picture of salvation, this legal righteousness is far from the only aspect. God's primary purposes toward humanity are not legal, but relational and filial…"[144] O'Connor shared with the Eastern Church and the fore-bearing Medieval Church in Europe a predilection toward the "personal aspect of salvation" as opposed to the semantics of the law.[145] Augustine's system of grace, the "most personal [in that it] was the first to synthesize the great theories of the Fall, grace, and free will," was the point of departure for O'Connor as Roman

---

[142] Aquinas' *Summa Theologiae* is analogous with Augustinian doctrine on this point: "It is…a mark of His unbounded goodness that God allows evil to exists and draws from it good. …[E]vilness isn't in any way included in God's will, but is a consequence of our free choice abandoning our relationship to God's will" (*Selected Philosophical Writings*, ed. and trans. Timothy McDermott [Oxford: Oxford University Press, 1993] 202, 296).

[143] St. Augustine of Hippo qtd. in G. R. Evans, *Augustine on Evil* (Cambridge: Cambridge University Press, 1982) 167.

[144] Donald Fairbairn, *Eastern Orthodoxy Through Western Eyes* (Louisville: Westminster John Knox Press, 2002) 117.

[145] Ibid.

Catholic.[146] It is a decisive remove when we consider the history of the Church in the West, which some critics describe as "the history of the progressive elimination of Augustinism."[147]

The relative ecunemicism of the early church was disrupted by the political division of the Roman Church (Western Latin) and the Orthodox Churches (Eastern Greek) in the eleventh century. Its theology was parsed once again in the sixteenth century with the establishment of the first Reformation Churches. The most lasting interpretation of Augustine and Aquinas with regard to the "American religion" has been Calvin's. His reading of Augustine, notably the latter's *On the Free Choice of the Will* (*De Libero Arbitrio*) and *On the Gift of Perseverance* (*De Dono Perseverantiae*), radicalizes the medieval notion of predestination. For Augustine, predestination is the joint action of God's infallible foreknowledge (*præscientia*) and His immutable decree (*decretrum*) of eternal happiness.[148] Allan Fitzgerald and John Cavadini rightly note that, by predestination, Augustine did not imply a divine foreknowledge of human deeds which would preclude the freedom of human will. Rather predestination is the "preparation of grace by God," a "gift" that can ultimately be rejected by free will.[149] Those who forsake the grace offered them by the Deity "are forsaken; by a just and secret judgment of God," Augustine wrote, "they are given over to their free will, not having received the gift of perseverance."[150] Unlike Calvin's, Augustine's doctrine of predestination rests on the free choice of human will to accept or reject God's salvific grace: "[T]he

---

[146] Eugène Portalié, "Teaching of St. Augustine of Hippo," *The Catholic Encyclopedia*, Vol. II (New York: Robert Appleton Company, 1907). *www.newadvent.org*. http://www.newadvent.org/cathen/02091a.htm (accessed 8 November 2010).

[147] Friedrich Loofs qtd. in Eugène Portalié, "Teaching of St. Augustine of Hippo," *The Catholic Encyclopedia*, Vol. II (New York: Robert Appleton Company, 1907). *www.newadvent.org*. http://www.newadvent.org/cathen/02091a.htm (accessed 8 November 2010).

[148] Allan D. Fitzgerald and John C. Cavadini, *Augustine Through the Ages: An Encyclopedia*, 2nd ed. (Grand Rapids: William B. Eerdmans Publishing, 1999) 678.

[149] Ibid.

[150] St. Augustine of Hippo, *De Correptione et Gratia* qtd. in *Fathers of the Church*, ed. John Joseph Gavigan (Washington, D.C.: Catholic University of America Press, 2002) 297.

predestined are called by some certain calling peculiar to the elect, and…they have been elected before the foundation of the world; not because they were foreknown as men who would believe and would be holy, but in order that by means of that very election of grace they might be such…"[151]

The Medieval Church in East and West understood preordination as a reciprocal action in which God co-works with the elect.[152] In this belief, the Christian church shares a heritage with the Hebrew Pharisees. The historian Flavius Josephus observed that: "[W]hen they determine that all things are done by fate, [the Pharisees] do not take away the freedom from men of acting as they see fit; since their notion is that it [has] pleased God to make a temperament whereby what he wills is done, but so that the will of man can act virtuously or viciously."[153] Orthodox doctrines regarding free will defend the Judaic claim that "to act what is right, or the contrary, is principally in the power of men, although fate does co-operate in every action."[154] "[E]ven the possibility of sin," Baron von Hügel wrote:

> arises, not from the freedom of the will as such, but, on the contrary, from the imperfection of freedom; and…there are doubtless reasons connected with the power of God or with His knowledge (concerning what will, upon the whole, produce a maximum of a certain kind of spiritual happiness), why He chose, or permitted, the existing scheme of imperfect liberty amongst human souls.[155]

O'Connor makes the point through inversion: her protagonists' seek orthodox truth even as they conceptualize that seeking in terms

---

[151] St. Augustine of Hippo, *De Praedestinatione Sanctorum* qtd. in *Nicene and Post-Nicene Fathers of the Church*, Vol. V, ed. Philip Schaff (New York: Cosimo, Inc., 2007) 516. See also St. Augustine of Hippo, *Enarrationes in Psalmos* qtd. *in Nicene and Post-Nicene Fathers of the Church*, Vol. VIII, no. XI (New York: Cosimo, Inc., 2007) 498.

[152] St. Augustine of Hippo, *De Praedestinatione Sanctorum* qtd. in Schaff, 516.

[153] Flavius Josephus, *Jewish Antiquities*, trans. William Whiston (Ware: Wordsworth Editions, Ltd., 2006) 774.

[154] Flavius Josephus, *History of the Destruction of Jerusalem or The Wars of the Jews* (Whitefish: Kessinger Publishing, 2004) 132.

[155] Baron Friedrich von Hügel, *Essays and Addresses on the Philosophy of Religion: First Series* (New York: E. P. Dutton, 1949) 221.

of dualities. Theirs is a Manichaeism clothed in the modern idiom of intellectual nihilism and civic gnosticism.

O'Connor's Misfit is her most direct indictment of the modern cosmology that holds man to be self-providential and God to be little more than a moral allegorism. The convict agrees with his captive, the Grandmother—Jesus *would* help him if he prayed—but he chooses to resist. "'I don't want no hep,' he [says]. 'I'm doing all right by myself.'"[156] Because he had not been at the tomb with the Magdalene nor in Jerusalem with the disciples, the Misfit could not assert absolutely that Jesus had been raised from the dead. Uncertain if he, as a son of Adam, is resurrected in Christ, the Misfit will consent only to his own judgment and follows a private sense of righteousness which declares, even if there is no pleasure in his choice, that he is doing *all* right himself. His demand for positive knowledge inverts Calvin's assurance of preordinate salvation. He is tellingly both executioner and confessor: "It ain't right I wasn't there because if I had been there I would of known…and I wouldn't be like I am now."[157] His choice of meanness follows his inability to abide the mystery of his faith. That choice, devastatingly punctuated by the grandmother's fateful gesture, comes clear not in the Calvinist decree that "eternal life is fore-ordained for some, eternal damnation for others"[158] but in the belief of the Jews and the early church that "mercy and judgment [are] manifested in the very wills [of men] themselves."[159]

Calvin's misappropriation of Augustine's and Aquinas' defense of predestination is in part to blame for the perception of O'Connor, as per her Misfits, as profoundly hard-hearted. Calvin brings a strange sense of divine sadism to the doctrine in which God calls all men to be saved but not with the intention of extending unconditional salvation. "There is a general call," Calvin claimed, "by which God invites all equally to himself through the outward preaching of the word—even those to whom he holds it out as a savour to death, and as the occasion for severer condemnation."[160] To

---

[156] O'Connor, "A Good Man Is Hard to Find," *Complete*, 130.

[157] Ibid., 132.

[158] John Calvin, *Institutio* qtd. in Niesel, 234.

[159] St. Augustine of Hippo, *De Praedestinatione Sanctorum* qtd. in Schaff, 5:503–504.

[160] John Calvin, *Institutio* qtd. in Niesel, 239.

a lesser degree, Luther interprets predestination as the saving grace of "man's will…in bondage."[161] "[N]ow…God," he declared, "has taken my salvation out of control of my own will and put it under the control of His, and promised to save me, not according to my working or running, but according to His own grace and mercy…"[162] The early reform churches here departed from the orthodox tradition in which salvation is the result of a shared effort in the wills of man and God. Interaction between man and Deity is removed from the material realm and displaced into a speculative ever-after of pure spirit. "Whatever holds down and confines the senses to the earth," Calvin claimed, "is contrary to the covenant of God: in which, inviting us to Himself, He permits us to think of nothing but what is spiritual."[163] Calvinism, in its most extreme manifestation, resurrected the dualistic theology of the Manichees in its insistence upon the dislocation of body and spirit; all matter, and most urgently the body, must be transcended to attain spiritual justification and redemption. O'Connor was stridently orthodox on this point, echoing the Church Fathers' conviction in the total redemption of the world, especially the biological temple of the body, through the life and death of the Christ. Jesus' "incarnation itself," John Thiel writes, "was a testimony to the goodness of Creation, and in the resurrection of the body, an affirmation of the created goodness, and so salvational worthiness, of the entire human person."[164]

O'Connor's fiction, particularly her late work, is imbued with a biblical revivalism which points to pre-schism orthodoxy. In *The Violent Bear It Away*, she made overt connections between her fictive prophets and Old Testament figures including Moses, Joshua, Daniel, Elijah, Elisha, Habukkuk, and Ezekiel. In "Parker's Back," O. E. and his wife are foiled with the Old Testament figures Obadiah, Elihu, Sarah, and Ruth. Orthodox saints like Jerome who appears in

---

[161] Martin Luther, *The Bondage of the Will* qtd. in Niesel, 240.

[162] Ibid., 240–41.

[163] John Calvin, *Commentary on the Last Four Books of Moses*, 1863–1880, v. 24:387 qtd. in James J. Buckley, et al., eds., *The Blackwell Companion to Catholicism*, 70.

[164] John E. Thiel, "The Development of Doctrine," *The Blackwell Companion to Catholicism*, ed. James J. Buckley, Frederick Christian Bauershmidt, and Trent Pomplun (Malden: Blackwell Publishing Ltd., 2007) 252. See also Bishop Irenaeus of Lyons, *Against Heresies*, Vol. V, Book V, 1.1 (Whitefish: Kessinger Publishing, 2004) 7–8.

"Why Do The Heathen Rage?" are coupled with more oblique nods toward ecumenism, for instance Hazel Motes's birthplace in Eastrod, Tennessee, his monkish self-chastisement, and his impassioned pseudo-Protestant evangelism. There are such cross-millennial foils as Mrs. May and Mrs. Greenleaf, the former "a good Christian woman" of no faith, the latter a modern day Margery Kempe, as well as the Straight Gospel Sarah Ruth and her Byzantine icon-wearing husband.[165] O'Connor's oeuvre is, in this respect, a literary attempt at ecumenism in which the entire history of the Christian faith, from its beginnings amongst the Jewish tribes to its translation by the Eastern Fathers, medieval and Renaissance scholars, and O'Connor's own "Instant Uplift" moderns, is made to ring through a contemporary resetting of scripture.[166] Her Southern Protestants are more insistently orthodox in their intimacy with the Bible than many Protestants and Catholics contemporary to her would have been. As Ralph C. Wood suggests, O'Connor did not write regional Protestantism straight; her intention was not to typify the Southern religion as something exceptional either in its conservatisms or its liberalisms but rather to reveal the recurring analogy of orthodox Christianity irrespective of the exceptionalism of a certain sect.[167] O'Connor found a point of reference more resonant with her two-testament Catholicism in the peculiar and fragmented American orthodoxy we call fundamentalism than could be found in the Mass. Wood correctly attributes a critical "heterodoxy" to O'Connor's book reviews, and the same can be seen to extend into the core of her fiction. "I do not use the word [heterodox] tamely," Wood writes, "to mean nothing more than 'unorthodox' nor pejoratively to indicate heresy, but positively to imply a certain critical distance from the central Catholic tradition of Thomistic humanism."[168]

---

165 O'Connor, "Greenleaf," *Complete*, 316.

166 O'Connor, "Novelist and Believer," *Mystery*, 165.

167 Ibid., 164.

168 Wood, "The Heterodoxy of Flannery O'Connor's Book Reviews," *The Flannery O'Connor Bulletin* 5 (1976): 3–4.

Section 2: "The Church Without Christ": O'Connor and the American Religion[169]

Somewhat in spite of the Catholic tradition, O'Connor invested her art in the Southern mode of evangelicalism and its refusals to divorce the Old Testament from the New or to prioritize the significance of the gospels. Like Eastern Orthodox Christians, O'Connor's fundamentalists draw from the image history of the Hebrew books to illuminate the Christ story with prophetic implication. The author was no doubt aware of Southern revivalists like Samuel P. Jones and Oral Roberts—the forerunners of the third "Great Awakening"—and the often militant fundamentalist movements which dislocated themselves from liberal and moderate-leaning sects. Though she was skeptical of the long-term viability of such charismatics, O'Connor was far more damning of the mainstream "liberal religion."[170] At the 1963 "Symposium on Religion in Art" at Sweet Briar College, O'Connor apparently got "a stomach full" it.[171] "The Devil," she wrote to the Fitzgeralds, "had his day there."[172] She recalls how she had, "waded in and gave them a nasty dose of orthodoxy," one which she was sure the audience found "quaint."[173] Her address, "Novelist and Believer," unapologetically condemns the "vaporization of religion in America" starting with Emerson's proclamation, "in 1832, that he could no longer celebrate the Lord's Supper unless the bread and wine were removed..."[174] O'Connor insisted to the contrary upon the continuity of the mattered and supernatural worlds in which there is one "unlimited" God "who has revealed himself specifically" and who, in her words, is "the object of ultimate concern."[175] The dislocation of that God from His intercession in the lives of men is to make Him the God, not of Abraham, Isaac, and Jacob, but of a hypothetical Everyman who bears no name or history but exhibits admirable manners. Such a

---

[169] O'Connor, *Wise Blood*, 105.
[170] O'Connor, *Habit*, 510.
[171] Ibid.
[172] Ibid.
[173] Ibid.
[174] O'Connor, "Novelist and Believer," *Mystery*, 161.
[175] Ibid.

man is not troubled by holy commandments nor "evil intelligence" but is appropriately respectful to the mythos thereof.[176]

O'Connor's orthodoxy was wholly intolerant of divulging itself of reality for the sake of the liberal Christian, however admirable his "spirit of ecumenism."[177] As in the early church, she interpreted the Old Testament drama as ongoing and counter-illuminating of the gospels and the present real and read the signs of the Hebrew books with intent to literal application, not symbolic reflection. Conversely, the prevailing civil religion aligned itself with a secular revisionism which gave ascendancy to the rationale of the national rhetoric. Increasingly the legitimacy of the national credo was gauged by how well the American dream paid out to the dreamer as opposed to faithfulness in the godliness of the dream itself.[178] As O'Connor demonstrated with such characters as Mrs. May and Ruby Turpin, one practices a civil religion for the sake of symbolic moral consequences, not actual ones.

Despite its strong ties to scripture, the South was in no way immune to the influence of secular religion. O'Connor bemoaned the slippage of fundamental Protestantism into constructs of social decency and deviance. "[T]he traditional Protestant bodies of the South," she wrote, "are evaporating into secularism and respectability and are being replaced on the grass roots level by all sorts of strange sects that bear not much resemblance to traditional Protestantism—Jehovah's Witnesses, snake-handlers, Free Thinking Christians, Independent Prophets, the swindlers, [and] the mad..."[179] The modern South adapted the business cunning of the post-war American Christian with the performance savvy of the Southern evangelical to produce the televangelist. Undergirding the choreographed pageantry was the invocation, by personalities like Billy Graham and Tammy Faye, of the Southern tradition of preaching as storytelling. Though critical of the televangelists recreating Christian rituals into a lucrative form of theatre, O'Connor

[176] Ibid., 168.

[177] Ibid., 166.

[178] Jon Lance Bacon describes the disjoint between the "American way," Catholicism, and Protestant Fundamentalism in his essay, "A Fondness for Supermarkets: *Wise Blood* and Consumer Culture," *New Essays on Wise Blood*, ed. Michael Kreyling (New York: Cambridge University Press, 1995) 25–49.

[179] O'Connor, *Habit*, 407.

accounted for the region's predominance as a storytelling section by its retention of the Old Testament and the willingness of its folk to be moved or at the very least entertained by the biblical drama. "[T]he Southerner's way of looking at things," she wrote, "[has been conditioned by]…the Hebrew genius for making the absolute concrete."[180] From the colonial period, the *belles lettres* of the South has been informed by the poetics of scripture. Faulkner cited the *King James Bible* as his primary stylistic influence, and O'Connor could point to the Douay version as the text which "saved [her] so many years in learning to write."[181] Unlike her predecessor's, O'Connor's fiction recalls the Hebrew genius in its plotting more so than its style. With her unequivocal "one cylinder syntax," she analogized the biblical drama, not by altering the scale of its play or by enlisting the help of supernatural phenomena, but by retelling the tale that recurs in each of the holy books, the tale of one man coming face to face with an unknown absolute.[182] Even as the New South was reading the Bible with an increasingly allegorical bent, the influence of grandmothers like Sam Jones's who had read the good book "thirty-seven times on her knees" could not be easily "shaken off."[183] "The fact that the South is the Bible Belt," O'Connor told Joel Wells, "is in great measure responsible for its literary preeminence now."[184] "To be great storytellers," she later wrote, "we need something to measure ourselves against… Men judge themselves now by what they find themselves doing. …For the purposes of fiction, [we require] guides [that] exist in concrete form, known and held sacred by the entire community. They have to exist in the form of stories which affect our image and our judgment of ourselves."[185] Even if it was, by mid-century, a shadowy influence, the scriptures remained the backdrop for the totalizing narrative of American identity. "Not only did the civil religion of the 1950s melt particularized historic faiths into a thin religious gruel," Wood notes, "it also made even the

---

[180] O'Connor, "The Catholic Novelist in the Protestant South," *Mystery*, 202.

[181] O'Connor, *Habit*, 139.

[182] Ibid., 292.

[183] O'Connor, "The Catholic Novelist in the Protestant South," *Mystery*, 202.

[184] O'Connor qtd. in *Conversations*, 87.

[185] Ibid.

most secular Americans into allegedly religious people. As President Eisenhower once declared, 'Our government makes no sense…unless it is founded in a deeply felt religious faith—and I don't care what it is.'"[186] The fear of God had been effectively replaced with the fear of apparent impiety. Good Christian values, not biblical verse, were the bywords of the modern faith, replacing the fiery visions of the desert prophets with a wooly image of right-living through a church-confined Christ.

Accustomed to a bloodless Christianity, O'Connor's immediate audience expected her fiction to communicate the soft redemption of the modern Buddy Christ.[187] Even her family, some of which were as dogmatic in their worship as O'Connor was herself, welcomed a degree of levity in her retelling of certain parables. When "The Life You Save May Be Your Own" was adapted into a tele-play in 1956, O'Connor was appalled at the changes made to her plot, especially the tacking on of a redemptive ending in which Shiftlet returns to the diner to collect his abandoned idiot-wife. "All my kinfolks," she admitted to Hester, "are going to think that it is a great improvement over the original story."[188] O'Connor's adversity to sentimental invocations of Christian morality and such secular correlatives as (successful) capitalism and humanist utilitarianism set even practiced readers like Hawkes searching out her debt to the Devil. The perversity Hawkes attributes to O'Connor's theology is more telling of his perception of the status quo than it is of the violence inherent to Flannery's "Christian realism." "You say," O'Connor argued, "that one becomes 'evil' when one leaves the herd. I say that depends entirely on what the herd is doing."[189] Flannery's theology does not conform to the American inclination to link material and social prosperity with good faith; it harkens instead to the blood sacrifice of the Hebrew God and the transcendent cost of that historical act. The victim is never simply an individual—a grandmother from middle Georgia or a young soldier from east Tennessee—but also the embodiment of the dark portal of Christian sacrifice that opens onto the conjoint mystery of the finite life of the

---

[186] Wood, *Christ-Haunted*, 19.

[187] *Dogma*, dir. Kevin Smith, Lions Gate Entertainment, 1999. Director Kevin Smith parodies the marketing of the civic Christ in this feature.

[188] Ibid., 195.

[189] O'Connor, *Habit*, 456.

body and the infinite life of the soul. O'Connor confessed to having approached the mysteries from the instance of individual suffering and destruction in order to make sensible the broadest sense of the Christian real. Her victim-heroes espoused an orthodox reality very much at odds with the glory-bound real touted by the American religion.

O'Connor's own theological criticisms were not limited to secularized Protestantism; she interrogated the rhetorical missives of her own church with the heightened scrutiny of an insider and was particularly disparaging of the manner in which the scriptures were transmitted in the Roman liturgy. "[W]e hear [the Bible]," she remarked, "read at Mass, bits and pieces of it are exposed to us in the liturgy, but because we are not totally dependent on it, it has not penetrated very far into our consciousness nor conditioned our reactions to experience."[190] The conventional Catholic O'Connor takes on an ironical cast when her criticism of that most Catholic of documents, the Roman catechism, is taken into account. Constructed to indoctrinate an illiterate laity, the catechism presupposed an intellectual remove between members of the clergy and lay people. The scriptures transmitted in the Mass are an abbreviated, church interpreted scripture. O'Connor was desirous of a more immediate interaction with the Bible in addition to the catechism, a desire reinforced undoubtedly by the impassioned command her Protestant neighbors had of the Old Testament. Her call for a biblical (as opposed to a liturgical) revival in the church was one of the few occasions in which she was directly critical of Roman dogma. Such an un-Catholic reproof underscores the complexity of O'Connor's relationship with the church and the inner conflict she must have felt criticizing the mainstay of ritual Catholicism while also continuing to practice its decrees. The author's recrimination of the liturgy also betrays the distance between her own beliefs, those of her immediate family, and of American Catholics more generally. "It would be foolish," she wrote, "to say there is no conflict between [one's own eyes and the eyes of the Church]. There is a conflict, and it is a conflict we escape at our peril, one that cannot be settled beforehand by theory or fiat or faith. We think that faith entitles us to avoid it,

---

[190] O'Connor, "The Catholic Novelist in the Protestant South," *Mystery*, 202.

when in fact, faith prompts us to begin it, and to continue it until, like Jacob, we are marked."[191] For O'Connor, the Catholic must wrestle with his faith, "like Jacob with the angel, until he has extracted a blessing" or else possess only the semblance of faith whose seemliness is its only reward.[192] The disjoint between O'Connor's somewhat militant faith and the "vapid" Catholicism of the modern American Church manifest itself most keenly in her writing life where her inclinations toward a more ancient orthodoxy translated into an aesthetic interpreted variously as un-Christian, un-American, and, in its recurring death-endedness, technically precipitous. "Maybe in fifty years, or a hundred," she mused:

> Catholics will be reading the Bible the way they should have been reading all along. I can wait that long to have my fiction understood. The Bible is what we share with all Christians, and the Old Testament we share with all Jews. This is a sacred history and our mythic background. If we are going to discard this we had better quit writing at all.[193]

It has been more than sixty years since the publication of O'Connor's best known works, *Wise Blood* and *A Good Man is Hard to Find*, and as she anticipated her critics have begun reevaluating the texts against an increasingly heteroglot Christian vision. The shift in emphasis does not discount the Roman influence in O'Connor's thinking, but it does make the appropriate distinction between the author's creative intellect and her religious practice. Certainly, there was a degree of overlap between the two, but it would be short-sighted to say that O'Connor's religious dogmatism precluded a broader intellectual fidelity. "I write with a solid belief in *all* the Christian dogmas," [194] she told Shirley Abbott at the outset of her career and would remain, throughout her writing life, ever-mindful of becoming an "unthinking Catholic," one who, when "brought up in [a] sheltered Catholic communit[y] with little or no intellectual contact with the modern world [is] apt to suppose that truth as Catholics know it is the order of the day except among the naturally

---

[191] O'Connor, "Catholic Novelists and Their Readers," *Mystery*, 180.

[192] O'Connor, "The Catholic Novelist in the Protestant South," *Mystery*, 198.

[193] O'Connor qtd. in *Conversations*, 87.

[194] O'Connor, *Habit*, 147. Italics in typescript.

perverse."[195] Always effecting a broader contact outside of the parish, O'Connor did not, like many self-proclaimed Catholic writers, close her own eyes in an attempt to "see with the eyes of the Church."[196] She warned that the writer who depends upon church dogma to impart his meaning ends by creating "another addition of that large body of pious trash for which we [Catholics] have so long been famous."[197]

O'Connor's catholic vision did not assume, as she supposed conventional Catholic writers might, a seamless or definite resolution for mankind. Indeed the moment of revelation comes for many of her characters with the painful onset of self-awareness by which some measure of the soul is revealed as imperfect and needful of a refashioning that far exceeds the boundaries of the narrative. In "Everything That Rises Must Converge," O'Connor's self-righteous bachelor of arts, Julian Chestny,[198] requires an extremely dramatic push (his mother's shock-induced coronary) to free him momentarily from the nearsightedness of intellectual pride. The young man's consciousness does not break through its own constructed real until he is on his knees, watching in helpless agony as his mother dies. The scene marks his "entry into the world of guilt and sorrow," but Julian's vision, although profound, is not equated to his salvation.[199] The internal transformation he experiences is transitory and incomplete, and in spite of his ingress into an alternative and bizarrely coincident reality, there is no implication that Julian's awakening has reached its endpoint. There is, in fact, a strong insinuation to the contrary that he will revert to the security of his prior reality, but with a painfully altered vision. The tone of the closing line suggests that the next turn of the revelatory process will not take so dramatic a push to complete.

"Everything That Rises Must Converge" is among the more secular of O'Connor's tales, invoking the otherworldly as an internal function of the protagonist not necessarily predicated by biblical

---

[195] O'Connor, "Catholic Novelists and Their Readers," *Mystery*, 185.

[196] Ibid., 180.

[197] Ibid.

[198] O'Connor does not declare from which line—maternal or paternal—the Chestny name originates, but it is significant, nevertheless, of Julian's ties with the paling Southern aristocracy.

[199] O'Connor, "Everything That Rises Must Converge," *Complete*, 420.

prophecy. The story's catholic significance lies in its replacement of the Church in the temple of the individual body, and one particularly inhospitable to grace. A likeness to Christ, O'Connor asserts with Julian, does not necessitate an aspiration to Christ as mankind was not created to be perfect in love. "[L]ove and understanding are one and the same only in God," she confided to Hester in fall 1963. "I love a lot of people, understand none of them. This is not perfect love but as much as a finite creature can be capable of."[200] Though his love for his mother is dulled tremendously by his misunderstanding of her, Julian is judged least by his imperfect affection. His capacity for self-reformation endows him with moral and dramatic worth, however late-coming. Herein lies the crux of the human drama for O'Connor. Irrespective of theological parameters, man is inevitably confronted by an unknown which exceeds his understanding and control; he must make a conscious decision to accept the bearing of revelation by pushing back the boundaries of his real or reject that intervening reality by retreating into his self-made real. Many of O'Connor's characters, including Mr. Head, the Misfit, Sarah Ruth Parker, Mrs. May, and Mr. Fortune opt for the latter, in some instances unto death. "Human nature," O'Connor reasoned, "vigorously resists grace because grace changes us and the change is painful."[201]

The resistance to self-disinterested change and the rare undertaking of the same is the subject of O'Connor's fiction much to the exclusion of any theological exposition on the nature of grace. "Grace can't be experienced in itself," O'Connor wrote to Hester in 1958. "[I]n a story all you can do with grace is show that it is changing a character."[202] She went on to say that she was, "much more interested in the nobility of unnaturalness than in the nobility of naturalness.[203] "...I will take just as much naturalness as I need to accomplish my purposes," she wrote, "no more..."[204] She concluded in noting, "The violent are not natural."[205] Even reluctant ascetics like Hazel Motes and Francis Marion come to bear away the inclination

---

[200] O'Connor, *Habit*, 543.
[201] Ibid., 307.
[202] Ibid., 274.
[203] Ibid., 343.
[204] Ibid.
[205] Ibid.

in man's damaged nature to remain damaged but apparently free, an inclination fulfilled in the author's lifetime by the disinheritance of the self from the Judeo-Christian myth. Such a disavowal denies that the individual has suffered any damage that cannot be explained by socio-economics.

O'Connor was inclined to name the parameters of her dramatic system in explicitly Christic terms, but her adaptation of the Christian cosmos and its particular symbology did not inhibit her complimentary employ of mytho-poetic traditions which predate Christianity. Thomas Merton famously aligned O'Connor's work with the Greek dramatist's Sophocles in his "prose elegy."[206] More recently, Montgomery correlates O'Connor's fiction with Greek poetics and pagan cosmology, arguing that the author's debt to the classical sense of dramatic justice shows itself in the self-responsible action of her heroes. When forced to choose between the "lesser of two evils," O'Connor's protagonists, like Aeschylus' Agamemnon, are made "aware that the flaw in the universe [which has driven them to such a choice] is at least partly in [themselves]."[207] The crisis of revelation operates two-fold: it shows the reality of men to be skewed to private inclinations, and in so doing it remarks that "man is less than the gods and doomed therefore to self-delusion."[208]

Man in conflict with himself and with God (or the gods) is certainly an ancient theme and one that Montgomery uses to liken O'Connor to Aeschylus and Homer. He is correct in his assessment that in the realm of her fiction, the author's aesthetic interests superseded any of her theological motivations. As an artist, O'Connor's ultimate concern was the dramatic virtue of her heroes which, like Odysseus', "[didn't] have to do with whether there is, in fact, a Poseidon as opposed to no god at all, but that [the hero] possess[ed], in addition to his sense of rightness, the courage of self-responsibility."[209] We admire the same self-possession in Huck Finn

---

[206] Thomas Merton, "Flannery O'Connor—A Prose Elegy," *The Literary Essays of Thomas Merton*, ed. Patrick Hart (New York: New Directions, 1981) 159–61.

[207] O'Connor, "Some Aspects of the Grotesque in Southern Fiction," *Mystery*, 49.

[208] Ibid.

[209] Marion Montgomery, "A Sense of Violation: Notes Toward a Definition of 'Southern' Fiction," *On Matters Southern: Essays About Literature*

when, "siding with Jim," he says, "All right then, I'll go to hell."[210] "Huck," Montgomery notes, "is firmly of the belief that he may very likely go to hell for his act."[211] The same pattern is echoed in Tarwater's "final temptation" at the lakeside when he must choose to save a life or take a life and thereby lose his own temporarily or permanently.[212] "His is Agamemnon's dilemma and Huck's put squarely in Christian terms," Montgomery argues. "[T]o baptize the child is to be enslaved...to the terrible Christ that haunts him for Adam's sin; to drown the child is to become enslaved to...that more terrible Devil whose name is Nada who art in Nada..."[213]

Whether or not O'Connor's fiction can be said to have a Christian intentionality, "drama," Montgomery notes, "is not created or sustained by faith;" the structure of her narratives owes more to the poetics of Aristotle than to the scriptures.[214] As in theatrical tragedy, O'Connor's stories are driven by the plotting of incident and action more so than a "moral purpose" inherent to a particular character.[215] The quality of a man's character, by Aristotelian aesthetics, is "subsidiary to [his] actions" as "life consists in action, and its end is a mode of action, not a quality. ...[I]t is by [his] actions that [he is] happy or the reverse."[216] O'Connor's heroes exhibit the defining attribute of tragedy in that their will to action comes from a certain ignorance which sets into motion a sequence of incidents. That particular sequence brings about an ultimate, enlightening reversal. The grandmother's actions in "A Good Man Is Hard to

---

and Culture, 1964–2000, ed. Michael M. Jordan (Jefferson: McFarland, 2005) 49.

[210] Ibid.

[211] Ibid.

[212] Ibid., 51. The scene reenacts one of O'Connor's favorite biblical paradoxes, that of gaining one's life (in Christ) by losing it (in self-possession): "For those who want to save their life will lose it, and those who lose their life for my sake, and for the sake of the gospel, will save it" (Mark 8:35, *NRSV*).

[213] Montgomery, "A Sense of Violation," 51; Ernest Hemingway, "A Clean, Well-Lighted Place," *The Complete Short Stories of Ernest Hemingway* (New York: Scribner, 1987) 291.

[214] Montgomery, "Flannery O'Connor and the Jansenist Problem in Fiction," 442.

[215] Aristotle, *Poetics*, trans. S. H. Butcher (New York: Cosimo Inc., 2008) 12.

[216] Ibid.

Find"—her secreting onboard Pity-Sing the cat, her conjuring the Tennessee plantation, and her recognition of the Misfit—originate the family's gruesome end, however innocent her intentions. The pattern remerges in later stories: in "A View of the Woods," Mr. Fortune's spiteful sale of his son in law's coveted pastureland incites Pitts to beat Mary Fortune who, doubly alienated by her grandfather, retaliates in like violence; in "Greenleaf," Mrs. May's priority of the wellbeing of her farm leaves her unloved and untended by her two sons and scornful of the easy success of the Greenleaf boys. Clearing off the Greenleaf bull is her last stand to principle. All three stories demonstrate complex action in which some change of fortune is accompanied by a reversal, a knowledge-endowing recognition, or both.[217] The change of fortune suffered by O'Connor's heroes is "subject always to [the] rule of probability or necessity" as opposed to theological determinism.[218] Even in stories with an overt Christological significance like "Parker's Back," the reversal linked to Christ's recognition is only mystically felt and then by O. E. alone. The substantive Christ is shown to be displaced from the world of action; in His place, a vague moral analogue functions as an element of landscape. When O. E. returns home to offer his remade flesh to Sarah Ruth, he is beaten mercilessly, and in that moment of misunderstanding, he realizes the nature of his husbandly love and of Christ's sacrifice. He weeps with the knowledge that he must "throw away everything," including his wife, and follow Christ's "all-demanding" eyes back to the bodily cost of redemption.

O'Connor's own story-telling genius functions as a collaborative mythology in which a multitude of collectively held story-systems are merged. These include the tragicomic cosmology of the Greeks, the sublime realism of the Hebrews and the Desert Fathers, the moral logic of Medieval Europe and the American New Canaan, and the consumerist ideologies of the New South and the greater Cult of Progress. Using a fine-grain of naturalistic detail and an uncannily lifelike idiomatic diction, O'Connor integrates the ethos of ancient and modern civilizations with especial regard to the viability of their defining mythology. She suspends the modern hyper-empirical sense of the world by subverting the intentions of

---

[217] Ibid., 19–20.

[218] Ibid., 20.

positivist materialist characters like Mrs. May and Mrs. Cope and reestablishing a more mysterious system of valuation by which the worthiness of a thing, sentient or insentient, visible or invisible, is dependent upon how completely it reveals the sublime interconnectivity of all things. O'Connor's manipulation of objects, like Joy/Hulga's wooden leg and Mrs. Chestny's felt hat, recalls the operation of Aristotle's "objects of recognition."[219] In his *Poetics*, the philosopher declared that, "Even inanimate things of the most trivial nature may in a sense be objects of recognition."[220] The ultimate reversal in "Good Country People" comes when the locus of Joy/Hulga's pride is stolen away by one she assumed she would outmaneuver both intellectually and physically; the absence of the leg makes her cognizant of the baselessness of her vanity. The function of the inciting object in "Everything That Rises Must Converge" is more complex. Julian's mother recognizes her hat atop the head of a black woman, is initially flustered at the coincidence, and then recovers her dignity, Julian supposes, by imaging the woman was "a monkey that had stolen her hat."[221] The old woman remains unaware of her error until her foil asserts her own dignity with a well-placed blow.

O'Connor's objectification of the dramatic reversal also recalls the image theory of early Byzantine iconography. Orthodox Christianity prior to the iconoclastic controversies of the eighth and ninth centuries "perceived [the holy icon] as matter imbued with *charis*, or divine grace."[222] "It stands for an admixture of presence and absence," an "imprint" which "enacts divine presence (essence) in its making and in its interaction with the faithful."[223] Objects which interact with and create transfiguration in O'Connor's heroes mimic the icon's essentialist relationship to an ultimate reality. As in Byzantine worship, O'Connor's iconic objects effect a "synesthetic experience in which the whole body is engaged."[224] "The icon," Bissera Pentchera writes, "is just an imprint of form, but it simulates

---

[219] Ibid., 21.

[220] Ibid.

[221] O'Connor, "Everything That Rises Must Converge," *Complete*, 416.

[222] Bissera V. Pentchera, "The Performative Icon," *The Art Bulletin* 88/4 (December 2006): 631.

[223] Ibid.

[224] Ibid.

the divine essence through the interaction of its imprinted surface with the changing ambience."[225] Its "surface…resonates sound, wind, light, touch, and smell" between itself and the viewer and is continually going through "a process of becoming…and performing before the faithful.[226] Joy/Hulga's leg, like the icon, imprints human form and analogizes divine incarnation. "If you want to say that the wooden leg is a symbol," O'Connor wrote, "you can say that. But it is a wooden leg first, and as a wooden leg it is absolutely necessary to the story. It has its place on the literal level of the story, but it operates in depth as well as on the surface. It increases the story in every direction…"[227] O'Connor described her intention to create a tangible matrix for several levels of actuality in terms of a Thomist realism in which the sensory and moral senses are engaged simultaneously. She attributed an incarnational significance to scripture which extended into the world of matter. "The author of Holy Writ," Aquinas stated in the *Summa*:

> in whose power it is to signify His meaning, not by words only (as men can also do), but also by things themselves. …[T]hings signified by…words have themselves also a signification. …[T]hat first signification whereby words signify things belongs to the first sense, the historical or literal. That signification whereby things signified by words have themselves also a signification is called the spiritual sense, which is based on the literal and presupposes it.[228]

Following Augustine's theorem, Aquinas further divides the spiritual sense into allegorical, moral, and anagogical denotations. Aquinas' scriptural exegesis, like Augustine's, has its basis in the writings of early Christians and church doctors.

> [A]s the Apostle [possibly Paul] says (Heb. x. 1) the Old Law is a figure of the New Law, and Dionysus says (Cæl. Hier. i) *the New Law itself is a figure of future glory*. …Therefore, so far as the things of the Old Law signify the things of the New Law, there is the allegorical sense; so far as the things done in Christ, or so far as the things which signify Christ, are types of what we ought to do, there

---

[225] Ibid., 632.

[226] Ibid., 631–32.

[227] O'Connor, "Writing Short Stories," *Mystery*, 99–100.

[228] St. Thomas Aquinas, *Summa Theologica*, "The Nature of Sacred Doctrine," trans. The Fathers of the English Dominican Province (New York: Cosimo Inc., 2007) 7.

is the moral sense. But so far as they signify what relates to eternal glory, there is the analogical sense.[229]

O'Connor echoes the sentiment of the early church by way of Aquinas in her paraphrase of St. Gregory I. In the essay "Catholic Novelists and Their Readers" she characterizes Medieval exegesis in her recollection of the sixth century pope: "St. Gregory wrote that every time the sacred text describes a fact, it reveals a mystery."[230] She went on to warn of the dangerous proclivity of the "religious" sense of artificially separating "[j]udgment...from vision, nature from grace, and reason from imagination."[231] While such divisions are by no means uniquely Catholic, O'Connor's criticisms were especially intended for parochial Romans of an artistic inclination. She complained of the shortcomings in the American establishment for producing any Catholic intellectuals to equal Bernanos, Mauriac, Maritain, Picard, or Guardini. "The Americans seem just to be producing pamphlets for the back of the Church (to be avoided at all costs) and installing heating systems..."[232] She conceded that there were "a few good resources" like Fordham University's *Thought*, and also that there was much "Catholic intellectual potential" in her native South, but ultimately the cultural mainstream produced "very few centers for it to revolve around."[233] So-called "enlightened Catholicism" seemed forthcoming only retrospectively as notable Catholic laymen, like Merton and Dorothy Day, gave currency to the wisdom of the early church.[234]

For her part, O'Connor determined to effect the Church Fathers' "anagogical vision" in which "different levels of reality" can be seen in "one image or one situation."[235] Such an "attitude" toward visible and invisible realities, O'Connor mused, disposed the intellect to "a

---

[229] Ibid.

[230] O'Connor, "Catholic Novelists and Their Readers," *Mystery*, 184.

[231] Ibid.

[232] O'Connor, *Habit*, 231.

[233] Flannery O'Connor, "Correspondence with Mrs. Frank Gafford," 16 May 1962, MS 59, Box 2, FF 1, *Flannery O'Connor Collection*, Manuscripts, Archives, and Rare Books Library, Emory University, Atlanta.

[234] Webster Schoot, "Flannery O'Connor: Faith's Stepchild," *The Nation* 201 (13 September 1965): 142–44, 146, in *Flannery O'Connor: The Contemporary Reviews*, ed. R. Neil Scott and Irwin H. Streight (Cambridge: Cambridge University Press, 2009) 291.

[235] O'Connor, "The Nature and Aim of Fiction," *Mystery*, 72.

way of reading nature which included most possibilities."[236] Critics including Carol Shloss, Sarah Gordon, and John F. Desmond have debated the efficacy of O'Connor's work in reproducing her desired anagogical aesthetic. Shloss makes her case with the most infamous of O'Connor's inciting objects, the Heads' "artificial nigger." "The meaning of the encounter," she writes, "...is unambiguously rendered. Nothing is left hidden. ...The reader is not left to surmise an extraordinary significance for the statue. ...He is told straightforwardly."[237] Gordon is more sympathetic to O'Connor's concluding exposition and states that the statue is "the catalyst for reconciliation. If we take the end of the story at face value," she continues, "we conclude that the chipped and battered figure suggests the mystery of human suffering and thereby summons Mr. Head to a recognition of his own weakness and dependence on God. In this way the story moves to the anagogical level."[238] Desmond concurs with Gordon, remarking that the statue "best realizes all the anagogical potentialities for the image. ...Through the statue, Mr. Head discovers not only the meaning of his present actions but also the ultimate significance of those actions within the cosmic framework of redemption."[239]

The statue does affect a kind of reconciliation; whether or not that change can be read from a specifically Christian point of view as the penultimate paragraph of the story dictates, is little supported by preceding instances of internal dialogue. Indeed, Mr. Head seems only to think Christianly after his nephew's denial; in the shadow of the boy's retracted love, he "felt he knew what time would be like without seasons and what heat would be like without light and what man would be like without salvation."[240] This revelation is then curiously underwritten by the "artificial nigger." Even as the object reunites Mr. Head and Nelson in likeness it reveals the collusion of

---

[236] Ibid., 72–73.

[237] Carol Shloss, *Flannery O'Connor's Dark Comedies: The Limits of Inference* (Baton Rogue:
Louisiana State University Press, 1980) 122.

[238] Sarah Gordon, *Flannery O'Connor: The Obedient Imagination* (Athens: University of Georgia
Press, 2003) 143.

[239] Desmond, *Risen Sons*, 49.

[240] O'Connor, "The Artificial Nigger," *Complete*, 268.

their identities, not in terms of a mutual benevolence of spirit but with regard to a host of mutual weaknesses. Both uncle and nephew share a delusion of urban wisdom; both deny, with words and with cold indifference, their kinship, and both find timely relief in the familiar shade of one denied still more than themselves. Nelson's ultimate response to the statue is to retreat to the known evils of the home place: "Let's go home before we get ourselves lost again," he tells his uncle, and upon returning declares, "I'm glad I've went once, but I'll never go back again."[241] The narrator implies a more complete transformation for Mr. Head, one brought on by "agony" and consummated in a self-awakening "action of mercy [which] covered [the old man's] pride like a flame and consumed it."[242] Significantly, the narrative opens with Mr. Head awash in the same "miraculous" moonlight that graces the close of the tale, but he is unmoved to meditate upon the health of his immortal soul or the workings of divine providence. To the contrary, he reflects upon his own experience-won "moral intelligence," which seems every bit as secular as Tom T. Shiftlet's.[243] It is as if the moonlight, in its final reflection of Christian mercy, has also imparted a peculiarly Catholic vocabulary to Mr. Head's most private thoughts.

Rarely did O'Connor allow her theologizing to subsume her dramatic instinct in such a way, so rarely, in fact, that the exposition which extends beyond the moment of dramatic catharsis takes on an air of deliberateness. She admitted to Ben Griffith in 1955 that she had written the story "a good many times, having [had] a lot of trouble with the ending."[244] She also noted having sent drafts of her stories to Mrs. [Allen] Tate who, she wrote, "is always telling me that the endings are too flat and that at the end I must gain some altitude and get a larger view. Well the end of 'The Artificial Nigger' was a very definite attempt to do that and in those last two paragraphs I have practically gone from the Garden of Eden to the Gates of Paradise."[245] She concluded by saying that she was "not sure [the story] is successful" but that she "mean[t] to keep trying with other

---

[241] Ibid., 269, 270.

[242] Ibid., 270.

[243] O'Connor, "The Life You Save May Be Your Own," *Complete*, 149.

[244] O'Connor, *Habit*, 78.

[245] Ibid.

things."[246] The following summer she "insist[ed]" that "The Artificial Nigger" was "a story in which there is an apparent action of grace" which was "equally successful" as her next story, "Good Country People."[247] Two years later she wrote to Maryat Lee that "The Artificial Nigger" was her "favorite" and "probably the best thing [she would] ever write."[248] O'Connor's anxiety regarding her readers' misapprehension of grace is here moderated by the narrative's inbuilt moral exposition, though somewhat at the expense of dramatic symmetry. The final act of the story turns, not upon Mr. Head's self-judgment or even his homecoming with the forgiving Nelson, but upon the point of sympathetic defeat where nephew implores uncle, at the foot of the miserable statue, to "explain once and for all the mystery of existence."[249] Mr. Head "open[s] his lips to make a lofty statement," some explanation of the race problem perhaps or justification for his disavowal of the boy, but instead he "hear[s] himself say, 'They ain't got enough real ones here. They got to have an artificial one.'"[250] The statement is a more befitting resolution than the succeeding comprehension of sin as the Heads' kinship is reestablished in their collusion in a less than virtuous ideology. Just as he had declared the "coffee-colored man" a "nigger," Mr. Head instructs Nelson to recognize "nigger statuary" as exotic, mysterious, and essentially inferior.[251] The child is wise to consider his grace-touched uncle with "suspicion" "under the shadow of his hat brim;" the divine will may well be omnipotent in its handling of creation, but in the realm of the story such a complete and miraculous change of sensibility smacks of human, not holy, contrivance.[252] More is accomplished by the simple collaboration of profane, finite being and sacred, infinite being whereby the objectified (black) man reveals a continuity between persecutor and victim, created and Creator. "For O'Connor," Peter Hawkins writes, "the ordinary vulgar world is sacramental: it is the place where God [the sublime] is present… This world is profane only when it is

---

[246] Ibid.

[247] Ibid., 160.

[248] Ibid., 209.

[249] O'Connor, "The Artificial Nigger," *Complete*, 269.

[250] Ibid.

[251] Ibid., 254; O'Connor, *Habit*, 101.

[252] O'Connor, "The Artificial Nigger," *Complete*, 270.

viewed as independent of its source."[253] "Things are funny," Lynch added, "precisely because they can recall the relation between God and themselves. ...[T]o recall this incredible relation between mud and God, is, in its own distant, adumbrating way, the function of comedy."[254]

O'Connor's insistence upon a practical kinship between the immediate reality of the mattered world and the transcendent reality of the Kingdom distinguishes her art from allegory in which "one [visible] fact points to another" visible fact.[255] O'Connor directed her readers to follow the interpretive tack of thirteenth century theologians like St. Thomas and Hugh of St. Victor who could detect "different levels of reality in one image or situation": the allegorical, the "tropological, or moral," and the anagogical.[256] O'Connor patterned her aesthetic upon the medieval anagoge in which a visible fact "leads above" to an invisible one and in so doing describes "the Divine life and our participation in it."[257] "The action or gesture" which reveals the anagogic, O'Connor asserted, would "transcend...any neat allegory that might have been intended or any pat moral categories which the reader could make. It would be a gesture which somehow ma[kes] contact with mystery."[258] Many of O'Connor's anagoges are unambiguously scriptural: in *Wise Blood,* Hazel Motes reverses Jesus' miracle, blinding himself so that he might see; in "A Circle in the Fire," Mrs. Cope invites destruction like the house-proud Job; and in "The Displaced Person," Mr. Guizac is sacrificed as Christ was so that the law of men might rule.

Nevertheless, the author's professed "anagogical vision" was overwhelmingly received as a dire sort of naturalism in which substance and corresponding action are examined for their literal and moral significance but not for their intimation of a super-reality whose historicity was itself reduced to a psychological weakness. O'Connor anticipated her readers' predilection for naturalist, topical

---

[253] Peter Hawkins, *The Language of Grace: Flannery O'Connor, Walker Percy, and Iris Murdoch* (Cambridge: Cowley Publications, 1983) 23.

[254] Lynch, *Christ and Apollo,* 109.

[255] O'Connor, "The Nature and Aim of Fiction," *Mystery,* 72.

[256] Ibid.

[257] Ibid.; O'Connor, "A Reasonable Use of the Unreasonable," *Mystery,* 111.

[258] O'Connor, "A Reasonable of the Unreasonable," *Mystery,* 111.

fiction, confiding to Hester that "the hardest thing for the writer to indicate is the presence of the anagogical which to my mind is the only thing that can cause the personality to change."[259] To her credit she persisted in a universalist vision by "say[ing] a plague"—even in such topical pieces as "Everything That Rises..."—"on everybody's house."[260] Just as the "divine deeper meaning [of the scriptures]" can be misconstrued at its most transparent level, the actual stuff of O'Connor's fiction, the "startling figures" of "death-in-life" and "life-in-death" that drive her protagonists onward to or away from their ultimate realities, can be constricted to their immediate significance.[261] For O'Connor's speculative "average reader," death can only mean death. The literal result of Francis Marion's drowning the child Bishop and Mr. Fortune's striking his granddaughter dead is of prime significance.[262] This is not to say that the literal is subordinate to the anagogic; on the contrary, the literal is the tangible expression of the meaningfulness of existence. Indeed, the paradox facing readers "[un]equipped to experience [the anagogic]" is the concomitance of an ultimate significance within an immediate and seemingly negligible frame. "[T]he chief difference," O'Connor remarked, "between the novelist who is an orthodox Christian and the novelist who is merely a naturalist is that the Christian novelist lives in a larger universe. He believes that the natural world contains the supernatural. And this doesn't mean that his obligation to portray the natural is less; it means it is greater."[263] To reveal the presence of an enlarged real within the mundane, O'Connor engineered her plotting to culminate in an extreme or violent action which forces the personality into a position of ultimate choice. "[T]he man in the violent situation," she wrote regarding "A Good Man Is Hard to Find," "reveals those qualities least dispensable to his personality, those qualities which are all he will have to take into

---

[259] O'Connor, *Habit*, 503.

[260] Ibid., 537.

[261] Hugh of St. Victor qtd. in Jane Chance, *Medieval Mythography: From Roman North Africa to the School of Chartres, A.D. 433–1177* (Gainesville: University of Florida Press, 1994) 36;

O'Connor, "The Fiction Writer and His Country," *Mystery*, 34; "The Nature and Aim of Fiction," *Mystery*, 72.

[262] O'Connor, "Writing Short Stories," *Mystery*, 95.

[263] O'Connor, "Catholic Novelists and Their Readers," *Mystery*, 175.

eternity with him; and since the characters in this story are all on the verge of eternity, it is appropriate to think of what they take with them."[264] The significance of gesture and personality is underwritten by the author's assumption of a mythos held in common by characters as contrasting in belief and vocation as the faith-healing Mrs. Greenleaf and the stoic school teacher George Rayber. When such characters "hold sacred history in common," O'Connor claimed, "they have ties to the universal and the holy, which allows the meaning of their every action to be heightened and seen under the aspect of eternity."[265] If we read the murders in "A Good Man Is Hard to Find" as the author suggests, they appear to carry a double significance. In an immediate, tropological sense, the shootings are indeed gruesome and ethically appalling, but in so far as the universe is principally unending and transcendental, they seem to matter only incidentally. The significant event to the orthodox mind is not physical death as the body will inevitably expire but the transcendence of the ultimate form of being which is irreducible: the soul. Even in suffering the "creative deaths" which realign the ego with divine consciousness, the soul "must subsist through abandoning itself."[266] The death of the body analogizes the relativity of immediate concerns and the necessary transition from one state of being to another. "There are three different levels on which life can be lived," Lynch writes:

> First, there is the level of surfaces and superficiality, above pain and problem, on which...we have...as a technological nation, tried to live. Secondly, there is a level much deeper than this (where pain is indeed confronted, and chaos too), which is...to be equated with what is today so often grimly called "the human situation." ...Thirdly, there is a still deeper level of human existence, a place where the human spirit "dies" in frequent real helplessness; and this we may call the really tragic level of existence. ...[T]he theologian says that it is the place of faith. By this he means that there is a point to which the mind must come where it realizes that

---

[264] O'Connor, "A Reasonable Use of the Unreasonable," *Mystery*, 114.

[265] O'Connor, "The Catholic Novelist in the Protestant South, *Mystery*, 203.

[266] Pierre Teilhard de Chardin qtd. in Christopher F. Mooney, "Blondel and Teilhard de Chardin: An Exchange of Letters," *Thought* 37/147 (Winter 1962): 549. See also Kinney, 181; Pierre Teilhard de Chardin, *The Phenomenon of Man*, trans. Bernard Wall (New York: Harper Perennial, 2008) 261.

> it is no match for the full mystery of existence, where, therefore, it suffers a death; it is only at this point that it will consent to put on the mind of God—as that mind is given us through the revelation of the Christian mysteries—and thus rise to a higher knowledge and insight. Here the points of death and life coincide in the one act. In this sense Christian faith has the tragic at its very core and is never a simple or easy intellectual act. It is always an extremely complicated mixture of dying and living; at no stage in the whole life of faith can death be screened out. The theologian also says that the third level...is the place of hope...the meeting ground of the tragic awareness of helplessness in the human will and its taking up (in the same moment) the strength of God. ...The discovered weakness becomes a gate to the infinite. But the weakness [of mortality] is permanent, and hence a permanent gate, not to be discarded in the name of some fraudulent and cheap leaping out of the skin of our helplessness into the arms of God.[267]

James J. Buckley remarks that the tradition of Catholic eschatology, particularly after the death of Aquinas in 1274, began to consider the human being "not as two things (body and soul) but as body 'formed' by soul."[268] The human body is iconic of the divine soul; just as Christ's flesh is indivisible from his Godliness, the human form exemplifies a natural weakness and a supernatural ascendancy. "Not even in the tomb," Buckley writes, "does God abandon the body."[269] Neither does O'Connor. Her most vital characters, some at the point of death, communicate through their bodies: the grandmother reaches out to touch the homicidal Misfit, Mary Fortune challenges her grandfather with a pounding of tiny fists, Mrs. Greenleaf prays flat-faced upon the earth for the entire world, and the rebel O. E. Parker "puts on" Christ.

O'Connor's view of death as a progressive experience drew her to theologians such as Lynch and Pierre Teilhard de Chardin who interpreted biblical history as ongoing and detectable to the most nonreligious of natural sciences, evolutionary biology. Both suggest an ascendant complexity of material being and consciousness in human experience through the ages. In his controversial study *The Phenomenon of Man*, Teilhard de Chardin describes the universe as evolving irreversibly toward an "Omega Point" in which

---

[267] Lynch, *Christ and Apollo*, 79–80.

[268] Buckley, "The End," *The Blackwell Companion to Catholicism*, 377.

[269] Ibid.

individuized beings are super-animated and integrated in a cosmic body. Chardin's theoretical universe reinterprets the Orthodox *Logos;* like Christ, the Omega Point antedates the creation of the universe and exists as its own cause beyond the constraints of temporality and locality. The Omega Point is the expression of God's personality as definitively autonomous and self-reflexive. The animal intellect rises irresistibly toward personalization—the process by which mankind "takes possession of itself as of an object endowed with its own particular consistence and value: no longer merely to know oneself; no longer merely to know, but to know that one knows"—and is synthesized, at the highest point of its evolution, with the rest of created consciousness into a universal collective.[270] Chardin's universe is essentially "personal."[271] Its energies radiate toward a "supreme consciousness" which manifests itself in humankind at the "highest degree" of "perfection of our consciousness—the illuminating involution of the being upon itself."[272]

Ordained a Jesuit priest, Chardin's theology bears the influence of Ignatian spirituality as well the ritual asceticism of Desert Fathers St. John Cassian and St. John Chrysostom. The Jesuit brotherhood was founded at the outset of the Counter-Reformation movement with the intention of inspiring internal reform. St. Ignatius outlined a series of meditative practices in his *Spiritual Exercises* which were derived from hermetic rituals of the Early Church such as the "Jesus prayer" of St. John Climacus' *Ladder of Divine Ascent*. Like the Desert Fathers', Jesuit spirituality was based upon the persistent invocation of the Christian mysteries with especial attention given to the Incarnation. Catholic and Eastern spirituality espouse a common "way" to God, a co-active progression of spiritual states by which the imperfections of the senses are purged, the consciousness is illuminated, and the soul is united in love with the "All."[273] An almost identical pattern is apparent in O'Connor's narratology: the protagonist is introduced with a definitive sensory weakness (Mr. Fortune is blind to the value of the woods, Ruby Turpin is self-

---

[270] Chardin, *The Phenomenon of Man,*165.

[271] Ibid., 257.

[272] Ibid., 258.

[273] Ibid., 259. See also Moine de l'Eglise d'Orient, *Orthodox Spirituality: An Outline of the Orthodox Ascetical and Mystical Tradition,* 2nd ed. (Crestwood: St. Vladimir's Seminary Press, 1978) 36.

justifying in her prejudices, and Joy/Hulga assumes a supreme intelligence), he is made aware of his fault (Mr. Fortune is denied in violence by his granddaughter, Ruby Turpin is struck down by the accusatory Mary Grace, and Joy/Hulga is duped by a simple con), and, dead or alive, he enters into a purgatorial "dark night of the soul." O'Connor was much taken with St. John of the Cross and read several accounts on his life and works, including Fr. Bruno's *Saint John of the Cross* (1932) and *Three Mystics: El Greco, St. John of the Cross, and St. Teresa of Avila* (1949). In the Rev. Louis Bouyer's *The Spirit and Forms of Protestantism* (1956), she marks a quotation of St. John's which criticizes the human want of individuized actualization: "The disposition required for union with God does not consist in understanding, tasting, feeling, or imagining God; it consists solely of purity and love, that is, *of complete submission of the will and absolute detachment from all for the sake of God alone*."[274] St. John's sentiment is repeated in Chardin's notion of "creative death" by which man becomes detached to the things of nature by virtue of nature itself; "in the sphere of nature itself," he wrote, "there is a power of renunciation," the beginning of which is "imposed by Christ on every member of His Body."[275] But as Chardin explains in the final chapters of *The Phenomenon of Man*, renunciation is not synonymous with dissolution; the Omega Point "in its ultimate principle, can only be a *distinct Centre radiating at the core of a system of centres;* a grouping in which personalisation of the All and personalisations of the elements reach their maximum, simultaneously and without merging, under the influence of a supremely autonomous union [italics in translation]."[276] According to Chardin, the "fatal" mistake of modern man is his confusion of "*individuality with personality*."[277] The error is one O'Connor perceived in herself in spite of her dogmatic training; she confessed to Hester that the "negativity" of

---

[274] St. John of the Cross qtd. in Rev. Louis Bouyer, *The Spirit and Forms of Protestantism* (Westminster: Newman Press, 1956) 94. See also Kinney, *Flannery O'Connor's Library*, 61.

[275] Pierre Teilhard de Chardin qtd. in Mooney, "Blondel and Teilhard de Chardin," 549. See also Kinney, *Flannery O'Connor's Library*, 181.

[276] Chardin, *The Phenomenon of Man*, 262–63.

[277] Ibid., 263.

her stories was "in large degree personal" and that her "disposition" was "a combination of Nelson's and Hulga's." [278]

At the point of crisis, O'Connor observed that few people, herself included, found themselves "as adequate to the situation as [they] thought [they] would be."[279] The confessional writings of church doctors such as Sts. Augustine and Jerome and the meditations of mystics including Sts. John of the Cross and Ignatius of Loyola affirmed her view that even men of exceptional spiritual bearing were prone to egoism. The often fatal striving of O'Connor's modern man imparts the triumphalism of the industrial West as a false boon. The material and intellectual successes of characters like Mrs. McIntyre and George Rayber are profoundly disadvantageous, provoking them to participate, by way of a canny negligence, in the deaths of two innocents. Rayber is a remarkable case because "the strongest of [his] psychological pulls are in the direction that he does not ultimately choose."[280] He imagines himself a child "still waiting on Christ," able to control his "terrifying love as long as it had its focus in Bishop, but if anything happened to the child, he would have to face it in itself. Then the whole world would become his idiot child."[281] Ultimately, Rayber succeeds in rationalizing himself out of love. He allows Tarwater to take the child from him, and when he hears Bishop's raking howl, he "wait[s] for the raging pain…to begin, so that he could ignore it, but he…fel[t] nothing."[282] Both men are equally reprehensible, driven to violence by an individuized principle of justice. Rayber attempts to drown Bishop so that the child might be delivered from a false-started existence, and Tarwater achieves the same to prove himself free of his prophetic calling. The experience of Bishop's death is one that effects both men acutely. The boy's father is lost to a self-defensive apathy, and his cousin is made an unwitting baptist, submitting, at the last possible moment, to a purpose that exceeds his pride. O'Connor describes the outcome

---

[278] O'Connor, *Habit*, 101.

[279] Ibid.

[280] Ibid., 488.

[281] Flannery O'Connor, *The Violent Bear It Away* (New York: Farrar, Straus & Giroux, 1960) 182.

[282] Ibid., 203.

with characteristic concision in a letter to Alfred Corn: "Tarwater wrestles with the Lord and Rayber wins."[283]

More startling to the modern sensibility, perhaps, than her implication that death is progressive—a correlative as opposed to a definitive experience—is O'Connor's suggestion that, despite its being essentially interruptive and isolating, death is very likely advantageous. She describes Bishop's final cry as transcending the scene, "rising out of its own momentum as if it were escaping finally, after centuries of waiting, into silence."[284] When the Greenleaf bull pierces Mrs. May through her heart and side, her consciousness shifts from the creature to the distant tree line. The narrator describes her as having "the look of a person whose sight has been restored but who finds the light unbearable."[285] Mr. Greenleaf finds her humped over the animal "as if she were "whispering some last discovery into [his] ear."[286] With her execution looming, the grandmother recognizes the Misfit as "one of [her] own babies" and reaches out to touch him.[287] O'Connor's "spiritual poetics" positions dramatic resolution at a point which almost always transcends the real time of the narrative.[288] This idiosyncrasy, perhaps more so than any other, offsets O'Connor's work from the prevailing teleology of the American short story. While critics like Frank O'Connor and Charles E. May theorize the short as a compressed sequence of crucial actions which result in the character being forever changed, Flannery's work implies that the character, by way of this crucial action, is literally entering into forever. The definitive irony of her stories lies in the general protagonistic urge to resist the inevitable dissemination of the self into eternity, in Lynch's words the "mad attempt at privacy" which poses as the "ultimate of the finite."[289] Pieces like "A Good Man Is Hard To Find" challenge preconceptions about the purpose and form of the short narrative in that its implied

---

[283] O'Connor, *Habit*, 488.

[284] O'Connor, *Violent*, 202.

[285] O'Connor, "Greenleaf," *Complete*, 333.

[286] Ibid., 334.

[287] O'Connor, "A Good Man Is Hard to Find," *Complete*, 132.

[288] Robert Gianonne, *Flannery O'Connor, Hermit Novelist*, rev. ed. (Columbia: University of South Carolina Press, 2010) 92.

[289] Lynch, *Christ and Apollo*, 80.

resolution exists outside of the bounds of immediately sensible time and experience.

Farrell O'Gorman attributes O'Connor's unconventional structuring to a "Catholic theory of fiction" which he describes, in tandem with Ross Labrie, as "essentially continuous with 'the Catholic imagination in American literature.'"[290] Distinguished by its perception of the sacred as contiguous with and "somehow involved in the secular," the Catholic imagination has fostered a narrative realism which stands in counter point to naturalism and romance. "[T]he romantic 'mainstream' of American literature," Paul Giles argues further, "is essentially Protestant and...there exists alongside it a 'competing antiromantic Catholic tradition.'"[291] "[A] full understanding of American Catholic literature 'will problematize that rigid affiliation between American literature and an ideology of romanticism...'"[292] O'Connor is at a further remove from the traditions of Emerson and Dreiser having been influenced as much by her native South as by the doctrines of the Catholic Church. The Southern imagination has been described historically and fictively as remarkably tolerant of creative distortion. In her lecture entitled "Writing Short Stories," O'Connor claimed that, "A great deal of the Southern writer's work is done for him because our history lives in our talk. In one of Eudora Welty's stories a character says, 'Where I come from, we use fox for yard dogs and owls for chickens, but we sing true.'"[293] Southern talk, which has its foundation in elaborative tale-telling, proclaims a truth that maintains its integrity to the real in spite of its relativity to the teller. O'Connor described her own aesthetic as novelistically unorthodox, intent upon the vitality of a character more so than his emulation of a typical life. In her 1960 lecture at Wesleyan, she declared that:

> The writer who writes within what might be called the modern romance tradition may not be writing novels which in all respects partake of a novelistic orthodoxy; but as long as these works have

---

[290] Farrell O'Gorman, *Peculiar Crossroads: Flannery O'Connor, Walker Percy, and Catholic Vision in Postwar Southern Fiction* (Baton Rouge: Louisiana State University Press, 2007) 104.

[291] Paul Giles qtd. in O'Gorman, *Peculiar Crossroads,* 106.

[292] Ibid.

[293] O'Connor, "Writing Short Stories," *Mystery,* 105. See Welty's short story, "The Hitch-hikers."

> vitality, as long as they present something alive, however eccentric its life may seem to the general reader, then they have to be dealt with; and they have to be dealt with on their own terms.[294]

O'Connor's "modern [Catholic] romance" is seemingly a contradiction of terms in that its intended "deeper" realism is intensely naturalistic. She retains the predictive quality of Dreiser's and Crane's sociology but also broadens the frame of environmental influence to include an implied reality that both predates and exceeds the material existence of mankind. The laws of natural science are not irrelevant to O'Connor—as an orthodox Christian, the atomistic nature of the universe is the first and final intimation of a transcendent real—but the mattered world is only descriptive of reality. It is not the end of the real itself. "[W]hen I know what the laws of the flesh and the physical really are," O'Connor confided to Hester in 1955:

> then I will know what God is. ...I am always astonished at the emphasis the Church puts on the body. It is not the soul she says that will rise but the body, glorified. I have always thought that purity was the most mysterious of the virtues, but it occurs to me that it would never have entered the human consciousness to conceive of purity if we were not to look forward to the resurrection of the body, which will be flesh and spirit united in peace, in the way they were in Christ. The resurrection of Christ seems the high point in the law of nature...[295]

O'Connor's Christian realism engages Orthodoxy's defining paradox—that the Holy Spirit is actually and mystically present in the world. To be realistic (in a Christian sense) about nature, one has to allow for the coincidence of a super-nature. O'Connor's fictionalized Protestantism is generally too moderate to entertain supernatural interventions, benevolent or otherwise. Even Hawthorne's consummate Puritan romance divests the Spirit of its material action. In Giles's words, "Protestant romance dissolves the mundane world into a more lucid spiritual allegory."[296] "Catholic realism," on the other hand, "invests the mundane world itself with

---

[294] O'Connor, "Some Aspects of the Grotesque in Southern Fiction," *Mystery*, 39.

[295] O'Connor, *Habit*, 100.

[296] Giles qtd. in O'Gorman, *Peculiar Crossroads*, 106.

sacramental significance."[297] Protestantism's tendency to allegorize the biblical drama may derive from its doctrine of predestination in which the souls of men are described as fitted immutably to either ascendancy in heaven or damnation in hell. O'Connor condemned the doctrine, calling it a "double predestination" and "strictly a Protestant phenomenon."[298] She recalls the ninth chapter of Paul's letter to the Romans which "is held by the Church to refer not to eternal reward or punishment but to our actual lives on earth, where one is given talent, wealth, education, made a 'vessel of honor,' and another is given the short end of the horn, so to speak—the 'vessel of wrath.'"[299] Verses twenty-two through twenty-four suggest that creation is cooperative in man's free will; the Deity suffers alike the actions of men of wrath and mercy so that an ultimate glory might be revealed. "What if God," Paul asks, "desiring to show his wrath and to make known his power, has endured with much patience the objects of wrath that are made for destruction; and what if he has done so in order to make known the riches of his glory for the objects of mercy, which he has prepared beforehand for glory…?"[300] The Protestant tradition has read Paul's "destruction" as a final judgment which can only deliver the soul into the abyss of the unredeemed. Human depravity is therefore indicative of God's immediate absence. Conversely, orthodox Christians (Catholic and Eastern) interpret human error as the requisite event for God's ongoing and personal advent in the world. "[God] does not predestine any soul to hell," O'Connor wrote to Alfred Corn in 1962, admitting that her conviction of the efficacy of grace, especially within the realm of Purgatory, comes from the "teaching authority" of the Church.[301] "If left to myself," she said, "I certainly wouldn't know how to interpret Romans IX."[302]

Although the Eastern Church does not acknowledge the term "purgatory" it shares a mystical belief with the Catholic Church in the soul's purification after death. "[T]he Eastern Orthodox problem with 'purgatory,'" Laurent Cleenewerck states, "is not so much the

[297] Ibid.
[298] O'Connor, *Habit*, 488.
[299] Ibid.
[300] Rom. 9:22–24, *NRSV*.
[301] O'Connor, *Habit*, 488–89.
[302] Ibid., 489.

idea of mercy after death as the legal concepts, terminology, and dogmatization used to express it."[303] To Orthodox, the intermediate state between death and resurrection is understood as a process of "purification or growth, or both" and "is not necessarily a place of punishment."[304] Both traditions believe that prayer and Eucharistic sacrifice benefit the individual soul in its movement toward deification. Unlike Protestant eschatology, "justification must be complimented by sanctification."[305] Erwin Fahlbusch describes Purgatory as the "continuation and completion of this process of sanctification after death. This purgation is not a replacement of grace by works but the painful process by which grace accomplishes its work precisely as grace."[306] Only those "who have believed in Christ" can avail of grace after death.[307] "[H]ell," O'Connor put it, "is what God's love becomes to those who reject it."[308]

That man can reject God, even if he was "made…to love Him," is very much the engine that drives O'Connor's fiction. "It takes two to love," she wrote. "It takes liberty. …No hell, no dignity."[309] To make the point emphatically, O'Connor posited her least upstanding characters, deviant murderers like Hazel Motes and the Misfit, as ultimately the most redeemable. In spite of their destructive behaviors, Christ and the consequence of His New Covenant are profoundly real to them. They may assert an immediate freedom by rejecting Christ, but they cannot displace what Hazel calls a "natural" want of redemption.[310] "Cutting yourself off from Grace," O'Connor wrote, "is a very decided matter, requiring a real choice, act of will, and affecting the very ground of the soul."[311] Hazel and

---

[303] Laurent Cleenewerck, *His Broken Body: Understanding and Healing the Schism Between the Roman Catholic and Eastern Orthodox Churches* (Washington, D.C.: Euclid University Press, 2008) 350.

[304] Ted A. Campbell, *Christian Confessions: A Historical Introduction* (Louisville: Westminster John Knox Press, 1996) 54.

[305] Erwin Fahlbusch and Geoffrey William Bromiley, *The Encyclopedia of Christianity*, Vol. IV, trans. Geoffrey William Bromiley (Grand Rapids: Wm. B. Eerdmans Publishing, 2005) 455.

[306] Ibid.

[307] Ted Campbell, *Christian Confessions*, 54.

[308] O'Connor, *Habit*, 354.

[309] Ibid.

[310] O'Connor, *Wise Blood*, 224.

[311] O'Connor, *Habit*, 389.

the Misfit suffer with the knowledge that they will "pay" for their sins, and their actions suggest they have already begun to pay, but men like Tom T. Shiftlet believe only in the retribution of men (which can be outrun). He operates entirely upon a self-judging code of "moral intelligence." O'Connor said she "could fancy a character like the Misfit being redeemable, but a character like Mr. Shiftlet as being unredeemable."[312] He is "of the Devil," she put it, "because nothing in him resists the Devil."[313] As such, he will face what the "preachers" called "eternal death."[314]

Shiftlet is one of the few "unredeemable" protagonists in O'Connor's oeuvre; the majority of characters who "win" their psychological freedom are secondary or tertiary figures. O'Connor's reasoning is technical. "If there is no possibility for change in a character," O'Connor wrote to Hester in 1957, "we have no interest in him."[315] "[Y]ou can't just posit a moral moron and expect the reader to have interest."[316] He must be capable "of feeling the difference between right and wrong" in order to sin.[317] "Sin," she concluded, "is interesting but evil is not. Sin is the result of an individual's free choice, but evil is something else."[318] George Rayber chooses to dislocate himself from the world by abandoning his one emotive tie to it and in so doing "kill[s] the little bit of good in him…"[319] He cannot help but feel the physical vibration of his son's death throes, but the once excruciating psychological effect of paternal denial he has managed to squelch completely. Rayber has entered a state of total self-justification in which "there would be no pain," and yet he is physiologically overwhelmed. O'Connor leaves him at the close of part two "collapsed" in a symbolic death.[320] The psychic death of George Rayber reiterates the connectivity, so much emphasized in orthodox Christianity, between physiological and cognitive ascension. He is at once an exaggeration of the "ideal"

---

[312] Ibid., 350.

[313] Ibid., 367.

[314] O'Connor, *Wise Blood*, 211.

[315] O'Connor, *Habit*, 199.

[316] Ibid.

[317] Ibid.

[318] Ibid.

[319] Ibid.

[320] O'Connor, *Violent*, 203.

modern hero and a swan song for the pre-modern man of place.[321] He is "the outsider" amongst his Christ-haunted kin but is utterly at home in a nondescript city.[322] "His experience is rootless" but punctuated by the imposition of an alternative reality at Powder Head.[323] "He can go anywhere," but he returns to his uncle's burnt-out homestead, intent upon making a terminal proof of his unbelief.[324] Conversely in Rayber's final inward-turning action there is confirmation that "[t]he borders of his country are the sides of his skull."[325]

Writing the "modern hero," even one as actively one-dimensional and stylized as George Rayber, was a challenge for O'Connor, particularly to her orthodox sensibility which would have found the school teacher's willful death-in-life an affront to the collective transcendence of the universe, what Chardin called "the Mass upon the World."[326] O'Connor told editor Catherine Carver that in writing the novel, "Rayber ha[d] been the difficulty all along." She would "never manage to get him as alive as Tarwater and the old man…"[327] Troublesome as he may have been to O'Connor's dramatic sense, Rayber's relative lifelessness is ultimately a symptom of his egoism. So advanced is his commitment to an internally constructed real, he is finally unwilling to engage the reality of his son who is implicitly reflexive of an absolute intelligence. Had O'Connor shifted Rayber to the position of central actor, he would have been unable to sustain a narrative of transcendental teleology; his arrival at a condition of zero-conflict does not conform with the author's concept of heroism as exceeding the frame of the story, in some instances surpassing death. Joy/Hulga and Asbury Fox exhibit a Rayber-like rationale, but when they are met with an unavoidable transformative event their internal realities are exploded, not confirmed. Whether or not they suffer physical death, protagonists such as Joy/Hulga and Asbury are purgatorial in character. Sudden,

---

[321] O'Connor, "The Catholic Novelist in the Protestant South," *Mystery*, 199.

[322] Ibid.

[323] Ibid.

[324] Ibid.

[325] Ibid., 200.

[326] Pierre Teilhard de Chardin qtd. in O'Connor, *Habit*, 521.

[327] O'Connor, *Habit*, 327.

cataclysmic textual resolutions give way to an impending progress to occur extratextually within a space as speculative as Roman Limbo. The narratives' supertemporality suggests that conflicts which exist between the incoherent desires of the individuized self and the cohesive impetus of the universe might be interrupted by death, but they are not extinguished by it.

O'Connor's fictive purgatory is begun in life by each of her "interleckchuls," but for many of her lapsed Protestants it commences in death or in a terrible proximity to the death of another.[328] The independent business women, Mrs. May, Mrs. Flood, and Mrs. McIntyre each partake of a cosmology which begins and ends in the individuized personality. All three have actively disassociated themselves from the larger community in everything but ritualized courtesies and presume to bear no responsibility to a collective real. Their ethics are based upon a utilitarian pleasure-principle; as Mrs. Flood puts it, "what's right today is wrong tomorrow and…the time to enjoy yourself is now so long as you let others do the same."[329] She justifies her social *laissez-faire* with the remark that she is "as good…not believing in Jesus as a many a one that does."[330] Mrs. May and Mrs. McIntyre have shed their childhood faith and replaced it with an agnostic pragmatism that intimates Mrs. Flood's live-and-let-live humanism, but it also insists upon an absolute control of their respective environments and the other individuals who inhabit it. Property is made an extension of the ego which threatens to subsume the humanity of the property-less for the sake of an unobtainable mastery. Characters like Mrs. May and Mrs. McIntyre reveal the self-interested motivation of outwardly "good country people." In isolation, their actions seem to be driven by a somewhat admirable logic of practical efficiency, but cumulatively they effect horrors which subvert the prevailing culture of Protestant truism and turn the accusatory gaze of the moral majority back upon itself.

While Richard Chase and Leslie Fiedler celebrated the hero in American literature for his alien qualities, O'Connor's heroes divest the gothic tradition of its romantic flight from civilization. Fiedler defines "the typical male protagonist" of American fiction as "a man

[328] Ibid., 574.

[329] O'Connor, *Wise Blood*, 221.

[330] Ibid.

on the run, harried into the forest or out to sea, down the river or into combat—anywhere to avoid 'civilization,' which is to say, the confrontation of a man and woman which leads to the fall, to sex, marriage, and responsibility."[331] O'Connor's protagonists are not frontiers-folk in search of a strange new world. They seem, rather, to have been abandoned to a world already spent, one whose religion has collapsed beneath the weight of so many conflicting individualisms and whose manners are based, not upon a sense of collective struggle toward the good, but a crass market survivalism. Unlike the modern gothic hero, O'Connor's protagonists are associated with an originating locale; they belong somewhere and are identified by an almost irrational compulsion to hold fast or return to a particular place. So doing, the hero is at once self-isolating and self-deciphering in his collusion with place. "In general," Fiedler writes:

> the symbols and meanings [of the gothic] depend on an awareness of the spiritual isolation or the individual in a society where all communal systems of value have collapsed or have been turned into meaningless clichés. There is a basic ambivalence in the attitude of the gothic writers to the alienation which they perceive. On the one hand, their fiction projects a fear of the solitude that is the price of freedom; and on the other hand, an almost hysterical attack on all institutions which might inhibit that freedom or mitigate the solitude it breeds.[332]

O'Connor made use of the "machinery and décor" of the gothic romance, but she was by no means ambivalent to the spiritual alienations suffered by her protagonists and was famously vocal regarding its cause and aftereffect. While attentive to the limitations inherent to a character's environment and social training, she did not count these as detriments to his achieving a sense of the real which extends beyond the self. Indeed, it is by the very particulars of a discrete personality in place and time that humanity takes on a universal dimension. It would be difficult if not impossible to sympathize with a hero who exists in an abstracted locale and speaks in a language of "purely private experience."[333] Fiction, especially gothic romance, must ground itself in a strong social idiom if it is to

---

[331] Fiedler, *Love and Death in the American Novel*, 26.

[332] Ibid., 131.

[333] O'Connor, "The Catholic Novelist in the Protestant South," *Mystery*, 199.

reveal any sort of intangible reality. O'Connor remarked that many young writers, particularly in the South, "would like to set their stories in a region whose way of life seems nearer the spirit of what they think they have to say, or better, they would like to eliminate the region altogether and approach the infinite directly. But this is not even a possibility."[334]

Since the rise of Transcendentalism, American aesthetes have ventured to recreate and also to elevate the real in two ways, first by positioning the artwork's figurative mechanisms at an intersect with the mattered world and second by implying a significance considerably beyond that realm. O'Connor resisted the trend by endeavoring to show the sublimity of the art object as concurrent with matter. Even at its most symbolic turns, her fiction posits the infinite as contiguous with the finite material of the story, not as an exceptional, objectified extension of material reality. She considered the dislocation of self from locality for the sake of artistic objectivity a damaging disregard for the creatureliness of man and the substantive way he perceives and makes sense of the universe. O'Connor's instinct was always to sink into place—a likely result of her orthodoxy regarding the Last Days. The Second Coming does not herald the spontaneous creation of a new world but the transfiguration of the old by which all matter, animate and inert, becomes completely realized. Being is eternally conserved in time and brought to an absolute state of synchronicity by the "full biological reality [of] love," in Chardin's words "the affinity of being with being."[335]

O'Connor's sacramental worldview has been criticized as an artistic limitation despite her counter-claim that her commitment to Catholic doctrine left her "free entirely to observe, ...to look at the [world] we already have and to show exactly what [I] see..."[336] When she delivered her talk "The Catholic Novelist in the Protestant South" at Georgetown, an audience member remarked that the concept *Catholic novel* was a limiting one and that the novelist, like Whitman, should be alien to nothing. "All I could say to him," O'Connor recalled, "was, 'Well, I'm alien to a great deal.' 'We are limited human beings,' she went on to say, 'and the novel is a

---

[334] Ibid., 198.

[335] Chardin, *The Phenomenon of Man,* 264.

[336] O'Connor, "Catholic Novelists and Their Readers," *Mystery,* 178.

product of our best limitations. We write with the whole personality, and any attempt to rise above belief or above background, is going to result in a reduced approach to reality.'"[337] In his study *The American Novel and Its Tradition*, Chase concurs that fiction divorced from the social reality of men can only produce melodrama. "It is [the] thick collaboration of the strands of human experience which makes a 'culture,'" he writes, "and it is this sense of a culture or the illusion of one that makes the context of tragedy. Without it you have melodrama which might be called tragedy in a vacuum."[338] O'Connor was fundamentally dependent upon the South as an informing culture. The mechanical orthodoxy of her fiction, reminiscent of the religious fatalism of the Greeks, has its basis in her contrasting the mythos of Southern and catholic religions. Like the ancient dramatists, O'Connor evoked the sublime through a ritualized stylization of her perceived real. Mr. Fortune's forsaken woods are envisaged as "gaunt trunks...raised in a pool of red light."[339] Asbury Fox's illusions are "torn" free by a "fierce" bird-shaped water stain.[340] An "old sow" and her brood reveal a "secret life" to Ruby Turpin.[341] The biblical motifs in these and other stories establish a figurative connect between O'Connor's fictive South and scriptural symbolism. They bring the tragic aspect of the Christian narrative to the fore, which is to say that sacrifice alone can effect salvation. Sacrifice is set to motion in O'Connor by a prevailing ignorance in man, the pride of self which presumes to bend the real so definitely it is no longer an immovable plane upon which a man acts but a hyper-reality of his own making. Whether man's desires are as virtuous as Sophocles's Antigone or as whimsically selfish as those of O'Connor's fictive grandmother, tragedy reveals man as indefatigably romantic; he will long for what he has judged should be rather than what is.

As O'Connor attests in her fiction, mankind's collective delusion of impending satisfaction plays out in a borderland between the now

---

337 O'Connor, "The Catholic Novelist in the Protestant South," *Mystery*, 193.

338 Richard Chase, *The American Novel and Its Tradition* (Baltimore: Johns Hopkins University Press, 1957) 41.

339 O'Connor, "A View of the Woods," *Complete*, 348.

340 O'Connor, "The Enduring Chill," *Complete*, 382.

341 O'Connor, "Revelation," *Complete*, 508.

shadowy Deism of the "Christian" state and the media made hyper-realities of post-capitalism. "The American writer," Fiedler writes:

> inhabits a country at once the dream of Europe and a fact of history; he lives on the last horizon of an endlessly retreating vision of innocence—on the "frontier," which is to say, the margin where the theory of original goodness and the fact of original sin come face to face. To express this "blackness ten times black" and to live by it in a society in which, since the decline of orthodox Puritanism, optimism has become the chief effective religion, is a complex and difficult task.[342]

O'Connor also links the degradation of the modern's dramatic sense with the paling of his religious orthodoxy, though she would likely have extended Fiedler's "decline" retroactively to include the fallout from the Great Schism. Christian orthodoxy was thereby radically effected by the pressures of individual interpreters, the most divisive of which—Rome's demand for papal infallibility—signifies a more general movement in Christian culture toward personally inflected heterodoxies. In the arts, "the older and more accurate idea of tragic movement," Lynch noted, "has been completely reversed both in theory and practice" so that the "dignity and strength of man [which] had been the subject material of first acts" is now the subject of the last.[343] The "tragic figures" of the modern narrative have become "incurably romantic" and "vaguely theological," "vindicated by neither history nor experience."[344] "Ours is an age," Gable adds, "of case histories. Characters in fiction are not responsible to a Supreme Being; they simply have experiences."[345] And yet there is an impulse, not sated by naturalism, to divine a universal significance from the typical. "There is," O'Connor wrote, "something in us, as storytellers and as listeners to stories, that demands the redemptive act, that demands that what falls at least be offered the chance to be restored. The reader of today looks for this motion, and rightly so, but what he has forgotten is the cost of it."[346]

---

[342] Fiedler, *Love and Death in the American Novel,* 27.

[343] Lynch, *Christ and Apollo,* 70.

[344] Ibid.

[345] Mariella Gable, O.S.B., "Ecumenic Core in Flannery O'Connor's Fiction," *The American Benedictine Review* 15/2 (June 1964): 131.

[346] O'Connor, "Some Aspects of the Grotesque in Southern Fiction," *Mystery,* 48.

O'Connor was famously critical of the "general" (American) reader, citing his dulled aesthetic sensibilities as the motive for her literary antagonisms. Her fiction portrays the so-called American way of life as long on Christian rhetoric and short on actual charity, a culture based upon a false religious homogeneity that justifies the fierce individualism of its market culture with moral cliché. "To affirm the possibility of dissent," Bacon argues, "...O'Connor had to distinguish her form of religion from the ones that dominated American culture during the 1950s. *Wise Blood* attacks the dominant forms, suggesting that American religion had been appropriated by the 'salesman's world.'"[347] If O'Connor was to engage the American psyche, she had also to engage the tradition of romantic, totalizing narratives that describe the nation's origin, its purpose, and its destiny. Although it seemed a somewhat unrealistic narrative in an era defined by social scape-goating, the mythos of the New Jerusalem remained a primary shaper of the modern American identity, whether an individual responds to the myth unaffectedly or ironically. Underlying the American legend is a presumption to divine right by means of a determined, mutual individualism. Here and here alone can man aspire to previously unthinkable freedoms and to the credit of the national blessing that he has an inalienable right to pursue his own happiness, however destructive it may be to the collective good. The transmission of these values in American politics and popular culture has installed a distinct sense of participation in the individual, a sense of organic inclusion in the national folkway. Persistent in her orthodoxy, O'Connor linked American post-Christianity with the historical bearing of the Judaeo-Christian tradition. She wrote, "has formed us in the west; we are bound to it by ties which may often be invisible, but which are there nonetheless. It has formed the shape of our secularism; it has formed even the shape of modern atheism."[348] Every social posture effected by modern man was, to O'Connor's mind, an outgrowth of the biblical drama. He is as easily swayed by false deity as the Edomites of Baal, as covetous of earthly power as Herod, and potentially as wicked. Such a resolved literalism distinguished O'Connor's orthodoxy from a more conventional American Christianity,

---

[347] Bacon, "A Fondness for Supermarkets...," 39.

[348] O'Connor, "Novelist and Believer," *Mystery*, 155.

including parochial Catholicism, which tended to allegorize scriptural history. The civically-minded state religion emphasized moral righteousness (the Law), but O'Connor's orthodoxy, rather like the prophesying of a churchless Fundamentalism, was intent upon the filial nature of creation (God's originating love). Her Thomist humanism stood in particular contrast to the state's religious pragmatism whereby the mystical elements of orthodoxy are whittled down to indiscriminate moral aphorisms. Christianity thus intellectualized speaks to only half the man, that half which is governed by reason, and leaves the unreasonable soul, which is moved by love, touched only superficially by a depersonalized sentiment. Ironically the American gospel demands of itself brotherly love but values that love for its utility alone, which is to say its ability to dispose the intellect to noble activity (the propagation of a material goodwill) and disregards the negative efficacy of love, that is the irrational compulsion of men to act for the sake of an immaterial good. One has only to compare the philosophies of St. Thomas and Ben Franklin to appreciate the distance between catholic and American perceptions of the good. "[A]ll Franklin's moral attitudes," Max Weber writes in his famed *Protestant Ethic,* "are coloured with utilitarianism. Honesty is useful, because it assures credit; so are punctuality, industry, and frugality, and that is the reason that they are virtues. ...[A]n unnecessary surplus of...virtue would evidently appear to Franklin's eyes to be an unproductive waste."[349] St. Thomas, on the other hand, showed more concern for what man could make of himself as opposed to what he could make for himself. His intellectual facilities, no matter how useful, are not the primary motivator of the good. "[L]ove, which pertains to the will," he wrote, "is a more intense motion than knowledge, which pertains to the intellect, because knowledge assimilates but love transforms..."[350]

O'Connor described the transformative power of love in terms of mankind's inimitable liberty, recalling Aquinas' contention that "free will does not mean one will, but many wills conflicting in one man."[351] "Freedom," even when it is wielded by one as apparently

[349] Max Weber, *The Protestant Ethic and the Spirit of Capitalism,* trans. Talcott Parsons (Mineola: Courier Dover Publications, 2003) 52.

[350] St. Thomas Aquinas, *Selected,* 554.

[351] O'Connor, "Author's Note to the Second Edition," *Wise Blood,* 6.

remorseless as the Misfit, "cannot be conceived simply."[352] It is bent ultimately upon reparation in love, but in the space of a lifetime, or indeed a short narrative, its ends are left incomplete, hinted at, but never consummated by the final act. "Miss O'Connor leaves her fictions open to the real world finally," Montgomery concludes. "Even her agents have left open to them a final contingency: Hell or Purgatory."[353] To her credit, O'Connor does not differentiate between salvation theologies; nowhere does she insinuate that a particular doctrinal model—Catholic, Protestant, or Orthodox—is more or less beneficial to her heroes' self-revelation. Indeed, her most developed characters preach a strange fusion of pre-Enlightenment orthodoxy and Southern Protestantism. "In yourself right now," Hazel Motes says, "is all the place you've got. If there was any Fall, look there, and if there was any Redemption, look there, and if you expect any Judgment, look there, because they all three will have to be in your time and your body and where in your time and your body can they be?"[354] Hazel's synchronistic collusion of biblical history, prophesy, and real time calls to mind the liturgical practice of the Eastern and Roman churches while his conclusive skepticism suggests Protestant empiricism. Mason Tarwater affords another example of O'Connor's ecumenism. He secrets himself in the woods of Powderhead to "thrash…out his peace with the Lord" like a modern Jerome but prophesies with a distinctly Protestant vocabulary, using idiomatic phrases like "the bread of life" and the "Redemption."[355] Even determinably anti-religious characters like George Rayber and Asbury Fox demonstrate flashes of various modes of Christian indoctrination.

O'Connor orientated her narratives as if a more traditionalist biblical discourse was still at the centre of American ideology despite its being beset on all sides by a competing secular-humanism. Orthodoxy, like Mason Tarwater's, was an entity verging on extinction. In response, O'Connor was happy to show that in the supposed heartland of Christian fanaticism, secularism was winning the day and not least in the rural South. One might expect a certain

---

[352] Ibid.

[353] Montgomery, "Flannery O'Connor and the Jansenist Problem in Fiction," 448.

[354] O'Connor, *Wise Blood*, 166.

[355] O'Connor, *Violent*, 16, 19.

religious disengagement in urban communities, but O'Connor overturns the city/country binary: more than half of her non-believers are country folk. She demonstrates the extent to which both settings have assimilated the commercial rhetoric of modern secular discourse. The advertisement was among her favorite devices, and she used its ubiquity to draw an ironic parallel between the hectic neon of the city and the grim biblical forewarnings of the backwater. In *Wise Blood,* these signs appear unfailingly at moments of transition, first when Hazel enters the foreign city, the determined no-preacher, and again when he escapes it in the high rat-colored Essex. Their function is double-headed, pointing on the one hand to the superficial action of a consumption-based culture and on the other to the ancestral worship of sacred signs. Hazel is bombarded when he disembarks the train by "frantic" electric lights which read: "PEANUTS, WESTERN UNION, AJAX, HOTEL, CANDY, ...WHITE."[356] The billboards and shop fronts in Taulkinham entice with a bold-faced literalness, identifying Hazel as consumer and alerting him to what he needs and why. "For the most part," Bacon writes, "[M]aterialism defines the existence of Hazel and the other characters [in *Wise Blood*]. Their lives are circumscribed by the material world, understood in two ways—as a world in which the spiritual has no place, as a world in which everything is for sale."[357] Such commercial inscriptions imply a tangible lack in Hazel and suggest as reparation a simple equation of exchange, but the signs he encounters on hay sheds and roadside markers in the second half of the novel are underwritten with ambiguity. Their message is of a different pitch entirely, advertising immaterial needs suggestive of a metaphysical lack that persists despite man's material saturation.

Hazel's reaction to the modern scene—his combative rejection of established religious and secular ideologies and his eventual divining of a personal Jesus—is prototypical of what might be called a protestant Orthodoxy. When he is met by a particular declarative marker in the novel's penultimate chapter, Hazel responds in a manner not unlike the Misfit's.[358] He "saw" that it said "Jesus Died for YOU" and "deliberately did not read [it]."[359] The intimacy of such

---

[356] O'Connor, *Wise Blood*, 29–30.

[357] Bacon, "A Fondness for Supermarkets...," 35.

[358] Ibid., 207.

[359] Ibid.

a decisive proclamation is offensive to Hazel's insistently discrete rationale. If Christ had in fact died for the sake of an indiscriminate "YOU," the self-preserving logic of biological man is "thrown…off balance."[360] Rather than accept the personal responsibility inherent to a Jesus-altered universe, Hazel attempts to recreate the real in a Church Without Christ, a "church that the blood of Jesus doesn't foul with redemption."[361]

Like the Misfit, Hazel was not a born blasphemer, but lacking substantial proof of his inherited faith, he seeks justification in the world. At the age of ten, he makes his first test of the Motes's fire and brimstone evangelism by enacting a secret repentance, not subtly reminiscent of the Desert Fathers'. Transgressing beyond a second inner veil, Haze peers down into a "lowered place" at a fat woman "squinting" in a black-lined casket.[362] His mother sets upon him with a stick as soon as he returns home. Thighs still smarting from his mother's punishing blow, Hazel begins to conceive of his sin, not as an immediate and peculiar transgression, but as a wrong accountable to all men. He "forgot the guilt of [beholding the naked woman in] the tent for the nameless unplaced guilt that was in him" and responds with self-mortification. He fills his heavy church shoes with stones, laces them up tightly, and walks a mile through the woods.[363] Mrs. Motes's chastisement had been ineffectual. "Jesus died to redeem you," she'd said, letting the rod fly, and Hazel had been "like part of the tree" he'd "stood flat against," unmoved and muttering, "I never ast him [sic]."[364] He is skeptical of the puritanical enthusiasm of American Protestantism for executing divine judgment and seeks instead the direct pronouncement of God in a self-determined, solitary subjection. Alone in the wilderness with his pain, Hazel "thought, that ought to satisfy Him."[365] But "[n]othing happened. If a stone had fallen he would have taken it for a sign," but it did not.[366]

Hazel is unique to O'Connor in that he persists in his anticipation of signs despite their reluctance to appear at will. He is a

---

[360] O'Connor, "A Good Man Is Hard to Find," *Complete*, 132.

[361] O'Connor, *Wise Blood*, 105.

[362] Ibid., 62.

[363] Ibid., 63.

[364] Ibid.

[365] Ibid., 63–64.

[366] Ibid., 64.

man actively without belief but faithful, and at the end of his creek-side vigil, he puts his stone-filled shoes back on and walks another half mile. The sign he anticipated—as a stone falling from the heavens—is itself remarkable because it recalls Islamic literary traditions more insistently than it does Christian ones. According to Muslim tradition, a pure white stone fell from Heaven and came to rest in the Garden of Paradise. On this sacred site, Adam and Eve erected the first house of worship. When the pair transgressed against God, the stone grew dark with sin. In the time of Noah, a Deluge was sent to purify the world of men, and the stone was taken back into Heaven and later revealed by the archangel Gabriel to Abraham.[367] The black rock is now the eastern cornerstone of Islam's holiest site, the *Ka'bah* at Mecca.[368] The structure itself predates "the historical appearance of Islam in the seventh century;" archeological "evidence suggests it did not differ significantly from other temples that had once been vital to the ancient civilizations of the Middle East, including that of Yahweh-Elohim in Jerusalem."[369]

Christian lore tells of a stone which fell from the archangel Lucifer's crown as he waged war in Heaven. The stone, known as the *lapsit exillis*, was "cut into the shape of a bowl by a faithful angel."[370] This Holy Grail is said to have been given to Adam before his expulsion from Paradise. The Crusaders called the Grail the "Blazing Star" and regarded it as a symbol of Godly omniscience as well as the fiery descent of those who covet divine knowledge.[371] Hazel's pride to authority through first-hand knowledge is as acute as The Misfit's; he reproofs supernatural Law by citing his exclusion from its human genesis. He had not requested Jesus' saving death and therefore considered himself exempt from God's demands. Nevertheless, Hazel attempts to subdue his pride by demonstrating a

---

[367] See Francis E. Peters, *Judaism, Christianity, and Islam: The Classical Texts and Their Interpretation*, Vol. III (Princeton: Princeton University Press, 1990) 112–14.

[368] *The Holy Qu'ran*, 2:125–2:128, *The Koran*, rev. ed., trans. N. J. Dawood (London: Penguin Books, 1995) 22.

[369] Juan Eduardo Campo, *Encyclopedia of Islam*, illus. ed. (New York: Infobase Publishing, 2009) 419.

[370] Julius Evola, *The Mystery of the Grail: Initiation and Magic in the Quest for the Spirit* (Rochester: Inner Traditions, 1996) 84.

[371] Albert Pike, *Morals and Dogma of the Ancient and Accepted Rite of Scottish Freemasonry* (Sioux Falls: NuVision Publications, LLC, 2004) 18–19.

visceral awareness of guilt but is unsuccessful. He waits in the underbrush of the Edenesque stream-side hollow, expecting a particular kind of divine intercession, one which alludes to the creation of a church but also foreshadows a more substantial fall,Hazel's initiation of a Godless church and his eventual rejection of a subverted faith of "no truth."[372]

After running down Solace Layfield with his rat-colored Essex, Hazel sets out for a city not yet enlightened by his preaching. He explains to a gas station attendant that "it was not right to believe anything you couldn't see or hold in your hands or test with your teeth. He said he had only a few days ago believed in blasphemy as the way to salvation, but that you couldn't believe in that because then you were believing in something to blaspheme."[373] Hazel has destroyed the emblem of the civil religion and with it the false prophecy of Onnie Jay's "Holy Church of Christ Without Christ," that is "if you want to get anywheres [sic] in religion, you got to keep it sweet."[374] Onnie Jay succeeds where Hazel fails; he is a true believer in the Cult of Progress. He sees "how a new [jesus]," one which "unlocked that little rose of sweetness inside you," "would be more up-to-date."[375] Mankind, for O. J. Holy, achieves significance by moving forward, creating new faiths to complement each new age, not by looking back, as Hazel is compelled to do, to the morbid practices of a less advanced religion. "It don't make any difference how many Christs you add," Onnie Jay proclaims, "...if you don't add none to the meaning, friend."[376] "The unredeemed are redeeming theirselves [sic] and the new jesus is at hand!"[377] Even in his aspiration to unbelief, Hazel resists the aptly named Shoats' revisionist blasphemy. "There's no such thing as any new Jesus," Motes insists. "That ain't anything but a way to say something."[378] There is only one Jesus in the gospel of Hazel Motes, and "[n]othing matters but that [He] was a liar," he declares.[379]

---

[372] O'Connor, *Wise Blood*, 165.

[373] Ibid., 206.

[374] Ibid., 157.

[375] Ibid., 153, 158.

[376] Ibid., 157.

[377] Ibid., 167.

[378] Ibid., 158.

[379] Ibid., 105, 148, 152.

Assured that his word of no truth can repeal the Word of the gospel, Hazel invests himself in the rhetorical freedoms of that peculiarly American ambition—the private automobile. "Nobody with a good car needs to be justified."[380] "Nobody with a good car need[s] to worry about anything..."[381] But Hazel did not have a good car. The Essex had "a leak in the gas tank and two in the radiator" and a puncture in one of the rear tires, but all the same he is intent to imagine that he and the automobile have a common destiny. The two will co-animate one another into new life, Hazel willing the car into action and the machine bestowing upon him its vague authority. "[T]his car is just beginning life," he remarks to the station attendant as if it were a spirited thing. "A lightning bolt couldn't stop it!"[382]

Hazel's boast invokes the Devil's legendary fall. In the gospel of Luke, Jesus tells his disciples, "I beheld Satan as lightening fall from heaven."[383] The young prophet and his fast-expiring Essex are doomed to meet with a comparably sinister authority, and before Motes can breach the town limits a "red pleasant face[d]" patrolman pulls him over.[384] He demands a license Hazel does not have and then lures him onto an embankment and out of the car. "I think you could see better if you was out," the patrolman says, heralding the immediate destruction of Motes's vision to freedom and his coming blindness. He pushes the Essex over the embankment, and it breaks apart in the "burnt pasture" below.[385] With the physical momentum of his ideology in pieces, Hazel's "knees bent under him;" his face "reflected the entire distance across the clearing and beyond," from the over-turned car and the charred pasture, to the "blank gray sky that went on, depth after depth, into space."[386] His mission of no truth had run up against the hard fact of evil, an evil which, for no reason other than meanness, had single-handedly obliterated the totem of his spiritual sovereignty. The only direction Hazel has left to travel is inward, and to make permanent that pilgrimage, he blinds himself with lime. Hazel's landlady, the Sodom-evoking Mrs. Flood,

---

[380] Ibid., 113.
[381] Ibid., 206.
[382] Ibid., 207.
[383] Luke 10:18, *KJV*.
[384] O'Connor, *Wise Blood*, 208.
[385] Ibid., 209.
[386] Ibid.

wonders "what possible reason [a] sane person [could] have for wanting to not enjoy himself anymore?"[387]

Wise Blood somewhat aggressively draws the reader's attention to the constructedness of both secular and religious discourse and to the strange symbiotic relationship between these two. "In fact," Weber argued:

> the *summum bonum* of [the Protestant] ethic, the earning of more and more money, combined with the strict avoidance of all spontaneous enjoyment in life, is above all completely devoid of any eudæmonistic, not to say hedonistic, admixture. It is thought of so purely as an end in itself, that from the point of view of the happiness of, or utility to, the single individual, it appears entirely transcendental and absolutely irrational. Man is dominated by the making of money, by acquisition as the ultimate purpose in life. Economic acquisition is no longer subordinated to man as the means for the satisfaction of his material needs.[388]

The "natural relationship" between man and his vocation is reversed so that the means of his striving for material success becomes the end of his spiritual actualization.[389] "The earning of money within the modern economic order," Weber attested, "is, so long as it is done legally, the result and the expression of virtue and proficiency in a calling; and this virtue and proficiency are the real Alpha and Omega..."[390] What's more, religion itself, in one form or another, has always been big business in the United States, and big business is made bigger—particularly in the South—by its pronouncement of God-entrustedness. The more the American ethic grew in its association with economic freedom, the more it distanced itself, practically and semantically, from its initially Puritanical motivations.[391] By mid-century, "President Eisenhower's Council of Economic Advisors Chairman [Arthur F. Burns declared that], 'the American economy's ultimate purpose [was] to produce more

---

[387] Ibid., 211.

[388] Weber, *The Protestant Ethic and the Spirit of Capitalism,* 53.

[389] Ibid.

[390] Ibid., 54.

[391] Bakhtin noted a similar shift in the Renaissance when the "manifestations of this life [in literature] refer...to the isolated biological individual," or to put an even finer point on it, "the private, egotistic 'economic man'" (*Rabelais and His World,* trans. Hélène Iswolsky [Bloomington: Indiana University Press, 1984] 19).

consumer goods,'" a very different mandate than that of Jefferson's humanist deism.[392] If the idea of America was still contained by the image of John Winthrop's "City on a Hill," it was because of the salable value of the hill itself, not the spiritual value of a symbolic proximity to God.

O'Connor's fiction documents precisely this twilight aspect of the national consciousness—the mytho-religious impulse—which America has worked so actively to exorcise from its "progressive liberalism." She concurred with her friend, Roman convert Allen Tate, that the ascendant faith in material progress was a "bad" one because it reduces creation to a function of "infallible" utility and can prescribe only consumptive ends.[393] "We know," Tate wrote:

> that the cult of infallible working is a religion because it sets up an irrational value; it is irrational to believe in omnipotent human rationality. Nothing infallibly works, and the new half-religionists are simply worshiping a principle, and with true half-religious fanaticism they ignore what they do not want to see—which is the breakdown of the principle in numerous instances of practice. It is a bad religion, for that very reason; it can predict only success.[394]

Conversely, the religion of the "whole" man predicts both success and defeat by taking into account inevitable "failures."[395] It is "realistic" in a manner completely foreign to the prevailing Calvinist-derived ethic; where the latter divides humanity into heathen and Elect, the religion of the whole man (which has the look of Christian orthodoxy) considers mankind as a common race evenly beset by "the traditional experience of evil."[396] "The concrete evidence of the human being," Robert Heilman contested, "is that he does not change much, that he may actually be harmed by the material phenomenon usually implied by progress, and that in any case his liability to moral difficulty remains constant."[397]

The so-called Southern Fall seems to have encouraged a certain moral skepticism with regard to the self-Electing American gospel,

---

[392] Arthur F. Burns qtd. in Annie Leonard, director, *The Story of Stuff,* 2009.

[393] Tate, "Remarks," 158.

[394] Ibid.

[395] Ibid., 159.

[396] Ibid.

[397] Heilman, "The Southern Temper," 6.

but that skepticism was felt most insistently in the region's least reputable of subcultures: the "shouting fundamentalists."[398] O'Connor suggested having discerned "a good deal more kinship with backwoods prophets" then "with those politer elements [in the mainstream] for whom…religion has become a department of sociology or personality development."[399] "It seems to me," she wrote, "that the Catholic Southerner's experience of living so intimately with the division of Christendom is an experience that can give much breadth and poignance to the novels he may produce."[400] She departs from the "felt superiority of orthodoxy" inherent to parochial Catholicism in her recognition of "the human aspiration" of "faith and passion" that manifests itself in the "extreme individualism" of "Southern life."[401] Writing catholically is not a case of "subtract[ing] one theology from another" but of realizing the "invisible Church" in its broadest spectrum.[402] "These [Protestant] people," she was convinced, "make discoveries that have meaning for us" not in spite of the idiosyncrasy of their doctrines, but very likely because of it.[403]

By mid-century, the United States could effectively be called a "post-Christian" culture in which even the Bible Belt South was enthusiastically exchanging the most basic of Christian traditions for a theoretical church whose priorities were social integration and a radical open-endedness.[404] The Universalist and Unitarian Churches which were conjoined in the late fifties proclaimed a "universal reconciliation" amenable to orthodoxy but challenged the conception of God as triune in nature, at times positing modalist and pantheist manifestations. Universalism also rejected the traditional concept of Hell, Roman Purgatory and the related notion of in-death purification of Eastern Orthodoxy as well as certain liturgical rites including Chrismation and Confirmation. Of the seven orthodox sacraments only two, Baptism and the Holy Eucharist, were retained,

---

[398] O'Connor, "The Catholic Novelist in the Protestant South," *Mystery*, 207.

[399] Ibid.

[400] Ibid., 206.

[401] Ibid.

[402] Ibid., 207.

[403] Ibid.

[404] Ibid., 209.

but their exact nature was the cause of sustained debate within opposing sects and were popularly considered to be non-sacramental memorials of Christ's sacrificial death and resurrection as opposed to intimations of His Real Presence.[405] In effect, Jesus was reduced to the status of "teacher," an ironical model citizen who is remembered for his sermons of unifying peace, not his razing of the Temple. Dislocated from its scriptural roots, "Free Thinking Christian[ty]" approached inevitable moral difficulties, not with a historical sense of providential significance, but with despair or a misplaced hope for Instant Uplift.[406] O'Connor observed that the religious sense was "bred out" of her compatriots "double quick by the religious substitutes for religion."[407] In stories like "The Displaced Person" and "The Life You Save May Be Your Own," she carries the rationale of modernity's half-religions to their logical conclusion, which is to say that man is self-perfectible to the point of global genocide and catastrophic economic depression. Here was the advanced human sensibility self-destructing on an almost inconceivable scale despite the cheerful sloganing of international commerce. The "ills and mysteries of life" had not "fall[en] before the scientific advances of man."[408] On the contrary, O'Connor's was "the first generation to face total extinction because of these advances."[409] The modern age was one afflicted by a sense of pandemic suffering, as if, O'Connor mused, "the whole world… [was] going through a dark night of the soul."[410]

Flannery's antidote came in a form most jarring to the modern conceit by revealing man, in spite of his industrial triumphalism, as merely human. She resisted the editorial call for American writers to create a species of men befitting the "strongest nation in the world" who reflect the joys of "unparalleled prosperity" and an "almost classless society."[411] "The writer whose position is Christian, and

---

[405] The Anglican Church is exceptional among Protestant sects in its affirmation of the Real Presence in the Communion rite irrespective of transubstantiation.

[406] O'Connor, *Habit*, 407; and "Novelist and Believer," *Mystery*, 165.

[407] O'Connor, *Habit*, 300.

[408] O'Connor, "Some Aspects of the Grotesque in Southern Fiction," *Mystery*, 48, 41.

[409] Ibid., 41.

[410] O'Connor, *Habit*, 100.

[411] O'Connor, "The Fiction Writer and His Country," *Mystery*, 29–30.

probably also the writer whose position is not," O'Connor hazarded, "will begin to wonder...if there could not be some ugly correlation between our unparalleled prosperity and the stridency of these demands for a literature that shows us the joy of life. He may at least be permitted to ask if these screams for joy would be quite so piercing if joy were really more abundant in our society."[412] O'Connor's aim, quite to the contrary of *Life* magazine's 1957 mandate, was not merely to show man at his ease in the modern scene but to dramatize the whole man beneath and beyond his material illusions. "What these editorial writers fail to realize," she said, "is that the writer who emphasizes spiritual values is very likely to take the darkest view of all of what he sees in this country today. For him, the fact that we are the most powerful and the wealthiest nation in the world doesn't mean a thing in a positive sense."[413]

At a remove from the religious mainstream, O'Connor was particularly attentive to the disassociation between the ideological ambition of American Christianity, that is to create a Kingdom of Heaven on earth, and modernity's religious economics. Any mystical implication of "man return[ing]...to the state God created him in" was being steadily displaced by the presumption that the Kingdom, in the shape of material convenience in surplus, had been realized.[414] The self-prioritizing aspect of human nature was envisaged as a condition fortuitous to the market culture, not as a spiritual detriment. Indeed, the materialist religion functions by "leaving out" or heroizing "the terrible radical human pride that causes death."[415] The Southern canon gives us the example of men like Thomas Sutpen and Ty Ty Walden, the tragic gallant and fool respectively, brought to ruin by the *ignis fatuus* of a salable peace. O'Connor's critique of American acquisitiveness is more nuanced. When Mrs. May and Mark Fortune attempt to preserve and supplement private ownership, it is with the intention of promoting a general prosperity in which "Christian" values of duty and propriety are transmitted by example. By no coincidence do they affect a damning semblance of control while invoking the blessing of Progress.

---

[412] Ibid., 30.

[413] Ibid., 26.

[414] O'Connor, *Habit*, 307.

[415] Ibid.

According to the laws of O'Connor's fictive universe, individuals act out of a willful depravity regardless of whether they are conspiring to power like Francis Tarwater and Tom T. Shiftlet or clinging to it like Mrs. May and Mrs. McIntyre. Nevertheless, O'Connor's stories are full of hope for the life of the whole man, even if it is often a hope for "life-in-death."[416] In a fashion not unlike the gospels of the New Testament, O'Connor's narratives employ simple naturalistic analogies to correlate relatively unexceptional human experiences with extraordinary instances of sublime intercession. Upon this intersecting plane of experience, the extraordinary exists in real time. O. E. Parker's theophany manifests itself in a dawning sky, Asbury Fox's in a water stain, and Ruby Turpin's in a pig parlor. As St. Mark did in his gospel, O'Connor was careful to differentiate between *chronos*, the "ordinary passing moments of time," and *chairos*, "the moment of opportunity."[417] She described this point of collusion as the "peculiar crossroads where time and place and eternity somehow meet."[418] To effect such an expansive vision, one capable of implying in its depth of structure the intersection of the infinite with the human experience of time, O'Connor developed a narrative strategy in which human action is raised to the power of ultimate significance. "I have discovered that what is needed to make stories 'work,'" she wrote in 1961:

> is an action that is totally unexpected, yet totally believable; it would have to be one that was both in character and beyond character; it would have to suggest both the world and eternity. ...While predictable, predetermined actions [manners] have a comic interest for me, it is the free act, the acceptance of grace particularly, that I always have my eye on...[419]

The actions and reactions of personalities to the a-religious existential crises of the modern scene were O'Connor's primary interest. In spite of the fact that modern civilization in the West was "exactly a setting in which nothing is so little felt to be true as the reality of a faith in Christ," O'Connor did not attempt to recreate or

---

[416] O'Connor, "The Nature and Aim of Fiction," *Mystery*, 72.

[417] Patrick J. Flanagan, *The Gospel of Mark Made Easy* (Mahwah: Paulist Press, 1997) 31.

[418] O'Connor, "The Regional Writer," *Mystery*, 59.

[419] O'Connor, "In the Devil's Territory," *Mystery*, 115, 118.

abandon the contemporary scene.[420] On the contrary, she was decidedly beholden to modern conventions, both material and social, in her endeavors "in making the divinity of Christ seem consistent with the structure of all reality."[421] The author's interlinking of Roman terminology, in particular the words grace and mystery, with her poetics remains a point of contention for that line of criticism intent upon reading the author as doctrinaire Catholic. While the term grace implies an indebtedness to the liturgical rhetoric of the Church, e.g. the apostolic tradition and the more general process of denotation by way of dialogue within the parish, O'Connor maintained that grace is a reality that cannot be "experienced in itself" either spontaneously or by means of doctrinal rituals.[422] "[W]hen you go to Communion," she explained to Hester in 1958, "you receive grace but experience nothing; or if you do experience something, what you experience is not grace but an emotion caused by it. Therefore in a story all you can do with grace is to show it is changing a character."[423]

The concept of Christian mystery is itself deliberately indistinct and common to all orthodox traditions. The Mysteries of the faith—the Immaculate Conception, the Incarnation, the Resurrection and Ascension, and the Assumption of Saint Mary—are to be beheld (albeit at a remove through the symbolic practices of the Holy Liturgy) and meditated upon but not explained. The Catholic reverence of mystery so often associated with the Medieval Church can be traced still further to the tribal worship of the Hebrews, the contemplative asceticism of the Copts and Desert Fathers, and the Orthodox invocation of the uncreated energies of God. The Eastern Church tellingly "follow[s] the Greek *mysterion*" in its declaration of the sacraments and does not place as much differential emphasis upon institutional and private conferrals of grace as the Roman tradition.[424] Jesuit theologian Dennis Smolarski attests that in Orthodox teaching:

---

[420] O'Connor, *Habit*, 290.

[421] Ibid.

[422] Ibid., 275.

[423] Ibid.

[424] Dennis Chester Smolarski, *Sacred Mysteries: Sacramental Principles and Liturgical Practice* (Mahwah: Paulist Press, 1995) 1.

> the various liturgical rites called *sacraments* or *mysteries* only mirror the ultimate mystery of Christ and his sacrificial life, death, and resurrection. And in a sense, whatever mirrors the presence of Christ and the power of God in our world can be considered a *sacred mystery*, whether it is a sacred gesture, such as the imposition of hands, a sacred object, such as an icon, or a sacred activity, such as proclaiming the word.[425]

We are reminded by Smolarski of the "imposition" of the grandmother's hands, of O. E. Parker's fleshy icon, and of the Tarwaters' preaching of the Word. The Protestant Church traditionally recognizes only two liturgical sacraments, the Baptism and the Lord's Supper, and some sects, the Quakers, for instance, have forgone sacramental worship entirely, yet it is from this point of contention that O'Connor draws a line of affinity between orthodox and Protestant traditions. For better or worse, prophets like Hazel Motes and the Tarwaters do not delimit their search for Christ to scripture or liturgy and are conferred their respective "sacraments" by a world very much outside of the institutional church. Documenting the sacramental real almost to the exclusion of Roman practice alienated O'Connor somewhat from her co-catechumens. "A good many Catholics," she observed, "are put off [by *The Violent Bear It Away*] because they think the old man, being a Protestant prophet, so to speak, has no hold of the truth. They look at everything in a confessional way…"[426] O'Connor did not conceive so narrowly of Christian truth and determined to show, regardless of her own confession, the sacramental life in vigorous attendance amongst non-sacramental Christians.

O'Connor's orthodoxy shared a further ancestral link to Celtic Christianity which grew out of an insular spiritual geography untouched by the invading armies of the Roman Empire. From the advent of St. Patrick in the early fifth century to the conciliar streamlining of the faith in the early tenth century, Christianity in Ireland was propagated by a decentered, wandering church which imagined itself as a dynamic organism reflexive of the universe as the "transfigured image of God."[427] Although she balked at the

---

[425] Ibid.

[426] O'Connor, *Habit*, 536.

[427] Anthony Duncan, *The Elements of Celtic Christianity* (Longmead: Element Books Ltd., 1992) 74, 76.

American obsession with Irishness, particularly the "Over Irish" well-to-do in her birthplace of Savannah, O'Connor was heir to the mythos of middle Ireland which her great-grandparents, both maternal and paternal, carried with them from County Tipperary. Her paternal grandfather and great-grandfather, John Flannery and Patrick O'Connor, and her maternal grandfather and great-grandfather, Peter James Cline and Hugh Donnelly Treanor, immigrated from a famine-gripped Ireland to Georgia in the mid-1800s.[428] The most enduring of customs to survive their journey were the families' ancestral Catholic faith and the exceptional lyricism of Hibernian English. The native Irish idiom constitutes a circuitous story-bent manner which evolved from Old and Middle Irish grammatical structures and, during the British occupation of the island, the *Geailge* speaker's begrudgingly becoming an English speaker.

Emblematic of the Irish language is the way in which its grammar seems to encourage embellishment through indirection. Breaks between clauses and implications of a change of state invite the speaker to create a scenario. In this way, little amongst the Irish is merely said; rather it is told. Whether or not O'Connor's immediate ancestors spoke *as Gaeilge*, they would have inherited indirectly this sense of language as essentially a telling device. Their resistance to the denotative nature of English is characterized by their manner of naming things. The descriptive nuance of the language inclined early Irish Catholicism toward an object relative mysticism. The mystery of a thing's beingness, preserved through the tellingness of the language, predisposed the Irish to that most Christian of mysteries, the Incarnation.

Critics such as Christina Bieber Lake and Warren Coffey insist that if O'Connor inherited anything from her Irish line, it was a "decidedly 'Jansenist' cast of mind."[429] The author herself described Irish Catholics as particularly "infected" with a "love of asceticism" because "all of the Jansenist priests were chased out of France at the

---

[428] Melissa Simpson, *Flannery O'Connor: A Biography*, 2.

[429] Ibid., 84. See also Lake, *The Incarnational Art of Flannery O'Connor*, 22; Warren Coffey quoted in Marion Montgomery, *Why Flannery O'Connor Stayed Home: The Prophetic Poet and the Spirit of the Age* (Peru: Sherwood Sugden and Co., 1981) 234.

time of the Revolution and ended up in Ireland."[430] Rev. Brian Van Hove argues, nonetheless, that, "There is no reason to believe Ireland was an outpost for Jansenism as we understand it."[431] I suspect that O'Connor's distancing herself from the Irish Church had a good deal to do with its presumably Calvinist cast, but the characterization of Irish Catholics as guilt-mongering ascetics is a misleading one. Van Hove draws a distinction between the "cultural rigorism" of Celtic religiosity and Jansenism: "At the peak of the Jansenists' strength, Ireland was either isolated or resistant to such a movement. …[T]he Irish forged a genuine lay spirituality instead of a passive receptivity to theological ideas."[432] The revisionist view of Irish Catholicism makes Tate's initiating suggestion that O'Connor was a "temperamental" Jansenist rather unsubstantiated. His projected emphasis upon the depravity of man, especially man's salvation by fire, misinterprets O'Connor's rendering of Augustine and her narrative adaptations of Southern fundamentalism.[433] O'Connor adhered to a more "Thomistic position" which preserves the orthodox "distinction between foreknowing and forewilling," the lack of which "gives rise to Calvinist or Jansenist heresy" and the denial of "free will as well as the possibility of resisting insistent grace."[434] "One may believe, as Miss O'Connor does," Montgomery argues, "that the Misfit has a capacity for grace greater than that of the grandmother. One may even suppose the possibility, perhaps even the probability, of the Misfit's conversion; but one does not thereby conclude his rescue an inevitable dictate of inexorable grace."[435]

On this point, O'Connor's theology was in line with Vatican II in its rephrasing of a core belief of the early Church in saying, "God's free initiative demands man's free response."[436] If, O'Connor

---

[430] O'Connor, *Habit*, 304.

[431] Rev. Brian Van Hove, S.J., "Jansenism, the Liturgy, and Ireland," *Christus Regnat* 3/1 (Christmas 2009): 15–18. *www.ignatiusinsight.com*. http://www.ignatiusinsight.com/features2010/bvanhove_jansenism_jan2010.asp (accessed 13 August 2010).

[432] Ibid.

[433] Allen Tate qtd. in O'Gorman, *Peculiar Crossroads,* 104.

[434] Montgomery, "Flannery O'Connor and the Jansenist Problem in Fiction," 441.

[435] Ibid., 439.

[436] *Catechism of the Catholic Church* (London: Continuum International

speculated, a writer is to be truly "Catholic," he will "not see man as determined…[or] totally depraved. [He] will see him as incomplete in himself, as prone to evil, but as redeemable when his efforts are assisted by grace."[437] O'Connor's theology is here reminiscent of the fictive Jesuit Ignatius Vogle's who declared, "There is…a real probability of the New Man, assisted, of course, …by the Third Person of the Trinity."[438] Despite her praise of Pascal, O'Connor did not "think that the Jansenist influence [was] healthy in the Church."[439] She observed that in Ireland the movement "[did not] seem to breed so much a love of God as a love of asceticism."[440] She remained as critical of extremist Augustinism within the Roman tradition as in the Reformation movements and faulted both with operating in faith "from an incomplete understanding of sin."[441] They "seem to demand…that the Holy Ghost be translated at once into all flesh" and also that some flesh is irredeemably corrupt.[442] O'Connor pares the issue to the controversial doctrine of Original Sin, noting that "Catholics often act as if that doctrine is always perverted and always an indication of Calvinism. They read a little corruption as total corruption."[443]

O'Connor's own rendering of the doctrine emphasizes man's inheritance of the consequences of Adam's free choice but not necessarily the inheritance of his guilt. Man is not "damned by God" in O'Connor's universe; he is damned by himself.[444] The "cost" of his redemption is not penitence in guilt but in love, of bringing the free will gradually back into its original state of union with God by a determined straining against his "disordered passions."[445] The phrase "disordered passions" is preferred in the Eastern Church to Roman "concupiscence" which implies a somewhat fatalistic inclination to evil. O'Connor's sacramentalism invokes the Orthodox conception of mankind as participant in the redeeming glory of the

---

Publishing Group, 2002) 435.

[437] O'Connor, "The Catholic Novelist in the Protestant South," 196–97.

[438] O'Connor, "The Enduring Chill," *Complete*, 360.

[439] O'Connor, *Habit*, 304.

[440] Ibid.

[441] Ibid., 307.

[442] Ibid.

[443] Ibid., 516.

[444] Ibid., 507.

[445] O'Connor, *Habit*, 336.

Incarnation. Humanity is understood, not as a scourge upon creation, but as the impetus for a new kind of creation in the context of Christ's dual nature. O'Connor criticized modern Christianity and its "religious substitutes" for having "no sense of the power of God that could produce the Incarnation and the Resurrection."[446] "[M]odern people," she claimed, "are all so busy explaining away the virgin birth and such things, and reducing everything to human proportions that in time they lose even the sense of the human itself."[447] O'Connor's use of violence, therefore, was not a remark, as Tate and others have suggested, to the effect of man's necessity of the severest kind of punishment but a technical strategy employed to make visible a force which exists independently of man but which has no greater affinity than man and so seems to emanate from him. Shortly after the publication of *The Violent Bear It Away*, O'Connor wrote to Andrew Lytle, saying:

> I have got to the point now where I keep thinking more and more about the presentation of love and charity, or better call it grace, as love suggests tenderness, whereas grace can be violent or would have to be to compete with the kind of evil I can make concrete. At the same time, I keep seeing Elias in that cave, waiting to hear the voice of the Lord in the thunder and lightning and wind, and only hearing it finally in the gentle breeze, and I feel I'll have to be able to do that sooner or later, or anyway to keep trying…[448]

This particular correspondence suggests that O'Connor's vision was terminologically Catholic, but in its dealing with the experience of evil it relied more intently upon Orthodox theology. Like the Roman Church, Orthodoxy recognizes Satan as the "Father of Evil," but rather than foregrounding mankind's inability to resist evil in the Garden or in the world, Orthodox stress humanity's complete integration in the process of Deification, a process principally involved in restoring man to God, not punishing him for a foreknown failing in his nature. The letter also indicates a continued evolution in O'Connor's theological and aesthetic thinking during the final years of her life. While we can only speculate as to the personal impact her extra-Roman study effected, there is a considerable amount of textual evidence, most notably in narratives

---

[446] Ibid., 300.

[447] Ibid., 299–300.

[448] Ibid., 373.

which attempt to document orthodox sacraments that suggests, at least poetically, O'Connor was willing to partake of a broader Christian tradition in order to illuminate her catholic ideology. In the following three chapters, I will attempt to show that evidence, first through the author's handling of the baptismal rite in "The River" and *The Violent Bear It Away*, second with her exploration of the Eucharist and the sacrament of marriage in "Parker's Back," and lastly the presentation of charity in "Why Do the Heathen Rage?"

Chapter 3

"Just As It Is or Nothing": Flannery O'Connor's Ugly Jesus[1]

The celebration of the Eucharist is a sacramental tradition which underpins each of O'Connor's fictions, even when, as in "A Good Man Is Hard to Find" and "The Life You Save May Be Your Own," its transformational effects are implied to be efficacious beyond the material substance of the text itself. Befittingly, O'Connor administers her "Mass upon the world" to non-Catholics and without the trappings of the liturgical Eucharistic sacrifice.[2] Proper to what might be called a desert orthodoxy, O'Connor intimates the transcendent symbolism of Christ in the mattered world and the ministers of His body, men and women "as ordinary as...the fishermen apostles."[3] She once called her second novel, *The Violent Bear It Away*, a "very minor hymn to the Eucharist;" in much the same spirit she composed two late works, "Why Do the Heathen Rage?" and "Parker's Back."[4] Whereas the sacrament of baptism is the *modus operandi* in the novel, in these later stories O'Connor engages the mystery of the Incarnation by way of the sacraments of marriage and penance. The romance-inspired conversion that is left unaccomplished in "...the Heathen..." is consummated in "Parker's Back" where the performance of marriage acts as the impetus for O. E.'s transfiguration in putting on Christ.[5]

Early drafts of "Why Do the Heathen Rage?" feature another tattooed man, a Mr. Gunnels who bears the sagging head of Matthias Grünewald's Christ on his back.[6] "The face, wet with Gunnels's

---

[1] O'Connor, "Parker's Back," *Complete*, 522.

[2] Teilhard de Chardin qtd. in O'Connor, *Habit*, 521.

[3] O'Connor, *Habit*, 337

[4] Ibid., 387.

[5] Gal. 3:27, *KJV*.

[6] Matthias Grünewald, *The Crucifixion*, 1512–1515, oil on wood panel, Isenheim Altarpiece, Musée d'Unterlinden, Colmar, France. Scala Archives, Florence, Italy. Art Resource, New York, 2006. *www.artstor*.org. http//:library.artstor.org.elib.tcd.ie.library/secureViewImages?id=4iFCeTg4

sweat," integrates the mythos of mankind's fall from grace and his redemption in the new Adam.[7] "By the sweat of your face," the Book of Genesis reads, "you shall eat bread until you return to the ground," but penance and, certainly, death are far from the thoughts of O'Connor's painted men.[8] The inheritance of original sin is writ large in both Parker and Gunnels. They are set to toil, like Adam before them, over the needs of corruptible bodies, and yet they persist in the human vanity of will. If there is a refrain to be heard in these stories it is the warning of Ben Sira that, "Pride is the beginning of sin."[9]

Judeo-Christian scripture proclaims that only an act of ultimate humility can reestablish the balance of man's initial grace, overcoming death by passing through it.[10] Composed so near to her own death, it is not surprising that O'Connor's final story should resolve in humility and very particularly in the long and arduous process of one man's "bringing [his] Will into God."[11] She worked alternately on "Parker" and "...the Heathen..." from 1962 until her death, the latter, in many ways, a staging ground for the more complex meditations which appear in "Parker's Back." O. E. shares Gunnels's compulsion to exhibition, as proud of the great cats and cannon-mounted eagle that adorn his arms as Gunnels's is the unseen Christ on his back. He suffers, as Gunnels does, for the Christ he bears, but O. E. is pierced to the depths of his soul by the Byzantine Christ, grimly aware that he must submit to those "all-demanding eyes" whereas Gunnels's anguish is merely cosmetic.[12]

NCciJy8laCt2KngqVXkhflt6eQ%3D%3&userId=gjJDfzUv&zoomparams= (accessed 20 February 2010).

[7] Flannery O'Connor, "Why Do the Heathen Rage?" N. date, MS 228a, 33, *Flannery O'Connor Collection*, Russell Library, Georgia College & State University, Milledgeville.

[8] Gen. 3:19, *NRSV*.

[9] Sir. 10:13, *NRSV*.

[10] Sir. 10:12, *NRSV*.

[11] Jacob Boehme, *The Signature of All Things; Of the Supersensual Life; Of Heaven and Hell; Discourse Between Two Souls*, trans. John Sparrow, rpt. ed. (Whitefish: Kessinger Publishing, 1992) 262.

[12] O'Connor, "Parker's Back," *Complete*, 522. See *Christ Pantocrator Icon*, ca. 12th century, mosaic, Kariye Djami, Istanbul, Turkey. Wikimedia, 11 August 2005. *www.wikipedia.org*. http://en.wikipedia.org/wiki/File:Chora_Christ_south_coupole.jpg (accessed 14 May 2011).

He claims to have been tricked, like O. E. fears he might have been, by the tattooist. "It ain't the Jesus I picked out," he says and intends to get his "twenty fi' dollars" back.[13]

O'Connor deliberated at considerable length over the actual cost of Parker's tattoo, contemplating prices as steep as fifty dollars but settling upon twenty, ten for each day's work.[14] The correlation between actual cost and value is a literal one to Gunnels's mind, but in "Parker's Back" there is a decided shift from farcical literalization to actual effect that intimates both the literal and mystical costs of the Incarnation. The formula of good-old-boy made God-man is radically deepened in Parker whose conjoining with Christ coincides with the eventual restoration of his sense of evil, a sense O'Connor believed crucial to interpreting the "redemptive act."[15] The price of Parker's ultimate restoration will be paid out in the negative currency of abstinence. At skin-depth, O. E.'s icon has its function as a sign of visible transfiguration—Christ has become his flesh—but its greater import is its establishing an analogy between Christ's and O. E.'s passion. Only after he concedes to the icon, a choice he makes with Sarah Ruth in mind, does O. E. see himself, not as "something haphazard and botched," but as a masterwork of creation.[16] He becomes an *eikon* of Christ who is Himself the *eikon* of God.

O. E. Parker is of the same cloth as O'Connor's original unwitting prophet Hazel Motes, an enthusiastic sinner unconvinced of the reality of sin, driven by an obscure positivist principle. He did not intend to "get himself legally tied up," most especially with a woman.[17] When he finds himself consenting to marry Sarah Ruth, he consoles himself in reasoning, "You could leave the one you were married to as easy as one you weren't."[18] He conceives of the marriage pact as another contractual snare, a legal formality that

---

[13] O'Connor, "Why Do the Heathen Rage?" MS 228a, 35.

[14] Flannery O'Connor, "Parker's Back," N. date, MS 205a, 17, *Flannery O'Connor Collection*, Russell Library, Georgia College & State University, Milledgeville.

[15] O'Connor, "Some Aspects of the Grotesque in Southern Fiction," *Mystery*, 48.

[16] O'Connor, "Parker's Back," *Complete*, 514.

[17] Ibid., 511.

[18] Flannery O'Connor, "Parker's Back," N. date, MS 204d, 2, *Flannery O'Connor Collection*,

Russell Library, Georgia College & State University, Milledgeville.

could be shrugged as readily as those of the United States Navy and the Methodist Church. To be married, enlisted, even baptized are states binding only when you are physically unable to flee. But after O. E. weds his onion-skinned beloved, he begins "to have the feeling that there was some hidden flaw in [his principle], and that when he got ready to leave her, there would be something to prevent him."[19]

That something is the mysterious attraction between O. E. and Sarah Ruth whose natures are at once inverse and parallel and whose temperamental deflections and syntheses are described by their given names. Sarah was the name conferred upon Sarai, Abraham's wife, after Yahweh forged His covenant with the Hebrews by giving their patriarch an heir. From the once barren old woman the tribe of Israel came and, after many trials, produced one to redeem all men, but it is not Sarah Ruth's anticipated pregnancy that conjures Parker. He has abandoned all of the women he has had, observing that they "soured usually between five and eight months."[20] He stays with Sarah Ruth not because she is, at last, one who would "stay sweet," but because she was "vinegar from the first," able to give form to his dissatisfaction by making him feel, for the first time in his life, the hot twinge of liability.

Our first glimpse of O. E. and Sarah Ruth establishes a pictorial composition correspondent with both Old Testament symbology and Orthodox iconography. The situation of the couple's rented house, high up on an embankment and solitary except for a single pecan tree, recalls the exile of Israel in the wilderness. The pair have made their home in a relative desert beyond the encroachments of state and church and beyond the temptations of the city save for the regular shooting by of automobiles. As her name suggests, Sarah Ruth has been longer in the wilderness; she has learned from real hunger to strain, as St. Thomas put it, "against mere nature."[21] When the story opens, she is seated on the porch floor with Parker on the step below her "some distance away."[22] Their staggered placement evokes the icons of St. John at Mt. Patmos where the Evangelist is

---

[19] Flannery O'Connor, "Parker's Back," N. date, MS 204b, 3, *Flannery O'Connor Collection*,
Russell Library, Georgia College & State University, Milledgeville.

[20] O'Connor, "Parker's Back," MS 204d, 2.

[21] St. Thomas qtd. in O'Connor, *Habit*, 343.

[22] O'Connor, "Parker's Back," *Complete*, 510.

said to have written the Book of Revelation and also Christ's Transfiguration on Mt. Tabor, the sight of which compels the apostles Peter, James, and John to their hands and knees.[23] A third analogue is the icon of Jacob's *Ladder of Divine Ascent* upon which angels and, in later iconography, Orthodox monks climb to achieve the Kingdom of Heaven.[24] The twelfth century icon depicting Jacob's vision at the Monastery of St. Catherine is most striking in parallel to the spiritual drama suffered by Parker.[25] The ladder is thronged with souls ascending, some just above the pull of the earth, others very nearly delivered into the awaiting arms of Christ. In O'Connor's narrative, Parker is beset by at least one demon; he ascends but with a shackle about his neck.

The *Ladder* icon became the template for the fourth century monk St. John Climacus' *Scala Paradisi*. Especially revered in the Orthodox eremitic tradition, Climacus' treatise reflects upon the rigors of monastic life and the spiritual illumination its dogmas seek to achieve. Climacus describes thirty stages of spiritual ascent beginning with the penitent's casting off of the carnal vices—gluttony and fornication—and the more insidious spiritual vices—avarice, anger, dejection, listlessness, and the principle vice, pride—and culminating in his gradual assimilation of the holy virtues until he has reestablished his initial semblance with the Godhead.[26] Each

---

[23] See *St. John at Patmos*, ca. late 15th century, tempura on wood panel, Trinity-Sergiev Monastery. Private collection. *The Bridgeman Art Library*, n. date. http://www.bridgemanart.com/image.aspx?img=1FE8B9ED-104D-48F5-A0FD-B7E9DE692973 (accessed 15 March 2011); Theophanes the Greek, *The Transfiguration of Christ*, ca. early 15th century, tempura on wood panel, Tretyakov Gallery, Moscow, Russia. Art History Survey Collection, n. date. *www.artstor.org*. http://library.artstor.org.elib.tcd.ie/library/secureView-Images?id=8DhbZCk2NzYrJSEnd1N7Q38rXXsvelQ%D&userId=gjJDfzUvzoop (accessed 15 March 2011).

[24] See Gen. 28:10–18, *KJV*.

[25] See *The Heavenly Ladder of St. John Climacus*, ca. 12th century, tempura and gold on panel, Monastery of St. Catherine, Mt. Sinai, Egypt, Erich Lessing Culture and Fine Arts Archives, Art Resource New York, 2006. *www.artstor.org*. (http://library.artstor.org.elib.tcd.ie/library/secure/V iew-Images?id=%2FThWdC8IywtPygFTx5RnksX3wqeF0%3D&userId=gjJDfzUv&zompaams = (accessed 1 May 2011).

[26] See St. John Cassian, "On the Eight Vices," *The Philokalia: The Complete Text*, ed. and trans. G. E. H. Palmer, Philip Sherrard, and Kallistos Ware, Vol. I, illus. ed. (New York: Macmillan, 1983) 73–93.

step brings the novice closer to his intended likeness with Christ, the model of spiritual perfection whose "hidden years" of prayerful contemplation are commemorated by the thirty-rung ladder.[27] "[T]he phrase 'after His image,'" St. John Damascene wrote of the creation of man, "...refers to the side of nature which consists of mind and free will, [a quality which cannot be lost or denigrated by sin], whereas 'after His likeness' means likeness in virtue so far as this is possible."[28]

Sarah Ruth may not be a monk transfigured—she is neither voluntarily poor nor introspective with regard to her own need for spiritual growth—but her ascetic posturing does effect a profound change in her husband. At the outset of their story, Parker counts his wife's puritanism amongst her unfavorable qualities, suspicious that she "actually liked the things she said she didn't."[29] He cannot see a logic of return in suffering for the sake of a removed salvation; in fact, "he didn't see it was anything in particular to save him from."[30] But even without faith in the redemption, Parker intuits that Sarah Ruth has achieved, through the rigors of poverty and abstinence, an elevated state of awareness. Despite her bizarre sense of what to do with God's free gift of grace, Sarah Ruth has learned how to "put herself in the way of being receptive to it" by first accepting her situation and then by practicing further "self-denial."[31] She is a poorly creature outwardly, and yet she does not suffer from her husband's compounding anxieties of self-disgust. Parker begrudges her this seniority—she is, after all, S. R. to his O. E.—yet he remains, just below her, in uneasy anticipation.

The bond that holds Obadiah Elihue to Sarah Ruth is figuratively ancestral. As Abraham and Sarah did before them, they

---

[27] Norman Russell, "St. John Climacus," *The Westminster Dictionary of Christian Spirituality*, ed. Gordon S. Wakefield (Westminster: John Knox Press, 1983) 89.

[28] St. John Damascene and St. Hilary of Poitiers, *Nicene and Post-Nicene Fathers of the Christian Church: Hilary of Poitiers, On the Trinity & On the Synods; John of Damascus, Exposition of the Orthodox Faith*, 2nd Series, Vol. IX, ed. Philip Schaff and Henry Wace, trans. Rev. E. W. Watson, Rev. L. Pullan, and Rev. S. D. F. Salmond (Grand Rapids: Wm. B. Eerdmans Publishing Co., 1980) 476.

[29] O'Connor, "Parker's Back," *Complete*, 510.

[30] Ibid., 518.

[31] O'Connor, *Habit*, 336.

have gone from their fathers' houses and participate, conscious of it or not, in God's covenant that "all peoples on the earth shall be blessed through Abraham."[32] Parker "did not believe in God but…he knew enough of the Bible…[to know] what His ways were."[33] His ironical respect for the Word further upsets his faith in regaining his freedom. "What would you do if I walked off and left you?" he asks his wife one night in bed, and like the biblical Ruth she replies, "I'd follow along behind. …If you were in China you'd still be married to me."[34] Sarah Ruth's wifely claim is an answer to Parker's silent prophesy. "Who in God's name would marry [this raw-boned girl]?"[35]

The shame Parker feels with regard to his baptismal name becomes a part of his suffering over "the problem of marriage."[36] Both remind him of his obligation to the God in whose name he was baptized. Obadiah was a minor prophet who administered Ahab's royal household, and when the queen, Jezebel, began to slaughter the prophets of the God of Israel, Obadiah hid one hundred of these men in caves and fed them. He stood against the royal household, placing his faith in the God of his ancestors, not in the false-god Baal, and was chosen to prophesy against Edom primarily because he was an Edomite himself. In spite of his being surrounded by the sacrilege of idol worship, Obadiah remained a faithful servant to Yahweh, going back at the prophet Elijah's command to confront Ahab.[37] In a vision, he sees Edom destroyed by the fiery wrath of God: "The pride of thine heart hath deceived thee, thou that dwellest in clefts of the rock, whose habitation is high; that saith in his heart, Who shall bring me down to the ground? Though thou exalt thyself as the eagle, and though thou set thy nest among the stars, from thence will I bring thee down, saith the Lord."[38]

Vainglorious in his painted flesh, Parker imagines he has outpaced the justice of the world of men by virtue of his physical assertions and the coming world of the Judgment by virtue of his

---

[32] Gen. 12:3, *KJV*.
[33] O'Connor, MS 205a, 3.
[34] Ruth 1:16–19, *NRSV*; O'Connor, "Parker's Back," MS 204d, 8.
[35] O'Connor, "Parker's Back," *Complete*, 516.
[36] O'Connor, "Parker's Back," MS 204d, 7.
[37] 1 Kings 18:7–8, *NRSV*.
[38] Obad. 1:3–4, *KJV*.

unbelief. He stands behind his adolescent apostasy, affecting to be neither bound by nor attentive to the Law of the commandments. Sarah Ruth immediately brings to light the hollowness of Parker's conceit, albeit inadvertently, by mistaking his tattooed eagle for a chicken.[39] She is drawn to this most amateur of O. E.'s tattoos because it makes visible the basest of his human desires: to control being by enacting creation itself. The eagle is an iconic attribute of St. John and befits O'Connor's hero as a totem of apocalyptic vision, that is of the world, most especially the world of the self, transfigured. Parker's swelling dissatisfaction is bound to his compulsion to remake himself; each of his tattoos is an insistence of being, a painful and lasting sign of willfulness and corporeality. To "forsake God and to exist in oneself—...to be pleased with oneself—is not immediately to lose all being; but it is to come closer to nothingness," Augustine wrote in *The City of God*.[40] With every assertion to being he makes, Parker feels more intensely his essential nonbeing, and with every act of rebellion he has asked, "Who shall bring me down to the ground?" Sarah Ruth obliges, "knock[ing] the last Goddammit lopsided out of his mouth" and, sometime later, thrusting his groping hands "away with such force...that he [finds] himself flat on his back on the ground.[41]

Sarah Ruth's violent denials of Parker's sins recall the advent of a sword-bearing Christ. "Love should be full of anger," St. Jerome told his fellow monk Heliodorus upon the latter's leaving the Syrian desert.[42] Jerome admonished him for retreating to the shade of church hierarchy rather than stay in the full sun of desert life, but in his youth, Jerome had much in common with Heliodorus and still more with O. E.[43] The privileged son of a wealthy landowner, he enjoyed all of the pleasures of the Roman empire and cultivated a "habit of delicate food" and women which haunted him all his years

---

[39] O'Connor, "Parker's Back," *Complete*, 515.

[40] St. Augustine of Hippo, *City of God Against the Pagans*, ed. R. W. Dyson (Cambridge: Cambridge University Press, 1998) 609.

[41] O'Connor, "Parker's Back," MS 205a, 3; and "Parker's Back," *Complete*, 518.

[42] St. Jerome qtd. in O'Connor, "Why Do The Heathen Rage?" *Complete*, 486.

[43] Heliodorus became the first bishop of Altinum in the fourth century.

in the wilderness.[44] His most enduring "passion" was for classical Roman literature, particularly the works of Virgil and Cicero.[45] When he set out for the desert the contents of his library were the only possessions he labored to carry. Having renounced the corporeal "vanit[ies] of his former pursuits and the irregularity of his life [in Rome]," Jerome took a vow of celibacy and entered into monastic life.[46] Despairing at the death of two fellow penitents and the retreat of Heliodorus, Jerome was "seized with a grievous sickness, [and] in the heat of a burning fever, fell into a trance or a dream, in which he seemed to himself arraigned before the dreadful tribunal of Christ."[47] The judge "thereby condemned him to be severely scourged by angels" for persisting in his study of "pagan" literature.[48] Certain icons depicting Jerome, such as Francesco Francia's *Crucifixion with Sts. John and Jerome*, situate the saint so that his bared back—the locus of his deepest suffering—is revealed to the viewer.[49]

If O. E. can be said to have a patron saint it is the vision-spurred penitent Jerome. Parker has taken his own vow of repentance; in his marriage to Sarah Ruth, he has promised a constancy of spirit which overrides the least of his habitual vices. He also shares in the saint's inability to refrain from his most enduring passion, the tattoo. He is beset, as Jerome was, by "violent temptations," the most consuming of these the desire to abandon his wife and return to a life of more or less guiltless immoderation. Like a monk in his cell, Parker becomes so preoccupied with the desire for peace he loses both sleep and

---

[44] Stefan Rebenich, *Jerome: The Early Church Fathers* (London: Routledge, 2002) 26. See also Desiderius Erasmus, *The Collected Works of Erasmus; Patristic Scholarship, the Edition of St. Jerome*, ed. James F. Brady and John C. Olin (Toronto: University of Toronto Press, 1992) 49; Alban Butler, *The Lives of the Saints*, Vol. II (New York: Benziger Brothers, 1894) 327.

[45] Alban Butler, *The Lives of the Fathers, Martyrs, and Other Principle Saints*, Vol. II, ed. and trans. F. C. Husenbeth (London: Henry and Co., 1857) 416.

[46] Ibid.

[47] Ibid.

[48] Ibid.

[758] See Francesco Francia, *Crucifixion with Saints John and Jerome*, 1485, oil on wood panel, Collezioni Comunali d'Arte, Bologna, Italy. Lib-Art, n. date. *www.lib-art.com*. http://www.lib-art.com/artgallery/5601-crucifixion-with-sts-john-and-jerom-francesco-francia.html (accessed 14 May 2011).

flesh.[50] Jerome's self-description not long before his revelation of heavenly judgment is very much the image of the man in O'Connor's story "two or three mornings" before the cataclysm in the field:[51] "My face was pale with fasting; yet my will felt violent assaults of irregular desires: in my cold body and in my parched-up flesh, which seemed dead before its death, concupiscence was able to live."[52] Jerome struggled to bring his own flesh into submission whereas Parker's aim is "to bring Sarah Ruth to heel" *with* his flesh.[53] Having suffered her denials since their first meeting, Parker's consciousness is overwhelmed by a sense of urgency in finding "exactly the right" image which would make him undeniable to Sarah Ruth.[54] "[H]is eyes took on a hollow preoccupied expression."[55] In a state of intense concentration, he circles the field with the tractor, his mind "on a suitable design for his back," his vision doubled "as if he had eyes in the back of his head."[56] At this moment of preternatural cognizance, Parker is "propelled" into a still more unworldly space, the borderland between life and death. "All at once he saw the tree reaching out to grasp him."[57] He lands "on his back while the tractor crashed upside down into the tree and burst into flame....He could feel the hot breath of the burning tree on his face."[58]

Parker's ordeal combines revelation from both the Old and New Testaments: Moses' vision of the burning bush and Christ's "breathing" the Holy Spirit unto his disciples after he was risen from the tomb.[59] Both passages have a pentecostal significance. In Exodus, God reveals his name to Moses, "I am that I am," a name which reveals the essence of the Holy Spirit itself and the life of that Spirit

---

[50] Alban Butler, *The Lives of the Fathers, Martyrs, and Other Principle Saints*, 2:414; O'Connor, "Parker's Back," *Complete*, 519.

[51] O'Connor, "Parker's Back," *Complete*, 520.

[52] Alban Butler, *Lives of the Fathers, Martyrs, and Other Principle Saints*, 2:415.

[53] O'Connor, "Parker's Back," *Complete*, 520.

[54] Ibid.

[55] Ibid.

[56] Ibid.

[57] Ibid.

[58] Ibid.

[59] Exod. 3:2–5; John 20:22, *KJV*.

in its mortal likeness.[60] In John, Jesus comes to his disciples to grant them peace in the sight of his resurrection. "Peace be unto you: as my Father hath sent me, even so send I you. And when he had said this, he breathed on them, and saith unto them, Receive ye the Holy Ghost..."[61] The "hot breath of the burning tree," the figurative essence of God, terrifies Parker; he "scrambled backwards, ...eyes cavernous" with experiential knowledge of "the God Who Is."[62] "[I]f he had known how to cross himself he would have done it."[63]

In "Parker's..." sister story, "Why Do The Heathen Rage?" St. Jerome appears explicitly, but he has only a passing effect. Walter, the narrative's offish protagonist, is much taken by the saint's *Letters*, especially his image of the warrior-Christ, but he cannot long maintain Jerome's angry love. Stricken to belief by the "bloody" face on the hired man Gunnels's back, Walter welcomes a "fresh satanic breeze" of haughty indifference which "seemed...to be blowing through him, chilling the passions that a few moments before had threatened to kindle in him."[64] Walter is not the first of O'Connor's heroes to be unambiguously linked with the devil. Rufus Johnson claims to be "in [Satan's] power" in "The Lame Shall Enter First," and Francis Marion takes directives from an apparitional devil and, for a time, becomes the embodiment of evil in *The Violent Bear It Away*.[65] But Walter's stunted conversion is unique in O'Connor in that it is framed in terms of the pre-schism church. A late manuscript states that:

> Walter knew the Fathers of the Church, he had assisted at Nicaea and at Chalcedon. He had explored the intricacies of Light with Bonaventure; he knew where Aquinas and Duns Scotus would part company. He had seen the path turn downward with Abelard and illogic enter...mashed and grotesquely...eloquent with Luther. He had been active at Trent. He had adhered always to the most orthodox line but never once, never for the slightest moment, had it

[60] Exod. 3:14, *KJV*.

[61] John 20, 21, 22, *KJV*.

[62] O'Connor, "Why Do The Heathen Rage?" *Complete*, 520; and *Habit*, 93.

[63] O'Connor, "Why Do The Heathen Rage?" *Complete*, 520.

[64] O'Connor, MS 228a, 35.

[65] O'Connor, "The Lame Shall Enter First," *Complete*, 450; and *Violent*, 24, 165.

> occurred to him, even remotely, to believe any of it; or that there was the least danger of his doing so.[66]

Walter's theology, prior to his witnessing Gunnels's bared back and the tattoo his mother calls "an offent [sic] against religion," is purely intellectual.[67] But before the image of the dead Christ, he loses his Stoic's nerve. "The pictures [he'd taken that day to benefit an epistolary ruse] came back from the photographers all clear expect the one of Gunnels's back. On that one Walter's hand had veered. The face was visible but as through a veil."[68] Walter has seen Christ in a way his mother and Sarah Ruth cannot—both deny Jesus the reality of His ruined flesh and demand "Christ didn't look like that"—but Walter is not willing to endure the pain of effort necessary to transfigure the soul, "to see," as O'Connor put it, "the selfish side of [himself] in order to turn away from it."[69] The violence of Desert Fathers like Jerome is an imitation of the violence of Christ come to judge those who would judge themselves. This, O'Connor wrote, "is the violence of love, of giving more than the law demands, of an asceticism like John the Baptist's, but in the face of which even John is less than the least in the kingdom..."[70]

Orthodox call St. John the Forerunner, the last prophet of the Old Testament who proclaimed "a baptism of repentance for the forgiveness of sins" before the coming judgment of Christ.[71] St. Jerome was not baptized himself until the age of nineteen perhaps "for fear of the responsibilities incurred by [the rite]."[72] Parker's mother conferred the sacrament upon him as an infant. He postpones his active initiation by deferring the sacrament of marriage. His second given name, Elihue, emphasizes his penchant for self-justification. The biblical Elihu chastises Job for accusing God of finding "occasions against him."[73] Suffering the loss of his estate, his

---

[66] O'Connor, "Why Do the Heathen Rage?" N. date, MS 226b, 21, *Flannery O'Connor Collection*, Russell Library, Georgia College & State University, Milledgeville.

[67] O'Connor, "Why Do the Heathen Rage?" MS 228a, 32.

[68] Ibid., 21.

[69] O'Connor, *Habit*, 430.

[70] Ibid., 382.

[71] Mark 1:4, *NRSV*.

[72] Rebenich, *Jerome: The Early Church Fathers*, 4.

[73] Job 32:2, *NRSV*.

family, and his health, Job charges God with unjustly punishing a "clean" man, but Elihu rebukes him, asking: "Why do you contend against God, saying, 'He will answer none of my words?' For God speaks in one way, and in two, though people do not perceive it."[74] Like Sarah Ruth's, Elihu's preaching is well intentioned but not without fault; St. Gregory would call him "faithful, but yet arrogant…saying right things in a wrong way."[75]

O. E.'s priority of vision is a needful challenge to Sarah Ruth's straight Gospel. O'Connor made a similar challenge to her audience at the Southern Literary Festival in spring 1962, declaring that, "We need to make contact with our sources, and I mean sources that go back farther than Thomas Jefferson and Rousseau and Descartes and Luther."[76] Parker is a man of displaced tradition in which the "prophetic voice" is as vital as any science. He attempts to subdue his wife, not with philosophic rationales or scriptural proofs, but by showing her the Word become flesh. Nevertheless, his master stroke succeeds only in inciting Sarah Ruth to a more brutal enactment of Mosaic law. In this regard, Parker's wife is representative of a sort common to O'Connor's South; she preaches Jesus with Luther's self-assuredness in election and with Calvin's distrust of the flesh. There is no room in such faith for sinner or Savior. To make discernible the "prophetic voice" of the early church, O'Connor had to contend, not only with the preaching of actual Sarah Ruths, but also with Ruby Turpins and Mrs. Mays—the good Christian women who were as committed to their civic religion as they were to unbelief.[77] And there were still others like *Wise Blood*'s false prophet Asa Hawks who proclaimed a salvation instant upon conversion. O. E. dramatizes O'Connor's convictions to the contrary. "I believe," she wrote Maryat Lee, "in the resurrection of the body. I also believe in it before it gets

---

[74] Job 32:2; 32:13–14, *NRSV*.

[75] St. Gregory the Great, "An Exposition on the Book of Blessed Job," *A Library of the Fathers of the Holy Catholic Church, Anterior to the Division of the East and West*, ed. Edward Bouverie Pusey, John Keble, and John Henry Newman, trans. members of the English Church (Oxford: J. H. Parker, 1847) 6.

[76] Flannery O'Connor, "The Catholic Novelist in the Protestant South," 20 April 1962, MS 271a, 12–13, *Flannery O'Connor Collection*, Russell Library, Georgia College & State University, Milledgeville.

[77] Ibid., 2.

that way…"[78] O. E. must begin his resurrection to life in life, which is not to say that he has "gone and got" the New South's automatic, bloodless religion, nor that he has been "saved."[79] He has only begun to accept a subordinate position to his instinct's "ultimate concern" of the living God revealed,[80] but is nonetheless a crucial part of the divine process, a "living and continuous link from the ancient to the modern world" which seeks experiential knowledge of the self as coactive with the ultimate reality.[81]

The hesychasts of the early church committed their lives to such knowledge and sought to "to circumscribe the incorporeal in [their] bod[ies]."[82] From the Greek *hesychia* meaning silence or rest, these men "of stillness" placed especial emphasis on the body as the conduit of *theosis*. Breathing exercises, fasts, and self-flagellation were integrated into their ritual prayer so that the spirit might be brought into an awareness of the body as inherently weak and yet interconnected with God.[83] "[T]he goal…is not the disincarnation of the mind, but a transfiguration of the entire person—soul and body—through the presence of the incarnated God…"[84] Parker is indifferent to his body previous to his visit to the fair; he had "never before felt the least motion of wonder in himself."[85] When he sees the tattooed man, his body transfigured in undulating color, Parker begins to intuit a connectivity between the flesh and the "unique reality" of illumined Being.[86] He endeavors to illuminate himself by imitating the tattooed man but is afflicted, with each new design, by a growing sense of ineffectuality. Not until he is catapulted to the nearside of death does O. E. see himself as a man lost in his freedom

---

[78] O'Connor, *Habit*, 227.

[79] O'Connor, "Parker's Back," *Complete*, 524.

[80] Flannery O'Connor, "Some Notes on the Combination: Novelist and Believer," March 1963, MS 266b, 3 alt., *Flannery O'Connor Collection*, Russell Library, Georgia College & State University, Milledgeville.

[81] O'Connor, "Catholic Novelist in the Protestant South," MS 271a, 2.

[82] Climacus qtd. in St. Gregory Palamas, *The Triads*, ed. John Meyendorff, trans. Nicholas Gendle (Mahwah: Paulist Press, 1983) 44.

[83] Norman Russell, "St. John Climacus," *The Westminster Dictionary of Christian Spirituality*, ed. Gordon S. Wakefield (Westminster: John Knox Press, 1983) 189.

[84] Palamas, *The Triads*, 3.

[85] O'Connor, "Parker's Back," *Complete*, 513.

[86] Palamas, *The Triads*, 63.

who will suffer alone. His peculiar theistic curses—"Jesus Christ in hell!" and "Jesus God Almighty damm!"—become an actual prayer of affirmation—"GOD ABOVE!"[87] His brush with death, like Jerome's, inspires a vision of his unrepentant soul scourged by heaven and ultimately left to burn, like his shoe, "by itself."[88]

O. E.'s is significantly a waking vision. Brought down bodily, he seeks his penance at the hands of the tattooist in his flesh, but the internal working of his transformation is begun before the first needle prick. His decision to transfigure himself in a manner invisible to his own pride and to do so (ostensibly) for the sake of his wife marks a radical change in motive. He has begun to reflect, in facial tics and sunken flesh, the decrepitude of his inner being, but in this diminished state, Parker is burgeoning in strength of spirit. He is no longer like to "nothingness" in love for himself but rather like to Christ in love for another.[89] At the threshold of the tattoo parlor he appears, not as a puffed up old sailor, but as a "hollow-eyed creature" intent upon an image that would interrupt the cycle of his dissatisfaction, a "religious subject…that Sarah Ruth would not be able to resist."[90] He considers a Bible with an "actual verse" printed on an open page but decides Sarah Ruth would balk, saying, "Ain't I already got a real Bible?"[91] Whether conscious of it or not, Parker eventually hits upon the very thing his wife doesn't have, a vision of God incarnate.

O. E. seeks out the town's most renowned tattooist precisely for his skill; such a man could render the God Who Is just as He is.[92] The artist is himself aligned with St. Jerome, boasting a tattoo of "a miniature owl atop his head. "[P]erfect in every detail," the owl "served him as a show piece."[93] One of Jerome's iconic attributes, the owl suggests artisanal wisdom but also "sinful pride, [and] eroticism."[94] It is a creature remarkable for its viability in opposing

[87] O'Connor, "Parker's Back," *Complete*, 511, 520.

[88] Ibid.

[89] St. Augustine of Hippo, *The City of God Against the Pagans*, ed. R. W. Dyson (Cambridge: Cambridge University Press, 1998) 609.

[90] O'Connor, "Parker's Back," *Complete*, 519, 521.

[91] Ibid., 519.

[92] Ibid., 522.

[93] Ibid., 521.

[94] Hope B. Werness, *The Continuum Encyclopedia of Animal Symbolism in Art* (New York: Continuum International Publishing Group, Inc., 2006) 308.

realms, at once associated with darkness and light, devilry and sanctity as in Cosimo Tura's *Saint Jerome*.[95] As if courting his own demons, Parker demands the intricate Byzantine icon which, the artist tells him, will "cost [him] plenty."[96] Although it is, at this moment, an unconscious analogy, the same costly desire binds Parker to ice pick-eyed wife and staring Jesus.[97] They both come at him prepared to do violence, to knock his vision free of the easy assurance of intoxicated egoism.

Sarah Ruth's introductory blow so blurs Parker's vision he thinks he has been attacked by a "giant hawk-eyed angel."[98] In an early draft of the story he sees her as a "fierce shimmering figure against a background of pure gold, ...bare feet seeming not to touch the ground and...hand gripped as if upon a fantastic weapon."[99] Appearing in the vestige of an icon, Sarah Ruth communicates the possibility of transfiguration just as the icon communicates the "reality...revealed in the transfiguration on Mount Tabor."[100] The scene recalls St. Jerome's desert visions in which he hears the heralding trumpet of the apocalypse and suffers flagellation at the hands of two strap-wielding angels.[101] In later versions O'Connor

---

See also Hieronymus Bosch, *St. Jerome at Prayer*, 1505, oil on wood panel, Museum voor Schone Kunsten Ghent, Belgium. University of California, San Diego, n. date. *www.artstor.org*. http://library.artstor.org.elib.tcd.ie/library-secureViewImages?id=8CJGczI9NzldLS1WEDhzTnkrX3kt113cyc%3D&userId=gjJDfzUv&zoomparams= (accessed 3 March 2011).

[95] See Cosimo Tura, *Saint Jerome*, ca. 1470, oil and egg tempura on wood panel, The National Gallery, London, UK, n. date. *www.nationalgallery.org*. http://www.nationalgallery.org.uk/paintings/cosimo-tura-saint-jerome (accessed 12 March 2011).

[96] O'Connor, "Parker's Back," *Complete*, 522.

[97] Walter's mother fears that everything her son's "generation took to had to be ugly. Ugly music, ugly pictures, and now it occurred to her [after reading the underlined paragraph in St. Jerome], an ugly Jesus" (Flannery O'Connor, "Why Do the Heathen Rage?" N. date, MS 227c, 11, *Flannery O'Connor Collection*, Russell Library, Georgia College & State University, Milledgeville).

[98] Ibid., 511–12.

[99] O'Connor, MS 204d, 3.

[100] Ouspensky and Lossky qtd. in Zubeck, "Back to Page One in 'Parker's Back,'" 96.

[101] See Bernardino Mei, *The Vision of St. Jerome*, 1657–1660, oil on canvas, private collection. Web Gallery of Art, n. date. http://www.wga.hu/art/

reconsidered drawing so stark a parallel between the antagonistic Sarah Ruth and the illuminating light of the Godhead. She rewrote the scene several times, altering Parker's perception of his assailant to more and more creaturely incarnations with a definite body and earthly features: first a "supernatural creature," then a "heavenly" one "from above," and finally a "giant hawk-eyed angel."[102] Parker must go, like Hazel Motes, "backwards to Bethlehem," and his first step is a push back into momentary submission by Sarah Ruth and the angry love of the third commandment.[103] Parker is stricken to the ground four times by his beloved, twice directly and twice indirectly. As each of his falls attest, he cannot displace himself from the persistance of his vanity, so proud of his debt to the vice itself that he combats his discontent by paying further homage to it. Ultimately, Parker is drawn to one who can sufficiently disorder his vision so that the cause of his dissatisfaction might be revealed. Sarah Ruth's disinterest in tattoos and crass advances makes her unique amongst his lovers. Her disregard is a powerful motivator, more powerful than her physical assaults. She beats Parker's will into sustained submission not so much by her violence as by her disavowal which silently holds him accountable for each of his betrayals: of holiness in blasphemy and faith in apostasy, of sanctity in lust and love in wrath, and of Judgment in self-idolatry.

The first of Parker's sins—taking the Lord's name in vain—Sarah Ruth dispatches with her broom. Her weapon might be a reference to the tree under which Elijah collapsed, spent by his flight from the murderous Jezebel. The prophet prays to God that he might die and is visited instead by an angel who spurs him on his journey to Mt. Horeb.[104] Atop the peak, the Lord beckons Elijah to bear witness as He passes by.[105] There "was a great wind, so strong that it was splitting mountains..., but the Lord was not in the wind; and after the wind...there was a fire, but the Lord was not in the fire; and after the fire a sound of sheer silence. ...Then there came a

---

m/mei/vision_j.jpg (accessed 27 February 2011).

[102] O'Connor, MS 205a, 2; "Parker's Back," *Complete*, 512.

[103] O'Connor, *Wise Blood*, 219; "Parker's Back," *Complete*, 511.

[104] O'Connor, "Parker's Back," *Complete*, 516.

[105] The long-view that so troubles O. E. as he sits on Sarah Ruth's porch is reminiscent of Elijah's flight and his coming near God atop the lone mountain.

voice..."[106] Elijah's revelation comes out of silence and foreshadows what Parker must achieve without the prodding of his wife. Although she acts as messenger, hastening Parker on his pilgrimage, Sarah Ruth is all wind and fire. Too often she crowds out the presence of the living Word with her own preaching. St. John Climacus called such "talkativeness" the "throne of vainglory...[and] the darkening of prayer."[107] Sarah Ruth's sin is to assume the glory of the Word as her own to transmit. She is, in this regard, like to the commune-dwelling Oona Gibbs of "Why do the Heathen Rage?" Walter befriends her through the post in the guise of a black man (a hypothetical tattoo), and when she reveals her personal theology, "[i]t came to Walter quietly...that what the woman had done was to abrogate the place of God and set herself up where it had been. He had not up until that moment been a believer. He realized now, with a shudder, that he was...a Christian bound for hell."[108] Sarah Ruth's fault is as indispensable to Parker's revelation; her insistence upon man's culpability, most especially his incurring debt, drives Parker into a more profound silence. Where he had easily matched his wife's evangelism with faith in self-salvation—each of her quotations he deflects with a ready curse—the total silence of the Deity unnerves him.

Parker's second sin of lust is met by Sarah Ruth's immovable will. She insists not only upon the necessity of marriage but the manner in which its corporeal pleasures are meted out: with reserve and under the cover of natural darkness.[109] But her husband's ultimate sin of pride requires a kind of mercy she does not yet understand, a mercy which explodes the Thou Shalt Not tenor of Mosaic Law and institutes a new law, one that sacrifices itself, not for an abstract good, but for the actual good of the sinner. As St. John wrote in his gospel, "The law indeed was given through Moses; grace and truth came through Jesus Christ."[110]

---

[106] 1 Kings 19:11–13, *NRSV*.

[107] St. John Climacus, *The Ladder of Divine Ascent*, trans. Colm Luibheid and Norman Russell (Mahwah: Paulist Press, 1982) 158.

[108] Flannery O'Connor, "Why Do the Heathen Rage?" N. date, MS 222, 29, *Flannery O'Connor Collection*, Russell Library, Georgia College & State University, Milledgeville.

[109] O'Connor, "Parker's Back," *Complete*, 529.

[110] John 1:17, *NRSV*.

Unlike Sarah Ruth's, Parker's penitence finds its inspiration in active revelation, not indoctrinated Word. One might even go so far as to say Sarah Ruth's expert knowledge prevents her seeing through the Word to "a light which illumines…the ears themselves."[111] Such "illumination," St. Palamas asserts, "can be possessed by a kind of ignorance rather than knowledge."[112] Parker's ignorance is a trenchant sort and one based on the priority of "his own sound judgment," but it, nonetheless, predisposes him to the cavernous introspection of desert life in which "silence" becomes a "language itself."[113] The story's first and final dialogues are marked by Parker's demand that Sarah Ruth "shut [her] mouth."[114] What began as a subconscious desire to experience again the gaping rapture he felt, first at the sight of the man at the fair and later at the sight of Sarah Ruth, becomes a conscious demand for silence.[115] On the artist's table, he lay awake "imagining how Sarah Ruth would be struck speechless by the face on his back…"[116] Parker's first encounters with divine stillness, however, bring him anything but peace. Shaken by the reflection of the "straight, all-demanding" face on his back, a face "enclosed in silence," he retreats to the false confidence of drink at the pool hall. When his fellow carousers pull up his shirt and reveal the stern face, there "was a silence…which seemed to Parker to grow from the circle around him until it extended to the foundations of the building and upward through the beams of the roof."[117] Christ has come unannounced to raze the temple, but the veil is let drop back over His face and the troubling silence made a joke.[118] Parker responds to his guffawing comrades with a command. "Aaa shut up," he tells them, but it isn't until these very devils cast him out that Parker begins to connect his sudden aversion to foul language with a

---

[111] Palamas, *The Triads*, 61.

[112] Ibid., 63.

[113] O'Connor, "Parker's Back," *Complete*, 522, 524.

[114] Ibid., 510, 529.

[115] Sarah Ruth seems to restore Parker to the state of gaping innocence he knew before his adolescent rows and his later stint with the Navy. See "Parker's Back," MS 204b, 3; and "Parker's Back," *Complete*, 513.

[116] Ibid., 525.

[117] Ibid.

[118] In St. Mark's Gospel, the temple veil is rent in two at Christ's death, and the Roman Centurion, a pagan not unlike Parker, is moved to declare that the dead man is the Son of God. See Mark 15:38–39, *NRSV*.

more profound change.[119] Prostrate in the back alley, he perceives the continuity between each of his revelations: the silent instinct which had led him to the carnival tent and the Naval yard, to Sarah Ruth and the all-demanding Christ, was a single instinct. It had led him "in rapture," in fear, and in "grumbling" submission to the self not as idol but as icon, a conduit of the holy "light," St. Gregory Palamas wrote, "which is the splendor of the deified flesh...[and] which enriches and communicates the glory of the divinity."[120]

The thought which "brings [Parker] slowly to his feet" is appropriately of his wife, the fleshy icon of Christ and mankind as bridegroom and beloved.[121] However imperfect, Sarah Ruth is the tangible connection between O. E. as a son of Adam and O. E. as son of God, the motivation of his desire to sacrifice all of his lesser "goods"—his drinking and wandering and womanizing—for the greater good of giving himself in marriage. "She would know what [Parker] had to do."[122] At dawn on the third day, O. E. returns home as to a strange country and in a strange transparent skin, hungry for the one he is bonded to in flesh so that she might see him. "Let me in!" he yells. "You know me."[123] He "puts his head to the keyhole, but it was stopped up with paper."[124] Sarah Ruth refuses to acknowledge him; she gets out of bed and asks from behind the barred door, "Who's there?"[125] The story's climax reads like an inverted "Song of Songs" in which Parker is bride and icon of Christ and Sarah Ruth the ironical beloved who will turn h/Him away:

> I sleep, and my heart watcheth: the voice of my beloved knocking: Open to me, ...my love. I have put off my garment, how shall I put it on [again]? ...My beloved put his hand through the key hole, and my bowels were moved at his touch. I arose up to open to my beloved: I opened the bolt of my door to my beloved: but he had turned aside, and was gone. My soul melted when he spoke: I sought him, and found him not: I called, and he did not answer me.[126]

---

[119] Ibid., 527.

[120] Ibid.; Palamas, *The Triads,* 62.

[121] O'Connor, "Parker's Back," *Complete*, 527.

[122] Ibid.

[123] Ibid.

[124] Ibid.

[125] Ibid.

[126] Song of Sg. 5:2–6, *Douay-Rheims*.

Parker denies to answer Sarah Ruth's call three times, having revealed his abbreviated name and has been thrice denied himself. He has "put off the garment" of the persona O. E. and turns back to that most primeval of theistic symbols, the rising sun "as if he expected someone behind him to give him the answer."[127] "The sky had lightened slightly and there were two or three streaks of yellow floating above the horizon. Then as he stood there, a tree of light burst over the skyline. Parker fell back against the door as if he had been pinned there by a lance."[128] O. E.'s vision of "uncreated light," so like to Moses', is not merely symbolic of divine proximity, it is a "direct encounter with the living God."[129] At this moment, O. E. is assimilated to Christ; he suffers the pain of the fifth "holy wound" and asserts his given names. "[A]ll at once he felt the light pouring through him, turning his spider web soul into a perfect arabesque of colors."[130] Parker's "mixed human nature, which was assumed by the Lord, has taken its seat on the right hand of divine majesty in the heavens, being full of glory not only (like Moses) in the face, but in the whole body."[131] He has become, as Palamas said of the hesychasts, "all light and is assimilated to what [he] sees, or rather, is united to it without mingling, being [himself] light and seeing light through light."[132]

The revelation of his transfigured body is fleeting as O. E.'s will retains the habit of its vices. The light of perfect illumination, Palamas tells us, "does not endure with the imperfect;" its sight is fleeting even for the saints.[133] "There is a difference," Palamas wrote, "between illumination and a durable vision of the light, and the vision of things in the light, whereby even things far off are accessible to the eyes, and the future is shown as already existing."[134] This double reality, at once achieved and forthcoming, is the ultimate revelation in which all matter is directly engaged with the Deity. O.

---

[127] O'Connor, "Parker's Back," *Complete*, 528.

[128] Ibid.

[129] Hunt, "Byzantine Christianity." *The Blackwell Companion to Eastern Orthodoxy*, ed Ken Parry. New York: John Wiley and Sons, Inc., 2010, 91.

[130] O'Connor, "Parker's Back," *Complete*, 528.

[131] Macarius of Egypt qtd. in Palamas, *The Triads*, 76.

[132] Palamas, *The Triads*, 64.

[133] Ibid.

[134] Ibid.

E.'s glimpse of total communion—of his body as a "garden of trees and birds and beasts"—spurs him to offer himself, not as a transitory object of desire, but as an icon of the world transfigured for his beloved to consume.[135] But Sarah Ruth's vision is limited by the old Law. Her fundamentalist leanings lead her to assume that her fallen husband, if he does not live entirely in the shadow of the Law, will be justly damned. "For the old Adam," she could have said with Luther's followers, "as an intractable, pugnacious ass, is still a part of [him], which is to be coerced to the obedience of Christ, not only by the doctrine, admonition, force, and threatening of the Law, but also oftentimes by the club of punishments and troubles, until the sinful flesh is entirely put off."[136] Undeniably, the process of divinization is only begun in Parker. Even repentant, it is hard to imagine his becoming entirely without sin. His significance lies very much in his fault; he is the counterpoint to Mosaic Law, forgiven in sin but not at the point of perfection. He is representative of the Orthodox conviction that the commandments were given to reveal what is possible for mankind in concert with the grace of God. Parker is therefore a testament to virtue in the negative which, as Aquinas put it, is "made perfect in [the] weakness...of our body."[137]

In an unpublished draft of "The Catholic Novelist in the Protestant South," O'Connor noted that, "A religion based entirely on the Bible creates distortions, for the Bible was meant to stand but not to stand alone."[138] Indeed, Parker's conversion would make hardly a sound if he had not first, like the Solomon of Ecclesiastes, made a test of pleasure.[139] His homecoming is significant precisely because of the singularity of his path which begins with his anxious flight from the "big lighted church," stagnates in his drunken furlough, doubles back to his native South, and finally retreats to a

---

135 O'Connor, "Parker's Back," *Complete*, 528.

136 The Evangelical Lutheran Church, *The Book of Concord: or, the Symbolical Books of the Evangelical Lutheran Church*, ed. Henry Eyster Jacobs (Philadelphia: The United Lutheran Publication House, 1911) 599.

137 St. Thomas Aquinas, *Selected Philosophical Writings*, ed. and trans. Timothy McDermott (Oxford: Oxford University Press, 1993) 395–96.

138 Flannery O'Connor, "The Catholic Novelist in the Protestant South," N. date, MS 274a, 10, *Flannery O'Connor Collection*, Russell Library, Georgia College & State University, Milledgeville.

139 Eccles. 2:1, *NRSV*.

red clay desert.[140] It is this human quality of O. E.'s, his being a particular man in need of a particular kind of mercy, that Sarah Ruth overlooks. She is conscious of only the narrow way and judges her husband's wide and haphazard circuit as merely sinful. Her theology is not equipped for the prophet whose faith is often slow in coming and never without the tandem pain of turning continually from earthly loves and of doubt. She demands Parker give his true name and yet refuses to acknowledge that man, part dissident, part visionary, who shares with her one flesh.

Once inside, Parker "set[s] about lighting the kerosene lamp;" a "yellow glow envelope[s]" the couple, not unlike the conjoined haloes of light in the iconic *Encounter of Sts. Joachim and Anne*.[141] Their embrace is unique among Orthodox icons in that it celebrates the conjugal source of Christ. Joachim and Anne, aged and childless, reunite after solitary petitions to God, clasping one another with passionate reverence at the conception of their daughter Mary. "The scene," Paul Atkins Underwood writes, "…has a higher significance than the mere return of Joachim, for the inscription [*The Conception of St. Anne*] marks it as the prelude to one of the momentous events in the Incarnation, namely, the conception of the God-bearer…."[142] O'Connor's narrative again inverts Apocryphal scripture; when O. E. returns from the wilds of the city, he is not welcomed into the arms of his pregnant wife. She denies him even a glance. "I ain't got to look at you," she says. Parker quietly maneuvers around her hard-heartedness.[143] "'Look at this' he says, 'and then I don't want to hear no more out of you.'"[144] O. E. turns his back to his wife, revealing the Byzantine Christ. She "growl[s]" at the sight of it: "I might have known… [M]ore trash."[145] In anguish, Parker yells, "Don't just say that! *Look* at it!"[146] "In the beginning was the Word" and "the Word was God," Sarah Ruth tells us, but the Word also "became flesh and

[140] O'Connor, "Parker's Back," *Complete*, 513.

[141] See *The Conception of St. Anne*, Novgorod School, ca. 15th century, egg tempura on panel,

Museum of Icons, Recklinghausen, Germany.

[142] Paul Atkins Underwood, *The Kariye Djami*, Vol. I (New York: Taylor & Francis, 1967) 65.

[143] O'Connor, "Parker's Back," *Complete*, 529.

[144] Ibid. Italics my own.

[145] Ibid.

[146] Ibid.

lived among us."[147] Parker alone has begun to engage the mystery of the Incarnation, the mystery of Christ as "the word between the silence of God and the understanding in the Spirit."[148] But even faced with so literal an analogy, Sarah Ruth's vision cannot penetrate the skin. She sees the brazen serpent but not the sacrifice.

Just as Sarah Ruth fulfils Parker's silent prophesy of marriage, *she* intimates the coming of the Christ, fulfilling, through her ultimate rejection, "all…the Lord had spoken through the prophets."[149] To bear the suffering of Jesus Obadiah Elihue has first to endure rejection—his bitter casting out by his pool hall cronies and his wife.[150] Only after this final rejection is O. E. suitably humbled; forsaken by his last refuge, he is left "right at the beginning" of a new life and very likely a new vocation.[151] Sarah Ruth's denial has shown him how to begin in faith by showing him first what faith is not. Hers is a religion in which faith seems superfluous. Rather it is an absolute and unsearchable truth of holy indictment located exclusively between the Books of Genesis and Revelation and accomplished long ago. There is no call for her to "leap," as O. E. must, into "a worse unknown."[152] To seek God in the world is, for Sarah Ruth, to tempt sin. Her ironical marriage to O. E. might be a sign of a latent sense of incompatibility in a faith that preaches the forgiveness of sins through human sacrifice but denies that faith its humanity. O. E.'s instinct, like O'Connor's, is to start with the flesh, to go into the desert himself and live the revelation. Like Jerome in his translation of Solomon's wedding song, O. E. says of Christ, "I don't wish Him to speak to me through Moses nor through the prophets; let Him take my body, let Him kiss me in the flesh."[153]

---

[147] John 1:1, 1:14, *NRSV*.

[148] Denis McBride, *The Gospel of Luke: A Reflective Commentary* (Dublin: Dominican Publications, 1991) 137.

[149] Matt. 1:22, 22:4, *NRSV*.

[150] Jürgen M. Moltmann writes in *The Crucified God*, "If those who follow Jesus are to take 'their cross' on themselves, they are taking on not only suffering and a bitter fate, but the suffering of rejection" ([London: S.C.M., 1977] 55).

[151] O'Connor, *Habit* 359.

[152] O'Connor, "Parker's Back," *Complete*, 521.

[153] St. Jerome, *The Satirical Letters of St. Jerome*, Vol. I, trans. Paul Carroll (Chicago: Henry Regenery Co., 1956) 121.

Chapter 4

"Lest Ye Be Born Again":

Heretical Baptism in "The River" and *The Violent Bear It Away*[1]

Flannery O'Connor's exposition of penance in her first novel *Wise Blood* and in the stories "Parker's Back" and "Why Do the Heathen Rage?", while harrowing, comes with a degree of expectation. There is a sense of authorial retribution in the suffering dealt to Hazel, O. E., and Walter that seems justifiable mechanically if not ethically, but in O'Connor's attempts to dramatize the sacrament of baptism in "The River" (1953) and *The Violent Bear It Away* (1960), suffering befalls the apparently innocent. The sense of justice that relieves some of the pain the reader bears with the penitent is left void in death, and the Christian edict of the needful sacrifice is tainted by the senselessness of accident and malice. In both texts, the performance of the baptism rite finds its resolution in an actual death. The orthodox ritual of symbolic burial with Christ is made literal while the mystery of bodily resurrection is shrouded in intentions at once sinister and guileless. To be born again to everlasting life is, for Tarwater and Harry/Bevel, an act that cannot be practicably separated from blasphemy.

Almost exclusively O'Connor's fiction figures within the precarious territory of contiguity between salvation and damnation. For characters as dissimilar as Hazel Motes, Joy-Hulga, and Mrs. Turpin, revelation is the direct result of rational blasphemy carried in practice to its conclusion and ultimately backfiring. Hazel rails against the orthodox pretext of Original Sin but in his sustained transgressions finds an inverse logic—that he is unclean in his very willfulness and must submit to a purifying penance. Joy-Hulga presumes supreme knowledge in her faithfulness to nothing, but her naïveté is revealed when the bumpkinish Manley Pointer reverses her seductions. Mrs. Turpin assumes her religious house is in order until the disaffected Mary Grace forces upon her an alternate vision of herself as an "old warthog…from hell."[2] Although the truth they

[1] John 3:3, *KJV*.

[2] O'Connor, "Revelation," *Complete*, 500.

seek in self-justification is symmetrically opposed to the truth they find, the way to revelation for O'Connor's heroes is very much the way of the blasphemer. As Hazel put it, "Blasphemy is the way to the truth…and there's no other way whether you understand it or not!"[3]

O'Connor's protagonists—deviants, intellectuals, and country women—all experience grace through the over-turning of their ritualized blasphemies. For the author, the baptismal rite was second in symbolic weight only to the Eucharist. It is a ritual that enacts the death and resurrection of the body that leaves an indelible seal upon the celebrant's soul, marking him as a new creature and a member of the mystical body of Christ.[4] To Roman Catholics, baptism "configures [the individual] to Christ." He is reborn supernaturally, unfettered from his biological inheritance of Original Sin. "Through the waters of baptism those who are born into this world dead in sin are…born again…[and] being stamped with a spiritual seal they become able and fit to receive the other Sacraments."[5] The Orthodox liturgy parallels Rome as regards the mystical rebirth that occurs at baptism, but Orthodoxy is careful to foreground the individual's participation in the actual death and resurrection of Christ in its rendering of Romans, chapter six: "…[D]o you not know that all [of us]…who were baptized into Christ Jesus were baptized into his death? And so, we were buried with him through baptism to death, so that just as Christ was raised from the dead by the glory of the Father, [likewise] we too might walk in newness of life."[6] For Orthodox Christians, the ritual of baptism describes "the personal

---

[3] O'Connor, *Wise Blood*, 152.

[4] *Catechism of the Catholic Church* (Libreria Editrice Vaticana, Citta del Vaticano, 1993) 1214, 1216. Vatican Publishing House, 1993. *www.vatican.va.* http://www.vatican.va/archive/ENG0015/__P3H.HTM (accessed 3 March 2011).

[5] Pope Pius XII, *Mystici Corporis Christi*, Section XVIII. Vatican Publishing House, 1990. http://www.vatican.va/holy_father/pius_xii/encyclicals/documents/hf_xii_enc_29061943mystici-corporis-christi_en.html (accessed 3 March 2011).

[6] Romans 6:3–4, *The Eastern/Greek Orthodox Bible*, 359. ed. Rev. Laurent Cleenewerck, St. Innocent Orthodox Church, Eureka, CA, 2008. *www.orthodoxanswers.org*. http://www.orthodoxanswers .org/eob/ (accessed 16 March 2011).

experience of Easter given to each man."[7] Active within the rite is the "real possibility to die and be 'born anew.'"[8] The inherited consequence of Original Sin, death, is washed away; the sense of hereditary guilt so emblematic of Pre-Vatican II Catholicism is absent from the Orthodox rite.

Chrismation, the sister sacrament of Orthodox baptism, is performed immediately succeeding the initiate's three-fold submersion. The priest makes the sign of the cross on the candidate's "forehead, eyes, nose, ears, lips, breast, back, hands, and feet" with oil (*chrism* or *myron*), anointing him as the kings of the Old Testament and Christ himself was anointed.[9] Confirmation is not deferred until "the age of reason"[10] as it is in the Roman liturgy, but both traditions hold that the baptismal rite is not fully realized until the initiate is confirmed and the grace conferred upon him by the sanctified waters is strengthened by the personal Pentecost of chrismation.[11] Confirmation, the Catholic catechism declares, "is necessary for the completion of baptismal grace…[for by this sacrament, the baptized] 'are more perfectly bound to the Church and are enriched with a special strength of the Holy Spirit.'"[12] Once the Orthodox initiate is confirmed by Chrismation, he is given the Sacrament of Sacraments, which is celebrated with both bread and wine. As in the Roman Church, the stuff of the Eucharistic ceremony is not "merely [an] intellectual or psychological symbol…of Christ's Body and Blood" but the manifestation of Christ's real presence.[13]

---

[7] V. Rev. Thomas Hopko, *The Orthodox Faith: Doctrine*, "Sacraments," Vol. I, n. page. Dept. of Religious Education. The Orthodox Church in America, 1996. *www.oca.org*. http://www.oca.org/OCchapter.asp?SID=2&ID=27 (accessed 3 March 2011).

[8] John 3:3, *EOB*, 236.

[9] *Catechism of the Catholic Church*, 1300.

[10] Joseph Delany, "Age of Reason," *The Catholic Encyclopedia*, Vol. 1 (New York: Robert Appleton Company, 1907). Kevin Knight, 2009. www.newadvent.org. http://www.newadvent.org/cathen/01209a.htm (accessed 4 March 2011).

[11] In the Roman rite, confirmation is preceded by a renewal of baptismal vows. See *Catechism of the Catholic Church*, 1298.

[12] Ibid., 1285.

[13] V. Rev. Thomas Hopko, *The Orthodox Faith: Worship*, "Holy Eucharist," Vol. II, n. page. Dept. of Religious Education. The Orthodox Church in America, 1996. *www.oca.org*. http://www.oca.org/ OCchapter.asp?SID=2&ID=27 (accessed 4 March 2011).

In both traditions, Holy Communion is the end point of all the other sacraments; all of the mysteries of the Christian faith are believed to radiate through this cumulative act. "All the rivers come from that one River and go back to it like it was the ocean sea," the evangelical Bevel Summers preaches, "and if you believe, you can lay your pain in that River and get rid of it because that's the River that was made to carry sin."[14] The mystical tradition that links Eastern and Roman orthodoxy has its locus in the Eucharistic mystery, and concomitant with the belief in the divinity of the bread of life is a metaphysics that deciphers the actual as an extension of the mystical. "All…reality is real to the extent that it is symbolical and mystical, to the extent that reality itself must reveal and manifest God to us."[15]

The initiates of "The River" and *The Violent Bear It Away* are both children, innocent in both experience and sensibility; Harry/Bevel is "four or five,"[16] hardly morally responsible, and Bishop Rayber is a child with Down's Syndrome "touched" with perpetual innocence.[17] Though she only hints at Harry's age in the text, O'Connor is very particular as to how he might be represented by an actual child in her correspondence with Robert Jiras, an independent filmmaker who attempted to adapt the story into a feature. She wrote that "the credibility of such a story depends on the age of the boy: a five year old child might reasonably be expected to believe that another world could be found under the river; a six year old one wouldn't."[18] It is significant that Harry has not reached the

---

[14] O'Connor, "The River," *Complete*, 165.

[15] Hopko, "Holy Eucharist," n. page.

[16] O'Connor, "The River," *Complete*, 158. In an earlier version of the story, Harry is said to be three years old. Flannery O'Connor, "Early Fragment of 'The River,'" N. date, MS 155, 1, *Flannery O'Connor Collection*, Russell Library, Georgia College & State University, Milledgeville.

[17] When Tarwater lashes out at the doting Bishop at the Cherokee Lodge, the matron tells him to, "'Mind how [he] talk[s] to one of them there…' as if he had profaned the holy." Old Tarwater interprets Bishop's condition as a blessing: "…the Lord gave [Rayber] one he couldn't corrupt" (Flannery O'Connor, *The Violent Bear It Away* [New York: Farrar, Straus & Giroux, 1955] 77, 155).

[18] Flannery O'Connor, "Correspondence with Robert Jiras," 29 August 1956, MS 59, Box 1, FF 39, *Flannery O'Connor Collection*, Manuscripts, Archives, and Rare Books Library, Emory University, Atlanta.

Roman age of discretion and yet is made to assume the responsibility of membership in the Church of Christ, which, in a mystical sense, means assuming Christ's Passion as a literal "member" of His body. The mystical efficacy of the sacraments here supersedes the particulars of church dogma. O'Connor was insistent upon underscoring the mystical import of the boys' baptisms as opposed to the mechanics of the rite by blending Orthodox, Roman, and Protestant traditions. What's more, neither child could be said to desire baptism in an ecclesiastical sense. Harry's self-baptism is the result of a deliberate but naïve rationale: if the Kingdom of Christ is in the river, he has only to go into the water to find it. He need "not fool with preachers anymore."[19] Bishop's attraction to the vehicle of baptism has a more immediate end: the overwhelming sensory pleasure of seeing and touching water itself. Fountain and lake draw the child to an instant reward, not a removed, ethereal salvation. There is something of the desert sensibility in Bishop; he perceives and interacts with the world in a way devoid of distracting calculation, very much to the contrary of his father's and his cousin's practical stoicism. He makes visible, in a way that Rayber and Tarwater cannot, the active presence of the Kingdom of God and the realm of the Devil in men. Take, for instance, his reactions to goodness and to evil—clinging whoops and stricken bellows—are appropriately guileless and faithfully repeated even when the goodness he seems to intuit in father and cousin is met with murderous intent.

In spite of his vaguely ennobling innocence, Bishop's sacrifice cannot be explained as a simple parallel to Christ's. The boy's death, however tragic, does not carry the gravity of penitential charity inherent to the Cross. Although Bishop does not function as a Christ figure in death—Tarwater must be sacrificed bodily himself before he is penitent—he is reminiscent of Jesus in life in that he is directed primarily by love. Even though this indiscriminate love leads Bishop to his death, his inability to choose that death, to respond, with head held under water, contrary to his instincts, makes him a victim not a martyr. "The shedding of blood," St. Thomas wrote, "is not in the nature of Baptism if it be done without charity."[20]

---

[19] O'Connor, "The River," *Complete*, 173.

[20] St. Thomas Aquinas, *Summa Theologica*, Part III, Ques. LXVI, Article XII, Reply to Objection II, n. page. *The Summa Theologica of St. Thomas*

It is crucial to both narratives that the sacrament of baptism occur outside a wilderness apart from the sterility of the city and the regalia of the church. "When I write a novel in which the central action is a baptism," O'Connor stated in 1963:

> I am very well aware that for a majority of my readers, baptism is a meaningless rite, and so in my novel I have to see that this baptism carries enough awe and mystery to jar the reader into some emotional recognition of its significance. To this end I have to bend the whole novel—its language, its structure, its action. I have to make the reader feel, in his bones if nowhere else, that something is going on here that counts.[21]

The sense of mystery O'Connor intends for the reader she first impresses upon Bishop and Harry, introducing them, not merely to the baptismal rite as a discrete event, but to the elemental nature of water with all of its symbolic and actual power. Ubiquitous and enduring, water, like fire, cleanses and sustains but also obliterates. From the beginning, "the Spirit of God moved upon the face of the waters," bringing creative light to darkness.[22] At Christ's baptism in the Jordan, the Spirit came "straightway up out of the water," the "heavens opened," and "the Holy Ghost descend[ed] like a dove" upon the son of man.[23] These verses from Exodus and the Gospel of St. Mark proclaim water as a conduit of the graciousness of God, but it also carries His wrath. The Deluge brought with it an "end of all flesh"; only the righteous house of Noah was spared.[24] In the time of Moses, the Spirit led Israel through the waters of the Red Sea, baptizing the people into new life in a promised land while Pharaoh and his men were buried beneath the waves.[25] For both Bishop and Harry, the double nature of water coincides, destroying as it purifies.

But first, water is a source of wonder. The experience of water, rushing and muddy, broad and deep, is without precedent for the suburbanites Harry and Bishop. At the Cherokee Lodge, Bishop goes

---

Aquinas, 2nd rev. ed., 1920, trans. Fathers of the English Dominican Province. Kevin Knight, 2008. http://www.newadvent.org/summa/4066.htm#article-12 (accessed 7 March 2011).

[21] O'Connor, "Novelist and Believer," *Mystery,* 162.

[22] Gen. 1:1–4, *KJV.*

[23] Mark 1:9–10, *KJV.*

[24] Gen. 6:13–17; 1 Pet. 3:17–21, *KJV.*

[25] Exod. 14:1–31; 1 Cor. 10:1–2, *KJV.*

into the water with Francis Marion, not primarily because Tarwater, the boy's standoffish antagonist turned steely care-giver, leads him, but because he is overcome by the strangeness of the lake itself. Harry's first sight of the river is akin to Bishop's in wondrous attraction. Breaking through the "bridle path" with Mrs. Connin, he spies the "broad orange stream where the reflection of the sun was set like a diamond."[26] O'Connor casts the scene with overtones of the marriage ritual, the child led like a bride to a new life of sacred union. In both stories the transmissive waters take on an air of otherworldliness, transfigured as if by magic from a clear flowing tap to a churning marl-red and a slick, solemn blackness. Such wonder at the world outside seems to have been completely "bred out" of Rayber and Harry's parents the Ashfields.[27] Rivers and lakes hold as much significance for them as the tenets and taboos of organized Christianity and are as easily disregarded as quaint throwbacks to a time before manicured sub-divisions, mass media, and Women's Lib.

O'Connor connects her generation's loss of wonder at the world with its loss of moral sensitivity. Rayber and the Ashfields parrot the cosmopolitan fashion of the day, that is to know everything and to care about nothing or at least appear to. "The moral sense," O'Connor wrote to Hester in 1955, "has been bred out of certain sections of the population like the wings have been bred off chickens to produce more white meat in them. This is a generation of wingless chickens, which I suppose is what Nietzsche meant when he said God was dead."[28] Perhaps this is why the author seems to favor child protagonists when writing stories which enact the sacraments. The movement of wonder within them is not met with counter-rationale; it is let flow. They haven't to work so hard against social breeding to come to revelation. In the case of young adults like Tarwater, Rufus Johnson, and Joy-Hulga mystery meets with an entrenched personal opposition. Each of them identifies internal resistance pridefully as the operation of their own assertive will. O'Connor meanwhile plays devil's advocate, literally associating her characters' anti-mysticism with the influence of demonic wile. Revelation, for these three, is accompanied by a humbling blow. Adults like Rayber and the Ashfields are spared the violent revelatory deaths of peers like Mrs.

---

[26] Ibid., 164.

[27] O'Connor, *Habit*, 90.

[28] Ibid.

May and the Mr. Fortune, but theirs is a false salvation which seems to justify the authorial implication that they are too far gone. Like the heretics in Dante's sixth circle of Hell, Rayber and the Ashfields suffer on indefinitely in self-satisfied confinement.[29] Even the false prophet, Asa Hawks concedes that, "The deepest places are reserved for blasphemers."[30]

The protagonists of "The River" and *The Violent Bear It Away* are both orphans, Tarwater literally and Harry figuratively. The elder boy was "born in a [car] wreck," and he clings to the high drama of his worldly entrance when no prophetic signs from above are forthcoming.[31] His father was a suicide. The:

> Lord had rescued him out of the womb of a whore and let him see the light of day…and then…having [saved him] once, He had gone and done it again, allowing him to be baptized by his great-uncle into the death of Jesus Christ, and then having done it twice [He] gone on and done it a third time, allowing him to be rescued by his great-uncle from the schoolteacher and brought to the backwoods and given a chance to be brought up according to the truth.[32]

Harry's early life has not been so remarkable, though he too was born of "heathen" parents.[33] There is no great uncle to pluck him from his parents' spartan flat where he waits, "patient and mute," his "eyes half closed" as if he's lived most of life in semi-darkness.[34] Harry has learned how to maneuver in the stale, shuttered air, absolutely silent, almost not existing, as his mother and father sleep off the evenings' cocktails. The boy is introduced by their joking negligence, his father thrusting him, arm awry in his coat, into the care of Mrs. Connin, his mother calling from the bedroom, not for her son but for an icepack. Ashfield darts his head from behind the bedroom door and calls, "Good-by, old man," moved to fatherly

---

[29] Dante Alighieri, *The Divine Comedy, Inferno, Canto* IX: 106–33; *Canto* X:1–15, trans. Charles H. Sisson, reissued (Oxford: Oxford University Press, 2008) 84–85.

[30] Flannery O'Connor, Manuscript of *Wise Blood*, N. date, MS 72, 11, *Flannery O'Connor Collection*, Russell Library, Georgia College & State University, Milledgeville.

[31] O'Connor, *Violent*, 41, 212.

[32] Ibid.

[33] O'Connor, Early Fragment of "The River," MS 155, 2.

[34] O'Connor, "The River," *Complete*, 158.

sentiment by Mrs. Connin's neck-craning. So unused is the boy to filial intimacy, he "jumped as if he'd been shot."[35]

The prime mover in the Ashfield universe is adult pleasure, and to this end it operates with chilling efficiency in spite of the fact that one of the trio is not yet past puberty. Harry's mother and father expect the boy to be the old man they project as adamantly as they expect him to feed and mind himself. He functions in "the place where he lives" like a distant relative turned squatter, not as one who is at home. When Mrs. Connin announces that the child "ain't fixed right," the painful implication of the Harry's needfulness is brought to bear while his hung arm and running nose point to more profound neglect.[36] "Well then for Christ's sake fix him," Mr. Ashfield replies, eager to hand off his responsibility to someone else.[37] Mrs. Connin takes Ashfield at his word. The country woman intends to "fix" the little boy, not just there in the doorway but for all time in baptism. In prelude she adjusts the child's coat and wipes at his nose with her handkerchief. "Some people don't care how they send one off," she exclaims. "You pervide [sic]."[38] She gives Harry what is likely her only handkerchief, and he presses her hand as she nods off on the street car, reassuring himself, perhaps, that Mrs. Connin is tired, not drunk, and that her charity is actual—not pitying or preachy and certainly not a joke. Her quotation of Abraham's words, "The Lord will provide," subtly foreshadows Harry's fate by drawing a parallel with Isaac, the would-be sacrificial lamb of Genesis.[39]

As if to signal his assuming a new life with a new set of expectations and realities, Harry christens himself Bevel. Mrs. Connin gushes over the "coincident" of the child's having the same given name as the preacher Bevel Summers she intends to take the boy to. With shared enthusiasm Harry confirms himself by repeating the name.[40] The coincidence is made all the more extraordinary because Bevel Summers is "not no ordinary preacher." He's a "healer," but you have to have faith to be healed, Mrs. Connin

---

[35] Ibid., 159.

[36] Ibid., 158.

[37] Ibid.

[38] Ibid., 159.

[39] Gen. 22:14, *NKJV*.

[40] O'Connor, "The River," *Complete*, 159.

explains. Her own husband, an ill unbeliever, was proof of the necessity of belief. "Will he heal me?"[41] Bevel asks and announces that he is hungry. The child's hunger pangs are two-fold issuing from body and soul, and Mrs. Connin treats both with an orthodox matter-of-factness imitative of the simple action of the Eucharist. To eat of the Bread of Life is to be confirmed in baptism, to be fulfilled in that rite and sustained eternally by the consummating love of the Spirit. Tarwater is afflicted with the same soul hunger though he resists it in name, sickening at the thought of the unimaginable fullness of actually eating the Bread and being sated by it in an oddly banal ever-lasting life. "The boy would have a hideous vision of himself sitting forever with his great-uncle on a green bank, full and sick, staring at a broken fish and a multiplied loaf." [42] "Had the bush flamed for Moses, the sun stood still for Joshua, the lions turned aside before Daniel only to prophesy the bread of life? Jesus? [Tarwater] felt a terrible...dread that it was true."[43] He felt "a slow warm rising resentment that...freedom had to be connected with Jesus and that Jesus had to be Lord."[44]

The thread of human resistance to grace is carried by the antagonistic Mr. Paradise in "The River," a nay-saying old man with bulbous tumors who presents himself at backwater healings to "show he ain't been healed."[45] Bevel associates the old man with the stampeding shoat which he is goaded to let loose by Mrs. Connin's three sons. If the reader missed the allusion to demonic power, O'Connor follows the shoat with the gospel according to Luke for "Readers Under Twelve." Bevel interprets Christ's works as Mrs. Connin does, with absolute literalness. Astonished, he listens to the account of Jesus' driving "a crowd of pigs out of a man, ...real pigs, ...gray and sour-looking. ...[He] had driven them all out of this one man."[46] St. Luke's gospel, which O'Connor tells Jiras Mrs. Connin's book would have to "hue with," has it that Christ drove "unclean spirits" from a man, and in his mercy consented that they reform in

---

[41] Ibid.

[42] O'Connor, *Violent*, 62. See also pgs. 122, 211, 213.

[43] Ibid., 21.

[44] Ibid., 21–22.

[45] O'Connor, "The River, *Complete*, 162.

[46] Ibid., 163.

the bodies of a nearby herd of swine.[47] There is a strong resonance between this gospel miracle and the sacrament of baptism, one that extends significantly to the damned. The legion of devils pray forgiveness to Christ that he might deliver them into the bodies of the pigs and not cast them "into the deep."[48] Christ "suffers" their beseeching and drives the demons from the body of the afflicted man and into the pigs. "Then went the devils out of the man, and entered into the swine: and the herd ran violently down a steep place into the lake, and were choked."[49] The demons' destruction is deliberately purgatorial. They have lost the dignity of a creaturely body but have been allowed to persist beyond the steeper fall into Sheol. Conversely, the afflicted man experiences a total exorcism of inherited and actual sin just as the catechumen does when he is baptized in Christ's Passion and reborn clean. Although the rite casts the demon of Original Sin into the abyss, the devils too experience a kind of baptism. They are compelled to acknowledge the power of the Spirit in Christ, naming Him when the disciplines yet denied Him, and thereby submitting themselves to the power of God. Even more to the point is their headlong rush into a purgatorial wilderness which mirrors the inverse call of Satan to the newly baptized Jesus into his trials in the desert. The unnamed man in Luke was "driven of the devil into the wilderness," and Christ himself, after he is baptized by John, is "immediately" driven "by the spirit into the wilderness" where he was tempted for forty days.[50]

By conjoining images of exorcism with images of the theophany implicit in baptism, O'Connor speaks to the complex nature of free will. That freedom "cannot be conceived simply" is apparent in the twin compulsion of the devils and the baptized Christ. The former are moved, as Christ was rising out of the river Jordan, to follow the Spirit into ungodly territory and to face the paradoxical limbo between devilish concession and God-given mercy. In "The River," limbo is made creaturely in the person of Mr. Paradise, a man who is at once a foil of the Devil and a testimony to Christ's compassion. His

---

[47] O'Conner, "Correspondence with Robert Jiras," 4 February 1958, MS 59, Box 1, FF 39, *Flannery O'Connor Collection*, Manuscripts, Archives, and Rare Books Library, Emory University, Atlanta; Luke 8:29, *KJV*.

[48] Luke 8:31–32, *KJV*.

[49] Luke 8:33, *KJV*.

[50] Luke 8:29; Mark 1:12–13, *KJV*.

name seems less ironic when we consider his closing act, his dashing into the churning water to save the child who has already slipped away. But even this gesture, with all of its fatherly overtones, is one which O'Connor was careful to play straight. She warns Jiras that, "...Mr. Paradise serves as the devil in this story even though he means well. Don't go and get Mr. Paradise too lovable please. He wants to save the little boy. That's the extent of his benevolence."[51]

Before he was given up to Mrs. Connin, Bevel's sense of salvation was clinical. He believed he had been made "by a doctor named Sladewell...who thought his name was Herbert, but this must have been a joke."[52] Here again the implication of a link between physical and spiritual health is taken up. The sentiment is felt more directly in an early fragment of the story in which the boy recalls his immunizations to a more damning Mrs. Connin:

> "Your people are heathens," [the old woman said].
> "What are heathens?" he asked.
> "Total unbelievers," she said.
> "Am I a heathen?"
> "Have you been baptized?"
> "I've been vacinated [sic]."
> "Not the same."[53]

Throughout "The River," O'Connor's concern for the right naming of things before God is suffused with a contrary sense that everything is in fact meaningless and part of an intricate, temporary farce. "They joked a lot where [the boy] lived. If he had thought about it before, he would have thought Jesus Christ was a word like 'oh' or 'damn' or 'God,' or maybe somebody who had cheated them out of something sometime."[54] It is quite a distance for Bevel to go, accepting the man in the sheet as maker not curse and to do so without the customary "we" of his dependent thinking as part of a unit. The woman O'Connor installs as minister to the child is called Connin, a name that does not inspire much faith in itself and which stands as the first of many nominal contradictions. The child is himself a paradox, at once naïve and calculating. He pockets Mrs.

---

[51] Ibid.

[52] O'Connor, "The River," *Complete*, 163.

[53] O'Connor, "Early Fragment of 'The River,'" MS 155, 2.

[54] O'Connor, "The River," *Complete*, 163.

Connin's beloved gospel reader and tips ash trays onto his mother's carpet, anticipating that if "he only emptied a few, she would think they had fallen."[55] Mr. Paradise, we find, is not merely devil but the devil converted. And the Ashfields, though their name conjures images of charred wasteland, also point to the resurrection and the sacramental of Ash Wednesday by which the first day of Lent is marked. On this occasion the faithful, bearing the sign of the cross, are asked to turn away from sin and to meditate upon Christ's temptation in the desert.

The woods stand in for the desert in O'Connor's fictive South. It is where the prophets Old Tarwater and Mr. Shiftlet (not Tom T.) go to pray and to "thrash…out [their] peace with the Lord."[56] It is where the child Rayber contemplated fleeing to escape his father and "the real world."[57] For Bevel the woods are the beginning of a "strange country," contiguous with his parents' world yet distinct.[58] The river that runs through the wood, "filthy" and quietly menacing, is also an extension of the mystical River of Christ's blood.[59] "If you ain't come for Jesus, you ain't come for me," the Reverend Bevel Summers proclaims, knee deep in the water. "If you just come to see can you leave your pain in the river, you ain't come for Jesus. You can't leave your pain in the river."[60] It is faith that heals—not the river—faith that is miracle and miracle-worker, one. Like Christ, Summers preaches against the miracle. He declares that if the people require miracles to have faith, they shall not be healed. To the blind man, the leper, and the bleeding woman Jesus said, "[T]hy faith hath saved thee, …thy faith hath made thee whole."[61] "The same blood that makes this River red, made that leper clean, made that blind man stare…" the Reverend calls across the water, "If it's the River of Life

---

[55] Ibid., 172.

[56] The Shiftlet of a fragmentary manuscript parallels Old Tarwater in his determined but often shadowy indoctrination of his son Woodrow. Flannery O'Connor, "Unidentified Fragment," N. date, MS 213a, 2, *Flannery O'Connor Collection*, Russell Library, Georgia College & State University, Milledgeville; *Violent*, 8.

[57] O'Connor, *Violent*, 76, 128.

[58] O'Connor, "The River," *Complete*, 164.

[59] Ibid., 173.

[60] Ibid., 165.

[61] Mark 10:51–52 and Luke 18:42; Matt. 8:2–3; Mark 5:34 and Matt. 9:22, *KJV*.

you want to lay your pain in, then come up... But don't be thinking this is the last of it because this old red river don't end here. This old red suffering stream goes on, you people, slow to the Kingdom of Christ."[62] Salvation was never instant and rarely complete in O'Connor's thinking; to be "saved" is to enter into the suffering of mankind not as one who seeks to be delivered from pain, transported from body to pure spirit, but as one who suffers *in* salvation. "[Y]ou do misinterpret me," O'Connor wrote Maryat Lee in 1957, "if you think I mean that it all ends in tattatatum and a tragic little pie. I believe in the resurrection of the body. I also believe in it before it gets that way..."[63] The River is a tangible Purgatory, and it courses by slow and soundless toward the centre of suffering, toward the Passion, initiating comers into a "new kind of suffering, not Purgatory as St. Catherine would conceive it (realization) but Purgatory at least as the beginning of suffering."[64] Even "redeemed," the pain rolls on in man through Christ to the *Logos* of God Himself. The Ashfields of the world subdue collective suffering with intoxicants, the Raybers with empiricism, certain that what causes pain, no matter its metaphysical reward, is not worth enduring. Indeed there are few in O'Connor's works who do not resist the trials of her purgatorial salvation, but in the author's words, "there is certainly no reason why the effects of redemption are plain to us and I think they usually are not. This is where we share Christ's agony where he was about to die and cried out, 'My God, why have you forsaken me?'"[65]

Unlike Rayber and his parents, Bevel goes the way of the disciple, not because he is an exceptional spiritual agent but because he is ignorant of what his seeking the Kingdom will mean actually or symbolically. The "servants of the Lord Jesus," Old Tarwater warns, "could expect the worse," and his young disciple Francis "could see that this was so."[66] But understanding is not necessary for the journey Bevel intends to take. He deserts the shuttered apartment. Alone and empty-handed but cannily purpose-driven, he pockets the car-token he'll need for the tram and considered a suitcase but

---

[62] O'Connor, "The River," *Complete*, 166.
[63] O'Connor, *Habit*, 227.
[64] Ibid., 118.
[65] Ibid.
[66] O'Connor, *Violent*, 62.

decided finally to leave it behind "because there was nothing from there he wanted to keep."[67] His movements are deliberate, endowed with an incongruous surety of adult objective. He catches the railcar at the corner and gets off "at the end of the line," anticipating that no one would be home at the Connin's to foil him.[68] As Christ's disciples were, Bevel is compelled to a narrow path; he understands as little about where it leads.[69]

The same "current of death" that spurs Bevel to the river runs "in [Tarwater's] blood," leading him along another narrow path to his personal Jerusalem at Powderhead. Once he has baptized Bishop by water and himself, twice, by fire,[70] he returns to the "ground that the Lord still held" a murderer, a minister, and the victim of an actual devil. He sees the "clearing…burned free of all that had ever oppressed him," a "forsaken place and his own," which stands as "the sign of a broken covenant."[71] Nevertheless, each of Tarwater's attempts to exorcise himself of Christ fail. He desecrates the body of his great-uncle, burning his corpse by setting his house afire, but Old Tarwater's friend Buford gathers the scorched bones and buries them beneath the sign of his Savior.[72] Tarwater then strikes out with violent action, drowning the innocent Bishop in a lake, but his malice is undercut by the words of the baptismal rite "that [had run] out of [his] mouth and into the water…of themselves."[73] "The fact that he had actually baptized the child disturbed [Tarwater] only intermittently and each time he thought of it he reviewed its accidental nature. …He considered that the boy was drowned and that he had done it, and that in the order of things, a drowning was a more important act than a few words spilled in the water."[74] O'Connor here toys with Augustine's theology in which he prioritizes the "remote and proximate matter" of baptismal water and ablution over the form of the ritual and any inconsistencies accidental to it. "When,

[67] O'Connor, "The River," *Complete*, 172.

[68] Ibid.

[69] Ibid., 172–73.

[70] O'Connor, *Violent*, 194, 232, 235.

[71] Ibid., 237.

[72] Ibid., 49–50. With pride, Tarwater imagines himself kin to Elijah, moving out into the night on the wings of a fiery chariot. See also pgs. 88, 240.

[73] Ibid., 209.

[74] Ibid., 221.

through ignorance, an accidental, not substantial, change has been made in the form (as *In nomine patriâ* for *Patris*), the baptism is to be held valid."[75] The sacrament "is so sacred," St. Augustine wrote, "that not even a murderer's administration contaminates it."[76] Despite having lived up to his name, sullying the lake with dark intention, Tarwater's performance of the ultimate blasphemy, destroying life, is sanctified by the life-saving action of baptism. When he sets fire to the "evil ground" where he was sodomized, this life-saving action is repeated. Tarwater experiences his own share in the Passion and is burned clean by the horrifying revelation of evil.[77] The day had come, as his great uncle had prophesied, "when a pit open[ed] up inside of [the boy] and [he knew] some things [he'd] never known before."[78] He has been "tried in the fire of his refusal…"[79]

To complete the circuit of his betrayal, Tarwater must return to the ashen clearing at Powderhead and renounce, once and for all, his allegiance with the Devil.

> "Go down and take it," his friend whispered. "It's ours. We've won it."…The boy shuddered convulsively. The presence was as pervasive as an odor, a warm sweet body of air encircling him, a violet shadow hanging around his shoulders. He shook himself free fiercely and grabbed the matches from his pocket. …He walked backward from the spot, pushing the torch into all the bushes…until he had made a rising wall of fire between him and the grinning presence.[80]

Only after his violation by the "lavender" man does Tarwater make the connection between his "violet[-eyed]" friend and Satan himself.[81] Old Tarwater had warned him that he "[was] the kind of

---

[75] "The Sacraments: Baptism," n. page. Ed Phillips, 2003. *www.ourcatholicfaith.org*. http://www.ourcatholicfaith.org/sacraments/baptism.html (accessed 21 March 2011).

[76] St. Augustine qtd. in St. Thomas Aquinas, *Summa Theologica*, Question LXVI, Article IX, Reply to Objection II, n. page. Kevin Knight, 2008. *www.newadvent.org*. http://www.newadvent.org/summa/4066.htm#article9 (accessed 20 March 2011).

[77] O'Connor, *Violent*, 232.

[78] Ibid., 67.

[79] Ibid., 220.

[80] Ibid., 237–38.

[81] Ibid., 215. Mr. Paradise is further associated with the demonic when described as having a "purple bulge on his left temple" (O'Connor, "The River," *Complete*, 166).

boy…that the devil is always going to be offering to assist, to give you a smoke or a drink or a ride, and to ask you your bidnis [sic]."[82] The man in the lavender suit does just that; he offers Tarwater a ride, then a smoke (these were "special" cigarettes), and a drink of bootleg liquor which the boy, now a bit dizzy, exclaims was "better than the Bread of Life!"[83] In less than five minutes he has defied his great-uncle and the God he has acted representative of three times, disregarding the old man's forewarning to "mind how [he took] up with strangers," to keep away from "poisonous liquor," and to "keep [his] bidnis [sic] to [himself]."[84] Tarwater has delivered himself into the hands of evil by the false conviction that he can pick and choose his way around evil, it being something he can mete out or evade as handily as judgment. He took the stranger to heart when he said, "[E]very day is Judgment Day," and began, from that moment, to act as devil and Lord both.[85] On the lip of Old Tarwater's shallow grave, he announces "in the voice of the stranger," "You can't be any poorer than dead."[86] He comforts himself with the thought, just dawning inside him, that his responsibilities to the old man and to God are irrelevant if he can sneak past ultimate Judgment. "No hand uplifted to hinder me from anything," he thinks to himself, "except the Lord's and He ain't said anything. He ain't even noticed me yet."[87]

On his way home to Powderhead, still wet to the knees from Bishop's murder-baptism, he boasts to a truck driver that on the place he is "in full charge. No voice will be uplifted." He goes on to explain how he "shouldn't never have left [the place] except [he] had to prove [he] wasn't no prophet… Now all [he has] to do is mind [his] own bidnis [sic] until [he dies]. [He] don't have to baptize or prophesy."[88] Tarwater is wrong, of course, and his incidental sentence is swift in coming and permanent. His violation in the sacred woods "force[s] him on to a final revelation. His scorched eyes no longer looked hollow or as if they were meant only to guide him forward. They looked as if, touched with a coal like the lips of a

---

[82] O'Connor, *Violent*, 58.

[83] Ibid., 227–30.

[84] Ibid., 58, 229.

[85] Ibid., 46.

[86] Ibid., 24.

[87] Ibid.

[88] Ibid., 210.

prophet, they would never see ordinary sights again."[89] At last the boy perceives the meaning of his great-uncle's words, "Even the mercy of the Lord burns."[90] St. John preached that Christ would come baptizing the penitent with the Holy Ghost and the sinner with fire. In fulfillment of the Baptist's prophesy, Francis Marion has required a three-fold baptism, his first by water and the Spirit, his last by fire. The Eastern Fathers believed that baptism by fire was "the literal fulfillment of the Pentecostal fiery tongues."[91] Only after he is illumined by fire does Tarwater attain the gift of holy prophesy. He can begin his life as a prophet having been purged of his desire for miraculous power, public renown, and freedom from his responsibility to the "New Dispensation" of Christ's law that is mediated by baptism.[92]

Befittingly, the boys' watery baptisms are followed by a revealing violence as the sacrament itself, transmitted by water, fire, or blood, "derives its efficacy…from Christ's Passion…"[93] O'Connor is explicit in her collusion of the three boys' suffering and Christ's. In the penultimate chapter of *The Violent Bear It Away*, she wrote, "[Tarwater's] eyes looked small and seedlike as if while he had been asleep, they had been lifted out, scorched, and dropped back into his head. His expression seemed to contract until it reached some point beyond rage or pain. Then a loud dry cry tore out of him and his mouth fell back into place."[94] Christ's forsaken cry echoes again in Bevel's confrontation with the river and Bishop's confrontation with Tarwater. Fearful that the Kingdom beneath it was "just another

---

[89] Ibid., 233.

[90] Ibid., 20.

[91] St. John Damascene, *An Exact Exposition of the Orthodox Faith*, Book IV, Chapter IX, n. page. St. Nicholas Russian Orthodox Church, McKinney, TX, 2008. *www.orthodox.net.* http://www.orthodox.net/fathers/exactiv.html#BOOK_IV_CHAPTER_IX (accessed 5 March 2011).

[92] St. Bonaventure qtd. by William Fanning, "Baptism," n. page. Kevin Knight, 2008. *www.newadvent.org.* http://www.newadvent.org/cathen/02258b.htm (accessed 20 March 2011).

[93] St. Thomas Aquinas, *Summa Theologica*, Ques. LXVI, Article XI, Reply to Objection I, n. page. Kevin Knight, 2008. *www.newadvent.org.* http://www.newadvent.org/summa/4066.htm #article11 (accessed 20 March 2011).

[94] Ibid.

joke," Bevel "[gives] one low cry of pain and indignation."[95] Bishop's "unmistakable bellow" breaks the quiet of the lake.[96]

The baptismal rite effects a needful transfiguration in each of the boys, one which O'Connor posits as unanswerable by anything less then the intercession of ultimate reality. For Bevel and Bishop the movement of transformation is "forward and down" into an actual watery burial.[97] In death, they are released from the living purgatory of unrequited filial love. The boys' destruction demonstrates the "painful contradiction" of Christian faith, that only in actual (albeit mystical) death can the body achieve everlasting life.[98] It is a belief intentionally inverse of nature which reveals the world as "made for the dead."[99] The transfigured Francis Marion rises, finally accepting of his calling, unexceptional as it is. He returns to the city, not as a newborn Elisha who multiplied loaves and raised the dead, but as the "hand…time [has] discover[ed]" to baptize the "ducked heads" of a nameless city and to turn them from their "hastening away from the Lord God…"[100] The infant Tarwater may have been baptized into blasphemy, his uncle Rayber turning him upside-down and repeating the ritual so that "Jesus [had] a claim on both ends," but his coming of age stands as a testimony to the indelible mark of "good blood" left by his first baptism.[101] "Blasphemy," the old man had told Rayber, "never changed a plan of the Lord's."[102]

The same redeemed blood courses through the school teacher in spite of his denials. He shares with his nephew the accident of a two-fold baptism. As an infant, his mother, a Methodist who "never overcame her upbringing" conferred the sacrament upon him, and at the age of seven—the age of Roman discretion—Old Tarwater "snatched" him away to Powderhead to baptize him in a stream.[103] "I've been born again," Rayber proclaimed to his father; "he could not go back…to town" with him.[104] Rayber Sr. responds with glib

[95] O'Connor, "The River," *Complete*, 173.

[96] O'Connor, *Violent*, 202.

[97] O'Connor, "The River," *Complete*, 173–74.

[98] Arseniev, *Mysticism and the Eastern Church*, 83.

[99] O'Connor, *Violent*, 16.

[100] O'Connor, *Violent*, 26, 35, 41, 80.

[101] Ibid., 59. See also pgs. 125–26.

[102] Ibid., 73.

[103] Ibid., 125–26.

[104] Ibid., 126–27.

condescension reminiscent of Harry/Bevel's parents: "'Glad you fixed him up, Mason,' he said. 'One bath more or less won't hurt the bugger.'"[105] Rayber's indoctrination at Powderhead insinuates itself upon his adult life persistently though he represents himself as one who has indeed overcome his upbringing. "'Good blood flows in his veins,' the old man said [to Francis Marion]. 'And good blood knows the Lord…and there ain't a way in the world he can get rid of it.'"[106] Rayber refers to his "good blood" as a family "affliction." "It lay hidden in the line of blood that touched them, flowing from some ancient source, some desert prophet or pole-sitter, until, its power unabated, it appeared in the old man and him and, he surmised, in [Tarwater]. Those it touched were condemned to fight it constantly or be ruled by it."[107] When he baptized Rayber at Powderhead, Old Tarwater transmitted the power of the sacrament to Rayber's blood, an action Rayber confesses to Francis Marion that "made a lasting scar."[108] The boy, on the other hand, tends to externalize his sense of divine power. It is alternately incarnate in the light of the sun and moon—reflections of the iconography of heavenly bodies as God's "immense silent eye"—and by silence itself, which "seemed…to be waiting patiently…until it should reveal itself and demand to be named."[109] Rayber's sense of divinity, though violently suppressed, expresses itself internally through his son as a "futureless…love without reason," a "love that appeared to exist only to be itself…"[110] In spite of himself, he "always felt with it a rush of longing to have the old man's eyes…with their impossible vision of a world transfigured…turned on him again. The longing was like an undertow dragging him backwards to what he knew to be madness."[111]

While the efficacy of the baptismal rite is uniform the circumstances and mechanics of each of the boys' baptisms are unique; each performance of the ritual belies the particular need of each child in its staging and structure. Tarwater's fiery baptism

---

[105] Ibid., 127.

[106] Ibid., 59.

[107] Ibid., 114.

[108] Ibid., 172.

[109] Ibid., 85–86.

[110] Ibid., 114.

[111] Ibid.

overturns his pride in choosing himself as savior, not Christ. His choice of self-salvation is significantly independent of Rayber's in that he still believes in the proximate reality of the Triune God.[112] Francis' turning away from God is a deliberate movement, encouraged by the "sibilant…breath" of a stranger-Devil.[113] "'The way I see it,' [the stranger] said, 'you can do one of two things. One of them, not both.' '…Jesus or the devil,' the boy said. 'No, no, no,' the stranger said, 'there ain't no such thing as a devil. …It ain't Jesus or the devil. It's Jesus or *you*.'"[114] The Reverend Bevel Summers makes a like demand of his congregation: "'Believe Jesus or the devil!' he cried. 'Testify to one or the other!'"[115] Tarwater is meanwhile seduced by the devil's keenest wile, that there is no such thing as a devil and no need to deny one by denying oneself. "Jesus or me," Tarwater repeats to himself and decides to go the way of the stranger, "not paying too much attention to [his] Redemption" and asserting himself, once and for all, as sovereign of his own deeds and desires.[116] The child Bishop is the radius around which Tarwater moves, "held" by his "morbid impulse" to baptize the boy and an equally strong impulse to destroy him.[117] "Before you was here, *I* was here," he says "in a slow emphatic voice" to Bishop on their first meeting.[118] He senses that he must proclaim his being against Bishop's or be drawn into the "strange waiting silence" of the *Logos* reflected in the child's eyes.[119] "The poor Soul," Jakob Böhme wrote, "is both afraid and ashamed to bring its Will into God…as fearing to be consumed by so doing."[120] Tarwater's greatest fear is to be "lost…forever" in the encroaching silence of an irresistible authority; Bishop becomes the locus of that fear, a nagging, tangible reflection of the divine Will. It "seemed to lie all around him like an invisible

---

[112] Ibid., 16, 70.

[113] Ibid., 237.

[114] Ibid., 39.

[115] O'Connor, "The River," *Complete*, 166.

[116] O'Connor, *Violent*, 39, 45.

[117] Ibid., 147, 151.

[118] Ibid., 32.

[119] Ibid., 160.

[120] Jakob Böhme, *Dialogues on the Supersensual Life: Dialogue III, Of Heaven and Hell*, n. page. The European Graduate School, 2007. *www.egs.edu*. http://www.egs.edu/library/jakob-dialogues-on-the-supersensual-life/dialogue-iii/ (accessed 22 March 2011).

country whose borders he was always on the edge of, always in danger of crossing."[121] In retaliation, Tarwater pits his will against the Deity's, first by denying recognition of holiness through contact. He "never looked lower than the top of [Bishop's] head except by accident..."[122] The "silent country appeared to be reflected in the center of [the little boy's] eyes. It stretched out there, limitless and clear."[123] By resisting the draw of those eyes, Tarwater could also resist his sense of obligation to his "first mission"—baptizing the child—and the rough life of a prophet.[124]

As disciplined as he is in his denials, none of Tarwater's posturing prepares him for a revelation which begins in Rayber's doorway and is deepened in the park. When he sees Bishop "shambl[ing]" around the hall, his:

> eyes widened and an inner door in them opened... He stood like one condemned, waiting at the spot of execution. Then the revelation came, silent, implacable, direct as a bullet. He did not look into the eyes of any fiery beast or see a burning bush. He only knew, with a certainty sunk in despair, that he was expected to baptize the child... He knew that he was called to be a prophet and that the ways of his prophecy would not be remarkable. His black pupils, glassy and still, reflected depth on depth his own stricken image of himself, trudging into the distance in the bleeding stinking mad shadow of Jesus, until at last he received his reward, a broken fish, a multiplied loaf.[125]

Tarwater "tried to shout 'NO'! but...the sound was saturated in silence, lost."[126] Thereafter he perceives the city landscape as replete with signs. The tabernacle banner seemed to chide him: UNLESS YE BE BORN AGAIN YE SHALL NOT HAVE EVERLASTING LIFE.[127] Even his reflection takes on a menacing sheen when it hovers in a bakery window, superimposed upon a single loaf of bread.[128] Under the counsel of his devilish friend, Tarwater "demand[s] an

---

[121] O'Connor, *Violent*, 160.

[122] Ibid.

[123] Ibid.

[124] Ibid., 9.

[125] Ibid., 91.

[126] Ibid., 92.

[127] Ibid., 109. See also pgs. 122–23.

[128] Ibid., 122.

unmistakable sign of the Lord."[129] The next day, as he and his surrogate family walk "deep…into the park…[Tarwater] began to feel again the approach of mystery," and he is confronted with the lion-spouted fountain.[130] "As soon as the dim-witted boy saw the water, he gave a whoop and galloped off toward it, flapping his arms…" and clambering into the pool.[131]

> The sun, which had been tacking from cloud to cloud, emerged above the fountain. A blinding brightness fell on the lion's…head and gilded the stream of water rushing from his mouth. Then the light, falling more gently, rested like a hand on [Bishop's] white head. His face might have been a mirror where the sun had stopped to watch its reflection.[132]

Tarwater is drawn forward despite his exertion of backward force, "moving blindly" as if "where [the little boy] was he only saw a spot of light."[133] His foot comes down on the edge of the pool just as Rayber snatches Bishop from the water. The child reacts by "split [ting] the silence with his bellow."[134] Tarwater's vision of Bishop "illumined" by holy light fades and is replaced by his own reflection. He tells the silent "cross-shaped" face he wasn't going to baptize the child, and his stranger-self answers, "Drown him then."[135] The thought tellingly "shock[s]" Tarwater, but it also mystifies him; drowning Bishop would appropriately free him from prophetic ordination as the single act which absolutely reverses his call. Instead of conferring everlasting life in symbolic death, he will bring about actual death as a symbol of the power in his own will. "No finaler [sic] act than this," the stranger tells him on the lake. "Once it's done, it's done forever."[136] Eager to "save himself from the fate [of the disciple]" and to preserve himself within "his own inclinations," Tarwater conspires not merely to say "NO" but to "do" NO.[137]

---

[129] Ibid., 163.

[130] Ibid., 164. The fountain is itself a nod to the penitence of St. Jerome, whose iconic attributes include the lion.

[131] Ibid. See also pg. 145.

[132] Ibid.

[133] Ibid., 146.

[134] Ibid., 165.

[135] Ibid.

[136] Ibid., 215.

[137] Ibid., 221.

The stranger's goading suggestions are now almost imperceptibly integrated to the boy's "underhead."[138] He has allowed his visionary sense to be to denigrated to fixation by his uncle and delusion by his "friend" who declared at the fountain side, "Well, that's your sign, ...the sun coming out from under a cloud and falling on a dimwit."[139] Minutes before he ushers Bishop onto the lake, Tarwater boasts to Rayber that he is under the influence of Evil itself. "With me, [the Word] fell on rock and the wind carried it away."[140] In Jesus' parable, Satan comes immediately after the Word is sown and steals away what God had planted along the "wayside" of men's hearts.[141] Sts. Matthew, Mark, and Luke each liken the Devil to "fowls of the air" who devour the seed of the Word with cunning and speed. Tarwater misremembers the parable and cites the wind. The slip is significant in that it belies the depth of conflict—here subconscious—between Tarwater's notion of self and the God of his upbringing. Scripture tells of the might of Yahweh as a wind that brings life; in Genesis, God "breathed into [Adam's nostrils] the breath of life," and in Revelation, the holy wind is taken away.[142] In Exodus, it brings protection. Godly winds carry plagues to Egypt, divide the Red Sea, and smite Pharaoh's army.[143] It also brings cleansing trials to the faithful. A violent wind destroys Job's family in order that he might be lead to a more perfect humility.[144] Finally, it brings revelation; the coming presence of the Lord is felt by Elijah as a passing gale, and in Psalms, the "stormy wind" is chief among the elements in "fulfilling His Word."[145]

For Rayber, the conflict between human and Godly Will plays externally in the person of Bishop. "The child," O'Connor's narrator tells us, "might have been a deformed part of himself that had been accidentally revealed."[146] Bishop manifests Rayber's lingering desire for belief and his equal and opposing desire to quash even the

---

[138] Ibid., 171.

[139] Ibid., 165.

[140] Ibid., 192.

[141] Luke 8:5–12; Matt. 13:3–19; Mark 4:3–16, *KJV*.

[142] Gen. 2:7; Rev. 7:1–3, *KJV*.

[143] Exod. 10:12–14, 10:18–20, 14:20–22, 15:9–11, *KJV*.

[144] Job 1:18–20, 37:20–22, *KJV*.

[145] 1 Kings 19:10–12; Ps. 148:8, *KJV*.

[146] O'Connor, *Violent*, 93.

memory of belief with "rigid ascetic discipline."[147] At once he conceives of the boy as "made in the image and likeness of God" and as a "mistake of nature," an "*x* signifying the general hideousness of fate."[148] Tarwater reacts to Bishop in parallel fashion, recoiling from the child's recognition and his touch, calling him a hog and a dog, and yet seeing him "illumined" with the light of revelation and possessed of the Spirit without having been baptized.[149] For both father and cousin, Bishop contains the painful implication of the Lord's Will. Both are compelled to kill him so that they might be freed of that implication. The logic of each man's undertaking to freedom reveals itself in the outcome of their violence against Bishop. Rayber's attempt to drown the child is motivated by a complex of abstractions, all of which rely upon Bishop's functioning as a non-being, better off dead than arrested in a state of unreason. But Bishop is every bit the creature his father is, and he asserts himself fiercely beneath Rayber's downward pushing hands. Not until the child is apparently dead, a limp body very nearly caught in an undertow, does Rayber experience the "complete terror" of his actual loss.[150] In contrast, Tarwater is achingly aware of Bishop as a created being, shrinking from his touch and avoiding his eyes lest he lose the nerve to destroy what he alternately fears and worships. To Tarwater, Bishop is a manifestation of the Godhead and an "afflicted" child, at once glorious and malformed.[151] He must reject Bishop completely in a final act in order to convince himself that "there is nothing for him to be born into."[152] But Tarwater has not been successful in displacing the Word of his great-uncle with the Pelagianism of his uncle. At his core, he does not believe that Bishop "won't rise again," that baptism is a "futile" rite, or that the only way to be born again is "through your own efforts."[153] He utters the words of baptism in a helpless admission that it is not for him to

[147] Ibid., 114.

[148] Ibid., 113, 117.

[149] "Illumined" is the name Orthodox give to the newly baptized. See Susan K. Wood, *One Baptism: Ecumenical Dimensions of the Doctrine of Baptism* (Collegeville: Liturgical Press, 2009) 109.

[150] Ibid., 142.

[151] Ibid., 154.

[152] Ibid., 172.

[153] Ibid., 110, 172, 194–95.

make himself straight nor is it any "part of his job to think for the Lord."[154]

Rayber's Stoical "deification of natural laws" leads to inaction and finally spiritual "dissolution."[155] At the Cherokee Lodge, he "had an instant's premonition that if he wished to save himself, he should leave at once,…the trip was doomed."[156] Yet Rayber remains, and what's more he allows Tarwater to take Bishop out onto the lake, knowing well what the older boy's vague pledge to "tend to [the child]" meant.[157] His plight demonstrates St. Augustine's proclamation that after the Fall man had become like to "nothingness."[158] "Being turned toward himself…" he exists "in himself—that is to be his own satisfaction…"[159] His "being [has become] more contracted…"[160] Doing nothing and feeling nothing, Rayber waits motionless on the hotel cot as for an apocalypse. "He had had this sense of waiting, kin in degree but not in kind, when he was a child and expected any moment that the city would blossom into an eternal Powderhead. Now he sensed that he waited for a cataclysm. He waited for all the world to be turned into a burnt spot between two chimneys."[161] Rayber sends Bishop to slaughter so that he might stop the flow of the "undertow of expectation" which reveals his being essentially "a child still waiting on Christ."[162] At the End of Days: "[a]ll he would be was an observer. …He told himself he was indifferent even to his own dissolution. …[T]his indifference was the most that human dignity could achieve, and…he felt he had achieved it. To feel nothing was peace."[163] When Rayber realizes that his son is drowned and that Tarwater has moved off to "meet his appalling destiny, he "stood…waiting for the raging pain…to begin,

---

[154] Ibid., 10, 114.

[155] Arseniev, *Mysticism and the Eastern Church,* 83; O'Connor, *Violent,* 200.

[156] O'Connor, *Violent*, 154.

[157] Ibid., 198.

[158] St. Augustine of Hippo, *City of God*, 609.

[159] Ibid., 609; St. Augustine of Hippo, *Nicene and Post-Nicene Fathers: St. Augustine, City of God, Christian Doctrine,* ed. Philip Schaff, Vol. II (New York: Cosimo, Inc., 2007) 273.

[160] Ibid.

[161] Ibid., 200.

[162] Ibid., 182.

[163] Ibid., 200.

so that he could ignore it, but he continued to feel nothing."[164] It was "not until he realized there would be no pain that he collapsed."[165]

While his uncle prevails against the pain of love, Tarwater at last submits to the "words…hidden in his bloodstream" and moves with them "toward some goal of their own."[166] One red river leads him to another, Christ's River of saving pain. What draws Harry / Bevel to the mystical river, on the other hand, is no ancestral call of wise blood; he is moved onward, not backward, by the current. He leaves behind a life tedious in its motivation to survival—"there was very little to do at any time but eat"—and without the slightest implication as to why it is so driven. He is aware of himself as superfluous to the apartment tableau, as something that cannot be counted among his parents' pleasures except as a passing amusement, reflecting back the ill-refinement of the outside world. He tries to engage in their detached condescension, grinning and rolling his eyes in the preacher's arms, then thrusting his face forward to exaggerate his taken name. "'My name is Bevvvuuuuul,' he said in a loud deep voice," but the preacher didn't smile.[167] Bevel has "the sudden feeling that this was not a joke. …From the preacher's face, he knew immediately that nothing the preacher said or did was a joke."[168] The child follows this revelation with routine evasion, nevertheless the lie seems also to seek justification. He tells the preacher "quickly," "My mother named me that," as if to say Summers could take it up with her, and not just for his name but his carrying on too.[169]

The devilish Mr. Paradise takes in the scene from the bumper of his "long ancient gray automobile"; he mocks the Reverend Summers and accuses him of being a sham healer who preaches, not for the people's relief, but for their money.[170] "Bevel stared at [Mr. Paradise] once and then moved into the folds of Mrs. Connin's coat and hid himself."[171] His action subtly marks his denial of Satan,

---

164 Ibid., 203.

165 Ibid.

166 Ibid., 61.

167 O'Connor, "The River," *Complete*, 167.

168 Ibid., 167–68.

169 Ibid., 168.

170 Ibid., 166.

171 Ibid.

which has a parallel in the apostolic tradition and in the contemporary orthodox baptismal rite. In the words of Tertullian, "When we are going to enter the water, but a little before, in the presence of the congregation…we solemnly profess that we disown the devil, and his pomp, and his angels."[172] Mr. Paradise is one of these dark angels, eager to sow doubt in the hearts of the faithful, but vulnerable himself to the transfigurative effects of the Holy Spirit. There is an ominous twinge to his pocketing the candy stick and stalking after the errant child, but whatever his initial intentions, he appears at the close of the story to be motivated by compassion.

What sets Bevel apart from Tarwater, Rayber, and Bishop is his free choice in accepting baptism. "'If I Baptize you,' the preacher said, 'you'll be able to go to the Kingdom of Christ. …You won't be the same again. …Do you want that?'"[173] The child says "yes" he does and thinks to himself, "I won't have to go back to the apartment, I'll go under the river."[174] It is clear that Bevel has no idea of the implication of his consent. He is shocked silent by the preacher's swinging him "upside down and plung[ing] his head into the water," holding him there while he said the "words of Baptism."[175] Still, there is an ironical truth to the boy's literal want of going under the river. He does so symbolically in the hands of the reverend and literally by his own volition; in both cases, he consents to be put under, and in both cases he does not anticipate death as the act's resolution. O'Connor implies that Bevel's ignorance of the spiritual and corporeal deaths that await him in the river is irrelevant: the sacrament has still been effectively conferred.

Of the children in O'Connor's baptismal stories, Bevel is the one most actively orphaned. Where Tarwater and the child Rayber rail against the filial bond of God as Father, Bevel seeks His familial love. There is in him none of the bitterness for freedom in choosing *not* to

---

[172] Tertullian, *De Corona*, Part III, trans. Jacques-Paul Migne, *Patrologia Latina*, Vol. II, Col. LXXVII, n. page. Early Church Texts, 2002. *www.earlychurchtexts.com.* http://www.earlychurchtexts.com/main/tertullian/traditional_christian_practices.shtml (accessed 29 March 2011). See also St. Basil the Great, *De Spiritu Sancto*, Ch. XI, Part XXVII. Christian Classics Ethereal Library, 2005. *www.ccel.org*. http://www.ccel.org/ccel/schaff/npnf208.vii.xii.html (accessed 29 March 2011).

[173] Ibid., 168.

[174] Ibid.

[175] Ibid.

be saved that we see in Hazel Motes, Francis Marion, and Rayber. Tarwater insists that he "ain't ast [sic] for no father" just as the teenage Rayber proclaims to his uncle and Hazel to his mother, though in different words.[176] Nor does Bevel share with Hazel, Tarwater, and Rayber an inflated sense of self-will. The preacher lifts him, silent but gasping, from the river, gives him a stern look, and says, "You count now. ...You didn't even count before."[177] Bevel's eyes, "dark and dilated" with fear, have about them a shade of the preacher's solemnity. He knows well how little he counted before, and now he intends to make good his claim to new life. For Bevel, the river effects the possibility of his desire to traverse between one realm of being to another—from not counting to counting—and also to remain there, an entity of discrete value forever. "[I]t is necessary," St. Basil the Great wrote: "that the continuity of the old life be cut. ...[I]n making a change in lives it seemed necessary for death to come as mediator between the two, ending all the goes before, and beginning all that comes after."[178] The continuity between Bevel's former life as Harry and his newly illuminated, "beveled" self is severed in baptism. The reverend immerses the boy once, a mode common to modern Roman Church and to most Protestant denominations. When Bevel returns to the river alone, he forces himself underwater three times. This triune immersion recalls the apostolic tradition of the early church, which is today practiced in Eastern Orthodoxy. By enacting both modes of the baptismal ritual, O'Connor implies a tangible connect between ancient and contemporary Christianity. She recalls the words of St. Gregory and St. Thomas, who said, "[B]oth single and triune immersion are lawful considered in themselves; since one immersion signifies the oneness of Christ's death and of the Godhead; while triune immersion

---

[176] Ibid., 106.

[177] O'Connor, "The River," *Complete*, 168.

[178] St. Basil the Great, *De Spiritu Sancto*, Ch. XV, Part XXXV, n. page in *Nicene and Post-Nicene Fathers, 2nd Series*, Vol. VIII. ed. Philip Schaff and Henry Wace (Buffalo: Christian Literature Publishing Co., 1895). Christian Classics Ethereal Library, 13 July 2005. *www.ccel.org.* http://www.ccel.org/schaff/npnf208.vii.xii.html (accessed 29 March 2011).

signifies the three days of Christ's burial, and also the Trinity of Persons."[179]

Each time Bevel plunges his head under the water, he comes up gasping and "choking," his self-baptism, a symbolic "descent into hell," marked by the same feeling of primeval confrontation he felt in the arms of the preacher.[180] "He…had to fight with something that pushed him back in the face."[181] But the "river wouldn't have him."[182] A dark notion befalls Bevel just as Mr. Paradise reaches the edge of the river, arms and voice uplifted, "shaking" the candy stick he'd brought as a lure like a "red and white club."[183] It was "just another joke," Bevel tells himself. He had "come for nothing."[184] He lets out a "low" cry of forsaken pain but is startled from his indignation by the approaching call of "something like a giant pig bounding after him."[185] Once more O'Connor aligns Mr. Paradise with demonic power. Terrified, the boy "plunge[s] under once and this time the waiting current caught him like a long gentle hand and pulled him swiftly forward and down."[186] He is drawn along by a placid but undeniable force akin to the "undertow" of desire in Rayber's and Tarwater's blood. "For an instant [Bevel] is overcome with surprise…"[187] Has he made a mistake in committing himself utterly to the power inside the river? "[T]hen since he was moving quickly and knew he was getting somewhere, all his fury and fear left him."[188] The dualistic Mr. Paradise cannot follow Bevel in his descent, but there is a hint as the boy disappears that the old man might be cleansed himself of at least one of his demons. He "star[es] with his dull eyes as far down the river line as he could see" for the place where the child might ascend.[189]

---

[179] St. Thomas Aquinas, *Summa Theologica*, Ques. LXVI, Article VIII, n. page. Kevin Knight, 2008. *www.newadvent.org*. http://www.newadvent.org/summa/4066.htm#article8 (accessed 29 March 2011).

[180] St. Basil the Great, *De Spiritu Sancto,* n. page.

[181] O'Connor, "The River," *Complete*, 173.

[182] Ibid.

[183] Ibid., 174.

[184] Ibid., 173.

[185] Ibid., 174.

[186] Ibid.

[187] Ibid.

[188] Ibid.

[189] Ibid.

Chapter 5

"Imagin[ing] a Vain Thing"

The Undeniable Body in "The Enduring Chill," "The Comforts of Home," and "Why Do the Heathen Rage?"

Flannery O'Connor's unfinished "third novel" "Why Do the Heathen Rage?" has been the source of much critical speculation, described by theorists including Marian Burns as an invaluable retrospective of the author's earlier work which does not necessarily evidence an aesthetic departure.[1] O'Connor composed the bulk of the text in her penultimate year, a fact that complicates critiques of the fragmented "...Heathen..." with occasionally romantic conjecture regarding the author's last word on such recurring themes as mankind's moral practicability and Christian eschatology. There is, of course, the danger of essentializing O'Connor's intentionality from that most romantic of perspectives—the artist approaching death. Since the addition of some three hundred and seventy eight pages of typescripts to the *Flannery O'Connor Collection* at Georgia College in 1978, "Why Do the Heathen Rage?" has revealed the author, not as one fatefully advancing toward her end with grand, pontifical gestures but as one getting on, for better or worse, with the business of writing. So little of the text made it to print for the simple reason that O'Connor, in the process of composing "Revelation," "Judgment Day," and "Parker's Back," revising (sometimes compulsively) extant works for the collection *Everything That Rises Must Converge*, and suffering, all the while, the practical interruptions of failing health, had neither the time nor the energy to devote to drafting and proofing, to say nothing of restructuring, the sometimes digressive "...Heathen..."

Burns has argued persuasively that, "there are reasons enough to suppose that even had O'Connor lived much longer, 'Why Do the

[1] See Marian Burns, "O'Connor's Unfinished Novel," rpt. in *Critical Essays on Flannery O'Connor*, ed. Melvin J. Friedman and Beverly Lyon Clark (Boston: G. K. Hall, 1985) 169–80.

Heathen Rage?' would never have been published as a novel."[2] There is little within the author's correspondence or indeed the manuscripts themselves to suggest that the "…the Heathen…" was intended to be developed into a novel; O'Connor had initially conceived of the piece as a companion narrative to a preceding short, "The Enduring Chill." The amended text "was to feature Asbury whose conversion," Burns contends, "…was originally to have been the premise for the third novel"; yet Asbury does not seem at all integrated or purposeful to the world of Walter Tilman in the way Enoch Emery is to Hazel Motes's Taulkingham. Rather the pair seem to be aspects of a single character, the intellectual in various attitudes of practical failure. There is a strange collusion of mannerism and desire, even of scenario, in which Asbury and Walter seem more or less interchangeable. In the earliest draft of "…the Heathen…" a third scholar, as ineffective and hen-pecked as Asbury and Walter, appears as protagonist—Julian (presumably of "Everything That Rises Must Converge)."[3] O'Connor's placement and replacement of these three characters in recurring scenes suggests that she was testing each voice relative to the crisis of a short narrative, not populating a novel with discrete, interactive voices. Furthermore, at no stage in the development of "…the Heathen…" does O'Connor elicit the sense of an anticipated ending so apparent in working drafts of *Wise Blood* and *The Violent Bear It Away*.[4] "What I had thought to do," she wrote to Dawkins in November 1963:

> was to use that ["The Enduring Chill"] to help explain Walter's character (the thing in *Esquire*). I may not do it, I may go on and rewrite ["Why Do the Heathen Rage?"] as a story and use it in the collection [*Everything That Rises Must Converge*]. My trouble right now is that I am beset by too many possibilities and can't make up my mind. I'd really like to turn "Why Do the Heathen Rage?" into a long story, without the "Enduring Chill" section, and use it in the collection but this all takes time.[5]

---

[2] Marian Burns qtd. in R. Neil Scott, *Flannery O'Connor: An Annotated Reference Guide to Criticism* (Milledgeville: Timberlane Books, 2002) 138.

[3] See Flannery O'Connor, "Why Do the Heathen Rage?" MS 216, n. date, 4; MS 217b, n. date, 5, *Flannery O'Connor Collection*, Russell Library, Georgia College and State University, Milledgeville, Georgia.

[4] Burns, 173.

[5] O'Connor, *Habit*, 546–47.

O'Connor exhibited an unprecedented degree of discomfort with "...the Heathen..." in each of its various manifestations, referring to the piece begrudgingly as the "Thing."[6] The version which appeared in the July 1963 issue of *Esquire* is little more than a sketch, redeemed in its brevity by a strong insinuation that even after the crisis of Tilman Sr.'s stroke his grown son Walter will persist in doing nothing and his wife will continue to bemoan that fact. The extended drafts extrapolate Walter's aimless scholarship by way of his "small, contemptible vice" of unsolicited, theatrical letter-writing, but the story's climax—the radically liberal Oona/Sarah Gibbs's "descen[t]" upon the Tilman farm—is continually deferred.[7] "O'Connor never seems to come to any decision as to what should happen at the dénouement. She seems," Burns writes, "to avoid the issue, instead repeatedly revising the details of the situation, the letters, and the characters."[8] We can only speculate as to which of the story's motifs so frustrated O'Connor's progress: was it the lack of understanding between parents and their children or between blacks and whites, liberals and conservatives or believers and non-believers? Certainly this is familiar territory for O'Connor; combinations of these nuclear tropes appear to some extent in all of her fiction. Stuart L. Burns observes in his review of the manuscripts that, "O'Connor was not embarked in any new direction" in the unfinished "...Heathen..."[9] The raw material of her tales remains constant, but occasionally the author did attempt a radical broadening of comic potential by "carefully not kill[ing] anybody off."[10] While the manuscripts cannot reveal any definitive intentionality they do yield an exceptional insight into O'Connor's hyper-critical mood as she undertook, from a particularly self-conscious posture, to adapt her aesthetic to new comic boundaries.

---

[6] Ibid., 504.

[7] Flannery O'Connor, "Why Do the Heathen Rage?" MS 220b, n. date, 1, *Flannery O'Connor Collection*, Russell Library, Georgia College and State University, Milledgeville, Georgia.

[8] Burns, 177.

[9] Stuart L. Burns, "How Wide Did 'The Heathen Rage'?" *Flannery O'Connor Bulletin* 4 (1975): 25–41. Qtd. in Scott, *Flannery O'Connor: An Anotated Reference Guide*, 140.

[10] O'Connor, *Habit*, 261.

The process began as O'Connor drafted and redrafted "The Enduring Chill," a story which gave her considerable trouble in resolving. She began work on the piece in autumn 1957 and would insist upon reworking the galleys three times from January to March the following year before she would allow Alice Morris, the then editor of *Harper's Bazaar*, to bring it to print. "I have a few things to do to the story yet," she wrote; "...I go from liking it to not liking it."[11] After the piece was published in the magazine, O'Connor confided to Maryat Lee that when she had seen "that last paragraph in print [she] knew instanter [sic] that it was too long."[12] "When I have another collection," she went on to say, "I am going to do some operating on it before I put it in."[13] Almost two years later in January 1960, O'Connor told Cecil Dawkins that, "The end of 'The Enduring Chill' ...still worrie[d her], particularly as someone who [had] read it recently thought that Asbury [had] died in the end."[14] And in November 1963, as she continued work on "...the Heathen...," O'Connor considers a more radical revision of the story. She remarked to Dawkins that she was "interested in keeping the situation of the boy coming home thinking he's going to die and in keeping the dialogue between him and Fr. Finn" apparently for the stalled "...Heathen..."[15] "If I find in the next month or so that I'm going to leave it as a story, I'll let you know..." she concluded.[16]

In her previous letter to Dawkins, O'Connor passed along the proofs of "The Comforts of Home," a story which parallels "...the Heathen..." at several crucial points. The tale of Thomas and Sarah Ham is likewise enamored of the ineffectual scholar trope O'Connor established in "Good Country People" and "The Enduring Chill" and was, at that time, continuing to plumb with George Rayber in *The Violent Bear It Away* and with Walter in "...the Heathen..." Thomas marks something of a departure in his will to power. Whereas Joy/Hulga makes a play of doing nothing as a means of showing her superiority and Asbury submits to fatalism, at the moment of crisis Thomas exhibits a sinister willingness to act out the

---

[11] Ibid., 256.

[12] Ibid., 293.

[13] Ibid.

[14] Ibid., 372.

[15] Ibid., 547.

[16] Ibid.

seeming merit of his own logic. Like Walter, he is a student of history, but his interest in the rise and fall of civilizations and their motivating ideologies is entirely theoretical. When his mother visits her "daredevil charity" upon him by taking in the rakish Sarah Ham, he psychologizes Christian faith to account for his own disgust.[17]

> The devil for Thomas was only a manner of speaking, but it was a manner appropriate to the situations his mother got into. Had she been in any degree intellectual, he could have proved to her from early Christian history that no excess of virtue is justified, that a moderation of good produces likewise a moderation of evil, that if Antony of Egypt would have stayed at home and attended to his sister no devils would have plagued him.[18]

In spite of Thomas's intellectualizing the good of virtue, he is quite literally possessed by a counter-inclination toward irrational ill-thought communicated to him in the form of his deceased father.

> Thomas was not cynical and so far from being opposed to virtue, he saw it as a principle of order and the only thing that makes life bearable. His own life was made bearable by the fruits of his mother's saner virtues—by the well-regulated house she kept and the excellent meals she served. But when virtue got out of hand with her, as now, a sense of devils grew upon him, and these were not mental quirks in himself or the old lady, they were denizens with personalities, present though not visible, who might any moment be expected to shriek or rattle a pot.[19]

It is the voice of his ogreish father which compels Thomas to act against his "love of good" to restore the comforts of his mother's well-ordered house by ousting, through some reasonable plot, the intruding "little slut" Sarah Ham.[20] "Several ideas for getting rid of her had entered his head but each of these had been suggestions whose moral tone indicated that they had come from a mind akin to his father's, and Thomas rejected them."[21] The narrator explains that Thomas had "inherited his father's reason without his ruthlessness and his mother's love of good without her tendency to pursue it. His plan for all practical action was to wait and see what developed," but

---

[17] O'Connor, "The Comforts of Home," *Complete*, 383.

[18] Ibid., 385–86.

[19] Ibid., 386.

[20] Ibid., 383.

[21] Ibid., 398.

the persistent imposition of his mother's shameless ward demands he act hastily and without his usual "bland" rationale.[22] "[O]utrageous...suggestions continued to come to him" amplified by his father's taunts. In the dead man's words he is, "Not enough to be a man," a "moron" too slow and too honest to act profitably and with conviction.[23] Finally he submits to the old man is memory and lies in a last ditch effort to defame Sarah Ham. "'I found [the gun] in her bag!' Thomas shouted. 'The dirty criminal slut stole my gun!'"[24] His mother pales "at the sound of the other presence in [Thomas's] voice," aware, it seems, that her son is lost now even to his stoic's virtue.[25] "Fire! the old man yelled," and "Thomas fired," so deluded in rage at his mother's betrayal that he "heard [the blast] as a sound...meant to bring an end to evil in the world."[26]

Walter intimates a further move toward radical liberalism for O'Connor's intellectuals in that he does not arrive, as Thomas does, at intellectual duplicity. He begins there. Walter had:

> no illusions about his own character. Once he had become convinced that his energy and ambition did not equal his talent and that he would never, as his mother said, 'make something of himself,' he had settled down with a sense of liberation, to be what he was—nothing much, but superior in that he knew it. He had a heart murmur, several allergies, and one or two other latent diseases that he could fall back on to explain his coming to terms with life at such an early age.[27]

Like Thomas, Walter "was not vicious and preferred right to wrong for it was usually less taxing," but he does not share his predecessor's morbid aversion to women.[28] In fact, Walter:

> thought a great deal about women but would not have liked to have to support one. Occasionally he went to the city for a pleasure trip, but he always returned depressed and with an unsettled feeling and for several days would do nothing but sit in the sun or wander through the woods, sunk in a kind of daze, watching the light as it settled in dappled patterns around him. Finally he would

---

[22] Ibid., 388.

[23] Ibid., 393, 402.

[24] Ibid., 403.

[25] Ibid.

[26] Ibid.

[27] O'Connor, "Why Do the Heathen Rage?" MS 217b, n. date, 5–6.

[28] Ibid., 6.

> return to himself and as if he had been saved from some dangerous encounter with the unknown, he would capture his view of himself and perhaps begin on another correspondence in which he would assume a new and fantastic personality.[29]

Walter's monkish retreatism and precious ailments are reminiscent not only of Thomas's intellectual compulsions but of Asbury's and Julian's with the crucial difference that Walter seems not to have forgone the pleasures of the body. Undoubtedly one of the reasons that O'Connor was so divided in her sense of Walter was her awareness that she was moving into the strange and sometimes unavoidably parodic realm of human sexuality. At this point in her writing life, she seems to accept sex as a driving force in human relationships which cannot be so definitively chased from the fictive bedchamber as it was by St. Thomas with a fiery poker.[30] O'Connor's friendship with the less than monogamous Robert Lowell and with Betty Hester, Maryat Lee, and Cecil Dawkins, all three of whom were openly gay, very likely prompted Flannery to reconsider sexuality in terms of charity and indeed beyond the doctrinal last word on what is "natural" or justifiable. O'Connor's boldness in pursuing these relationships, at least intellectually, in spite of the Church's condemnation of homosexuality, suggests further that while she endeavored to uphold Christian dogma she did not censor the influence of those who might have conflicting priorities. The "...Heathen..."'s antagonist, Oona Gibbs, is a direct adaptation of Maryat Lee, at times even using her private speech, and as such is uniquely demonstrative of the degree to which O'Connor's fictions were effected by and indeed infused with her relationships and her discourse with other people.

This is not to say that the sex act had not occurred in O'Connor before the advent of Walter. The hero of her debut novel, Hazel Motes, visits at least two "friendly" beds, but the manner in which he goes about the act—joylessly as if attending to some entirely inevitable and banal rite—saves O'Connor from having to speculate about the particularities of male desire. She seems to test the quality of a fictionalized, masculine desire with Thomas but instead of demonstrating his urges directly, she subjects her hero to an

[29] Ibid.

[30] In an early letter to Hester, O'Connor declared sympathy for the saint's conviction against carnal nature. See O'Connor, *Habit*, 94.

insistent, burlesque female gaze. "The quality of her look was such that it might have been her hands, resting now on his knees, now on his neck."[31] Thomas's defense is to avoid even the slightest contact with Sarah Ham; he makes a point of not looking into her winking eyes or touching her skin or inhaling her unmistakable odor. When the girl would ease into a throaty blues song, he would "frantically stuffle his ears with Kleenex."[32] Nevertheless he cannot help but be effected by the proximity of Miss Ham; his face constantly "flushed" at the thought of his outrageous "violation."[33]

Walter, on the other hand, is the initiator of his epistolary liaisons. The act of letter-writing seems itself a method of physical gratification. What began as "a sort of literary exercise" in which Walter wrote to strangers he considered not particularly "intelligent or honest," assuming various attitudes of admiration, develops into a role play galvanized by actual passion.[34] Having courted the radical humanist Oona Gibbs in the guise of a black man—a composite of imagined Negro significations and the borrowed photographic image of his father's care-giver, Roosevelt—Walter anticipates the girl's bodily presence as a man "making love through the mail to a woman he had never seen."[35] Not coincidently, it is "on the day the woman decended [sic] on them" that Walter appears to consummate his epistolary love.[36]

> Walter was upstairs in his room, sitting at his typewriter, finishing a letter to her. His big spectacled face was unnaturally flushed. Every now and then he paused and rubbed his hand gently over the bald spot at the top of his head, down across one of his steaming cheeks and under the fold of his chin. Then he would begin to type again. The words came furiously. His blue eyes

---

[31] O'Connor, "The Comforts of Home," *Complete*, 390.

[32] Ibid., 395.

[33] Ibid.

[34] Flannery O'Connor, "Why Do the Heathen Rage?" MS 218a, n. date, 5, MS 216, n. date, 4, *Flannery O'Connor Collection*, Russell Library, Georgia College and State University, Milledgeville, Georgia.

[35] O'Connor, "Why Do the Heathen Rage?" MS 220b, 1.

[36] Flannery O'Connor, "Why Do the Heathen Rage?" MS 220a, n. date, 1, *Flannery O'Connor Collection*, Russell Library, Georgia College and State University, Milledgeville, Georgia.

> seemed to sit far behind his spectacles... His blue plaid shirt stuck to his back with sweat.[37]

Walter's seeming climax is a far cry from Hazel's perfunctory execution of "the usual business," but it was one which apparently proved to be a step too far. [38] O'Connor crossed out the bulk of the passage. On one level, the author was almost certainly being ironical, perhaps responding in kind to the "ridiculous results" sometimes attendant to the "Freudian technique"[39] of literary anlaysis. If her friend William Sessions could make phalluses out of "lifted bough[s]" and "door handle[s]," she might comment by transforming the act of writing into a suggestively visceral onanism. Burns suggests that O'Connor's attempt at writerly hedonism ultimately derailed the narrative. She argues that the author "lavishes so much comic attention on Walter's letters that she loses sight of the plot."[40] For her part, O'Connor seems to have reconsidered the phallic gag, and on her next attempt shifts the emphasis from Walter's body to Eustis's—one of the Tilmans' black farmhands.

> [Walter's] face reddened and paled as he wrote. Every now and then he paused and rubbed his hand... Then he would begin to type again furiously. Occasionally he paused & glanced through the window. Out over the meadow, where Eustis was mowing. The negro shouted a song to the Lord over the rumble of the tractor, flung it out as if the Lord were sitting forward on the throne of heaven with his hand cupped to his ear to catch the words. Each time he looked, the sight of the Negro seemed to intensify...[41]

Very likely, this is the first time Walter has considered Eustis for any length as a man independent of his race with discrete abilities and insight, but his altered vision does not ultimately convert him to Oona's prescribed co-martyrdom. Instead it seems to bolster his "bent on destruction."[42]

> ...His eyes behind his glasses were green and intense. There was in them a kind of agonized impatience. He had the look of some one [sic] who is alleviating boredom with evil, but an evil that has

---

[37] Ibid.

[38] O'Connor, *Wise Blood*, 34.

[39] O'Connor, *Habit*, 407.

[40] Burns, "O'Connor's Unfinished Novel," 177.

[41] O'Connor, "Why Do the Heathen Rage?" MS 220b, 1.

[42] Ibid.

> slowly and uncertainly to make its own way and always with the danger of interference and the sudden raw appearance of…reality. It was reality he was looking for, the sudden explosion that was designed to tear down a veil.[43]

Walter's sense of the real is abstracted and, as his letter-writing attests, radically disembodied.

> Ever since he was ten, Walter had been writing to people he did not know. …As he grew older, his interest in prominent people ceased. The relatively obscure began to hear from him. Sometimes he assumed personalities that fit the interests of his correspondents but most of the time he wrote legitimate letters to people he considered to have integrity. He had more friends he had never seen than friends he had. The soul moves quickly without the body. Flesh is the greatest interference to love.[44]

Walter's fictive efforts to do away with the body are matched and ultimately overshadowed by the philosophy of the a-religious Oona. Following the vague doctrine of the "Fellowship Farm," she rejects the Eucharistic "value of what is least about us, our flesh."[45] "To her nothing mattered but the spirit of a person and she had seen from the first that [Walter's] spirit was beautiful and generous."[46] The reader's impression of Walter, on the other hand, is informed by private images of the man slinking about his father's place in "dirty soft-soled moccasins" so as not to be "wayla[id]" by the old man.[47] His mother observes uneasily that "[h]e had been home for three years, he was twenty-eight, and he had not done anything."[48] "His smile was…wide [and] thin," his face "heavy, his eyes "cloudless" and blue.[49] "The eyes, the smile belonged to a different kind of man

---

[43] Ibid.

[44] Flannery O'Connor, "Why Do the Heathen Rage?" MS 222, 23–24, n. date, *Flannery O'Connor Collection*, Russell Library, Georgia College and State University, Milledgeville, Georgia.

[45] O'Connor, *Habit*, 366.

[46] Flannery O'Connor, "Why Do the Heathen Rage?" MS 218e, n. date, 12, *Flannery O'Connor Collection*, Russell Library, Georgia College and State University, Milledgeville, Georgia.

[47] Flannery O'Connor, "Why Do the Heathen Rage?" MS 227c, n. date, 13, *Flannery O'Connor Collection*, Russell Library, Georgia College and State University, Milledgeville, Georgia.

[48] Ibid., 12.

[49] Ibid.

from any [his mother] had ever known. There was no innocence in them; they courted good and evil impartially; and no convention held them. God knows, she thought and caught her breath, what he might do."[50] There is little beauty or generosity to be found in Walter. To his credit, he is aware of his own "depravity" and appears to suffer acutely from it.[51] "The odiousness of what he was doing was palpable to [him]," nevertheless, he cannot resist the pedant's compulsion to correct Oona's error in attempting to love indiscriminately, to be "open…to everything."[52] She writes of her adopted "interdenominational, inter-racial" community that:

> Friendship is a weak word for [what we do]. We can't use the word love or people would think it was something fishy. Charity won't do because it sounds religious and we aren't. There's none of that kind of nonsense about this. This is all in us! In you and me! It's something we've got and the prize is right now. The salvation is right now. There's no eternal reward, no postponement. You rot when you die and you only live once and then you only live when you love.[53]

In his letters to Oona, Walter has rejected his own body, not necessarily out of shame for his status relative to Roosevelt's and Eustis's, but more likely out of his inability to make his own situation as noble as he imagines Roosevelt's might be had he been someone more like Walter. He envisions himself at the fringes of the Southern tableau, more or less passive in comparison to his parents in his role as "observer."[54] When Oona asks him to "[t]ell [her] about the South,"[55] to explain how "a white Southerner [can] stand…the shame of being an oppressor," Walter first answers from this vantage.[56]

---

[50] Ibid.

[51] O'Connor, "Why Do the Heathen Rage?" MS 222, 24.

[52] Flannery O'Connor, "Why Do the Heathen Rage?" MS 228b, n. date, 27, *Flannery O'Connor Collection*, Russell Library, Georgia College and State University, Milledgeville, Georgia; O'Connor, "Why Do the Heathen Rage?" MS 218a, 7.

[53] O'Connor, "Why Do the Heathen Rage?" MS 216, 5; and MS 222, 27.

[54] O'Connor, "Why Do the Heathen Rage?" MS 218a, 7.

[55] Oona's demand inevitably brings to mind Faulkner's Shreve McCannon, who famously asks Quentin Compson to, "Tell about the South" (William Faulkner, *Absalom, Absalom!* [London: Vintage Random House, 2005] 174).

[56] O'Connor, "Why Do the Heathen Rage?" MS 218a, 6.

> He wrote her that he was in a peculiar position to understand her philosophy, but that it was impossible to put it into practice in a section where selfishness was so much a way of life that it could no longer be recognized as such. There was enough truth in this to make the writing of it disagreeable to him and it was, at the same time, enough of a lie to justify his treating it as a joke. The thought of Miss Oona Gibbs living with Negroes on this place was comical.[57]

For Oona, the "race problem" can be rectified simply by disregarding the flesh and by extending "friendship" to "anyone" "anywhere, anytime."[58] She has failed to take account of the mannered "formality" which, in O'Connor's words, has been "a condition of survival" in the South since the fall of the Confederacy.[59] "White people and colored people are used to milling around together in the South," she told Gerard Sherry in 1963, "and this integration only means that they will be milling around together in a few more places. No basic attitudes are being changed.[60] In a subsequent interview with C. Ross Mullins she declared that:

> It requires considerable grace for two races to live together, particularly when the population is divided about fifty-fifty between them and when they have our particular history. It can't be done without a code of manners based on mutual charity. ...When you have a code of manners based on charity, then when the charity fails—as it is going to do constantly—you've got those manners there to preserve each race from small intrusions upon the other. The uneducated Southern Negro is not the clown he's made out to be. He's a man of very elaborate manners and great formality which he uses superbly for his own protection and to insure his own privacy. All this may not be ideal, but the Southerner has enough sense not to ask for the ideal but only for the possible, the workable. The South has survived in the past because its manners, however lopsided or inadequate they may have been, provided enough social discipline to hold us together and give us identity. Now those old manners are obsolete, but the new manners will have to be

---

[57] Ibid., 7.

[58] O'Connor, "Why Do the Heathen Rage?" MS 216, 5.

[59] O'Connor qtd. in C. Ross Mullins, "Flannery O'Connor: An Interview," *Jubilee* 11 (June 1963): 32–33, rpt. in Magee, ed., *Conversations*, 104.

[60] O'Connor qtd. in Gerard E. Sherry, "An Interview with Flannery O'Connor," *The Critic* 21 (June–July 1963): 29–31, rpt. in Magee, ed., *Conversations*, 102.

> based on what was best in the old ones—in their real basis of charity and necessity. In practice, the Southerner seldom underestimates his own capacity for evil. For the rest of the country, the race problem is settled when the Negro has his rights, but for the Southerner, whether he's white or colored, that's only the beginning. The South has to evolve a way of life in which the two races can live together with mutual forbearance. You don't form a committee to do this or pass a resolution; both races have to work it out the hard way.[61]

Walter has had the advantage of observing Southern manners, both good and bad, at close range and immediately brings Oona back to the unavoidable reality of the body. His method of hijacking Roosevelt's person operates on two presumptions: first that he can effectively fictionalize the "Negro" manner and second that if his "fictional sense" of black consciousness proved "inadequate," his interlocutor would not be able to tell the difference.[62] He "threw himself so wholeheartedly into the role that he wrote ten emotional pages without stopping."[63] "I couldn't tell you," he writes:

> how a white Southerner feels because I am a Negro Southerner. I work in the country for a white family, typical in every way of these parts. I nurse the old man. He has…a son 27 years old, who is an interesting slob-like character, and a school-teacher daughter a few years older, very bossy and self important. I am as good educated as any of them but you see how much good it does me. They furnish me with a shack on the place and I am far from the madding [sic] crowd and all that and save my money, but sometimes I think I can't stand it and will go beserk [sic] and maybe knock down their big fat son. The son doesn't work, he does tend a liquor store for a few hours every night and gets him some pocket money that way and buys a lot of paper back books which I then steal. One thing I give him credit for—he's not going to get in the rat race, he's a thinker but he doesn't see anything worth wasting his thought on, not this sinking ship anyway.[64]

Walter's intentions become more sinister in later drafts that are motivated by a nascent theological sensitivity. His initial reading of

---

[61] O'Connor qtd. in Magee, ed., *Conversations,* 103–104.

[62] Flannery O'Connor, "Why Do the Heathen Rage?" MS 228a, n. date, 30, *Flannery O'Connor Collection*, Russell Library, Georgia College and State University, Milledgeville, Georgia.

[63] O'Connor, "Why Do the Heathen Rage?" MS 218e, 10.

[64] O'Connor, "Why Do the Heathen Rage?" MS 228b, 27.

Oona's profession of friendship as a comic aspect of her character shifts radically to an affront upon divine hierarchy. "What enraged [Walter] was something basic, something that offended the order of the universe. The answer drifted toward him like a cloud...fully formed, fully rational, not wholly unexpected: this woman had abrogated the place of God... Her error was theological."[65] Walter had apparently been indoctrinated in childhood, but as an adult he regards his parents' respective churches (Tilman Sr. is a staunch Baptist and his wife a Methodist) as if they were "a joke."[66] In an attempt to instill the boy with "plain country virtues," Tilman Sr. bestowed upon Walter in his boyhood the responsibility of one of his sows. The animal "had been almost ready to farrow and the idea that [Walter] could prevent this came to him quite casually as he lay in bed one night. He sat upright in the dark, astonished."[67] Having "never poisoned anything before," Walter "[r]apidly ...went through the ten commandments in his mind. ...Nowhere was there anything about poisoning hogs, especially your own hog."[68] The episode marks the first ethical dilemma Walter will face and as such it reveals his emerging preoccupation with authorial godliness. He does in fact poison the sow, "and the shock changed his life," seemingly by redirecting his aspirations of predominance to the fictionalized realm of his letters.[69] Not until he is confronted with a personality as inclined to delusions of control—Oona declares that she'd "even like to have a negro baby somehow to become them"—that Walter realizes his own theological error.[70] He has made a vocation of turning actual people into pliable caricatures who he can influence with praise or blame. Once their reality becomes too insistent upon

---

[65] Flannery O'Connor, "Why Do the Heathen Rage?" MS 226b, n. date, 20, *Flannery O'Connor Collection*, Russell Library, Georgia College and State University, Milledgeville, Georgia.

[66] O'Connor, "Why Do the Heathen Rage?" MS 226b, 27. See also Flannery O'Connor, "Why Do the Heathen Rage?" MS 220b, n. date, 22, *Flannery O'Connor Collection*, Russell Library, Georgia College and State University, Milledgeville, Georgia.

[67] Flannery O'Connor, "Why Do the Heathen Rage?" MS 225e, n. date, 23, *Flannery O'Connor Collection*, Russell Library, Georgia College and State University, Milledgeville, Georgia.

[68] Ibid., 23–24.

[69] Ibid., 23.

[70] O'Connor, "Why Do the Heathen Rage?" MS 222, 28.

his orchestration, he can withdraw from the game unequivocally by creating his own death. "Whenever one of his mocked correspondents, from being a caricature, began to take on human lines—pathetic, undemanding, full of ridiculous encroaching love—Walter wrote DECEASED across the next letter he received and put it back in the mail, and for a time he would not debase himself again."[71] When his correspondence with Oona Gibbs got "out of hand," Walter moves to avert disaster with another staged death, "but he could not bring himself to put deceased across any of her letters."[72] "Ever since the first letter, he had been held fast in the snare of his own depravity."[73] Oona is the first of Walter's targets to elicit a counter-effect, a shock not unlike the one he experienced when he killed the sow. What he had done suddenly "mattered; and worse, the woman mattered."[74] "It was necessary that his system ward off the full force of the discovery he had made, but his logical mind was already sorting out the consequences."[75] The "worst" of these was "the Church and the place waiting for him in it."[76] The "truth" intimated by the circumstance "... did not so much occur to him now as it simply appeared...stunning and uncorrectable, something which he had in fact always known."[77] He had been, in Burns's words, "a susceptible personality already intellectually converted to an early form of Christianity, but yet to undergo spiritual conversion."[78] Having witnessed the effect of Oona's conversion—a phenomenon which forsakes sacred and political history to operate on unchecked emotion—Walter realizes the technical short-coming of his intellectual heathenism, the inverse of Friendship Inc.'s doctrine of brotherhood.

Walter's initial reaction is to resist conversion by undertaking to destroy the spirit of his adversary. He "call[s] upon the devil, also a believer, to help him..., intend[ing] to answer Oona Gibb's letter in

[71] Ibid., 24.

[72] O'Connor, "Why Do the Heathen Rage?" MS 217b, 4.

[73] O'Connor, "Why Do the Heathen Rage?" MS 222, 24.

[74] O'Connor, "Why Do the Heathen Rage?" MS 226b, 21.

[75] Ibid.

[76] Ibid.

[77] Ibid.

[78] Marian Burns qtd. in Scott, *Flannery O'Connor: An Annotated Reference Guide,* 138.

such a way that she would be brought down at least to human stature."[79] His usual "method" of "honest insult" would not suffice.[80] More than likely the commiserate Oona would turn any direct abuse into a means of fixing her philosophy upon him. He would have to ambush her from within her own apostasy, but "[h]e didn't know how. Real inspiration did not come to him until he was almost in front of the house and saw the back of Roosevelt's head like a black globe resting on the balustrade."[81]

Roosevelt's head appears disembodied and unconscious, an image which subtly analogizes Walter's appropriation of his mental being. The former's impersonation is a weak one, even taking into consideration the fact that O'Connor's own efforts to "get inside" Roosevelt's "head" are among the manuscripts' least convincing moments.[82] "Roosevelt Junior Hill" has a wooden quality of almost absent-minded resignation, his "face...masked with an indolence that barely covered the wariness behind it."[83] This is precisely the quality which seems to endear the apparently vagrant, half-blind Roosevelt to Tilman Sr. The boy, he liked to say, was, "Pure nigger."[84]

O'Connor had observed first-hand the self-preserving "indolence" of her mother's black employees. "The Negro's method of escape is foolproof," she said of longtime Andalusia resident Louise Hill.[85] "She can effect complete mental absence when she wants to—she's there, grinning, agreeing, but gone gone. No white person can cope with this, not even my parent. Least of all my parent..."[86] O'Connor seemed unable to conceive of Louise's private thoughts. Like Walter, she admits she could "only look at [blacks] from the outside."[87] "Who," she asks through Walter, "knew Eustis's thoughts, or Roosevelt's or Alice's[?]"[88] Not surprisingly O'Connor's fictional blacks share Louise's impenetrability; they are

[79] O'Connor, "Why Do the Heathen Rage?" MS 222, 29.

[80] O'Connor, "Why Do the Heathen Rage?" MS 225e, 23.

[81] Ibid.

[82] Sally Fitzgerald, "Introduction," *Habit*, xix.

[83] O'Connor, "Why Do the Heathen Rage?" MS 222, 20, 18.

[84] Ibid.

[85] O'Connor, *Habit*, 508.

[86] Ibid.

[87] O'Connor, "Why Do the Heathen Rage?" MS 228a, 30.

[88] Ibid.

performatively black, individuals defined by their reactions to the white understanding (and misunderstanding) of blackness. As such they cannot act independently of blackness as trope because the framing logic of O'Connor's narration is always situated on the white side of the performance. Roosevelt and Randall ("The Enduring Chill") play up the white conception of blackness while the "huge woman" on the bus ("Everything That Rises Must Converge") and the New York actor ("Judgment Day") attack that conception, but all four come away from confrontation with their privacy very much intact.[89]

Walter is confident that he can write convincingly from a black point of view because he assumes that education, even a poor education, would effect a change, turning a man like Roosevelt or Eustis into "[him]self but black."[90] "[A]n educated negro[,] even a half-educated one," he thought, "should be different. They were the ones who suffered. He should be able to get into such a mind."[91] Walter's charade is met with an unexpected reprove; rather than sympathizing with his black double, Oona chastises him for his effusive self-pity:

> Dear Walter Tilman, What a sniveling lump of self-pity you must be... It's quite likely that I could not stomach you for I have learned one thing in the last six months—only equals can be friends and you don't appear to be my equal and not because you're black. Black and white is just a detail, like fat and thin, as far as I'm concerned. ...For your information...I have no desire to arrange reality for other people though sometimes I would like to ask them why they don't arrange it for themselves. You, I doubt if you even vote. Are you registered? If you are have you made any effort to see that other negroes in your community register? You sound to me just like the type who complains and complains and never makes a move to do anything. ...I suppose you spend a lot of time envying that stupid son on the place there w[h]ere you work, wishing you were him. You sound like his double to me, only black, and without the place to do nothing on.[92]

---

[89] O'Connor, "The Enduring Chill," *Complete*, 379; "Everything That Rises Must Converge," *Complete*, 418; and "Judgment Day," *Complete*, 545.

[90] O'Connor, "Revelation," *Complete*, 491.

[91] O'Connor, "Why Do the Heathen Rage?" MS 228a, 30.

[92] O'Connor, "Why Do the Heathen Rage?" MS 228a, 28–29.

O'Connor here underlines the significance of the name "Walter," a designation in common usage from the late fourteenth to the nineteenth century meaning, in its verb form, "to turne or walter in myre as hogges doe."[93] The word also appears as a noun in the English clergyman John Knewstub's treatise, *A Confutation of Monstrous Heresies...* where it is used to denote the "wallowing place" itself.[94] "The Lord...reuengeth [reigneth] the shameful contempt and neglect of his truth: by sending numbers to their stie or walter againe."[95] In the context of Knewstub's usage, Walter is associated with the impending justice of a jealous God. There is a further analogy with the piece's title, the first words of psalm two which describe, in much the same tone as St. Jerome's in his letter to Heliodorus, Christ's coming in vengeance. The psalm reads:

> Why do the heathen rage, and the people imagine a vain thing? The kings of the earth set themselves, and the rulers take counsel together, against the Lord, and against his anointed, saying, Let us break their bands asunder, and cast away their cords from us. He that sitteth in the heavens shall laugh: the Lord shall have them in derision. Then shall he speak unto them in his wrath, and vex them in his sore displeasure. Yet have I set my king upon my holy hill of Zion. I will declare the decree: the Lord hath said unto me, Thou art my Son; this day have I begotten thee. Ask of me, and I shall give thee the heathen for thine inheritance, and the uttermost parts of the earth for thy possession. Thou shalt break them with a rod of iron; thou shalt dash them in pieces like a potter's vessel. Be wise now therefore, O ye kings: be instructed, ye judges of the earth. Serve the Lord with fear, and rejoice with trembling. Kiss the Son, lest he be angry, and ye perish from the way, when his wrath is kindled but a little. Blessed are all they that put their trust in him.[96]

The crux of Walter's story, as it is with so many of O'Connor's heroes, is bound up in his imagining "a vain thing," namely his authorial conceit. Walter presumes he can make sport of meddling in other's lives, even assume the life of another, and remain, by virtue of his relative anonymity and his ability to "die" at will, wholly

---

[93] John Withals, *Shorte Dictionaire for Yonge Beginners* (London: Ihon Kingstun, 1553) f. 11v/2.

[94] "Walter," n., *Oxford English Dictionary*, 2nd ed. (Oxford: Oxford University Press, 1992) n. page. *www.oed.com.* http://www.oed.com/view/Entry/225377 (accessed 14 September 2011).

[95] Ibid.

[96] Ps. 2:1–12, *KJV*.

detached. O'Connor seems to suggest with her title that Walter's transformation is one from imaginary kingship to the "heathen…inheritance" of Christ.

Oona's name, on the other hand, implies that she is indeed good in spite of her unorthodox means of serving the good. Oona is possibly an Anglicized version of the Irish *Úna,* a given name thought to be derived from the word *uan,* or "lamb." The name has also been linked to the Latin adverb *una,* meaning "in one" or "together."[97] In her dealings with Walter, Oona cannot know that he has misrepresented himself; nonetheless, she intuits a connect between the black "Walter" and his self-aggrandizing by proxy. Stunned at his own transparency, Walter retaliates by challenging Oona's credo. "He pointed out that it was possible to love almost anyone who was 2,000 miles away. On closer inspection, however, she would find him very black."[98] Unwittingly, Oona calls Walter's bluff by requesting he send his picture. Exchanging photographs, she wrote, would "make them that much closer and when she continued to write [to him] in the same way, he would see that she was as much a realist as himself."[99]

> The idea of sending her a picture intriegued [sic] Walter. He bought some film for his camera and took several pictures of his father and Roosevelt, he took one of his mother, standing with her hands on her hips, talking angrily to R[oosevelt] …and finally he got his mother to take one of him squatting under a tree. Just as she snapped the picture, he opened his mouth and squinted like a lunatic.[100]

Walter uses the photos as a supplementary medium through which he imparts a super-reality, exaggerating his own personal quirks and refining his parents' and Roosevelt's to create a more affecting fiction.

---

[97] Kevin Cawley, "Latin Dictionary and Grammar Aid," *University of Notre Dame Archives,* n. page. *www.archives.nd.edu.* http://www.archives.nd.edu/cgibin/lookit.pl?latin=una (accessed 14 September 2011).

[98] O'Connor, "Why Do the Heathen Rage?" MS 218e, 11.

[99] Flannery O'Connor, "Why Do the Heathen Rage?" N. date, MS 218f, 11, *Flannery O'Connor Collection,* Russell Library, Georgia College & State University, Milledgeville, Georgia.

[100] Ibid., 12.

The interplay between Roosevelt and Tilman is brought to the fore as one operating on a basic premise of condescension. Nonetheless there are signs of genuine affection between the pair as if both were happily complicit in a joke on the rest of the household and on the overbearing Mrs. Tilman in particular. "Get behind…my chair and try to look like you got good sense," the old man says when Walter appears with his camera.[101] "Roosevelt got behind the chair and stood there, grinning."[102] In the published excerpt of the story, Roosevelt is the only soul amongst Tilman's charges to be visibly effected by his homecoming from the hospital.

> Roosevelt, who from now on would be nurse instead of yard man, stood inside the door, waiting. He had put on the white coat that he was supposed to wear for occasions. He peered forward at what was on the stretcher. The bloodshot veins in his eyes swelled. Then, all at once, tears glazed them and glistened on his black cheeks like sweat. Tilman made a weak rough motion with his good arm. It was the only gesture of affection he had given any of them.[103]

Walter had only managed a "sloppy salute," preoccupied, his mother reckoned, with the dramatic potential of the scene.[104] "His eyes were on her, glittering just slightly behind his glasses. He had taken in every detail of Tilman's face; he had registered Roosevelt's tears, Mary Maud's confusion, and now he was studying her to see how she was taking it."[105] Walter's "squatting" self-parody gives outlet to his unspoken frustration at having resigned himself to a no-account life as Meadow Oaks' resident hanger-on. Both of his parents resent this choice. "If I could stand on my feet," Tilman said, "I'd run him off the place."[106] The old man had once paid a "considerable sum" to rescue Roosevelt from a chain-gang, but "[h]e would not have spent the same—or in fact a nickel—to get Walter off…"[107] Privately Mrs. Tilman admits that her son's hidden pursuits more than likely "had to do with nothing and that would draw him farther and farther away from what mattered and make him more and more

---

[101] O'Connor, "Why Do the Heathen Rage?" MS 228a, 40.
[102] Ibid., 41.
[103] O'Connor, "Why Do the Heathen Rage?" *Complete*, 484.
[104] Ibid., 483.
[105] Ibid., 484.
[106] O'Connor, "Why Do the Heathen Rage?" MS 227c, 12–13.
[107] O'Connor, "Why Do the Heathen Rage?" MS 222, 20.

ineffectual."[108] What mattered to Mrs. Tilman was the practical future of the farm, and "[a]ll Walter knew about the land was that is was underneath him."[109] The hired laborer Mr. Gunnels supposes that the young man, though seemingly able-bodied, was somehow challenged. "It was plain enough to Gunnels that the fellow had fits. He must have because if there wasn't something wrong with him, the old woman would have put him to work. She hated idleness worse than she hated sin."[110]

In a later draft, O'Connor underscores Walter's deliberate orchestration of a pictorial Southern romance. "…He bought a roll of film, so that he would have a good selection to choose from and then he set out to concoct a picture-story of his life at Meadow Oaks. …Let her get a look at Roosevelt and her sense of detail would become keener."[111] It is precisely the details of life on the Tilman farm that Walter is compelled to reorder or abandon. For instance: "The negroes' house looked entirely too substantial to serve his purposes. It was unpainted, but it had windows in it, a pleasant porch, and a good roof, and it was set back in a lacy grove of chinaberry trees. It would not attract anyone looking for radical poverty."[112] Walter opts to photograph a neighbor's tenant "shack" instead, which "sat, windowless in front, about a foot off the bare swept ground. …Three colored children sat in front of it, playing in the dirt."[113] He also arranges a bizarre trinity on his parents' front porch, his father in his wheelchair, Roosevelt, obediently "solemn," behind him, and Walter in the background.[114] Mrs. Tilman is reluctant to snap the shot; "You look like a tramp," she says to Walter, and "you ought to be directly behind your father's chair and Roosevelt behind you if you want him in it."[115] Walter protests: "'No!' he shout[s]. '…I want it just like I fixed it. …Leave em [sic] both the way they are and take the picture.'"[116]

---

[108] O'Connor, "Why Do the Heathen Rage?" MS 226b, 25.
[109] Ibid.
[110] O'Connor, "Why Do the Heathen Rage?" MS 228a, 35.
[111] Ibid., 30–31.
[112] Ibid., 35–36.
[113] Ibid., 37.
[114] Ibid., 41.
[115] Ibid.
[116] Ibid., 41–42.

Walter's temptation to fictionalize the real extends to Oona Gibbs; as he appropriates Roosevelt's image he supplies Oona with a number of imagined bodies. After reading her first letter he "began to conjure up unbidden a picture of this girl, small and dark with luminous brown eye[s] in a fragile face. He decided that actually she would have big teeth that stuck out, a receding jaw and wear large spectacles."[117]

In another draft he "visualized her [as] a large woman with a blonde pony-tail and a round childish face…," and later "he saw a girl with very large dark eyes, and experienced a moment of tenderness for this image before it faded and he was left with the original woman he had conjured up, the big blond pony-tailed arranger."[118] Mrs. Tilman is the one to insist upon Oona's person as a reality independent of Walter's imagination. The young woman represents a potentially dangerous variable, one capable by association of defaming the Tilman name should they be seen to be taking up with "[s]ome*body* peculiar."[119] "What kind of a woman…" was she?[120] Was she "married or single?"[121] "What [did] she do?"[122]

> "Walter," [Mrs. Tilman] said, "you've never seen this woman. You don't even know if she's white or black." "She couldn't be black," he murmured. …Slowly Walter's jaw slackened. She could easily be any shade between. She had not sent him the pictures of herself that he had asked for. He turned his face slightly away from the cutting eyes in front of him. A parade of horrors passed before him. The vision of a woman with negroid features arriving to visit turned his blood to lead. He sickened at himself. He had responded to something sensual in the letter, he had trapped himself. He had imagined after the third letter a delicate girl, ignorant and teachable, someone whose vulgarity was only skin deep. The soul travels rapidly through the mail, unencumbered with real flesh.[123]

It is unclear whether Walter has assimilated Oona's airy disregard for the body or has taken up, in a gesture of irony, her

---

[117] O'Connor, "Why Do the Heathen Rage?" MS 218a, 11.

[118] O'Connor, "Why Do the Heathen Rage?" MS 222, 23, 28–29.

[119] O'Connor, "Why Do the Heathen Rage?" MS 226b, 28. Italics my own.

[120] Ibid., 27.

[121] Ibid., 27–28.

[122] Ibid., 28.

[123] Ibid., 29.

belief that the real work of charity occurs "between heart and heart."[124] In her first letter she writes, "The heart can move like a wind in letters where it is not tied to the body."[125] Yet even as Oona's "unconventional" charity attempts to supercede the flesh, it recalls certain practices of the early Christian church and its surviving orthodoxies. The girl has, first of all, removed herself from the social mainstream, forsaking the attendant status of her career, and has joined a meditative cooperative, not unlike the monastery, whose aim is to promote goodwill indiscriminately. Secondly, she experiences a conversion whose high drama is reminiscent of Sts. Augustine and Jerome. On her way to work at a New York fashion magazine she is struck by the image of a "Puertorican" child, alone in an alleyway, Crisco tin in hand, "waiting for the garbage."[126] She had seen him there for three months, and then one day she "SAW" him with a forcefulness she describes as a lightning strike.[127] "And this," she wrote:

> is the thing. I didn't want to give him food. I wanted to stand there hungry with him. I wanted to say, "Look there are two of us waiting." Do you see? Yes you see. You wrote me the kind of letter you did and you see! The next morning I got up early and I was going to talk to him but when he saw me turn into the alley, he ran. I was all I deserved.[128]

Oona intuits, in a way that the intellectually "Orthodox" Walter does not, that charity requires a very literal sort of compassion, in Marion Montgomery's words "an enduring—a suffering with—in love out of faith and hope."[129]

In the last years of her life, O'Connor was preoccupied with the execution of charity. She wrote to Andrew Lytle in spring 1960, "I have got to the point now where I keep thinking more and more about the presentation of love and charity...," a presentation which has been problematized, in every age, by the human reluctance to

---

[124] Flannery O'Connor, "Why Do the Heathen Rage?" N. date, MS 218d, 6, *Flannery O'Connor Collection*, Russell Library, Georgia College & State University, Milledgeville, Georgia.

[125] Ibid.

[126] O'Connor, "Why Do the Heathen Rage?" MS 222, 26.

[127] Ibid., 26–27.

[128] Ibid., 27.

[129] Montgomery, *Hillbilly Thomist*, 94. See also pg. 279.

engage in a personal sacrifice for a non-personal good.[130] O'Connor confessed to such experiencing such reluctance herself. She wrote to Hester in spring 1959:

> The law of my great charity is that it operates in inverse ratio to the nearness of the object. Therefore I can tolerate Cecilia [an acquaintance who insisted upon reading aloud to O'Connor via the telephone] very well but as Billy [Sessions] gets closer and closer to interrupting my labors at ten o'clock tomorrow, I love him less and less.[131]

The following June she added, "I share your lack of love for the race of man, but then this is only a sentiment and a sentiment falls before a command."[132] O'Connor's personal anxieties concerning charity were very likely exacerbated by her inheritance of a less than sympathetic view of the "plight of the Negro." Her close friend, the "rebellious and unconventional" playwright Maryat Lee, challenged O'Connor's anti-liberalisms, most insistently her preference for a slower-moving, locally envisaged methodology of racial integration.[133] Virginia Wray suggests that Lee was a "very general model" for "...the Heathen..."'s Oona Gibbs.[134] She also links the story's "Fellowship Farm"/"Friendship Inc." to Koinonia, "an interracial farm community" located just over one hundred miles southwest of Milledgeville in Americus, Georgia.[135] "I wish somebody would write something sensible about Koinonia," O'Connor wrote to Hester: "...[A]s you say it is something regressive which is getting all the benefit of martyrdom. I think they should be allowed to live in peace but that they deserve all this exaltation I highly doubt."[136] Lee was not a part of the Koinonia cooperative; she was, however, a lifelong champion of racial integration. Having relocated from her native Kentucky to Harlem, she "threw herself into the

---

[130] O'Connor, *Habit*, 373.

[131] Flannery O'Connor, "Correspondence with Betty Hester," 14 March 1959, MS 1064, Box 1, FF 7, *Flannery O'Connor Collection*, Manuscripts, Archives, and Rare Books Library, Emory University, Atlanta.

[132] O'Connor, *Habit*, 335.

[133] Sally Fitzgerald, *Habit*, 193.

[134] Virginia Wray qtd. in Scott, *Flannery O'Connor: An Annotated Reference Guide*, 673.

[135] Ibid.

[136] O'Connor, *Habit*, 220.

black movement with all the fervor of her character."[137] She became a leading voice of the 1960s street theatre movement, enlisting local people, untrained in stagecraft, to perform in roles which might subvert socialized "masks." Lee recalled of Flannery that she "permanently became devil's advocate with me in matters of race, as I was to do with her in matters of religion. Underneath the often ugly caricatures of herself…I could only believe that she shared with me the sense of frustration and betrayal and impotency over the dilemma of the white South."[138]

O'Connor's most direct invocation of Lee to appear in "Why Do the Heathen Rage?" occurs in Oona Gibb's initial response to Walter's "spontaneous…enthusiasm."[139] Oona exclaims, "I've become free. I've broken through the ceiling of everything that suffocated me—conventions, manners, religion—and have suddenly like breaking into outer space, understood that nothing matters but that you be open to everything and everybody. For the first time in my life, I'm afraid of nothing."[140] In O'Connor's first correspondence with Lee in January 1957, she wrote:

> I'm glad you liked the stories of mine you read and felt that they weren't a dead-end taken. …I wonder if you can have thought the dead-end a likely possibility for me because of the orthodoxy, which I remember you said was a ceiling you had come through? I take it that what you have come through is some expression of orthodoxy. I have come through several of those myself, always with a deepened sense of mystery and always several degrees more orthodox.[141]

Nearly six years later in July 1962, O'Connor remarked that Maryat had once been "unable to respond to anything. Now," she told Hester, "she responds to everything, or anyway to much more."[142] Maryat's previous assertion of having "come through" various indoctrinations to a more complete spiritual freedom is here overturned by O'Connor who implies that such an indiscriminate

---

[137] Sally Fitzgerald, *Habit*, 194.

[138] Maryat Lee qtd. in Sally Fitzgerald, *Habit*, 193.

[139] O'Connor, "Why Do the Heathen Rage?" MS 218a, 6.

[140] O'Connor, "Why Do the Heathen Rage?" MS 222, 26. See also MS 218a, 6.

[141] O'Connor, *Habit*, 195.

[142] Ibid., 483–84.

openness might actually "impose...impediments to [spiritual] responsiveness."[143]

In "...the Heathen...," Walter is a literal devil's advocate to Oona's a-historical philosophizing. He exhibits other conspicuous authorial parallels, including a prestigious education and a stint away from home ostensibly in preparation for a career in fiction writing.[144] His primary occupation on the farm is to "research" the domestic dramas of the hired help, which he does almost entirely "through his mother."[145] As to the real work of the farm, Walter is utterly ineffectual and divides his time between manning the register at a roadside liquor store and his private duties as a "secular contemplative."[146] "[H]e reads or writes or just ambles around, watching the way the light falls like an old man looking at everything a lot before he dies."[147] O'Connor's own sensibilities, while certainly not secular, do suggest an under-welling of self-conscious unease with regard to her "peculiar" vocation and her considerable dependence upon her mother for practical support. Her correspondence also implies that, like Walter, O'Connor felt somewhat representative of a generation who have lost touch with practical concerns and who refused, out of a vague intellectual righteousness, to participate in certain unfashionable practicalities. Walter, for instance, "could no more give orders to Mr. Gunnels than he could fly—even if [his mother had] told him exactly what orders to give. ...He didn't know how to deal with the class of people the Gunnels were. She handled Mr. Gunnels very well, using with him the exact tone of voice to maintain his medium dignity and no more."[148] Walter did not share his parents' "instinct" to handle "trashy" types like the Gunnels, and certainly he lacked his mother's ability "to dress down the niggers" daily.[149] "[Mrs. Tilman] was aware that something between her father's time and her own had

---

[143] Ibid., 484.

[144] O'Connor, "Why Do the Heathen Rage?" MS 226b, 26.

[145] O'Connor, "Why Do the Heathen Rage?" MS 228a, 31.

[146] O'Connor, "Why Do the Heathen Rage?" MS 226b, 26.

[147] O'Connor, "Why Do the Heathen Rage?" MS 228a, 28.

[148] O'Connor, "Why Do the Heathen Rage?" MS 226b, 24.

[149] O'Connor, "Why Do the Heathen Rage?" MS 228a, 38, 35; and MS 218a, 9.

happened to the world to produce children like hers."[150] Walter himself observes, albeit in the guise of Roosevelt, that "his generation isn't sure of anything. They can't order a negro around and he can't say 'nigger' like his old man. What I mean is he's eaten up with guilt on account of me and the old man never felt an ounce of it in his life."[151] If Walter can be said to fictionalize O'Connor's personal difficulty with the "race problem," it should also be noted that she maintained, in spite of her hero's vacillation between the political far left and middle right, a conventionality that betrayed her ties to the South and the Catholic Church. She jested to Lee, saying, "The South is the place for you if you can keep yourself from running off to every sit-in or wade-in or kneel-in that is being held."[152] Even in her ribbing of Maryat's lust for social justice, O'Connor is sure to "say a plague on everyone's house"—the citified integrationists', the river-revivalists', and the genuflecting Catholics'.[153]

Walter's own relationship with Oona and the movement she is made to represent is anything but straightforward. "His image of her now after three months of steady correspondence varied erratically from complete repulsion to unsatiable [sic] imaginary lust..."[154] "[S]he had answered his letter," like Jerome had answered Heliodorus, "with a violence...of affection & disdain that would not be denied and the correspondence had continued, furious and personal."[155] "She had that radical kind of innocence that trails bloodshed behind it."[156] Oona's innocence, in its theological erring, explodes Walter's adopted "tone" of "cynical intelligent despair."[157] Her telling of her conversion effects profound physiological and psychic tremors in him: "[He] paled. He stared straight in front of him. His throat was instantly dry, his face grew even paler, he looked as if the country-side had dropped away from the rock he sat on and he and the rock were suspended over nothing...while a bolt of lightning flashed from the cloud and turned everything around

---

[150] O'Connor, "Why Do the Heathen Rage?" MS 226b, 25.
[151] O'Connor, "Why Do the Heathen Rage?" MS 228b, 27.
[152] O'Connor, *Habit*, 482.
[153] Ibid., 537.
[154] O'Connor, "Why Do the Heathen Rage?" MS 226b, 22.
[155] Ibid.
[156] O'Connor, "Why Do the Heathen Rage?" MS 228a, 30.
[157] O'Connor, "Why Do the Heathen Rage?" MS 218a, 7.

him glaring white."[158] Walter's experience of conversion significantly parallels Oona's, a nod perhaps by the author to her liberal friend that is suggestive of a respect (if not a validation) of non-sacramental charity. "I don't know," O'Connor told Hester in January 1961, "if anybody can be converted without seeing themselves in a kind of blasting anihilating[159] [sic] light, a blast that will last a lifetime." Though O'Connor made light of liberal rhetoric and remained throughout her confidence with Lee critical of leftist fanaticism, it is clear that she held Maryat in an esteem enjoyed by few of her friends. She saw her as one "full of [grace]," and her jibing seems a love-wrought attempt to help in providing the tradition-shrugging Lee a form with which to harness and direct her compassion. "Everything," O'Connor told her not long after their first acquaintance in January 1957:

> has to be diluted with time and with matter, even that love of yours which has to come down on many of us to be able to come down on one. It is grace and it is the blood of Christ and I thought, after I had seen you once, that you were full of it and didn't know what to do with it or perhaps even what it was. Even if you loved Foulkes [David Faulkes-Taylor, Lee's fiancé] and [Donald] Ritchie and me…equally and individually, it all has to be put somewhere finally.[160]

For O'Connor, mankind's practical love is amassed in the "invisible Church" where, in time and in matter, it will glorify all of creation. The universal transfiguration orthodox Christians anticipate has its basis in the very thing liberal crusaders, like Oona Gibbs, seek to jettison: the body. Liberal justice tends to put its emphasis on an abstractedly uniform human soul, but "[i]t is not the soul," O'Connor would remind Oona, "she [the Church] says will rise but the body, glorified."[161] "Our salvation," she went on to say, "is worked out on earth according as we love one another, see Christ in one another, etc. by works. This is one reason I am chary of using the word, love,

---

[158] O'Connor, "Why Do the Heathen Rage?" MS 226b, 20.

[159] Flannery O'Connor, "Correspondence with Betty Hester," 21 January 1961, MS 1064, Box 2, FF 4, *Flannery O'Connor Collection*, Manuscripts, Archives, and Rare Books Library, Emory University, Atlanta.

[160] O'Connor, *Habit*, 224–25.

[161] Ibid., 100.

loosely. I prefer to use it in its practical forms, such as prayer, almsgiving, visiting the sick and burying the death and so forth."[162]

Oona has a much more dramatic approach, confessing love to the unseen Walter after a single exchange. "The heart," she writes, "has no color. Write to me, dear Walter Tilden, for already knowing your beautiful and absurd heart, I love you."[163] Walter challenges her to put her hypothetical love into practice:

> "The only way you'll know," he [wrote], "is to come. Come and see. You won't stay. I can guarantee that. I can promise you that. You're a fool[.] You don't know your right hand from your left. I want you to come. Meadow Oaks is...waiting for you. It's] the place...for your revelation. You'll stay just long enough to look once & then you'll turn & run."[164]

Walter's inner-pedant longs to demonstrate the failings of Oona's philosophy, but he is coincidently mired in actual affection for her. His challenge, in this respect, is remarkably vulnerable: "Come and see me," he asks. "See me as I am, see how I have lied, and then set about loving me." But Oona never arrives. This is just as well for Walter because, in preparing his mother for the impending visit of a woman "fanatic" who "thumb[s] rides," he has a revelation of his own.[165] The strange woman could, as his mother curtly points out, very well be something *he* is unprepared for. The butt of his hoax it turns out is not the hapless Oona, but Walter himself. When his mother presents the possibility that his postal lover is black, Walter is made aware of his own secret prejudice.

> Guilt fastened upon him and with it...a full confrontation with...his revolting conversion. ...Unlike Paul he had not been thrown to the ground and blinded. He saw well or better than ever. What appealed to his intellect in theory did not appeal to his taste in fact. At the thought of Christ he winced and at the thought of the Church he shuddered and sickened. All spring he had been desperately courting disaster, ...tempting fate to keep his mind

---

[162] Ibid., 102.

[163] Flannery O'Connor, "Why Do the Heathen Rage?" N. date, MS 218d, 6, *Flannery O'Connor Collection*, Russell Library, Georgia College & State University, Milledgeville, Georgia.

[164] O'Connor, "Why Do the Heathen Rage?" MS 220b, 1.

[165] Flannery O'Connor, "Why Do the Heathen Rage?" N. date, MS 226f, 28, *Flannery O'Connor Collection*, Russell Library, Georgia College & State University, Milledgeville, Georgia; and MS 218a, 9.

> occupied, his senses engaged. Now, predictably, all that was backfiring. Automatic revenge was taking place.[166]

Walter's premonition is correct; if his intention was to maintain his fictional self, he would have done well to steer clear of the guileless Oona Gibbs.

> After a week's correspondence with her he had begun to suspect that in spite of the absurdity of the movement, she herself was inadvertently intelligent; and he had let himself slip into the letters. She had from the first addressed him…with an innocence that he found appalling [and had] expressed some of what must have been her inmost thoughts. Julian [Walter] was both shocked and attracted by honesty and afraid of it since it was infectious. He could not sustain the pose he had started and found himself writing her truths about himself which he had heretofore kept from his own attention.[167]

Wray has proposed that a similar phenomenon occurred between O'Connor and Lee, remarking that the playwright appears to have "caused O'Connor to soften her scathing critique of liberals."[168] While I disagree with the American Literature Association panel's assertion that the unfinished "…Heathen…" concludes with a "defense of liberalism," there is considerable evidence in O'Connor's personal letters to suggest that her friendship with Lee was a welcome challenge to her dogmatisms.[169] Lee embodied a somewhat "overpower[ing]" sort of charity rarely witnessed outside of Catholic religious orders, and O'Connor, even as she made attempts to temper the boldness of her friend's love, could not help but be drawn by the apparent ease with which Lee went at the practical making of friends in love.[170] Not quite six months after their first meeting in Milledgeville, Maryat wrote to O'Connor from New York: "Oh, Flannery, I love you. …Did you know that? I almost said it when we were standing by the fence, but I

---

[166] O'Connor, "Why Do the Heathen Rage?" MS 226f, 30.

[167] O'Connor, "Why Do the Heathen Rage?" MS 216, 5.

[168] Wray qtd. in Marshall Bruce Gentry, "ALA 1997 Panel Discussion: 'Flannery O'Connor and the Maryat Lee Letters,'" *CHEERS! The Flannery O'Connor Society Newsletter* 5/2 (1997–1998): 3.

[169] 1997 ALA Panel qtd. in Gentry, 3.

[170] Robert E. "Buzz" Lee qtd. in Jean W. Cash, "Flannery O'Connor: Art "Demand[s] Celibacy," *Postscript: A Publication of the Philological Association of the Carolinas* 15 (1998): 29.

was just too depressed and low and desperate, about work and family and etc. What would you have done if I had come up with it? Gone flippity flopping away on your crutches I bet."[171] O'Connor endeavors, like Walter, to bring Lee back to the reality of the body which is to say the needfulness of love to be mediated by time and substance. She seems suspicious of Lee's maintaining such fast-coming affection or her own ability to remain the object of Maryat's love. On several occasions she prompts Lee to come and see her at Andalusia as if to make a proof, to herself and to her friend, that "[c]harity is hard and endures."[172] O'Connor would likely have distinguished her companionship with Maryat as a possibility for "[p]ositive charity as opposed to flagellation and the hairshirt…[its being] harder and more wearing on the nerves…[but which] availeth more."[173] Maryat, like Oona, brushes O'Connor's "Christian realism" aside in her reply: "…I take you with or without the blood of the lamb, and still it is you I love and it is I that love you, and my heart leaps. Oh Flannery, your reply falls pitifully short, a ruse of bones, a chill breeze, inadequate, obfuscating, limp, full of cliches, the quaver of a solitary voice in the airless eternities and fog drifting over in sheets."[174] Not surprisingly, O'Connor defends her rejoinder by saying, "You are of course entirely right that the reply was inadequate and cliche-ridden. It always will be. These are mysteries that I can in no way approach…"[175] In turn, Maryat resists O'Connor's theological deflection, matching Flannery's insistence of a practical love with her own demand that O'Connor accept the free gift of her friendship:

> My dear girl, I am not attacking your *religion*—but your use of it. Surely you can't find in [Christian] dogma the argument that when someone says simply & clearly they love you that you are called upon to elaborate (needlessly) upon the ultimate significance of

---

[171] Maryat Lee qtd. in Cash, "Flannery O'Connor: Art 'Demand[s] Celibacy,'" 29.

[172] O'Connor, *Habit*, 308.

[173] Flannery O'Connor, "Correspondence with Betty Hester," 16 May 1959, MS 1064, Box 1, FF 7, *Flannery O'Connor Collection*, Manuscripts, Archives, and Rare Books Library, Emory University, Atlanta.

[174] Maryat Lee qtd. in Cash, *The Mind of the South*, 29–30.

[175] O'Connor, *Habit*, 227.

same. You may be a Catholic but you're acting like a damn Puritan or, just as bad, cautious intellectual.[176]

Walter seems, at various moments, to enact O'Connor's self-conscious intellectual caution, but ultimately Flannery was unwilling to follow Maryat's example and subject, even her fiction, to apostasy. She reverts Walter to the familiar territory of the scriptures, reaffirmed, it seems, in her belief that "the mind serves best when it is anchored in the word of God. There is no danger then of becoming an intellectual without integrity."[177] In September 1963, O'Connor admitted to John Hawkes, "I have been working all summer just like a squirril [sic] on a treadmill, trying to make something of Walter and his affairs and the other heathens that rage but I think this is maybe not my material..."[178] Quite unlike Asbury's and Thomas's, the structure of Walter's story is such that the major crisis is not the moment of conversion but some demonstration of the effect of that change. "I don't believe the fundamental nature changes, but that it's put to a different use when conversion occurs and of course," O'Connor wrote to Hester in 1956, "it requires vigilance to put it to proper use..."[179] Asbury finds that he cannot disembody his mind when it is revealed by the drawling Dr. Block that he will live, that "[b]lood" in fact "don't lie."[180] Thomas acts out a devilish impulse to restore his mother to his private use but accidentally shoots her dead. Suspended in shock above her body, Thomas can no longer deny his mother the dignity inherent to her flesh or the determinedness of her sacrifice.

Walter, on the other hand, is left without the physical manifestation of Oona's inciting body. In the final pages of several manuscripts, he frantically attempts to "head her off" with telegrams exclaiming all manner of catastrophe: "Do not come. Mother dying" one note reads, another "INFECTIOUS HEPATITIS. DO NOT COME. VERY DANGEROUS."[181] Walter fears that the prospect of calamity will entice rather than repel Oona, but the fateful "descent"

---

[176] Maryat Lee qtd. in Cash, "Flannery O'Connor: Art 'Demand[s] Celibacy," 30.

[177] O'Connor, *Habit*, 134.

[178] Ibid., 537.

[179] Ibid., 184.

[180] O'Connor, "The Enduring Chill," *Complete*, 367.

[181] O'Connor, "Why Do the Heathen Rage?" MS 226b, 29–31.

never occurs. The final manuscripts of "…the Heathen…" see O'Connor refining existing scenes and filling out, with short episodic asides, the routine of her protagonists' domestic life; she seems reluctant to speculate how Oona's arrival would effect Walter's universe. She opts instead to devote her energies to the burgeoning "Parker's Back," a story with definitive parallels to "…the Heathen…"'s Mr. Gunnels. "I have been writing eighteen years," O'Connor confided to Sister Gable in the midst of revising "…the Heathen…", "and I've reached the point where I can't do again what I know I can do well, and the larger things that I need to do now, I doubt my capacity for doing."[182] Whether it was for want of time or strength or desire that O'Connor left Walter's story untold we cannot say, but it is clear that she felt much comfort in returning to that most fundamental of Christian doctrines, the Incarnation, with O. E. Parker. It seems appropriate that O'Connor, in the last year of her life, would go "back to page one," as it were, to reflect upon the central mystery of her faith, leaving her imperfect execution of charity to be worked out in a realm of transfiguring grace not unlike the one she visited so relentlessly upon her heroes.[183]

O'Connor's final letter, scrawled less than a week prior to her death and left on her bedside table, was addressed to Lee. The playwright had received an anonymous telephone call; unsettled, she had confided in O'Connor who replied with characteristic equanimity: "Cowards can be just as vicious as those who declare themselves—more so. Dont [sic] take any romantic attitude toward that call. Be properly scared and go on doing what you have to do."[184] O'Connor's advice to Maryat has the savour of immediate experience. When we consider her situation as an unmarried and ailing woman writer, a third generation Irish American who came of age in the Atomic Era, who celebrated the Catholic Mass in a Protestant South, read Nietzsche alongside Aquinas, and entertained, in easy rotation, artists and academics, clergymen and fanatics on her mother's porch, we have a sense of the many interconnected pressures O'Connor felt herself writing amidst and at times against. Her vocation forced her into a tense coincidence both within and without the patriarchal traditions of Christianity in the West, of the

---

[182] O'Connor, *Habit*, 518.

[183] Zubeck, "Back to Page One in 'Parker's Back,'" 92.

[184] O'Connor, *Habit*, 596.

Southern and the American ethos, and of the O'Connor-Cline family. To write the real from this vantage, O'Connor followed her own advice and went on doing what she had to do with or without the blessing of her family, her church, and her audience. In a final scribble she told Lee, "Dont [sic] know when I'll send those stories. I've felt too bad to type them."[185] Six days later, O'Connor "received the Eucharist, and at some point during a very hot, very still Sunday, as her kidneys began to fail, was administered last rites by Abbot Augustine More of Conyers."[186] She passed away at 12:40 a.m. the following morning, August 3, 1964. The previous week, She had labored to finalize the revisions of "Revelation," "Judgment Day," and "Parker's Back," and with the life of her mind more or less fulfilled, O'Connor seemed peaceably to accept the end of the life of her body.

---

[185] Ibid.

[186] Gooch, *Flannery: A Life of Flannery O'Connor*, 368.

Chapter 6

Second Coming:

Flannery O'Connor in the Post-South and Europe

Flannery O'Connor has enjoyed a remarkable success in maintaining a devoted readership in the United States in the form of mainstream media, independent scholarship, and an increasingly pervasive virtual criticism which provides an instant platform for both amateur and professional theorists. The relative accessibility of her prose and the complex of "sunken" meaning inherent to her "one cylinder syntax" has contributed to O'Connor's sustained currency in the academy and among a wider lay audience.[1] From their first publication, not one of O'Connor's books has gone out of print; Farrar, Straus, and Giroux continue to produce updated editions while mass production presses, like Signet and Noonday, have helped to solidify O'Connor's place among the most influential voices of the modern American scene. In 1988, O'Connor's published works, including fiction, occasional prose, and a selection of correspondence, were collected by the *Library of America*.

Of the so-called Southern Gothicists, O'Connor is among the more prolific catalysts of discourse in the post-South, a status I would attribute to her unwillingness to engage region as a deterministic essentiality as well as her resistance to envisaging topical happenings as potential formulae for narrative drama or as conditions indispensable to the Southern real. Unlike Mitchell or Faulkner, O'Connor did not undertake to make the South a universal; nor did she, like McCullers or Caldwell, rely upon the mystique of Southern difference to legitimize the implication of an isolated, extraordinary reality. Her project was rather to depict universality *through* the local and the topical; consequently, O'Connor's fiction does not carry the same possibly damning priority of a meta-South. Her work has, as a result, stood up to regional deconstruction and has somewhat ironically benefited, at least in the mainstream, from the pop-cultural identification as classically Southern Gothic.

---

[1] O'Connor, *Habit*, 292.

In the past year, O'Connor Studies has seen a more insistent progression of increasing dynamism with respect to conventional baseline criticisms. Editor John J. Han's recent collection of essays titled *Wise Blood: A Re-Consideration* is a case in point. The opening piece, "Flannery O'Connor and the Question of the Christian Novel" by Debra L. Cumberland, maintains the customary reading of the author's "Christian vision" as demonstrative of a "Manichean universe...where the physical world (and hence the body) is viewed as evil."[2] While Cumberland acknowledges the "wide latitude of interpretation" inherent to the text, citing John Hawkes's determination that the book was "of the devil's party and Richard Gianonne's counter-claim that the work parallels the "experience of the desert fathers," she ultimately characterizes the novel in terms of long-established Calvinist/Manichean dualities.[3] "The insistence on fragmentation in *Wise Blood*—where the spiritual represents good and the physical evil," Cumberland writes, "—expresses itself most clearly in the relationship between Haze[l] and Enoch Emery. Haze[l] stridently denies God throughout the novel only to find it is God he sought all the time, while Enoch just as adamantly seeks out the physical world."[4] Cumberland is correct in her assertion that O'Connor's handling of Christian materials was actively transfigured mechanically and conceptually over time, but her reading of the interplay, or rather the lack of play, between Hazel and Enoch as descriptive of a firm disjoint between matter and spirit presumes that hero and foil should be read without irony with the Hazel ascending into a dark, "ambiguous...enlightenment" and Enoch descending into animalism.[5] Cumberland downplays the possibility of Hazel and Enoch as intentionally extreme modes of conversion, both of which are comic and terrible in their final isolation and partiality.

John D. Fitzgerald's essay, "This Protestant World: Flannery O'Connor's Portrayal of the Modern Protestant South in *Wise Blood*," leads with the customary statement that the "fiction is characterized by being distinctly Southern and distinctly Catholic" but goes on to

---

[2] Debra L. Cumberland, "Flannery O'Connor and the Question of the Christian Novel," *Wise Blood: A Re-Consideration*, ed. John J. Han (New York: Rodopi Press, 2011) 4.

[3] Ibid., 5.

[4] Ibid., 11.

[5] Ibid., 6.

develop a more nuanced and individual assessment of O'Connor's regionalism and spirituality.[6] Of particular interest is Fitzgerald's point on the author's "indictment of modernism" and the "extreme individualism that leads, eventually, to solipsism in the modern era."[7] He posits Hazel as violently representative of modern Protestantism's "tendency toward antinomianism" while his "would-be disciple, Enoch Emery, in desperate need of religious authority...follows the lead of his own 'wise blood.'"[8] I agree that Hazel's rejection of the orthodox tenet of Original Sin "unwittingly expresses the working philosophy of...Taulkinham," but I would argue further that Motes also demonstrates the possibility for meaningful discovery congenital to the "properly anti-clerical."[9] "[O'Connor's] critique [of modern Protestantism]," Fitzgerald notes in closing, "comes with the added weight of attempting to unite Christians both by highlighting differences between Catholics and Protestants while underscoring the similarities."[10]

Andrew Peter Atkinson's foregrounds his "...Defense of Jansenist Interpretations of *Wise Blood*" with a superlative recount of Cornelius Jansen's influence on John Calvin and the American Protestant and Catholic traditions more generally. He also makes a definitive contrast between orthodox Catholic theology *vis a vis* Aquinas and Puritan sensibilities and Reform theologies by underscoring the Catholic retention of Eastern Orthodoxy's sense of salvation as a dynamic phenomenon in which faithful co-work with God. "Orthodox Catholic, while agreeing [with Luther and Calvin] that salvation is by grace through faith, add that faith is worked out in love (Gal. 5:6). Salvation is not conceived as a static operation conducted on a passive humanity; rather, God works and Man moves toward God in mysterious co-operation."[11] Atkinson makes

---

[6] John D. Fitzgerald, "This Protestant World: Flannery O'Connor's Portrayal of the Modern Protestant South in *Wise Blood*," *Wise Blood: A Re-Consideration*, ed. John J. Han (New York: Rodopi Press, 2011) 25.

[7] Ibid., 28.

[8] Ibid., 28–29.

[9] Preston M. Browning, Jr. qtd. in John Fitzgerald, "This Protestant World," 31; O'Connor, *Habit*, 262.

[10] John D. Fitzgerald, "This Protestant World," 39.

[11] Andrew Peter Atkinson, "Virgil If Punched in the Gut: A Defense of Jansenist Interpretations of *Wise Blood*," *Wise Blood: A Re-Consideration*, ed. John J. Han (New York: Rodopi Press, 2011) 61.

the claim that in her representation of Motes O'Connor has "neglect[ed] the affirmation of creation's sustained goodness that the Catholic tradition teaches."[12] I would make the counter-claim that Hazel, although apparently uncooperative with the action of grace, does freely will his own redirection toward God. His method of self-mortification and determined isolation are flawed in that they dislocate Hazel from that portion of the goodness of creation immanent in Man, but they also indicate a crucial displacement of the ego reminiscent of the hermetic praxis of the Desert Fathers.

A similar progression away from critical conventions is being made in the realm of literary anthologies; Christopher J. MacGowan's *Twentieth-Century American Fiction Handbook* makes the crucial distinction that the generalized "Southern gothic tradition has its value, but has itself been accused of being an externally imposed stereotype."[13] He points out that Flannery O'Connor:

> along with Carson McCullers, ...Katherine Anne Porter, ...and Eudora Welty, is a writer often associated with the Southern gothic..., a genre that includes among its features a reaction against stereotypes of the antebellum South, and characters who are exaggerated, grotesque, or deeply disturbed—often by elements associated with Southern culture.[14]

MacGowan's preface of the Southern gothic marks a vital movement away from the essentialist interpretation of the South and Southernness toward a hermeneutic that is not only conscious of critical stereotyping but also of the "Southern" writer's self-awareness of his participation and identification (or his equally mindful non-involvement and disidentifcation) with the tropological South. The steady proliferation of Southern studies in European, Asian, African, and South American academics has been invaluable in challenging North American conventions in reading the South as the majority of this audience comes to know the region through the idiom of a particular author and his interpretation of a particular South. This text by text conceptualization of the South is not as inclined to generalize fictionalized communities and behaviors as inherent to the grander construction known as The South. When

---

[12] Ibid., 80.

[13] Christopher J. MacGowan, *The Twentieth-Century American Fiction Handbook* (Hoboken: Wiley-Blackwell Press, 2011) 364.

[14] Ibid.

French readers were first introduced to Hazel Motes in 1959, for instance, they had no immediate experience of street preaching. The phenomenon, associated in the United States almost exclusively with the South, inspired a unique thread of discourse in France and other European nations not necessarily linked to regional type-casts. Melvin J. Friedman suggests that O'Connor's idiom has a particular affinity to the French language and cites the predominance of non-English speaking studies of short fiction as a proponent to the sustained interest in O'Connor's work.[15] In an article featured in *The Biographical Dictionary of Contemporary American Catholic Writing*, Friedman notes the requirement of reading *A Good Man Is Hard To Find and Other Stories* for all advanced graduate students studying English and American literature.[16]

In her lifetime, O'Connor was keen to distribute her work to readers abroad, and succeeded, with the help of her editors Robert Giroux and Catherine Carver and her agent Elizabeth McKee, in reproducing her major works in Britain as well as securing translations of the same in France, Germany, Sweden, Italy, Spain, and Greece. O'Connor had aspirations of finding a market for her fiction in eastern Europe but eventually abandoned the project, apparently frustrated by political impositions. She considered McKee's suggestion that they place her first novel with Polish and Czech translators but decided, after some time, to "drop the matter of publishing [*Wise Blood*] in any Russian occupied country..."[17] Since her death, O'Connor's work has more than transcended the Iron Curtain, engaging a sweeping audience in eastern Europe, Asia, Australia, Africa, and South America. To date, her collected works have been translated into twenty-nine languages including Portuguese (European and Brazilian), Hungarian, Turkish, Danish, Polish, Norwegian, Hebrew, Japanese, and Swahili. The past decade has seen contemporary translations appear in Italy, Spain (in Castilian), and France, countries which have become unofficial hubs

---

[15] Melvin J. Friedman, "Flannery O'Connor in France: An Interim Report," rpt. in *Critical Essays on Flannery O'Connor*, ed. Melvin J. Friedman and Beverly Lyon Clark (New York: G. K. Hall, 1985) 130–37.

[16] Melvin J. Friedman, "Flannery O'Connor," *The Biographical Dictionary of Contemporary American Catholic Writing*, ed. Daniel J. Tynan (New York: Greenwood, 1989) 121–24.

[17] O'Connor, *Habit*, 151.

of O'Connor studies on the continent. Translators in all three countries have endeavored to make the whole of O'Connor's oeuvre, including her published correspondence and occasional prose, accessible to non-English speakers.[18] Critics including Friedman contend that the continued interest in O'Connor's work amongst the Spanish and French has its basis in a common sensibility which may be present in her British and German readers but for whatever reason does not translate well into their native idiom.[19]

More recently, Richard Gray and Waldemar Zacharasiewicz have worked together in compiling the most comprehensive transatlantic study to date entitled *Transatlantic Exchanges: The American South in Europe, Europe in the American South*. Published in 2007, the study includes essays from more than thirty contributors and explores the cross-currents extant between the South and Europe from the eighteenth century. Of particular note is Zacharasiewicz's essay, "Antecedents and Trajectories of Two Twentieth-Century Writers from Georgia in Europe" which compares the initial reception and contemporary appreciation of Flannery O'Connor and Carson McCullers on the continent.[20] Zacharasiewicz notes that O'Connor's suspicions about how she might be received in Soviet Bloc countries was well founded; "in the GDR edited by Hans Petersen: *Moderne amerikanische Prosa* (1967), …O'Connor…is represented by "A Late Encounter with the Enemy."[21] He posits that the author's "relative neglect of class and social issues helps to account for her lack of popularity in East Germany and elsewhere behind the Iron Curtain, in contrast to McCullers, who had a mass market there."[22] Zacharasiewicz's research suggests that a continued

---

[18] See Gretchen Dobrott Bernard, Rev. of *El Hábito de Ser* by Flannery O'Connor, ed. Sally Fitzgerald, intro. Gustavo Martín Garzo, trans. Francisco Javier Molina de la Torre (Salamanca: Ediciones Sígueme) 2004.

[19] See Melvin J. Friedman, "O'Connor in France: An Interim Report," rpt. in *Critical Essays on Flannery O'Connor*, ed. Melvin J. Friedman and Beverly Lyon Clark (New York: G. K. Hall, 1985) 130–37.

[20] See Waldemar Zacharasiewicz, "Antecedents and Trajectories of Two Twentieth-Century Writers from Georgia in Europe," *Transatlantic Exchange: The American South in Europe, Europe in the American South*, ed. Richard Gray and Waldemar Zacharasiewicz (Vienna: Austrian Academy of Science Press, 2007) 115–34.

[21] Ibid., 125.

[22] Ibid.

exploration of non-Southern interpretations of Southern authors including O'Connor can reveal invaluable information, not only about the texts themselves but also the disparate cultural and political context into which it has been assimilated.

With Southern Studies becoming an increasingly global field, future O'Connor scholarship should undertake to provide a complete map of the author's publication history to further interrogate the viability of regional identifications and interpretations. In conjunction, a more in depth review of recommissioned and revised translations and any linguistic synchronicities or divergences between O'Connor's English dialect and those of particular translated editions could substantiate a more concrete platform from which more amorphous concerns, such as "Southern" or "Catholic" thinking, might be considered. A broadening of collaborative transatlantic studies, like Jan Nordby-Gretlund and Karl-Heinz Westarp's *Flannery O'Connor's Radical Reality* and Zacharasiewicz and Gray's *Transatlantic Exchanges…*, will encourage further complication of the conventional "Southern Catholic" O'Connor by positioning her within the global context she engaged with as both aesthete and theologian.

It is my ultimate view that O'Connor's work reciprocates the contemporary non-essentialist movement in Southern studies, underlining the perils of allegiance to an essence-endowing South and the relative constructedness of regional identification and disidentification. Inbuilt in O'Connor's dramatic structuring is a dialogue that not only anticipates this movement but also performs the action of self-examination in its exploration of the overlapping constructs of region and nation, ideology and cosmology, modernity and eternity. Her narratives, in their deliberate interlinking of immediate and universal realities—most insistently those of Southern and American self-geneses and the implicitly co-effective history of "Creation" communicated by the Hebrew scriptures and the multi-form Christian church—demonstrate the complex and unstable discourse that undertakes to explain the Southern, the American, and the Christian real. The revelation of O'Connor's unpublished correspondence and manuscripts as evidenced in this study suggest a more intimate contention between the author's self-identification as a Southern writer and a Catholic, the critical delineation of her work within those traditions, and the increasingly ecumenical bent of her individual thinking than orthodox criticism allows. Like her denial-made prophets Hazel Motes and Francis Tarwater, O'Connor cannot be reduced to a determinism of her culture, Southern or Catholic.

In her correspondence with LaTrelle Blackburn, a master's student writing on her fiction at Duke University, O'Connor declared:

> I don't think of myself as having a "purpose as a Southern writer." My purpose as a writer is to write well and see as truly as possible and in as much as Southerners are the people I see, they fall under my general intention of seeing things as they are. There is nothing about this "purpose" that develops; it simply is... People write books on the subject of what is Southern literature and you can make a big thing of it, but I think probably an unsubtle definition like: Southern literature is literature in which Southerners are accurately reflected: is as good as any other. Using a definition like this, I wouldn't consider a book like "Clock Without Hands" or "Breakfast at Tiffany's" Southern literature, even though they are written by Southerners. I have an ingrained suspicion of "Southern" writers who sit in judgment on the South from up-state New York and such like places. The real Southern writer when he sits in judgment on the South is sitting in judgment on himself.[23]

At that time, O'Connor was composing her essay, "The Catholic Novelist in the Protestant South," which she later delivered at Georgetown University in 1963. In the essay, O'Connor picks up the thread of self-judgment, making the claim that storytelling requires "something to measure ourselves against, and this is what we conspicuously lack in this age."[24] She posits the prototypical Catholic as a counter, asserting that, "[he] has the natural law and the teachings of the Church to guide him," but she also makes the crucial distinction that, "for the writing of fiction, something more is necessary. For the purposes of fiction, these guides have to exist in a concrete form... They have to exist in the form of stories which affect our image and our judgment of ourselves."[25] In the penultimate year of her life, O'Connor reiterated the import of her self-judgment as

---

[23] Flannery O'Connor, "Correspondence with LaTrelle Blackburn," 1961–1963, MS 59, Box 2, FF 13, *Flannery O'Connor Collection,* Manuscripts, Archives, and Rare Books Library, Emory University, Atlanta.

[24] O'Connor, "The Catholic Novelist in the Protestant South," *Mystery,* 202.

[25] Ibid.

Southerner and Catholic with the distinction that her "Southern" sensibility was informed by her Catholicism and her Catholicism by the ecumenisms her aesthetic vision seemed to necessitate. We are reminded of the author's 1955 confidence to Andrew Lytle in which she declared, "[T]he only thing that keeps me from being a regional writer is being a Catholic and the only thing that keeps me from being a Catholic writer (in the narrow sense) is being a Southerner…"[26] In order to continue in deepening the significance of the author's work, O'Connor scholarship should endeavor, as the author did throughout her writing life, to examine the prolific communication between O'Connor's Southern and Catholic regionalisms and ecumenisms.

[26] O'Connor, *Habit*, 104.

Bibliography

Alighieri, Dante. *The Divine Comedy*. Translated by C. H. Sisson. Oxford: Oxford University Press, 2008.

Anderson, Sherwood. *Winesburg, Ohio*. Revised edition. New York: Penguin Books USA Inc., 1992.

Aquinas, St. Thomas. *Selected Philosophical Writings*. Edited and translated by Timothy McDermott. Oxford: Oxford University Press, 1993.

——. *Selected Writings*. Edited and translated by Ralph McInerny. London: Penguin Books Ltd., 1998.

——. *The Summa Theologica of St. Thomas Aquinas*. 2nd revised edition, 1920. Translated by Fathers of the English Dominican Province. *www.newadvent.org*. Kevin Knight, 2008. http://www.newadvent.org/summa/index.html.

Arseniev, Nicholas. *Mysticism and the Eastern Church*. Translated by Arthur Chambers. Oxford: A. R. Mowbry and Co. Ltd., 1979.

Asals, Frederick. *Flannery O'Connor: The Imagination of Extremity*. Athens: The University of Georgia Press, 1982.

Auerbach, Erich. *Mimesis: The Representation of Reality in Western Literature*. Translated by William Ropes Trask. 3rd edition. Princeton: Princeton University Press, 1953.

Augustine of Hippo, St. *The City of God Against the Pagans*. Edited by R. W. Dyson. Cambridge: Cambridge University Press, 1998.

——. *The Confessions of St. Augustine*. Translated by Edward B. Pusey. New York: Pocket Books, 1952.

——. *Nicene and Post-Nicene Fathers of the Christian Church: St. Augustine, Anti-Pelagian Writings*. Series I. XIV volumes. Edited by Philip Schaff. Translated by Peter Holmes, Robert Ernest Wallis, and Benjamin B. Warfield. New York: Cosimo Classics, Inc., 2007.

——. *Nicene and Post-Nicene Fathers of the Christian Church: St. Augustine, City of God & Christian Doctrine*. Series I. XIV volumes. Edited by Philip Schaff. Translated by Marcus Dodds. New York: Cosimo Classics, Inc., 2007.

Bacon, Jon Lance. *Flannery O'Connor and Cold War Culture*. Cambridge: Cambridge University Press, 1993.

——. "A Fondness for Supermarkets: *Wise Blood* and Consumer Culture." In *New Essays on Wise Blood*, edited by Michael Kreyling, 2–25. Cambridge: Cambridge University Press, 1995.

Bakhtin, Mikhail M. *The Dialogic Imagination: Four Essays*. Edited by Michael Holquist. Translated by Caryl Emerson and Michael Holquist. Austin: University of Texas Press, 1981.

——. *Problems of Dostoevsky's Poetics*. Edited and translated by Caryl Emerson. Minneapolis: University of Minnesota Press, 1984.

——. *Rabelais and His World*. Translated by Hélène Iswolsky. Bloomington: Indiana University Press, 1984.

Bell, Jason. "'An Island in the South': Tampa's Nineteenth-Century Regional Identity." European Association of American Studies, Biennial Conference, Dublin, March 2010. Unpublished conference paper.

Ben-Bassat, Hedda. "Flannery O'Connor's Double Vision." *Literature and Theology* 11/2 (June 1997): 185–99.

Bernard, Gretchen Dobrott. Rev. of *El Hábito de Ser* by Flannery O'Connor. Edited by Sally Fitzgerald. Introduction by Gustavo Martín Garzo. Translated by Francisco Javier Molina de la Torre. Salamanca: Ediciones Sígueme, 2004.

Best, Ernest. *Mark: The Gospel as Story*. Edinburgh: T & T Clark, 1983.

Bewes, Timothy. *Reification, or the Anxiety of Late Capitalism*. New York: Verso Publishing, 2002.

Bishop, John Peale, and Edmund Wilson. *The Undertaker's Garland*. New York: Alfred A. Knopf, 1922.

Bloom, Harold. *The American Religion: The Emergence of the Post-Christian Nation*. 2nd edition. New York: Chu Hartley Publishers, 2006.

Boehme, Jacob. *The Signature of All Things; Of the Supersensual Life; Of Heaven and Hell; Discourse Between Two Souls*. Translated by John Sparrow. Reprint. Whitefish: Kessinger Publishing, 1992.

Boles, John B. "The Southern Way of Religion." *Virginia Quarterly Review* (Spring 1999): 226–47. *www.vqronline.org*. *Virginia Quarterly Online*, 1999. http://www.vqronline.org/articles/1999/spring/boles-southern-way-religion/.

Bone, Martyn. *The Post-Southern Sense of Place in Contemporary Fiction*. Baton Rouge: Louisiana State University Press, 2005.

Bosch, Hieronymus. *St. Jerome at Prayer*. 1505. Oil on wood panel. Museum voor Schone Kunsten Ghent, Belgium. *www.artstor.org*. University of California, San Diego, n. date. Accessed 3 March 2011. http://library.artstor.org.elib.tcd.ie/librarysecureViewImages?id=8CJGczI9NzldLS1WEDhzTnkrX3ktc113cyc%3D&userId=gjJDfzUv&zoomparams=.

Bradbury, Malcolm. *The Modern American Novel*. Revised edition. New York: Penguin Books, 1994.

Brinkmeyer, Robert H. *The Art and Vision of Flannery O'Connor*. Baton Rouge: Louisiana State University Press, 1993.

——. "A Closer Walk with Thee: Flannery O'Connor and Southern Fundamentalists." *The Southern Literary Journal* 18/2 (Spring 1986): 3–13.

Brooks, Cleanth. *The Hidden God: Studies in Hemingway, Faulkner, Yeats, Eliot, and Warren*. New Haven: Yale University Press, 1963.

Buckley, James J., Frederick Christian Bauershmidt, and Trent Pomplun, editors. *The Blackwell Companion to Catholicism*. Malden: Blackwell Publishing Ltd., 2007.

Burns, Marian. "O'Connor's Unfinished Novel." In *Critical Essays on Flannery O'Connor*, edited by Melvin J. Friedman and Beverly Lyon Clark, 169–80. Boston: G. K. Hall, 1985.

Burns, Stuart L. "How Wide Did 'The Heathen Rage'?" *Flannery O'Connor Bulletin* 4 (1975): 25–41.

——. "'Torn by the Lord's Eye': Flannery O'Connor's Use of Sun Imagery." *Twentieth Century Literature* 13/3 (October 1967): 154–66.

Butler, Alban. *The Lives of the Fathers, Martyrs, and Other Principle Saints*. IV volumes. Edited and translated by F. C. Husenbeth. London: Henry and Co., 1857.

——. *The Lives of the Saints*. Vol II. New York: Benziger Brothers, 1895.

Caldwell, Erskine. *God's Little Acre*. London: Pan Books Ltd., 1958.

——. *Tobacco Road*. Athens: The University of Georgia Press, 1995.

Campbell, Debra. "Flannery O'Connor Is Not John Updike." *American Quarterly* 43/2 (June 1991): 333–40.

Campbell, Ted A. *Christian Confessions: A Historical Introduction*. Louisville: Westminster John Knox Press, 1996.

Campo, Juan Eduardo, editor. *Encyclopedia of Islam*. Illustrated edition. New York: Infobase Publishing, 2009.

Capote, Truman. *The Complete Stories of Truman Capote*. New York: Vintage Books, 2004.

——. *In Cold Blood: A True Account of a Multiple Murder and Its Consequences*. New York: Vintage Books, 1965.

——. *Other Voices, Other Rooms*. New York: Vintage Books, 1994.

Cash, Jean W. "Flannery O'Connor: Art 'Demand[s] Celibacy.'" *Postscript: A Publication of the Philological Association of the Carolinas* 15 (1998): 23–32.

Cash, Wilbur J. *The Mind of the South*. New York: Vintage Books, 1941.

Cassian, St. John. *The Philokalia: The Complete Text*. Edited and translated by G. E. H. Palmer, Philip Sherrard, and Kallistos Ware. IV volumes. Illustrated edition. New York: Macmillan, 1983.

Catechism of the Catholic Church. *www.vatican.va*. *Vatican Publishing House*, n. date. Accessed 3 March 2011. http://www.vatican.va/archive/ccc_css/archive/cate chism/ccc_toc.htm.

Cawley, Kevin. "Latin Dictionary and Grammar Aid." *www.archives.nd.edu*. *University of Notre Dame Archives*, n. date. Accessed 14 September 2011. http://www.archives.nd.edu/ cgibin/lookit.pl?latin=una.

Chance, Jane. *Medieval Mythography: From Roman North Africa to the School of Chartres, A.D. 433–1177*. Gainesville: University of Florida Press, 1994.

Chapman, C. Stuart. Rev. of *Flannery O'Connor and the Mystery of Love* by Richard Gianonne. *Modern Fiction Studies* 46/4 (Winter 2000): 1026–28.

Chapman, Geoffrey, ed. *Catechism of the Catholic Church*. London: Continuum Publishing Group, Ltd., 2002.

Chase, Richard. *The American Novel and Its Tradition*. Baltimore: Johns Hopkins University Press, 1957.

Chestnut, Allison Carol. "A Reading of *A Good Man Is Hard to Find* and *A Curtain of Green*: The Influence of Parable on Flannery O'Connor and

Eudora Welty." Diss. Louisiana State University, Baton Rouge, 1991. DAI 52 (1992): 2551A.

Christ Pantocrator Icon. ca. 12th century. Mosaic. Kariye Djami, Istanbul, Turkey. *www.wikipedia.org*. *Wikimedia*, 11 Aug. 2005. http://en.wikipedia.org/wiki /File:Chora_Christ_south_coupole.jpg.

Chryssavgis, John. *Light Through Darkness: The Orthodox Tradition*. London: Dartman, Longman & Todd Ltd., 2004.

Cleenewerck, Laurent. *His Broken Body: Understanding and Healing the Schism Between the Roman Catholic and Eastern Orthodox Churches*. Washington, D.C.: Euclid University Press, 2008.

Climacus, St. John. *The Ladder of Divine Ascent*. Translated by Colm Luibheid and Norman Russell. Mahwah: Paulist Press, 1982.

Cobb, James C. *Away Down South: A History of Southern Identity*. Oxford: Oxford University Press, 2005.

——. "An Epitaph for the North: Reflections on the Politics of Regional and National Identity at the Millennium." *The Journal of Southern History* 66/1 (February 2000): 3–24.

Collins, Kevin. *Catholic Churchmen and the Celtic Revival in Ireland, 1848–1916*. Dublin: Four Courts Press Ltd., 2002.

The Conception of St. Anne. Novgorod School. ca. 15th century. Egg tempura on wood panel. Museum of Icons, Recklinghausen, Germany.

Cornwell, Neil. *The Literary Fantastic: From Gothic to Postmodernism*. New York: Harvester and Wheatsheaf, 1990.

Council of Trent: The Canons and Decrees of the Sacred and Ecumenical Council of Trent (1848). Edited and translated by J. Waterworth. London: Dolman. *www.history.hanover.edu*. *Hanover Historical Texts Project*, 1995. http://history.ha nover.edu/texts/trent.html.

Dainotto, Roberto M. *Place in Literature: Regions, Cultures, Communities*. Ithaca: Cornell University Press, 2000.

Damascene, St. John. *An Exact Exposition of the Orthodox Faith*. *www.orthodox.net*. St. Nicholas Russian Orthodox Church, McKinney, Texas, 2008. http://www.orthodox.net/fathers/exactiv.html.

Damascene, St. John, and St. Hilary of Poitiers. *Nicene and Post-Nicene Fathers of the Christian Church: Hilary of Poitiers, On the Trinity & On the Synods; John of Damascus, Exposition of the Orthodox Faith*. 2nd Series. XIV volumes. Edited by Philip Schaff and Henry Wace. Translated by Rev. E. W. Watson, Rev. L. Pullan, and Rev. S. D. F. Salmond. Grand Rapids: Wm. B. Eerdmans Publishing Co., 1980.

Daniel, Scott. "Gender-Bending Innuendo and Mystical Theology in O'Connor's *Wise Blood*." *Flannery O'Connor Review* 4 (2006): 110–21.

Demetry, Rev. Constas H., D. D. *Catechism of the Eastern Orthodox Church*. *www.christusrex.org*. Fort Lauderdale: The Saint Demetrios Greek Orthodox Church, 31 January 2001. http://www.christusrex.org/www1/CDHN/cate chis.html.

Desmond, John F. "Flannery O'Connor and Simone Weil: A Question of Sympathy." *Logos* 8/1 (Winter 2005): 102–16.

——. *Risen Sons: Flannery O'Connor's Vision of History*. Athens: University of Georgia Press, 1987.

Dewey, Joanna. Rev. of *Mark: The Gospel as Story* by Ernest Best. *Journal of Biblical Literature* 105/2 (June 1986): 335–36.

Di Renzo, Anthony. *American Gargoyles: Flannery O'Connor and the Medieval Grotesque*. Carbondale: Southern Illinois University Press, 1993.

Duncan, Anthony. *The Elements of Celtic Christianity*. Longmead: Element Books Ltd., 1992.

The Eastern/Greek Orthodox Bible. Edited by Rev. Laurent Cleenewerck, St. Innocent Orthodox Church, Eureka, CA, 2008. http://www.orthodox-answers.org/eob/.

Edmonson III, Henry T. *Return to Good and Evil: Flannery O'Connor's Response to Nihilism*. Lanham: Lexington Books, 2002.

Egerton, John. *The Americanization of Dixie: The Southernization of America*. New York: Harper's Magazine Press, 1974.

Eggenschwiler, David. *The Christian Humanism of Flannery O'Connor*. Detroit: Wayne State University Press, 1972.

Erasmus, Desiderius. *The Collected Works of Erasmus; Patristic Scholarship, the Edition of St. Jerome*. Edited by James F. Brady and John C. Olin. Toronto: University of Toronto Press, 1992.

The Evangelical Lutheran Church. *The Book of Concord: or, the Symbolical Books of the Evangelical Lutheran Church*. Edited by Henry Eyster Jacobs. Philadelphia: The United Lutheran Publication House, 1911.

Evans, G. R. *Augustine on Evil*. Cambridge: Cambridge University Press, 1982.

Evola, Julius. *The Mystery of the Grail: Initiation and Magic in the Quest for the Spirit.* Rochester: Inner Traditions, 1996.

Fahlbusch, Erwin, and Geoffrey William Bromiley, editors. *The Encyclopedia of Christianity*. V volumes. Translated by Geoffrey William Bromiley. Grand Rapids: Wm. B. Eerdmans Publishing, 2005.

Fairbairn, Donald. *Eastern Orthodoxy Through Western Eyes*. Louisville: Westminster John Knox Press, 2002.

Faulkner, William. *Absalom, Absalom!* London: Vintage Random House, 2005.

——. *Light in August*. Revised edition. New York: Vintage International, 1990.

Feeley, Kathleen S.J. *Flannery O'Connor: The Voice of the Peacock*. Chapel Hill: Rutgers University Press, 1972.

Fiedler, Leslie A. *Love and Death in the American Novel*. 3rd edition. Harmondsworth: Penguin Books, 1984.

Fisher, James T. *The Catholic Counterculture in America, 1933–1962*. Chapel Hill: University of North Carolina Press, 1989.

Fitzgerald, Allan D., and John C. Cavadini. *Augustine Through the Ages: An Encyclopedia*. 2nd edition. Grand Rapids: William B. Eerdmans Publishing, 1999.

Fitzgerald, John D. "This Protestant World: Flannery O'Connor's Portrayal of the Modern Protestant South in *Wise Blood*." *Wise Blood: A Re-*

Consideration. Ed John J. Han. New York: Rodopi Press, 2011. 25–39.

Fitzgerald, Sally, ed. *The Habit of Being: Letters of Flannery O'Connor*. New York: Farrar, Straus, and Giroux, 1979.

Flanagan, Patrick J. *The Gospel of Mark Made Easy*. Mahwah: Paulist Press, 1997.

Flora, Joseph M., and Lucinda MacKethan, et al., editors. *The Companion to Southern Literature: Themes, Genres, Places, People, Movements, and Motifs*. Baton Rouge: Louisiana State University Press, 2002.

Foster, Shirley. "Flannery O'Connor's Short Stories: The Assault on the Reader." *Journal of American Studies* 20/2 (August 1986): 259–72.

Francia, Francesco. *Crucifixion with Saints John and Jerome*. 1485. Oil on wood panel. Collezioni Comunali d'Arte, Bologna, Italy. *www.lib-art.com*. *Lib-Art*, n. date. Accessed 14 May 2011. http://www.libart.com/artgallery/5601-crucifixion-with-sts-john-and-jerom-francesco-francia.html.

Francisco, Edward, Robert Vaughan, and Linda Francisco, editors. *The South in Perspective: An Anthology of Southern Literature*. Upper Saddle River: Prentice-Hall, 2001.

Friedman, Melvin J. "Flannery O'Connor." In *The Biographical Dictionary of Contemporary American Catholic Writing*, edited by Daniel J. Tynan, 121–24. New York: Greenwood, 1989.

——. "O'Connor in France: An Interim Report." Reprint in *Critical Essays on Flannery O'Connor*, edited by Melvin J. Friedman and Beverly Lyon Clark, 130–37. New York: G. K. Hall, 1985.

Gable, Mariella, O.S.B. "Ecumenic Core in Flannery O'Connor's Fiction." *The American Benedictine Review* 15/2 (June 1964): 127–43.

Gavigan, John Joseph, editor. *Fathers of the Church*. Washington, D.C.: Catholic University of America Press, 2002.

Gentry, Marshall Bruce. "ALA 1997 Panel Discussion: 'Flannery O'Connor and the Maryat Lee Letters.'" *CHEERS! The Flannery O'Connor Society Newsletter* 5/2 (1997–1998): 3.

——. *Flannery O'Connor's Religion of the Grotesque*. Jackson: University of Mississippi Press, 1986.

Getz, Lorine M. *Nature and Grace in Flannery O'Connor's Fiction*. Lewiston: The Edwin Mellen Press, 1982.

Gianonne, Robert. *Flannery O'Connor, Hermit Novelist*. Revised edition. Columbia: University of South Carolina Press, 2010.

Gilbert, Susanna. "'Blood Don't Lie': The Diseased Family in Flannery O'Connor's *Everything That Rises Must Converge*." *Literature and Medicine* 18/1 (1999): 114–31.

Gleeson-White, Sarah. "Revisiting the Southern Grotesque: Mikhail Bakhtin and the Case of Carson McCullers." *The Southern Literary Journal* 33/2 (2001): 108–23.

Golden, Robert E., and Mary C. Sullivan. *Flannery O'Connor and Caroline Gordon: A Reference Guide*. Boston: G. K. Hall & Co., 1977.

Gooch, Brad. *Flannery: A Life of Flannery O'Connor*. New York: Back Bay Books, 2009.

——. "Thirteenth-Century Lady." *Flannery O'Connor Review* 5 (2007): 23–34.

Goodwyn Jones, Anne, and Susan Van D'Elden Donaldson. *Haunted Bodies: Gender and Southern Texts*, 287–315. Charlottesville: The University of Virginia Press, 1997.

Gordon, Caroline. "Heresy in Dixie." *Sewanee Review* 76/2 (Spring 1968): 261, 263–97.

Gordon, Mary. "Is Flannery O'Connor a Catholic?" *Flannery O'Connor Review* 2 (2004): 1–3.

Gordon, Sarah. *Flannery O'Connor: The Obedient Imagination*. Athens: University of Georgia Press, 2000.

Gordon, Sarah, Craig Amason, and Marcelina Martin. *A Literary Guide to Flannery O'Connor's Georgia*. Athens: University of Georgia Press, 2008.

Gray, Richard. *The Literature of Memory: Modern Writers of the American South*. London: Edward Arnold Ltd., 1977.

——. *Southern Aberrations: Writers of the American South and the Problems of Regionalism*. Baton Rouge: Louisiana State University Press, 2000.

——. *A Web of Words: The Great Dialogue of Southern Literature*. Athens: University of Georgia Press, 2007.

——. *Writing the South: Ideas of an American Region*. Cambridge: Cambridge University Press, 1986.

Gray, Richard, and Owen Robinson, editors. *A Companion to the Literature and Culture of the American South*. Malden: Blackwell Publishing, 2004.

Gray, Richard, and Waldemar Zacharasiewicz, editors. *Transatlantic Exchange: The American South in Europe, Europe in the American South*, 115–34. Vienna: Austrian Academy of Science Press, 2007.

Greeley, Andrew M. *The Catholic Imagination*. Berkeley: University of California Press, 2000.

Gregory the Great, St. "An Exposition on the Book of Blessed Job." *A Library of the Fathers of the Holy Catholic Church, Anterior to the Division of the East and West*. Edited by Edward Bouverie Pusey, John Keble, and John Henry Newman. Translated by members of the English Church. Oxford: J. H. Parker, 1847.

Gretlund, Jan Nordby, and Karl-Heinz Westarp. *Flannery O'Connor's Radical Reality*. Columbia: University of South Carolina Press, 2006.

Grünewald, Matthias. *The Crucifixion*. 1512–1515. Oil on wood panel. Isenheim Altarpiece, Musée d'Unterlinden, Colmar, France. Scala Archives, Florence, Italy. *www.artstor*.org. *Art Resource, New York*, 2006. http//:library.artstor. org.elib.tcd.ie.library/secureViewImages?id =4iFCeTg4NCciJy8laCt2KngqVXkhflt6eQ%3D%3&userId=gjJDfzUv&zoomparams=.

Haddox, Thomas Frederick. *Fears and Fascinations: Representing Catholicism in the American South*. New York: Fordham University Press, 2005.

Han, John J., editor. *Wise Blood: A Re-Consideration*. Illustrated edition. New York: Rodopi Press, 2011.

Hargrave, Robert James. Orthodox Church of Tanzania, Archdiocese of Mwanza. Personal interview. 5 and 7 February 2011.
Harmless S.J., William. *Desert Christians: An Introduction to the Literature of Early Monasticism*. Oxford: Oxford University Press, 2004.
Harpham, Geoffrey. "The Grotesque: First Principles." *Journal of Aesthetics and Art Criticism* 34 (Summer 1976): 461–68.
Harris, George Washington. *Sut Lovingood. Yarns Spun by a "Nat'ral Born Durn'd Fool." Warped and Wove for Public Wear.* New York: Dick & Fitzgerald Publishers, 1867.
Harris, Joel Chandler. *Uncle Remus: His Songs and Sayings*. Revised edition. London: Osgood, McIlvaine & Co., 1895.
Hassan, Ihab. "The Existential Novel." *The Massachusetts Review* 3/4 (Summer 1962): 795–97.
——. *Radical Innocence: Studies in the Contemporary American Novel*. Princeton: Princeton University Press, 1961.
——. "The Victim: Images of Evil in Recent American Fiction." *College English* 21/3 (December 1959): 140–46.
Hauerwas, Stanley, and Ralph C. Wood. "How the Church Became Invisible: A Christian Reading of the American Literary Tradition." *Religion and Literature* 38/1 (Spring 2006): 61–93.
Hawkes, John. "Flannery O'Connor's Devil." *The Sewanee Review* 70/3 (Summer 1962): 395–407.
Hawkins, Peter S. *The Language of Grace: Flannery O'Connor, Walker Percy, and Iris Murdoch.* Cambridge: Cowley Publications, 1983.
Heavenly Ladder of St. John Climacus, The. ca. 12th century. Tempura and gold on wood panel. Monastery of St. Catherine, Mt. Sinai, Egypt. Erich Lessing Culture and Fine Arts Archives. *www.artstor.org.* Art Resource New York, 2006. http://library.artstor.org.elib.tcd.ie/library/secure/ViewImages?id=%2FThWdC8IywtPygFTx5RnksX3wqeF0%3D&userId=gjJDfzUv&zompaams=.
Hemingway, Ernest. *The Complete Short Stories of Ernest Hemingway*. New York: Scribner, 1987.
Hendin, Josephine. *The World of Flannery O'Connor*. Bloomington: Indiana University Press, 1970.
Hewitt, Avis, and Robert Donahoo. *Flannery O'Connor in the Age of Terrorism: Essays on Violence and Grace*. Knoxville: University of Tennessee Press, 2010.
Hoffman, Frederick J. "The Sense of Place." In *South: Modern Southern Literature and Its Cultural Setting,* edited by Louis D. Rubin, Jr. and Robert D. Jacobs, 60–75. New York: Doubleday, 1961.
Holman, C. Hugh. "Detached Laughter in the South." In *Comic Relief: Humor in Contemporary American Literature,* edited by Sarah Blacher Cohen, 87–104. Urbana: University of Illinois Press, 1978.
The Holy Bible. Douay-Rheims Version. American edition. Baltimore: John Murphy Co., 1899.

The Holy Bible. King James Version. King James Bible Online, 2011. *www.kingjamesbibleonline.org*. http://www.kingjamesbibleonline.org.

The Holy Bible. New King James Version. Nashville: Thomas Nelson, Inc., 1982. *www.biblegateway.com*. *The Zondervan Corporation*, 9 Sept. 2010. http://www.biblegateway.com/versions/New-King-James-Version-NKJV-Bible/.

The Holy Bible. New Revised Standard Version. Catholic edition. New York: Harper Collins Publishers, 1989.

Hopko, V. Rev. Thomas. "The Orthodox Faith: Doctrine." IV volumes. Dept. of Religious Education. *www.oca.org*. *The Orthodox Church in America*, 1996. http://www.oca.org/OCchapter.asp?SID=2&ID=27.

——. "The Orthodox Faith: Worship." IV volumes. Dept. of Religious Education. *www.oca.org*. *The Orthodox Church in America*, 1996. http://www.oca.org/O Cchapter.asp?SID=2&ID=53.

Howe, Irving. "The Southern Myth and William Faulkner." *American Quarterly* 3/4 (Winter 1951): 357–62.

Humphries, Jefferson. *The Metamorphoses of the Raven: Literary Over-Determinedness in France and the South since Poe*. Baton Rouge: Louisiana State University Press, 1985.

Humphries, Jefferson, and John Lowe, editors. *The Future of Southern Letters*. New York: Oxford University Press, 1996.

Hunt, Hannah. "Byzantine Christianity." *The Blackwell Companion to Eastern Christianity*. Ed. Ken Parry. New York: John Wiley and Sons, Inc., 2010.

Irenaeus, Bishop of Lyons. *Against Heresies*. V volumes. Whitefish: Kessinger Publishing, LLC, 2004.

Jackson, Robert A. "Religion, Idolatry, and Catholic Irony: Flannery O'Connor's Modest Literary Vision." *Logos* 5/1 (Winter 2002): 13–40.

James, Henry. "The Art of Fiction." In *The Art of Criticism: Henry James on the Theory and Practice of Fiction*, edited by William Veeder and Susan M. Griffin, 165–96. Chicago: University of Chicago Press, 1986.

Jansson, David R. "American National Identity and the Progress of the New South in *National Geographic Magazine*." *Geographical Review* 93/3 (July 2003): 350–69.

——. "Internal Orientalism in America: W. J. Cash's *The Mind of the South* and the Spatial Construction of American National Identity." *Political Geography* 22/3 (March 2003): 293–316.

Jefferson, Thomas. *A Jefferson Profile As Revealed in His Letters*. Edited by Saul Kussiel Padover. New York: John Day Co., 1956.

——. *Writings*. Edited by Merrill D. Peterson. New York: Literary Classics of the United States, Inc., 1984.

Jerome, St. *Ancient Christian Writers: The Works of the Fathers in Translation, The Letters of St. Jerome*. Translated by Thomas Comerford Lawler. Volume I, Number XXXIII. Westminster: The Newman Press, 1963.

——. *Latin Vulgate*. Translated by Douay-Rheims. *www.vulgate.org*. *Vulgate*, 2005. http://www.vulgate.org.

——. *The Satirical Letters of St. Jerome*. Translated by Paul Carroll. Chicago:

Henry Regenery Co., 1956.
Johansen, Ruthann Knechel. *The Narrative Secret of Flannery O'Connor: The Trickster as Interpreter*. Tuscaloosa: University of Alabama Press, 1994.
Josephus, Flavius. *History of the Destruction of Jerusalem or The Wars of the Jews*. Whitefish: Kessinger Publishing, LLC, 2004.
——. *Jewish Antiquities*. Translated by William Whiston. Ware: Wordsworth Editions, Ltd., 2006.
Kane, Richard. "Positive Destruction in the Fiction of Flannery O'Connor." *The Southern Literary Journal* 20/1 (Fall 1987): 45–60.
Katz, Claire. "Flannery O'Connor's Rage of Vision." *American Literature* 46/1 (March 1974): 54–67.
Kazan, Elia. *Panic in the Streets*. Twentieth Century Fox, 1950.
Kilcourse, Jr., George A. *Flannery O'Connor's Religious Imagination: A World with Everything Off Balance*. Mahwah: Paulist Press, 2001.
Kinney, Arthur F. "Flannery O'Connor and the Fiction of Grace." *Massachusetts Review* 27/1 (Spring 1986): 71–96.
——. *Flannery O'Connor's Library: Resources of Being*. Athens: University of Georgia Press, 2007.
Kirby, Jack Temple. *Media Made Dixie: The South in the American Imagination*. Revised edition. Athens: University of Georgia Press, 1986.
Knight, Kevin, editor. *The Catholic Encyclopedia*. XV volumes. New York: Robert Appleton Company, 1907. *www.newadvent.org*. Kevin Knight, 2007. http://www.newadvent.org/cathen/.
The Koran. Revised edition. Translated by N. J. Dawood. London: Penguin Books, 1995.
Kreyling, Michael. "Towards a 'New Southern Studies.'" *South Central Review* 22/1 (Spring 2005): 4–18.
Lake, Christina Bieber. *The Incarnational Art of Flannery O'Connor*. Macon GA: Mercer University Press, 2005.
Leonard, Annie. *The Story of Stuff*. Online documentary film. Directed by Louis Fox. Produced by Eric Priggen. *Free Range Studios*, 6 May 2009. http://www.storyofstuff .com/.
Lilley, James D., Brian Oberkirch, and Barry Hannah. "An Interview with Barry Hannah." *Mississippi Review* 25/3 (Spring 1997): 19–43.
Lock, Charles. "Double Voicing, Sharing Words: Bakhtin's Dialogism and the History of the Theory of Free Indirect Discourse." In *The Novelness of Bakhtin: Perspectives and Possibilities*, edited by Jørgen Bruhn and Jan Lundquist, 71–87. Copenhagen: Museum Tusculanum Press, 2001.
Longstreet, Augustus Baldwin. *Georgia Scenes: Characters, Incidents, &c., in the First Half Century of the Republic by a Native Georgian*. 2nd edition. New York: Harper and Brothers, 1850.
Lynch, William F., S.J. *Christ and Apollo: The Dimensions of the Literary Imagination*. New York: Sheed and Ward, 1960.
MacGowan, Christopher J. *The Twentieth-Century American Fiction Handbook*. Hoboken: Wiley-Blackwell Press, 2011.

Magee, Rosemary M., editor. *Conversations with Flannery O'Connor*. Jackson: University Press of Mississippi, 1987.

Marshall, Christopher D. *Faith as a Theme in Mark's Narrative*. Cambridge: Cambridge University Press, 1989.

Martin, Carter W. "The Catholic Commitment as a Phenomenological *Vorhabe*: Flannery O'Connor, n. date. "Sally Fitzgerald Papers." MS 1101, Box 53, FF 2. *Flannery O'Connor Collection*. Manuscripts, Archives, and Rare Books Library. Emory University, Atlanta.

——. *The True Country: Themes in the Fiction of Flannery O'Connor*. Nashville: Vanderbilt University Press, 1969.

Matterson, Stephen. Personal interview. 11 February 2009.

May, Charles E. *The Short Story: The Reality of Artifice*. New York: Routledge, 2002.

May, John R. "The Methodological Limits of Flannery O'Connor's Critics." *Flannery O'Connor Bulletin* 15 (1986): 16–28.

——. *The Pruning Word: The Parables of Flannery O'Connor*. Notre Dame: University of Notre Dame Press, 1976.

McBride, Denis. *The Gospel of Luke: A Reflective Commentary*. Dublin: Dominican Publications, 1991.

McCarthy, John F. "Human Intelligence Versus Divine Truth." *English Journal* 55/9 (1966): 1143–48.

McCown, Robert M. "Flannery O'Connor and the Reality of Sin." *Catholic World* 188 (January 1959): 285–91.

McKee, Katherine. *Global Contexts, Local Literatures: The New Southern Studies*. Durham: Duke University Press, 2006.

McMullen, Joanne Halleran. *Writing Against God: Language as Message in the Literature of Flannery O'Connor*. Macon GA: Mercer University Press, 1996.

McMullen, Joanne Halleran, and Jon Parrish Peede, editors. *Inside the Church of Flannery O'Connor: Sacrament, Sacramental, and the Sacred in Her Fiction*. Macon GA: Mercer University Press, 2007.

Mei, Bernardino: *The Vision of St. Jerome*. 1657–1660. Oil on canvas. Private collection. *Web Gallery of Art*, n. date. Accessed 27 February 2011. http://www.wga.hu/art/m/mei/vi sion_j.jpg.

Mencken, H. L. "The Sahara of the Bozart." In *The American Scene: A Reader*, edited by Huntington Cairns, 157–68. New York: Alfred A. Knopf, 1977.

Mills, Jerry Leath. "The Dead Mule Rides Again." *Southern Cultures* 6/4 (Winter 2000): 11–34.

Moltmann, Jürgen. *The Crucified God*. London: S.C.M., 1977.

Montgomery, Marion. "Flannery O'Connor and the Jansenist Problem in Fiction." *Southern Review* 14/3 (1978): 438–48.

——. *Hillbilly Thomist: Flannery O'Connor, St. Thomas, and the Limits of Art*. II volumes. Jefferson: McFarland & Company, Inc., Publishers, 2006.

——. Why Flannery O'Connor Stayed Home: The Prophetic Poet and the

Spirit of the Age. Peru: Sherwood Sugden and Co., 1981.

Mott, Sara. "Flannery O'Connor's Unique Contribution to Christian Literary Naturalism." In *Realist of Distances: Flannery O'Connor Revisited*, edited by Karl-Heinz Westarp and Jan Nordby Gretlund, 217–26. Langelandsgade: Aarhus University Press, 1987.

Muller, Gilbert H. *Nightmares and Visions: Flannery O'Connor and the Catholic Grotesque*. Athens: University of Georgia Press, 1972.

Mullins, C. Ross. "Flannery O'Connor: An Interview." *Jubilee* 11 (June 1963): 32–33. Reprint in *Conversations with Flannery O'Connor*, edited by Rosemary M. Magee, 103–107. Jackson: University Press of Mississippi, 1987.

Munk, Linda. "Understanding Understatement: Biblical Typology and 'The Displaced Person.'" *Literature and Theology* 2/2 (September1988): 237–53.

Neusner, Jacob, and Alan Avery-Peck. *The Blackwell Companion to Judaism*. Malden: Blackwell Publishing Ltd., 2000.

Niesel, Wilhelm. *The Gospel and the Churches: A Comparison of Catholicism, Orthodoxy, and Protestantism*. Translated by David Lewis. Philadelphia: Westminster Press, 1962.

Nova Vulgata. Bibliorum Sacrorum ed. The Vatican: Libreria Editrice Vaticana, 1979.

Oates, Joyce Carol. "The Action of Mercy." *Kenyon Review* 20/1 (Winter 1998): 157–60.

——. "The Visionary Art of Flannery O'Connor." In *Flannery O'Connor*, edited by Harold Bloom, 44–46. Philadelphia: Chelsea House Publishing, 1986.

O'Brien, Michael. *The Idea of the American South, 1920–1941*. Baltimore: Johns Hopkins University Press, 1979.

O'Connor, Flannery. "An Afternoon in the Woods." N. date. MS 1101, Box 58, FF 13. *Flannery O'Connor Collection*. Russell Library. Georgia College & State University, Milledgeville.

——. "Catholic Novelist in the Protestant South." Southern Literary Festival. 20 April 1962. MS 271a. *Flannery O'Connor Collection*. Russell Library. Georgia College & State University, Milledgeville.

——. "The Catholic Novelist in the Protestant South." November 1962. MS 274a. *Flannery O'Connor Collection*. Russell Library. Georgia College & State University, Milledgeville.

——. *Collected Works*. Edited by Sally Fitzgerald. New York: Library of America, 1988.

——. *The Complete Stories*. Edited by Robert Giroux. New York: Farrar, Straus & Giroux, 1978.

——. "Correspondence with Betty Hester." 1955–1964. MS 1064, Box 1–3. *Flannery O'Connor Collection*. Manuscripts, Archives, and Rare Books Library. Emory University, Atlanta.

——. "Correspondence with Mrs. Frank Gafford." 1962–1963. MS 59, Box 2, FF 1. *Flannery O'Connor Collection*. Manuscripts, Archives, and Rare Books Library. Emory University, Atlanta.

——. "Correspondence with LaTrelle Blackburn." 1961–1963. MS 59, Box 2, FF 13. *Flannery O'Connor Collection*. Manuscripts, Archives, and Rare Books Library. Emory University, Atlanta.

——. "Correspondence with Leo Zuber." 1959–1963. MS 1101, Box 58, FF 12. *Flannery O'Connor Collection*. Manuscripts, Archives, and Rare Books Library. Emory University, Atlanta.

——. "Correspondence with Robert Jiras." 1956–1959. MS 59, Box 1, FF 39. *Flannery O'Connor Collection*. Manuscripts, Archives, and Rare Books Library. Emory University, Atlanta.

——. "Early Fragment of 'The River.'" N. date. MS 155. *Flannery O'Connor Collection*. Russell Library. Georgia College & State University, Milledgeville.

——. *The Habit of Being*. Edited by Sally Fitzgerald. New York: Farrar, Straus & Giroux, 1979.

——. "How the Writer Writes." N. date. MS 59, Box 1, FF 1. *Flannery O'Connor Collection*. Manuscripts, Archives, and Rare Books Library. Emory University, Atlanta.

——. "Manuscript of *The Violent Bear It Away*." N. date. MS 188e, 188f, 189f, 190a, 190c, 190f. *Flannery O'Connor Collection*. Russell Library. Georgia College & State University, Milledgeville.

——. "Manuscript of *Wise Blood*." N. date. MS 31, 32, 40, 64, 67, 71c, 71d, 72, 85b, 86a, 86b, 91b, 102, 104f, 106a, 110a, 110b, 113b, 118a, 118b, 119h, 120, 130, 138, 142b, 147a, 148j. *Flannery O'Connor Collection*. Russell Library. Georgia College & State University, Milledgeville.

——. *Mystery and Manners: Occasional Prose*. Edited by Sally Fitzgerald and Robert Fitzgerald. New York: Farrar, Straus & Giroux, 1969.

——. "On the Significance of Being a Georgia Author." N. date. MS 59, Box 1, FF 6. *Flannery O'Connor Collection*. Manuscripts, Archives, and Rare Books Library. Emory University, Atlanta.

——. "Parker's Back." April 1965. MS 204b, 204c, 204d, 204f, 204g, 204h, 204i, 204j, 205a, 205c, 205d, 205e, 205f, 205g, 205h, 205i, 206a, 206b, 206c, 206d, . *Flannery O'Connor Collection*. Russell Library. Georgia College & State University, Milledgeville.

——. "The Problem of the Southern Writer." N. date. MS 59, Box 1, FF 2. *Flannery O'Connor Collection*. Manuscripts, Archives, and Rare Books Library. Emory University, Atlanta.

——. "Reviews." 1961. MS 293h. 9 December 1961. MS 293o, MS 293p. 27 May 1961. MS 293d. N. date. MS 293s. 2 March 1962. MS 294f. 17 March 1962. MS 294g. 24 October 1963. MS 295g. N. date. MS 295h. N. date. 295i. *Flannery O'Connor Collection*. Russell Library. Georgia College & State University, Milledgeville.

——. "Some Notes on the Combination: Novelist and Believer." March 1963.

MS 266a, 266b. *Flannery O'Connor Collection*. Russell Library. Georgia College & State University, Milledgeville.

——. "Unidentified Fragment." N. date. MS 213a, 213b, 213c, 213d, 213e, 213f. *Flannery O'Connor Collection*. Russell Library. Georgia College & State University, Milledgeville.

——. "Unidentified Fragment." N. date. MS 276, 281b, 281c, 281d, 283c, 283e, 283f. *Flannery O'Connor Collection*. Russell Library. Georgia College & State University, Milledgeville.

——. *The Violent Bear It Away*. New York: Farrar, Straus & Giroux, 1960.

——. "Why Do the Heathen Rage?" N. date. MS 216, 217b, 217g, 218a, 218d, 218e, 218f, 220a, 220b, 222, 225e, 226b, 226f, 227c, 228a, 228b, 232a, 232f, 234. *Flannery O'Connor Collection*. Russell Library. Georgia College & State University, Milledgeville.

——. *Wise Blood*. New York: Farrar, Straus & Giroux, 1949.

Odum, Howard W. *An American Epoch: Southern Portraiture in the National Picture*. New York: H. Holt and Company, 1930.

Odum, Howard W., and John MacLachlan. "Literature in the South: An Exchange of Views." In *Southern Renascence: The Literature of the Modern South*, edited by Louis D. Rubin, Jr. and Robert D. Jacobs, 83–111. Baltimore: Johns Hopkins University Press, 1953.

——. "Toward a Catholic Theory of Fiction: A Christian Realism of the 'Here and Now.'" In *Peculiar Crossroads: Flannery O'Connor, Walker Percy, and Catholic Vision in Postwar Southern Fiction*, 103–50. Baton Rouge: Louisiana State University Press, 2004.

Odum, Howard W., and Harry Estill Moore. *American Regionalism: A Cultural-Historical Approach to National Integration*. New York: H. Holt and Company, 1938.

O'Gorman, Farrell. "A Confederacy of Forces." *Notre Dame Magazine* (Autumn 2005): 52–57.

Orvell, Miles. *Flannery O'Connor: An Introduction*. Oxford: University of Mississippi Press, 1991.

Palamas, St. Gregory. *The Triads*. Edited by John Meyendorff. Translated by Nicholas Gendle. Mahwah: Paulist Press, 1983.

Parry, Ken, editor. *The Blackwell Companion to Eastern Christianity*. New York: John Wiley and Sons, Inc., 2010.

Pelikan, Jaroslav. *The Emergence of the Catholic Tradition (100–600)*. Chicago: University of Chicago Press, 1971.

Percy, Walker. *The Moviegoer*. 1961. New York: Quality Paperback Book Club, 1991.

——. *Signposts in a Strange Land*. Edited by Patrick Samway. London: Bellew Publishing, 1991.

Peters, Francis E. *Judaism, Christianity, and Islam: The Classical Texts and Their Interpretation*. III volumes. Princeton: Princeton University Press, 1990.

Pike, Albert. *Morals and Dogma of the Ancient and Accepted Rite of Scottish Freemasonry*. Sioux Falls: NuVision Publications, LLC, 2004.

Poe, Edgar Allan. *Edgar Allan Poe: Selected Tales*. Edited by David Van Leer. Oxford: Oxford University Press, 1998.

——. *Essays and Reviews*. Edited by Gary Richard Thompson. New York: Library of America, 1984.

Pope Pius XII. *Mystic Corporis Christi. www.vatican.va. Vatican Publishing House,* 1990. http://www.vatican.va/holy_father/pius_xii/encyclicals/documents/hf_p-xii_enc_29061943_mystici-corporis-christi _en.html.

Praeder, Susan Marie. Rev. of *Mark as Story: An Introduction to the Narrative of a Gospel* by David Rhoads and Donald Michie. *Journal of Biblical Literature* 103/3 (September 1984): 482–84.

Quinlan, Kieran. "O'Connor, Percy, and Orthodoxy." *The Southern Literary Journal* 38/2 (Spring 2006): 150–52.

Raiger, Michael. "'Large and Startling Figures': The Grotesque and the Sublime in the Short Stories of Flannery O'Connor." In *Seeing into the Life of Things: Essays on Literature and Religious Experience*, edited by John L. Mahoney, 242–70. New York: Fordham University Press, 1998.

Ransom, John Crowe. *Poems about God*. New York: Henry Holt and Company, 1919.

Rebenich, Stefan. *Jerome: The Early Church Fathers*. London: Routledge, 2002.

Reed, John Shelton. *The Enduring South: Subcultural Persistence in Mass Society*. Chapel Hill: University of North Carolina Press, 1972.

——. *Southern Folk, Plain and Fancy: Native White Social Types*. Athens: University of Georgia Press, 1986.

Reynolds, Guy. "There Are So Many Horrible Examples of Regional Writers, and the South Is Loaded: Flannery O'Connor 'Every Action Is Weighted with an Eternal Consequence.'" In *Twentieth Century American Women's Fiction: A Critical Introduction*, 114–45. New York: St. Martin's Press, 1999.

Rhoads, David, and Donald Michie. *Mark as Story: An Introduction to the Narrative of a Gospel*. Philadelphia: Fortress Press, 1982.

Richard, Mark. *Charity: Stories*. New York: Anchor Books, 1998.

——. *Fishboy: A Ghost's Story*. London: Hodder & Stoughton, 1993.

——. *The Ice at the Bottom of the World*. New York: Anchor Books, 1991.

Robillard, Douglas, Jr. "Rethinking the Catholic Imagination." *Modern Fiction Studies* 53/1 (Spring 2007): 174–82.

——, editor. *The Critical Response to Flannery O'Connor*. Santa Barbara: Greenwood Publishing Group, 2004.

Robinson, Owen. *Creating Yoknapatawpha: Readers and Writers in Faulkner's Fiction*. New York: Routledge, 2006.

Romine, Scott. *The Real South: Southern Narrative in the Age of Cultural Reproduction*. Baton Rouge: Louisiana State University Press, 2008.

Rubin, Louis D., Jr. "From Combray to Ithaca; or, The 'Southernness' of Southern Literature." *Virginia Quarterly Review* 66/1 (Winter 1990): 47–63.

——. "The Historical Image of Modern Southern Writing." *The Journal of*

Southern History 22/2 (May 1956): 147–66.

Rubin, Louis D., Jr., and Robert D. Jacobs, editors. *Southern Renascence: The Literature of the Modern South*. Baltimore: Johns Hopkins University Press, 1953.

"The Sacraments: Baptism." *www.ourcatholicfaith.org*. Ed Phillips, 2003. http:/ourcatholicfaith.org/sacraments/baptism.html.

Schaff, Philip, and Henry Wace, editors. *Nicene and Post-Nicene Fathers*. Series II. XIV Volumes. Buffalo: Christian Literature Publishing Co., 1895. *www.ccel.org. Christian Classics Ethereal Library*, 13 July 2005. http://www.ccel .org/ccel/schaff/npnf208.toc.html.

——. *Nicene and Post-Nicene Fathers of the Christian Church: Basil, Letters, and Select Works*. Series II. XIV volumes. Translated by Blomfield Jackson. New York: Cosimo Classics, 2007.

Scott, R. Neil. *Flannery O'Connor: An Annotated Reference Guide to Criticism*. Milledgeville: Timberlane Books, 2002.

Seinfeld, Alexander. *The Art of Amazement: Judaism's Forgotten Spirituality*. Los Angeles: Jeremy P. Tarcher, 2005.

Sessions, W. A. Rev. of *Flannery O'Connor: An Annotated Reference Guide to Criticism* by R. Neil Scott. *South Atlantic Review* 68/1 (Winter 2003): 131–35.

Sherry, Gerard E. "An Interview with Flannery O'Connor." *The Critic* 21 (June– July 1963): 29–31. Reprint in *Conversations with Flannery O'Connor*, edited by Rosemary M. Magee, 97–102. Jackson: University Press of Mississippi, 1987.

Shloss, Carol. *Flannery O'Connor's Dark Comedies: The Limits of Inference*. Baton Rouge: Louisiana State University Press, 1980.

Simpson, Melissa. *Flannery O'Connor: A Biography*. Westport: Greenwood Press, 2005.

Smith, Kevin, director. *Dogma*. Lions Gate Entertainment, 1999.

Smith, Mack. *Literary Realism and the Ekphrastic Tradition*. University Park: Pennsylvania State University Press, 1995.

Smolarski, Dennis Chester. *Sacred Mysteries: Sacramental Principles and Liturgical Practice*. Mahwah: Paulist Press, 1995.

Sonnenfeld, Albert. "Flannery O'Connor: The Catholic Writer as Baptist." *Contemporary Literature* 13/4 (Autumn 1972): 445–57.

Sontag, Susan. *Against Interpretation and Other Essays*. London: Andre Deutsch, 1987.

Spivey, Ted R. *Flannery O'Connor: The Woman, the Thinker, the Visionary*. Macon GA: Mercer University Press, 1995.

St. John at Patmos. ca. late 15th century. Tempura on wood panel. Trinity-Sergiev Monastery. Private collection. *The Bridgeman Art Library*, n. date. Accessed 15 March 2011. http://ww w.bridgemanart.com/image.aspx?img=1FE8B9ED-104D-48F5-A0FD-B7E9DE692973.

Staunton, John A. "Shadowing Grace in the Post-Southern South: 'A Roadside Resurrection' and Larry Brown's Narratives of Witness." *Religion and Literature* 33/1 (Spring 2001): 43–75.

Sturges, Robert S. "Indeterminancy of Literary Meaning in Medieval Culture, 1100–1500." In *Medieval Interpretation: Models of Reading in Literary Narrative, 1100–1500*, 1–31. Carbondale: Southern Illinois University Press, 1991.

Sundquist, Eric J., editor. *American Realism: New Essays*. Baltimore: Johns Hopkins University Press, 1982.

Tate, Allen. *Essays of Four Decades*. London: Oxford University Press, 1970.

——. *The Swimmers and Other Selected Poems*. London: Oxford University Press, 1970.

Tate, Allen, et al. *I'll Take My Stand: The South and the Agrarian Tradition*. 1930. Edited by Lewis P. Simpson. Baton Rouge: Louisiana State University Press, 1977.

Tertullian. *De Corona*. Translated by Jacques-Paul Migne. *Patrologia Latina*. CCXXII volumes. *www.earlychurchtexts.com*. *Early Church Texts*, 2002. http://www.earlychurchtexts.com/main/tertullian/traditional_christi an_practices.shtml.

Theophanes the Greek. *The Transfiguration of Christ*. ca. early 15th century. Tempura on wood panel. Tretyakov Gallery, Moscow, Russia. *www.artstor.org*. *Art History Survey Collection*, n. date. Accessed 15 March 2011. http://library.artstor.org.elib.tcd.ie/library/secure-ViewImages?id =8DhbZCk2NzYrJSEnd1N7Q38rXXsvelQ %D&userId=gjJDfzUvzoop.

Third Council of Baltimore (1891). *The Baltimore Catechism*. Number II. New York: Benziger Brothers, Inc. *www.boston-catholic-journal.com*. *The Boston Catholic Journal*, 2005. http://www.pcpbooks.net/docs/baltimore_ catech ism.pdf.

Tillich, Paul. "The Nature and the Significance of Existential Thought." *The Journal of Philosophy* 53/23 (November 1956): 739–48.

——. "The Religious Symbol." *Dædalus* 87/3 (Summer 1958): 3–21.

Toulson, Shirley. *The Celtic Alternative: A Reminder of the Christianity We Lost*. London: Rider Books, 1987.

Tresmontant, Claude. *A Study in Hebrew Thought*. Translated by Michael Francis Gibson. New York: Desclee, Co., 1960.

Trilling, Lionel. "Manners, Morals, and the Novel," *The Liberal Imagination: Essays on Literature and Society*. Oxford: Oxford University Press, 1981.

Tura, Cosimo. *Saint Jerome*. ca. 1470. Oil and egg tempura on wood panel. *www.nationalgallery.org*. *The National Gallery, London, UK*, n. date. Accessed 12 March 2011. http:// www.nationalgallery.org.uk/ paintings/cosimo-tura-saint-jerome.

Underwood, Paul Atkins. *The Kariye Djami*. IV volumes. New York: Taylor & Francis, 1967.

Van Hove, Rev. Brian, S.J. "Jansenism, the Liturgy, and Ireland." *Christus*

Regnat 3/1 (Christmas 2009): 15–18. *www.ignatiusinsight.com.* http://www.ignatius insight.com/features2010/bvanhove_jansenism_jan 2010.asp.

Van O'Connor, William. *The Grotesque: An American Genre and Other Essays.* Carbondale: The University of Southern Illinois Press, 1962.

——. "The Grotesque in Modern American Fiction." *College English* 20/7 (April 1959): 342–46.

Wakefield, Gordon S., editor. *The Westminster Dictionary of Christian Spirituality*. Westminster: John Knox Press, 1983.

Walker, Alice. "Beyond the Peacock: Reconstructing Flannery O'Connor." In *Search of Our Mothers' Gardens: Womanist Prose*, 42–59. New York: HBJ Publishers, 1983.

Ward, Graham. *Christ and Culture*. Oxford: Blackwell Publishing, 2005.

Ware, Timothy. *The Orthodox Church*. Revised edition. Harmondsworth: Penguin Books Ltd., 1982.

Watkins, Steven R. *Flannery O'Connor and Teilhard de Chardin: A Journey Together Towards Hope and Understanding in Life*. New York: Peter Lang Publishing, Inc., 2009.

Watson, Ritchie Devon. "Antebellum Race Mythology and the Development of Southern Nationalism." *The Southern Literary Journal* 35/1 (Fall 2002): 1–13.

Weber, Max. *The Protestant Ethic and the Spirit of Capitalism.* Translated by Talcott Parsons. Mineola: Courier Dover Publications, 2003.

Welty, Eudora. *Complete Novels*. Edited by Richard Ford and Michael Kreyling. New York: Library of America, 1998.

——. *Welty: Stories, Essays, & Memoir*. Edited by Richard Ford and Michael Kreyling. New York: Library of America, 1998.

Werness, Hope B. *The Continuum Encyclopedia of Animal Symbolism in Art*. New York: Continuum International Publishing Group, Inc., 2006.

Westarp, Karl-Heinz. *Precision and Depth in Flannery O'Connor's Short Stories.* Langelandsgade: Aarhus University Press, 2002.

Whitt, Margaret Earley. *Understanding Flannery O'Connor: New Perspectives.* Columbia: University of South Carolina Press, 1995.

Withals, John. *Shorte Dictionaire for Yonge Beginners*. London: Ihon Kingstun, 1553.

Wood, Ralph C. "The Catholic Faith of Flannery O'Connor's Protestant Characters: A Critique and Vindication." *Flannery O'Connor Bulletin* 13 (1984): 15–25.

——. "The Heterodoxy of Flannery O'Connor's Book Reviews." *Flannery O'Connor Bulletin* 15 (1976): 3–29.

——. "Such a Catholic." Rev. of *Flannery: A Life of Flannery O'Connor* by Brad Gooch. *National Review* 61/4 (March 2009): 38–42.

Wood, Susan K. *One Baptism: Ecumenical Dimensions of the Doctrine of Baptism*. Collegeville: Liturgical Press, 2009.

Wright, J. Robert, and Thomas C. Oden, editors. *Ancient Christian Commentary on Scripture: The Old Testament*. Volume IX. Downers Grove: InterVarsity Press, 2005.

Wynne, Judith F. "The Sacramental Irony of Flannery O'Connor." *The Southern Literary Journal* 7/2 (Spring 1975): 33–49.

Yaeger, Patricia. *Dirt and Desire: Reconstructing Southern Women's Writing, 1930–1990*. Chicago: University of Chicago Press, 2000.

Zubeck, Jacqueline A. "Back to Page One in 'Parker's Back': An Orthodox Examination of O'Connor's Last Story." *Flannery O'Connor Review* 8 (2010): 92–116.

Index